ATL Server: High Performance C++ on .NET

PRANISH KUMAR,
JASJIT SINGH GREWAL,
BOGDAN CRIVAT,
AND ERIC LEE

ATL Server: High Performance C++ on .NET

ISBN (pbk): 1-59059-128-3

Printed and bound in the United States of America 12345678910

Editorial Directors: Dan Appleman, Gary Cornell, Simon Hayes, Martin Streicher, Karen Watterson, John Zukowski

Assistant Publisher: Grace Wong

Project Manager and Copy Editor: Nicole LeClerc

Proofreader: Lori Bring

Compositor: Argosy Publishing

Indexer: Valerie Perry

Cover Designer: Kurt Krames

Production Manager: Kari Brooks

Manufacturing Manager: Tom Debolski

Distributed to the book trade in the United States by Springer-Verlag New York, Inc., 175 Fifth Avenue, New York, NY, 10010 and outside the United States by Springer-Verlag GmbH & Co. KG, Tiergartenstr. 17, 69112 Heidelberg, Germany.

In the United States, phone 1-800-SPRINGER, email `orders@springer-ny.com`, or visit `http://www.springer-ny.com`. Outside the United States, fax +49 6221 345229, email `orders@springer.de`, or visit `http://www.springer.de`.

For information on translations, please contact Apress directly at 2560 Ninth Street, Suite 219, Berkeley, CA 94710. Phone 510-549-5930, fax 510-549-5939, email `info@apress.com`, or visit `http://www.apress.com`.

The source code for this book is available to readers at `http://www.apress.com` in the Downloads section.

I'd like to dedicate this book to my lovely wife, Diana. She's a constant source of inspiration in my life. I'd also like to dedicate this book to my parents for everything they've done for me, as well as Ravinish and Camille for their love and support. Finally, I'd like to dedicate this book to all my family and friends: There are too many to mention, but I think of you always.

Pranish Kumar

I would like to dedicate this book to my parents. Thanks for believing in me, and thanks for not believing my first grade teacher when she told you I'd never make it into the honors classes.

Jasjit Singh Grewal

I would like to dedicate this book to Nei, my parents, and Andrei. Thank you for being there!

Bogdan Crivat

I would like to dedicate this book to my family, my friends, and the faculty and staff of the UWO Computer Science department, with whom I had the privilege of studying and, in many cases, restudying under. Thanks in particular to Hanan and Doug for your wisdom and patience!

Eric Lee

Contents at a Glance

Contents

Chapter 25 Developing HTTP Client Applications in ATL Server 441

Chapter 26 Securing Your Web Application 457

Chapter 27 ATL Server FAQ 467

Foreword

The Microsoft Active Template Library (ATL) was originally developed by Microsoft's Visual C++ team to meet the goal of providing component developers with a C++ class library that they could use to build compact COM-based components. The ATL team was able to achieve this goal by using object-oriented design and advanced C++ coding techniques. The release of ATL made it possible for developers to create components from a flexible and extensible C++ class library that were small in footprint and working set requirements. These were two very important characteristics considering that at the time, many developers were developing these components for the sole purpose of publishing them for download over the Internet. Internet users connected to the Internet via telephone modems (which was standard practice at the time) benefited greatly from this compact code because installing and running ATL components didn't require additional runtimes or a large DLL to be downloaded.

Soon after the original versions of ATL came out, I was fortunate enough to join the team of Microsoft developers who started to look at other parts of the Microsoft C++ class libraries to find feature areas where the techniques developed in the original versions of ATL could be applied to benefit Web application developers. We believed if we could apply the coding techniques and practices we learned in the development of ATL to a class library that could be used in applications on the server side of a Web application, that these Web applications would also benefit. Thus was born the idea for the ATL Server class library. The goals behind the development of ATL Server were to provide a lightweight, highly customizable, full-featured C++ class library for writing ISAPI-based applications; to provide a tightly integrated development experience; to separate the development of static content from the development of dynamic content; and to provide a best-of-breed platform for developing SOAP-based Web services. The library provides a complete set of features that enable C++ developers to create fast and flexible ISAPI applications for Internet Information Server (IIS).

The completion of this book represents a milestone in the evolution of ATL Server. The authors and I spent a significant portion of our lives developing this technology. It's incredibly satisfying to now see it in the hands of developers who will use it as the foundation for their work. Likewise, it's incredibly satisfying to see this book at last be made available to developers so that they may use it as a tool and as a guide to building ATL Server applications. By reading this book, you'll learn all the details of developing applications using the ATL Server class library. This book will help you get over the learning curve of using an advanced C++ class library to develop your Web applications, and it will open the door to the fun and excitement of writing Web applications that are faster than anyone else's!

Mike Dice
Development Lead, Microsoft Web Services

About the Authors

Pranish Kumar is currently a program manager on the Visual C++ Libraries team at Microsoft. He joined Microsoft in 2000, focusing on ATL Server. Before joining Microsoft, Pranish worked in different areas of software development in Sydney, Australia. He holds bachelor's degrees in computer science and electrical engineering from the University of New South Wales.

Outside of software development, Pranish enjoys single-malt whisky, cigars, and his continuous struggle to learn Romanian.

Jasjit Singh Grewal graduated in May 1999 from the University of Maryland at College Park with a degree in computer science. He joined Microsoft in June 1999 and began working on the Visual C++ Libraries team and, in particular, on ATL Server. During his time on the Libraries team, Jasjit contributed to nearly all aspects of the design and implementation of the ATL Server library and was the primary designer and implementer of the ATL Server Web services support. Jasjit's interests outside of software development are drawing, reading, and writing. He also enjoys playing roller hockey and hiking.

Bogdan Crivat is a software design engineer in the Data Mining Server Development team at Microsoft. Bogdan joined the ATL Server team at Microsoft in 1999, focusing mostly on the SOAP support and the SMTP support classes. He worked there until ATL Server was released (with Visual Studio .NET). Before Microsoft, Bogdan worked on large-scale client/server applications for Softwin, the largest Romanian software development company. He holds a bachelor's degree in computer science from the University of Bucharest, Romania.

When he's not working, Bogdan likes to read pretty much everything, and he especially enjoys reading about his recurring passion, the history of religions.

Eric Lee has worked in testing and development at Microsoft for just over 4 years. Before Microsoft, Eric worked at a small company in Toronto, Canada. Most of Eric's experience has been in GUI components and server-side programming. He holds a bachelor's degree in computer science from the University of Western Ontario.

Acknowledgments

WE WOULD LIKE TO THANK the many people who made this book possible. Many of these people offered great advice, reviewed chapters, and offered other forms of support to make this book happen.

First off we'd like to thank members of the Libraries team (past and present) who offered to review chapters for us and provided some great feedback on the book. A heartfelt thanks to our colleagues and friends Mike Dice, Momin Al-Ghosien, Walter Sullivan, Andrew Laucius, Jerry Weiler, and Sridhar Madhugiri. We'd also like to thank the rest of the Libraries team for their efforts in creating the library and their continued support.

We're also grateful to the various other people who either offered to review chapters and give us feedback on the book, gave us great feedback on the library itself, or both. We'd like to thank Todd Brooks, CTO and vice president of software development at Truistic Software, located in Houston, Texas, who has over 8 years of development experience with Microsoft technologies. We'd also like to thank Tomas Restrepo, a software developer at InterGrupo S.A., who is interested in object-oriented programming, design patters, C++, the .NET platform, and XML Web services. In addition, we'd like to thank Michael Guo, development manager for Microsoft Passport.

A very special thanks must go to Nicole LeClerc, our editor at Apress, who helped us turn our book around quickly. In addition, we must thank Kari Brooks, Grace Wong, Simon Hayes, and all the other great people at Apress who helped this book come to life. We also must thank Gary Cornell for approaching us with the idea of this book and pressuring us to get it finished, without ever actually pressuring us to get it finished.

Part One
Overview of ATL Server Features and Services

CHAPTER 1

Introduction to ATL Server

IT IS APPARENT THAT WEB APPLICATIONS will play a significant role in the future of software. Today's business Web sites must be tightly coupled with a company's other systems, such as databases that track inventory, ordering, and customer and business partner information. All of these business aspects need to be handled in real time over the Web.

In particular, the need for high-end mission-critical Web applications has begun to grow and shows no signs of slowing down. Companies with this need include not only Internet (dot-com) businesses that aim to make money with their Web sites and associated services, but also more traditional businesses that are exposing important internal subsystems on the Web (such as ordering and inventory management) to facilitate more efficient business transactions.

In this chapter we introduce you to the basics of the ATL Server library. You'll learn why you as a developer should choose ATL Server, and you'll examine some of the features that the library provides. You'll also take a look at a high-level overview of the architecture of an ATL Server application.

What Is ATL Server?

With Windows NT/2000 and Internet Information Services (IIS), Microsoft has introduced a platform capable of handling the mission-critical tasks described previously. Combine IIS with Internet Server Application Programming Interface (ISAPI) development and developers are capable of getting the flexibility, control, performance, reliability, and scalability they desire. Unfortunately, ISAPI development is difficult, and there's a lot of infrastructure that the developers themselves must provide before they can even think of working on their application logic.

With Visual C++ .NET, the Visual C++ libraries team has created a library that greatly aids ISAPI development. That library is ATL Server.

The ATL Server library has been designed to be a lightweight, thin wrapper over ISAPI. As such, the library allows developers to maintain complete control over their Web applications (by plugging directly into the underlying layers wherever they deem it necessary) while also greatly reducing development time by giving developers much of the code that they would normally have to write, test, and document themselves.

The ATL Server classes are well-contained, separate parts that come together to form a complete "framework" that helps developers create ISAPI applications much more productively. The classes are built on top of one another, with high-level functionality built on top of low-level functionality, so nothing is hidden and the pieces can be easily replaced and changed without affecting other portions of the application.

ATL Server doesn't use COM, nor does it require developers to have any COM knowledge to develop with it. It's predominantly a class library based on top of ISAPI using ATL. ATL Server does have some template usage, but this is reserved (compared to traditional ATL) mainly for areas of the library that require the flexibility that templates allow.

Who ATL Server Is For

The ATL Server library is designed for developers who need the high performance, control, and flexibility of ISAPI. It isn't designed to simplify your task by *hiding* the underlying technology; it's designed to simplify your task by providing a lot of code that you need to create a fully functional Web application—code you would otherwise have to write yourself.

ATL Server is a C++ library designed by and for C++ developers who need to create Web applications and Web services with the low-level control, flexibility, and performance that ISAPI provides. It is an unmanaged C++ library; it doesn't involve the .NET runtime in any way.

ATL Server isn't designed to provide a high level of abstraction. It's a layer of thin wrappers over ISAPI, and it doesn't hide or simplify the underlying technology; instead, it makes using this underlying technology more productive. There's no scripting language or abstracted object model here (although you could easily implement features like this on top of ATL Server).

What About Web Services?

Web services bring about a new philosophy in software design. They're basically functions that are exposed (and that can be called) over the World Wide Web through Hypertext Transfer Protocol (HTTP). Web services use Simple Object Access Protocol (SOAP) by default over HTTP to allow communication between clients and servers, even through firewalls.

Because you can treat Web services just like any other HTTP request (except for having to decode the request from SOAP and encode the response to SOAP), ATL Server is the perfect place in the Visual C++ libraries to provide support for them. Thus, ATL Server not only allows developers to create high-end Web applications, but it also allows them to create high-end Web services. Just as with the

Web application model, flexibility, control, reliability, scalability, and performance are all paramount in the design.

By taking advantage of the attribute feature in the Visual C++ .NET compiler, ATL Server makes Web service programming very similar to COM programming. This is made possible by the fact that Web services, like COM components, rely on having a well-defined interface and an interface description language (Web Services Description Language [WSDL] instead of Interface Definition Language [IDL]) to describe that interface with.

Not only does this attribute feature enable existing COM developers to leverage their knowledge of COM development when creating Web services, but it also makes it very easy to expose objects as both COM components and Web services. On top of this, developers can easily expose existing COM objects (or Web services) as Web services (or COM objects).

There are a few major advantages to having a native solution for Web services:

- Web services are just like regular Web application requests, except you need to be able to encode and decode SOAP. Developers needed a solution that would handle the networking, marshaling, transport, and other Web service issues for them on both the client and the server.

- Native Web services enable Web application developers using ATL Server (or ISAPI directly) to easily expose Web application functionality (or parts of their Web application) via Web services, which allows them to target a much broader market.

- Native Web services allow ATL COM developers to protect their existing investment in the knowledge they possess about developing and using components that rely on well-defined interfaces to communicate. They also help developers protect their existing code investment by making it easy to expose existing (and new) COM components as Web services. It's easy for ATL COM developers to expose Web services they develop in the future as COM components.

- Native Web services provide an ideal solution for developers who require the low-level control, flexibility, and performance that only a solution such as ATL Server can provide.

How ATL Server Compares with Traditional Solutions

There are three main traditional solutions for creating Web applications. We discuss these solutions in the following sections, as well as ATL Server.

CGI

Common Gateway Interface (CGI) provided one of the first ways to create Web applications, and it's still extremely popular, especially for developers on UNIX systems. CGI was designed to work on the UNIX systems that originally powered the Internet, and it creates one process for each request received. Unfortunately, this is very inefficient on Windows systems, as process creation is very expensive. As a result, CGI isn't an ideal solution for Windows systems.

ASP

Active Server Pages (ASP) is a more recent innovation designed to simplify Web application development on Windows. ASP is very popular for many of today's Web applications because it offers fast application development. Unfortunately, with ASP it can be difficult to separate Web logic and Web page design. Also, because ASP was designed to greatly simplify Web development, it suffers from some problems related to performance, control, and flexibility.

ISAPI

ISAPI is the underlying application programming interface (API) for Web development on Windows. It's therefore very powerful and controllable, and it has excellent performance characteristics. The problem with targeting ISAPI directly is that it doesn't provide any functionality for creating real Web applications, so developers end up spending a lot of time trying to get useful access to information such as cookies or form/query data, not to mention the framework code required to get an application running efficiently (thread pool, cache, and so on).

Other Solutions

More recently, JavaServer Pages (JSP) and ASP.NET were developed to help developers in the ASP segment who are looking for better performance, more control, and better application architecture than ASP provides. These solutions, however, lack the benefits of raw ISAPI. They still take away control and flexibility from the developer and suffer from many performance problems, much like their predecessor.

Another issue that arises with these solutions is their reliance on script. This reliance can create Internet Protocol (IP) issues for developers. For example, if a third-party site is running your application and some of your application logic is in script, then your IP is not as well protected as it is in a compiled image. Outside of IP issues, a reliance on scripting languages generally leads to a maintenance nightmare for all but one-off projects.

ATL Server

ATL Server provides a lot of common Web application functionality on top of ISAPI, without hiding the underlying ISAPI model and without costing the developer performance, control, or flexibility.

Among the functionality provided is an I/O completion port–based asynchronous thread pool. The thread pool provided in IIS is static (not strictly true, but you can't rely on it to grow and shrink to handle the application's requirements). When all the threads become busy, your Web server will stop accepting HTTP requests. To your customers (and in many ways to you), this is the same as your Web server going down. Therefore the IIS team recommends that developers create their own thread pool. This thread pool should take requests off the fixed-sized IIS thread pool to ensure that the IIS thread pool never becomes full.

Another piece of functionality is *caching*, which gets turned on by default and is used to make your application more efficient out of the box. Other examples of functionality that ATL Server provides are output page caching (for pages that have already been rendered), session state (with custom backing or built-in support for memory and database backup), and PerfMon counters.

The ATL ideal of lightweight, separate classes means that you can easily add ATL Server use to an existing ISAPI application or revert parts of an ATL Server application to straight ISAPI without requiring rewriting of any part of the application that isn't being converted. Therefore, if you don't like the ATL Server thread pool, caching, or session state, you can easily implement your own and slot it right in.

The ATL goal of flexibility in design is also very important. The classes are all stand-alone in functionality, and for the most part they aren't application specific. This means that you can use the caches in a general application (e.g., the memory cache for holding a lookup table) or you can use the thread pool to handle DirectPlay events (as some of the ATL Server developers did). Good use of templates means that it becomes easy to use classes in flexible ways. For example, with ATL Server Web services you can templatize on one of the HTTP stacks provided (WinINet, Custom, or MSXML) or create your own. Another great example of flexibility is the ability to use transports other than HTTP for your XML Web services—you can easily change to using TCP/IP or MSMQ as your transport mechanism.

The ATL goal of high performance is also very critical in the design of ATL Server. By designing for performance and testing performance (at both a class level and an application level), from the very start the library is well designed for handling the most demanding performance requirements.

How ATL Server Works

In this section you'll take a look at the architecture of an ATL Server application. We walk you through the basics of processing a request and then drill down in further detail into each of the components.

First, a client makes an HTTP request to a server (running Windows and IIS), as shown in Figure 1-1.

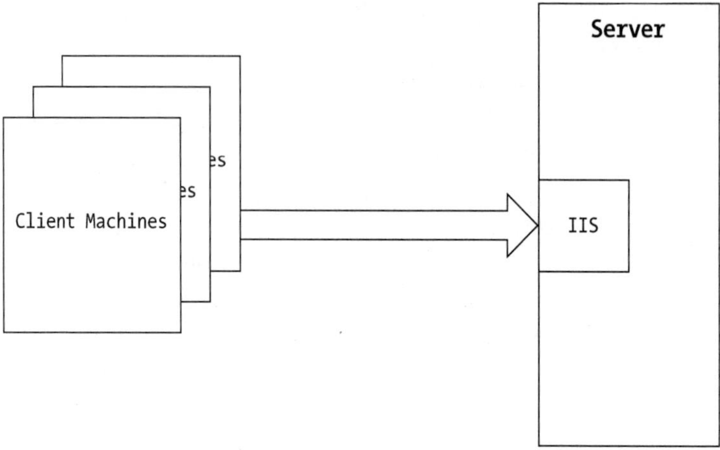

Figure 1-1. A client sending a request to a server

When the server receives the request, it passes it on to the appropriate ISAPI (extension) DLL. In Figure 1-2, you can see that the request is handed off to MyISAPI.dll.

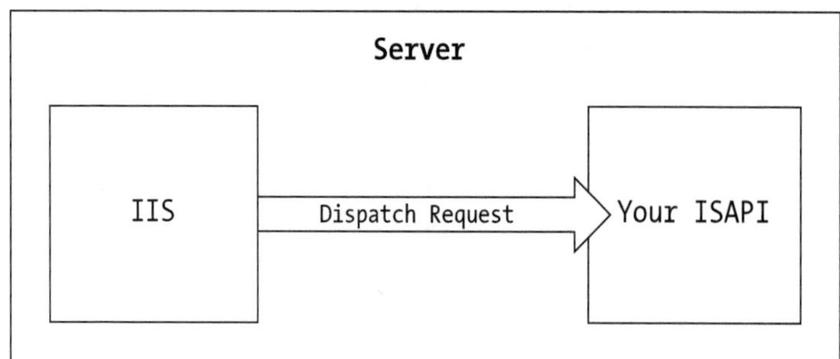

Figure 1-2. A request being dispatched to the ISAPI DLL

At its heart, the ISAPI DLL is designed to dispatch requests to the appropriate application DLL (see Figure 1-3). But the ISAPI DLL is capable of doing much more than this. Because it's common to all your application DLLs (all the application DLLs in any given virtual root [vroot]), it's a great place for providing cross-application features. An obvious example of a feature suitable for the ISAPI DLL is the various caches, so that each application DLL doesn't have to keep its own cache. Every vroot on your server that you enable has to point to one ISAPI DLL that will handle and dispatch the requests to this vroot.

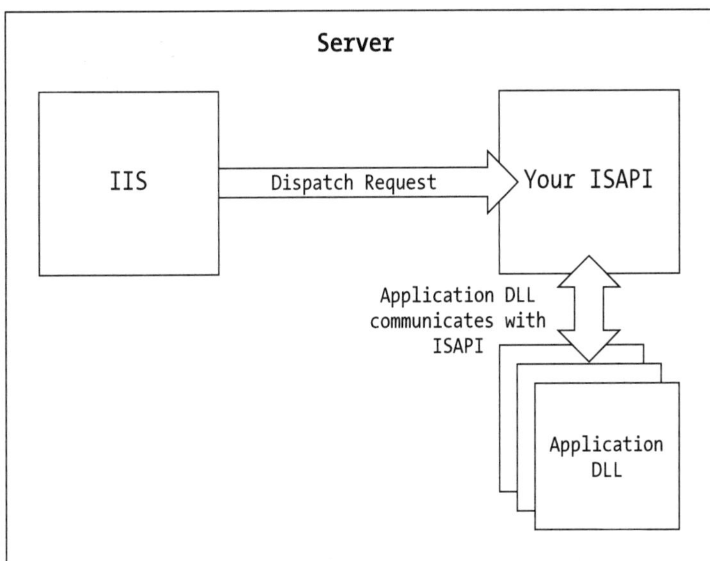

Figure 1-3. The ISAPI DLL dispatching a request to an application DLL

The ISAPI DLL is designed to dispatch requests, and in this case (an ATL Server application), the ISAPI DLL will dispatch the request to an appropriate application DLL. The application DLL is where the application logic resides. The reason for separating application DLLs from the ISAPI DLL is that the ISAPI DLL gets locked by IIS; therefore, in order to change the ISAPI DLL, the server needs to be restarted (via iisreset). Because restarting IIS on a server is a procedure that most companies don't want to do often (if the IIS process is resetting, then you'll lose all incoming client requests), ATL Server provides application DLLs that can be changed without needing to restart IIS, through a process referred to as *hot swapping*. In fact, the system has been designed so that when you change an application DLL, requests currently being processed will use the old application, and new requests will go to the new one. Not only does ATL Server provide this functionality, but it also handles flushing the DLL cache and resetting other appropriate components so you can make the change seamless.

Of course, if you really want to, you can combine the application DLL and ISAPI DLL into a single DLL, but outside of the file maintenance issue, there's no real advantage in doing this and you'll lose the ability to hot swap your application DLL.

The application DLL also has the ability to work with ATL Server *stencil* or *server response file* (SRF) files. SRF is a new file type created by the ATL Server team that is designed to make it easy to cleanly separate static and dynamic HTML content. SRF files are basically HTML files with dynamic tags that indicate where dynamic content is to be injected. (The stencil processor allows your application to spit into the HTML stream whenever a dynamic tag occurs.)

Figure 1-4 shows how SRF files fit into the picture with ISAPI and the application DLL.

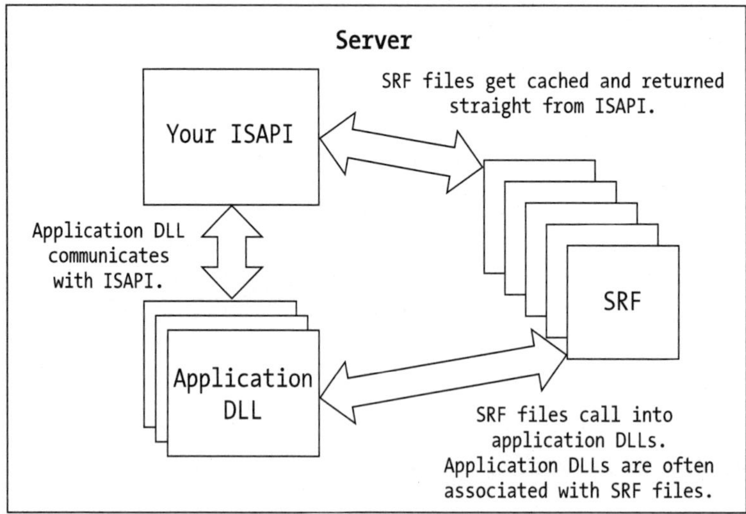

Figure 1-4. The relationship between ISAPI, the application, and SRF

It's important to remember that not only can these features (and subfeatures) be used separately in any appropriate applications, but also they're completely extensible. This means that whenever you want to add or modify the functionality they provide, it's always possible to do so. In the next sections, you'll briefly examine each of these components.

SRF Basics

SRF allows developers to easily create the user interface (UI) aspects of their Web applications. The file allows for the mixing of static HTML content with dynamic HTML content using the double brace tag syntax: {{}}. SRF also was designed to allow teams to completely separate layout design from development. This key design goal means that Web designers can work solely in the SRF files and developers can work solely in the code. Here's an example of a basic SRF file:

```
<html>
<head> Basic SRF </head>
  {{handler BasicSrf.dll/Example}}
  <body>
    Hello {{World}}
  </body>
</html>
```

We'll come back to the first tag in the preceding sample, but for now we'd like you to focus on the second tag. The second tag, `{{World}}`, will be associated with a method in your handler class (which we explain in a moment—for now, just think of it as any C++ method in a C++ class). The stencil processor is designed (like the rest of ATL Server) to be very efficient. In the interest of efficiency, the ATL Server design team decided to make the stencil processor parse an SRF file only once (i.e., it will only move forward through an SRF file, never backward). The advantage of this design is great performance, and the disadvantage is that you can't do some of the things you can with scripting files, such as have variables and variable parameters. This actually helps push you to keep application logic in the code and only layout information in the SRF file. The SRF file will make a call to the associated function (in your handler class) when it parses a tag.

You may be wondering why the double braces are good for denoting tags. Well, there are two main reasons. First, the braces are ignored by most HTML editors, which means that Web designers can focus on developing layout without worrying about dynamic content. Second, the braces can be placed anywhere within an HTML file, including within HTML tags (as you'll see later on), again without disturbing the use of layout or other HTML tools.

The SRF syntax includes some basic flow control and, as always, the model is completely extensible. The existing flow control, as well as the extensibility mechanism and everything else you may want to know about SRF files, is covered in Chapters 2 and 17.

Now let's examine the first tag in the preceding sample: `{{handler BasicSrf.dll/Example}}`. The first tag is required in all SRF files, and it must be the first noncomment tag. This is the handler tag, and it tells the stencil processor which application DLL will be handling requests for this file. It also tells the processor which class in that application DLL will handle requests. You can have more than one handler in an SRF file, but you must have at least one.

You can see that the BasicSrf DLL will handle requests for the example SRF file. In the code in our application DLL, we'll use a handler map to map the string `Example` with a handler class in our application. This class will then contain another map that will map the string `World` with a method in that class. To better understand how this works, you'll look at application basics and handler classes in the next section.

Application Basics

The application DLL is where the logic of your application resides. A single application DLL can contain one or more handlers. At this point, it's probably worth explaining exactly what a handler is. A *handler* is simply a class that derives from `CRequestHandlerT` (or, at a lower level, `IRequestHandlerImpl`) and is exposed via a handler map. A *handler map* is simply a mapping between text strings and the name of a class. The code for the handler map looks like this:

```
BEGIN_HANDLER_MAP()
  HANDLER_ENTRY("Example", CExampleHandler)
END_HANDLER_MAP()
```

The following code shows an example of an actual request handler:

```
class CExampleHandler : CRequestHandlerT<CExampleHandler>
{
public:
  BEGIN_REPLACEMENT_METHOD_MAP(CExampleHandler)
    REPLACEMENT_METHOD_ENTRY("World", OnWorld)
  END_REPLACEMENT_METHOD_MAP()

  HTTP_CODE ValidateAndExchange
  {
    return HTTP_SUCCESS;
  }

  HTTP_CODE OnWorld
  {
    m_HttpResponse << "World";
    return HTTP_SUCCESS;
  }
};
```

In this case, you can see that we're associating the text string Example with the class CExampleHandler. You'll notice that within the handler itself we have a REPLACEMENT_METHOD_MAP map that maps the text string World with a method, in this case the OnWorld method. Thus, whenever we use the {{World}} tag in an SRF file associated with this handler class (e.g., the SRF file from the previous example), the OnWorld method will be called with the capability to inject characters into the HTML stream at the point where the {{World}} tag occurs.

We can easily rewrite this handler to work with the new Visual C++ .NET attributes. We discuss attributes in more detail later on, but for now you should understand that they're basically a new design philosophy in Visual C++ that allows you to focus on your application logic and not on implementation details. You can view them as compile-time wizards. The compiler tells the attribute provider whenever it sees an attribute (and what the attribute is). When the compiler has finished parsing the class, it calls the attribute provider, which in turn injects code based on information about the class and its methods that it learns from the compiler. This allows for very rich and powerful code injections. You can view the injected code by using the /Fx compiler switch.

You can see that this attribute feature not only simplifies the implementation, but also helps create a more logical structure to the code, which makes the code easier to read and maintain. (Note, for example, that we no longer need the maps that generally exist in the .cpp file and not the header.) Here's an example of a request handler created using attributes:

```
[ request_handler("Example") ]
class CExampleHandler
{
public:
  HTTP_CODE ValidateAndExchange
  {
    return HTTP_SUCCESS;
  }

  [ tag_name(name="World") ]
  HTTP_CODE OnWorld()
  {
    m_HttpResponse << "World";
    return HTTP_SUCCESS;
  }
};
```

You can see in the preceding code that the attributes are denoted by square brackets [] and go on top of the class or method on which they interact. You'll see a lot more attributes throughout this book. In Visual C++ .NET, there are attributes to help with COM development, database development, ATL Server Web application development, and ATL Server Web service development.

Now that you understand the basics of handlers and SRF files, in the next section you'll explore the basics of the ISAPI DLL.

ISAPI Basics

Your ISAPI DLL is the DLL that receives all incoming requests (from IIS) and dispatches them to the appropriate application DLL. Because it's global to all your application DLLs, it's the perfect place for putting cross-application logic. (Application DLLs are spun off a thread pool per request, so if you want to store information permanently between requests, you need to put the information in a global store located in a permanent place such as the ISAPI DLL.) The permanent information and the cross-application logic includes, but isn't limited to, items such as your caches, session, and PerfMon counters.

You'll notice that there's no binary version of the ISAPI DLL; instead, the ATL Server Project Wizard generates the code for a simple yet fully functional ISAPI DLL for you. This allows (and encourages) you to customize your ISAPI DLL as you see fit. For more information on how to do this, please refer to Chapter 4.

The basic ISAPI DLL (with attributes) looks like the following:

```
[ module(name="Example", type="dll") ];
[ emitidl(restricted) ];

// The ATL Server ISAPI extension
ExtensionType theExtension;

extern "C" DWORD WINAPI HttpExtensionProc(LPEXTENSION_CONTROL_BLOCK lpECB)
{
  return theExtension.HttpExtensionProc(lpECB);
}

extern "C" BOOL WINAPI GetExtensionVersion(HSE_VERSION_INFO* pVer)
{
  return theExtension.GetExtensionVersion(pVer);
}

extern "C" BOOL WINAPI TerminateExtension(DWORD dwFlags)
{
  return theExtension.TerminateExtension(dwFlags);
}
```

Let's briefly look at what the three main functions here are for. The first function is `HttpExtensionProc`. This is your "main" application (i.e., the main entry point for your application). In the case of ATL Server, this function will queue HTTP requests on the thread pool and return `HSE_STATUS_PENDING` on a successful queue and `HSE_STATUS_ERROR` otherwise.

The second function is `GetExtensionVersion`. This function is called when your application is invoked on the server for the first time. It's used to exchange version numbers: the version your application is coded against and the version on the server. It also provides a short text description of your application. Because it's called on the first initialization of your application, it's useful for any initialization required, including thread pool and cache initialization. This function returns `TRUE` on success and `FALSE` on failure.

The third function is `TerminateExtension`. This function is called only when your application is terminated and is used for any cleanup and shutdown tasks required by your application. This includes freeing up any resources that your extension might have accessed. This function returns `TRUE` on success and `FALSE` on failure.

Other Features of ATL Server

This section provides a brief look at some of the features that ATL Server provides. Although this section isn't by any means a complete description, it should give you an excellent feel for the sort of functionality provided by ATL Server. We go into much more detail about each of these features (as well as some others) later in the book.

ATL Server provides a number of caches that you can customize for your specific application. Some of the out-of-the-box caches are as follows:

- The *database connection cache* allows you to cache your database connections and save network trips to your SQL Server machine.

- The *file cache* is very useful for caching files that can be quickly returned to the user by IIS. SRF files can be (and are by default) cached into files after their first processing and then passed back quickly as static files by IIS.

- The *BLOB cache* allows you to store binary large object (BLOB) data.

The session state facilities provided by ATL Server can back session state to any store that you desire. There are two storage techniques fully implemented for you, one being memory-backed session state and the other being database-backed session state. *Memory-backed session state* is great for single Web-server situations, as it provides a fast and efficient way of storing session. *Database-backed session state* is more appropriate for Web farm systems, as it's less vulnerable to corruption (through system failure, for example) than memory-backed session state. The nice thing about the session state is that the interfaces are identical, so moving between these two types of storage (or to or from your own custom storage) is seamless and requires changes to only two or three lines of code.

The ATL Server thread pool is used to take the burden off IIS's threads. Because IIS has a fixed number of threads and will block all incoming requests if these threads are busy, it's best to move all but static requests off to your own thread pool. The ATL Server thread pool is completely customizable—it's created at start-up and is dynamically resizable. The threads in this pool are completely asynchronous, so if you need to wait on an expensive call, you can send the thread back to the pool to process incoming requests and keep your Web application running at maximum efficiency. The thread pool is an excellent example of a feature that can be used outside of Web applications. For example, you could use this thread pool to handle DirectPlay events for a DirectX application (this was done by some of the developers on the ATL Server team).

The cookie helper functions are designed to make working with cookies easy and efficient. ATL Server lets you work with both single value and multiple value cookies. It provides simple set and lookup functions to make working with cookies trivial.

ATL Server also provides query and form helper classes. These classes are designed to help with all the tasks associated with working with query and form data. These tasks include validating the form and query parameters, and exchanging form and query parameters into member variables in your class.

The Simple Mail Transfer Protocol (SMTP) support provided by ATL Server makes it easy to compose and automatically send e-mail. SMTP is perfect for creating automatic confirmations and status messages.

The Web service support allows you to create unmanaged Web services. The ATL Server model takes advantage of the fact that Web services (like COM) rely on having an interface and an IDL. This knowledge has been used to make Web service development similar to (attributed) COM development. This protection of investment (in both knowledge and code) extends to making it easy to expose objects as both Web services and COM components. Thus, with ATL Server it becomes easy to expose existing or newly written COM components as Web services, as well as newly written Web services as COM components.

Web services represent a new direction in software development, and ATL Server is the tool that helps unmanaged C++ developers easily move to embrace this new technology if they so desire.

With the introduction of attributes, both COM and Web service development has become a lot faster, more readable, and more maintainable.

NTLM security support allows developers to take advantage of the security of the Windows NT Logon Manager. This feature makes it easy to secure sites with

Windows security, which is great for securing intranets and parts of your site that control administration features or contain privileged information.

There are also now wrapper classes for generating Windows PerfMon counters. PerfMon is the perfect way to store statistics about your Web site. The provided counters measure common statistics such as site hits and downloaded files, and the helper classes make it easy for you to add your own counters.

The ATL Server browser capabilities support is designed so that developers can take advantage of the capabilities of modern browsers without denying access to users with older browsers. An initialization file is used to set up the capabilities for different browsers, making it easy to modify browser support over time (including adding support for new browsers).

Along with the functionalities described in this section, ATL Server provides myriad of classes designed to make Web application development easier. Many of the features mentioned here build on lower-level ATL Server functionality. This lower-level functionality is almost always exposed to the developer so that he or she can build customized high-level features off these low-level bases. A good example of a great lower-level feature is the request/response classes, which are designed to make handling requests and generating responses much more efficient.

More on Performance

Performance was a very important goal for the ATL Server team. Throughout the design of ATL Server, the team was very focused on ensuring that the ultimate performance was maintained. All the areas of the library were individually tested to ensure great performance, and the library as a whole was consistently tested to ensure that great performance was being maintained.

One reason that performance was so critical in the design of ATL Server was the results of the Doculabs benchmark test. The Doculabs benchmark test, published in *PC Week* magazine, was designed to test the performance of a number of Web application implementations. The application used to measure performance was basically an online bookstore, with login, search, purchase, shopping cart, and checkout functionality. The test measured a number of high-end Sun Microsystems/Java solutions against two Microsoft implementations.

The test showed that the Visual Basic implementation (using ASP) was about twice as fast as the closest Java solution. The test also showed that the Visual C++ implementation (using ISAPI) was about twice as fast as the Visual Basic solution. Although this benchmark demonstrated that ISAPI and Windows 2000 (the Windows version used for the benchmark) had the performance capability to handle any application, it also brought to light a major problem with ISAPI: Implementing a real application with ISAPI was too difficult! The group of developers who created the ISAPI implementation complained about the time it took to write all of the "framework" code they required before they could even get started writing the application itself. In fact, because of the time constraints the developers were under for the benchmark, they weren't able to do an optimal job. If you download the ISAPI implementation code from the Microsoft Web site (`http://msdn.microsoft.com/library/default.asp?url=/library/en-us/dnnile/html/nilewp.asp`), recompile and rerun it, and then create the same application with ATL Server (in about 1 or 2 weeks versus several months for the original ISAPI implementation), the ATL Server version should be about 10 percent faster, as the team itself discovered when the ATL Server quality assurance (QA) team (none of whom had worked on the original application) did just that.

This benchmark and the problems encountered by the group doing the ISAPI implementation were key driving factors in the design of ATL Server, which is why maintaining hand-tuned ISAPI performance with the library was a key design goal. The ATL Server team definitely reached this goal, and in 99.99 percent of cases there should be no significant difference in performance between the hand-tuned ISAPI version and the ATL Server equivalent.

Many developers are interested in the performance of ASP.NET compared to ATL Server. Many issues are involved with comparing these two disparate technologies. ASP.NET is designed as an alternative to ASP and JSP, whereas ATL Server is designed for C++ ISAPI developers. Although specific performance issues will depend on your application setup and limitations (whether you're database bound, network bound, CPU bound, memory bound, and so on). ATL Server has been designed so that it has minimal dependencies and enables developers to write very high performance web applications and web services quickly and easily.

Basic Deployment

The deployment support in Visual C++ .NET is designed to simplify the deployment task for you. However, you should be clear on what's happening under the covers. IIS Manager is the administration tool that allows you to set up your Web application.

You'll want to create a virtual directory for your application and then set up some properties for this vroot. First, you'll most likely want to set the Application Security Protection option to Low (IIS). This means that your application will run within the IIS process (inetinfo.exe). Note that your application will be running with elevated privileges (as a system process) and will therefore be vulnerable to attack.

You could choose a higher security setting such as Medium or High, but unfortunately there's a significant performance penalty for doing this with IIS 5.0. The other problem with running in these higher settings is that your application will run in one (of many possible) DLL hosts. Luckily with F5 debugging in Visual C++ .NET, debugging applications running in an unknown DLL host isn't as difficult as it used to be. With IIS 6.0 (Windows .NET Server 2003) the IIS team has changed the out-of-process model and fixed many of the performance issues with running an application out-of-process. Therefore, running out-of-process makes a lot more sense on these newer (at time of this writing, unreleased) operating systems.

For more information on deployment, please see Chapter 7.

Debugging Web Applications

With the introduction of Visual Studio .NET, debugging Web applications has become remarkably easy. With F5 debugging, the debugger automatically attaches to the correct process, be it inetinfo.exe if you're running in-process with IIS or (the correct) one of several DLL hosts. The new detach feature allows you to detach from processes (as long as you have dbgproxy.exe running) without having to terminate and restart your Web server (inetinfo.exe).

Improvements in native debugging help developers of ATL Server applications and C++ developers in general. Examples of such improvements include automatic display of HRESULTs in the Watch window and improved Unicode support for global Web sites. There's also great Edit and Continue support, and the new ability to detach and reattach to processes, including inetinfo.exe.

Other improvements that are very useful (particularly for Web applications) include the ability to remotely debug applications and the ability to debug multiple processes (both local and remote) from a single IDE, which is great for debugging client/server applications such as Web services. In addition, the Visual Studio .NET product provides the WebDbg utility, which enables you to view the trace and assert messages that IIS traditionally attempts to hide from you.

For more information on debugging ATL Server applications, please see Chapter 15.

Attribute Basics

Attributes are a new feature in Visual C++ .NET. You've already seen what they look like—attributes are included within square brackets before the definition of the class or method they affect. In this section, you'll take a brief look at what they are.

You can view attributes as compile-time wizards. The compiler uses them to inject code into your application to complete the functionality desired. You can view what the compiler injects by using the `/Fx` compiler switch. This switch will save the files the compiler generates (i.e., a generated file with plain C++ and no attributes).

Attributes are designed not only to simplify implementation details (by letting you focus on application logic), but also to improve the readability and maintainability of your code. One way that attributes do this is the way that they keep all your code in one place, which means that changes to the code occur in only one place (as opposed to your needing to go and change the map and the class it relates to). The use of attributes has enabled the introduction of inline IDL (for COM developers) and has made COM development in general a lot easier and faster, without developers having to give up control. The database attributes reduce the legwork in accessing databases, and the ATL Server attributes help with the creation of Web applications (as you've seen) and Web services (as you'll see in Chapter 10).

Because attributes are new to Visual C++ .NET, we explain the code clearly whenever we use them in this book.

Conclusion

You should now have a good idea of what ATL Server is designed to do and what problems it's aimed at solving. You should also have a good grasp of the wide range of features that ATL Server provides. The basic syntax of an SRF file and a request handler (attributed and nonattributed) should be familiar to you, as well as the ideas incorporated into this architecture. You should also now be familiar with the new features of Visual Studio .NET that help make creating Web applications much simpler (e.g., compiler attributes and the debugger).

Throughout the rest of this book, we expand on the ideas presented in this chapter and we introduce some new ones. We designed this book in such a way that you can read through it (or most of it) to gain a useful understanding of the area(s) of ATL Server in which you're most interested. This book is intended to be a useful reference on each major area of functionality the library provides, so that you can refer to it while you work with the library.

In the next chapter you'll move on to learn more about SRF files, what they contain, and why they provide an excellent model for Web application design.

CHAPTER 2

SRF Files

Server Response Files (SRFs)[1] are a new file type created by the ATL Server team for storing dynamic and static HTML content in a single file. This new solution was designed to help completely separate the development of HTML layout (static HTML) from the development of dynamic HTML content.

Separating layout/design from code is a problem that has plagued Web development teams for many years. Finally there's a solution that allows Web designers to concentrate on HTML layout and design, and that enables developers to concentrate on writing the underlying C++ code. There's no longer any need for developers to tinker with the HTML layout files (SRF files), and there's no longer any need for designers to tinker with the code.

You saw a basic SRF file in Chapter 1, but here's a quick recap:

```
<html>
  <head> Basic SRF </head>
  {{handler BasicSrf.dll/Example}}
  <body>
    Hello {{World}}
  </body>
</html>
```

This simple demonstration application contains two tags. The first tag is the handler tag. This tag tells your ISAPI DLL which class in which application DLL will handle calls to this file. This handler class is simply a class inheriting from `IRequestHandlerT` (or commonly, `CRequestHandlerT`). It's required that you have at least one handler tag in your SRF file (you'll learn about using more than one handler later on in this chapter). It's also required that this handler tag be the first (noncomment) ATL Server tag encountered in the SRF file.

Now let's move on to look at the `World` tag. This tag calls into a method in your handler class, which in turn is able to spit output into the HTML stream at the

1. You can change the file type from .srf to whatever you like. You can find out more about doing this in Chapter 17.

location of this tag. That is, if you were to have the `World()` method spit the string "World!", your HTML stream (returned to the client) would look like this:

```
<html>
<head> Basic SRF </head>
<body>
  Hello World!
</body>
</html>
```

NOTE *The method itself may not be called* `World()`, *but for the purposes of this chapter, assume that the method being invoked in the handler class has the same name as the tag name in the SRF file. The subtleties of this will become clearer in Chapter 3.*

NOTE *Remember that ATL Server dynamic tags are server side, not client side. If you've used ASP before, you should be familiar with this concept.*

What makes the double brace syntax particularly nice is that not only does it get ignored by HTML editors (which makes Web design and layout an easier task), but it can also be used *anywhere* within an HTML file, making the following type of coding possible:

```
<img src="{{GetImage}}">
```

Flow Control

By examining many of the high-end Web applications on the Internet today, the ATL Server team discovered that most (almost all) Web pages require very simple flow control. This flow control is designed to be used to aid with HTML layout aspects as opposed to actual application logic.

For this reason, the ATL Server flow control system provides very limited flow control out of the box. This helps development teams keep application logic out of the SRF file, and it makes the stencil processor more efficient. In the ATL Server team's experience, this minimal flow control should be sufficient for 99 percent of Web applications.

Of course, if the provided flow control does fall short of your requirements, the flexibility and extensibility of ATL Server means that you can extend the flow control language to include new syntax. We demonstrate this capability later on in the book later on in Chapter 17. For now, let's look at the existing (provided) flow control and see how to go about using it.

If/Else Statement

One of the most useful flow control constructs is the `if` statement, with the `else` statement being a productive relative. An `if/else` block must be terminated with an `{{endif}}` tag.

The `if` statement is placed before the method name (i.e., the name you would normally use in the tag of the method that will be called to evaluate the `if` statement) and it generates the HTML nested within it only if the method returns `HTTP_SUCCESS`. If the method returns `HTTP_S_FALSE`, the corresponding `else` section (if it exists) will be rendered.

Listings 2-1 through 2-3 present some simple examples of `if/else` blocks and what the client would end up seeing based on return values.

Listing 2-1. Simple If Usage in a "Hello World" SRF File

```
<html>
<head> Basic SRF </head>
{{handler BasicSrf.dll/Example}}
<body>
  Hello {{if World}}World!{{endif}}
</body>
</html>
```

If the `World()` method returns `HTTP_SUCCESS`, then the client will see this:

```
<html>
<head> Basic SRF </head>
<body>
  Hello World!
</body>
</html>
```

If the `World()` method returns `HTTP_S_FALSE`, then the client will see this:

```
<html>
<head> Basic SRF </head>
<body>
Hello
</body>
</html>
```

NOTE *The* `World()` *method itself doesn't inject anything into the stream in the Listing 2-1 example—it simply returns success or false.*

Listing 2-2. Simple If/Else Usage in an SRF File

```
<html>
<head> Basic SRF </head>
{{handler BasicSrf.dll/Example}}
<body>
  Hello {{if World}}World!
  {{else}}Foo!
  {{endif}}
</body>
</html>
```

If the `World()` method returns `HTTP_SUCCESS`, then the client will see this:

```
<html>
<head> Basic SRF </head>
<body>
  Hello World!
</body>
</html>
```

If the `World()` method returns `HTTP_S_FALSE`, then the client will see this:

```
<html>
<head> Basic SRF </head>
<body>
  Hello Foo!
</body>
</html>
```

Listing 2-3. Using If/Else to Control Permissions in a Simple SRF File

```
<html>
<head> Basic SRF </head>
{{handler BasicSrf.dll/Example}}
<body>
  {{if LoggedOn}}
    Here is the classified information {{ShowInformation}}
  {{else}}
    Please Login
  {{endif}}
</body>
</html>
```

In Listing 2-3, the `LoggedOn()` method will check if the user is correctly logged on. If the user is correctly logged on, it returns `HTTP_SUCCESS`, thereby sending the following to the client:

```
<html>
<head> Basic SRF </head>
<body>
  Here is the classified information OUTPUT OF ShowInformation
</body>
</html>
```

If the `LoggedOn()` method fails (i.e., the user isn't logged on), then the user will be asked to "Please Login" and `ShowInformation()` will never even get called. What about if you use static HTML for the "classified information"? It still doesn't matter—the client has no way of getting the string "Here is the classified information" once the request to `LoggedOn()` has failed, because all processing is done on the server.

While Statement

The other statement that proves to be very useful in generating HTML layout is the `while` statement. This statement will continue repeatedly calling the method indicated and process the block (terminated with `{{endwhile}}`) until `HTTP_S_FALSE` is returned from the method.

The `while` statement is particularly useful for generating structures such as HTML tables, as you can see in the following example:

```
<html>
<head> Basic SRF </head>
{{handler BasicSrf.dll/Example}}
<body>
  <table>
    {{while AuthorsRemain}}
      <tr>
        <td>{{AuthorName}} </td>
      </tr>
    {{endwhile}}
  </table>
</body>
</html>
```

By now the logic presented here should be fairly straightforward. As long as `AuthorsRemain()` returns `HTTP_SUCCESS`, you'll generate another row in your HTML table. In this case, it's up to the `AuthorName()` method to inject data into the table (you'll learn how the method can do this in Chapter 3).

Here's an example of output the preceding code snippet might generate for the client:

```
<html>
<head> Basic SRF </head>
<body>
  <table>
    <tr>
      <td>Grewal </td>
    </tr>
    <tr>
      <td>Lee </td>
    </tr>
    <tr>
      <td>Kumar </td>
     </tr>
    <tr>
       <td>Crivat </td>
    </tr>
  </table>
</body>
</html>
```

Nesting Statements

As you would expect, there are no rules against nesting statements. End calls are matched with the last relevant opening of flow control. Thus, expressions like the following are perfectly valid:

```
{{if True}}
  {{if NestedTrue}}
    {{while NestedNestedTrue}}
      {{if NestedNestedNestedTrue}}
        Spit this text
      {{endif}}
    {{endwhile}}
  {{endif}}
{{endif}}
```

The formatting system you use should make it clear which `endif` goes with which `if` statement. As you would expect, `endif` or `endwhile` will be associated with the last opened `if` or `while` statement.

There's no limit on the number of nesting levels and the kinds of statements you can use within nested expressions. You can have `while` statements within `while` statements, `while` statements within `if` statements, `if` statements within `if` statements, `if` statements within `while` statements, and unlimited combinations of these.

Using More Than One Handler

By this stage you might be wondering what happens if you need to use more than one handler for your SRF file. Well, ATL Server has been designed to allow you to use as many handlers as you want in any SRF file.

All handlers after the first handler are considered subhandlers. You must list them after the initial handler, before you use any other tags. You denote them similarly to the main handler, except that you use the keyword `subhandler` instead of `handler`, and you give each subhandler a name to identify it. To use a method from a subhandler (instead of from the main handler), you must explicitly put the name identifier of the subhandler (otherwise, the stencil processor will assume that the method is in your main handler). The following example should help clear up any confusion:

```
<html>
<head> Basic SRF </head>
{{handler BasicSrf.dll/Example}}
{{subhandler Foo BasicSrf2.dll/Example2}}
```

```
<body>
  Hello {{World}}<br>
  Hello {{Foo.World}}
</body>
</html>
```

Hopefully this looks fairly straightforward (the syntax is designed to suit C++ developers). It should be clear that you first call the `World()` method in the `Example` class in BasicSrf.dll, and then you call the `World()` method in the `Example2` class in BasicSrf2.dll.

There's no reason why a subhandler can't point to the same DLL as the main handler, or to the same handler (in a different DLL), or even to the same handler in the same DLL (although the latter would mean that the subhandler was providing no additional functionality to the main handler).

There's no limit to the number of subhandlers you can use, the only caveat being that each subhandler must have its own unique identifier:

```
<html>
<head> Basic SRF </head>
{{handler BasicSrf.dll/Example}}
{{subhandler Foo BasicSrf2.dll/Example}}
{{subhandler Bar BasicSrf3.dll/Example}}
{{subhandler FooBar BasicSrf4.dll/Example}}
<body>
  Hello {{World}}<br>
  Hello {{Foo.World}}<br>
  Hello {{Bar.World}}<br>
  Hello {{FooBar.World}}<br>
  Hello {{Foo.World}}
</body>
</html>
```

The extra subhandlers in the preceding example work just as you would expect.

Subhandlers are very useful for breaking functionality out into generic application DLLs and generic handler classes. Thus, you might have a set of database application DLLs, and you could split these into separate handlers: handlers for reading from the database, handlers for inserting new elements into the database, and handlers for replacing or deleting elements in the database (or any number of similar partitions). Doing so enables you to better reuse code throughout your application.

Include Statements

Another feature that's often useful for creating real-world Web applications is the ability to include other HTML files. This not only reduces the complexity of individual HTML files (by separating information into other files), but it also, for many common items such as navigation bars, headers, and footers, allows developers to make one change in one place in one file and have it propagate throughout their Web site.

ATL Server allows you to include either HTML files or SRF files in any SRF file. The syntax for this is very simple, and the include takes place wherever you place this tag within your layout:

```
<html>
{{include header.srf}}
<body>
</body>
</html>
```

NOTE *You can use the* `include` *statement in conjunction with other features such as flow control in order to display includes only when certain conditions are met.*

CAUTION *An included SRF file will make use of handlers specified in the included file, and it will not take any settings from the parent file (into which it is included).*

Parameters

ATL Server's stencil processor provides support for parameters for your tags. There's no limit to the number of parameters you can give to a single method, and there's no restriction as to how you use them.

The syntax is based on C++ syntax and therefore should be quite straightforward:

```
{{simpleString(HelloWorld)}}
{{complexString( Hello, World,!)}}
```

You'll notice that these parameters are static (they can't be modified at runtime from user input, for example[2]). ATL Server supports only static parameters simply because this feature isn't designed to encourage application logic in the SRF file—it's primarily a layout/design/reusability tool.

For example, in the preceding example you might have a `simpleString()` method that has a set of built-in parameters that it recognizes and associates with a fixed output string (in this case it might spit out "Hello World!"). In the `complexString()` method you may take a number of parameters. Each of these parameters might represent a string that you want the method to spit into the stream; therefore, this would result in "Hello World!"

Note that because the `simpleString()` method takes a number of known parameters and basically looks for a match for which string to show, it's much simpler to implement than the `complexString()` method, which takes a variable number of arguments and then needs to convert these arguments into individual strings, concatenate these strings into a single larger string, and finally spit this into the HTML stream.

Static parameters are very useful for aiding code reuse because they make functions more generic. For example, say you have `{{Hello(1)}}`, `{{Hello(2)}}`, and `{{Hello(3)}}`. Each of these would call the `Hello()` method, but the result might vary based on which static parameter you gave it. For example, you might have

```
{{Hello(1)}} = "Hello"
{{Hello(2)}} = "Bonjour"
```

and

```
{{Hello(3)}} = "Guten Tag"
```

NOTE *The parameters don't have to be numbers. They could easily be strings. For example, you could use* `{{Hello(English)}}`, `{{Hello(French}}`, *and* `{{Hello(German)}}` *instead.*

2. The claim that parameters can't be modified at runtime isn't strictly true. It's possible to have methods in one SRF file and make changes to another SRF file (including changes to parameters). You could even have an SRF file change itself and force a refresh. However, this is a clumsy solution and usually indicates either badly structured SRF files or an attempt to move application logic into the SRF file.

Why No Variables?

At this point you're probably wondering where the variables are. Static parameters are useful, but what happens when you want to have dynamic parameters and other variables for storing things like user input? Well, the short answer is that ATL Server doesn't provide variables. Again, the model is extensible so you can add variables if you so desire, but you would have to do a lot of work and you would detract from some of the advantages of ATL Server.

Advantages of ATL Server

The first advantage of ATL Server is its performance. Because there are no variables in SRF files, and there are certain structural rules (e.g., handlers must appear as the first tags), the stencil processor needs to parse an SRF file only once. Thus, it parses the file while generating the HTML stream to be sent to the client. This process is extremely efficient and doesn't suffer from the big performance problems of systems that require multiple parses of the dynamic HTML file in order to render the static page to send back to the client. SRF files are basically as "static" as dynamic files can be (in terms of performance).

The second advantage relates to the issue of where your application logic is going to reside. ATL Server is designed for high-end Web applications. In this situation, you want your application logic where your best developers are (in your C++ shop). The emphasis is on having *all* the application logic go into the code and only layouts go into the SRF files. There are a number of major advantages to this, especially as your Web application begins to grow. Although scripting languages and other "Web languages" can appear powerful at first, they can quickly pull developers into a trap. Their syntax, though often friendly for rapid development, can be difficult to read (especially when it's nested within complex layout logic). On top of this problem, tasks such as debugging the application become an absolute nightmare, not to mention the loss of some of the foundations of object-oriented programming such as code reuse.

The ATL Server team ran into countless examples of large Web applications built with the application logic within the Web pages themselves. In all these cases, the development teams had lost the ability to maintain many of the complex pages in these applications. Beyond this, the teams had often become afraid of even touching some of the pages for fear of breaking their applications. The teams decided that they wanted to make it as difficult as possible for ATL Server users to fall into this trap of choosing small short-term gains that cause large long-term problems.

Because of this decision, it didn't make sense to provide support for variables in the SRF file. Not only does this help you provide your pages with high performance, but it also makes sure that you keep your application logic where it belongs: in the code!

Comment Tags

One final SRF tag we should cover quickly is the comment tag. Unlike HTML comments, which propagate through to the client, SRF comments are discarded on the server, which makes them very useful for annotating your SRF files with development comments.

Comment tags are the only type of tag excluded from most of the SRF processing rules. This means that you can have comment tags before your handler tag and comment tags between your subhandler tags, among other things.

The syntax for comment tags is based on the C++ syntax for comments:

```
{{//Here is a comment about the main handler}}
{{handler MainHandler/Main.dll}}
```

Conclusion

SRF files provide a great way for developers to separate the design task of page layout from the development task of implementing application logic. By allowing developers to mix static and dynamic content, and by providing a basic flow control and layout framework, SRF files make developing high-end Web applications easier than ever before.

By providing an extensible model, SRF files allow developers to add new functionality or modify the behavior of existing functionality in order to best meet their needs. The model provided is also lightweight and flexible, which makes it ideal for completing many tasks. These features also combine to make the SRF framework very useful as a starting point for many other projects—at its heart it's just a very simple and efficient yet powerful text replacement system. You'll learn more about some of these advanced uses for SRF files later in the book.

You'll learn more about SRF files when you take a look at handlers in the next chapter. By looking at SRF files in the context of handlers, it should become clearer to you how the ATL Server model works, and how the code "talks" with the SRF file and vice versa.

CHAPTER 3

Request Handlers

WITH SRF FILES, YOU HAVE the first half of the solution for creating complete a Web application (the HTML UI, design, and layout or front-end aspects). Request handlers are the part of ATL Server that completes the solution. They're classes that provide the back-end for your HTML front-end. They're where your application processing and logic reside. You should be familiar with the material presented in Chapter 2 before you read this chapter.

Like SRF files, request handlers are designed to be lightweight, powerful, efficient, extensible, and flexible. But what exactly is a request handler? A *request handler* is simply a class in your application that implements the `IRequestHandler` interface (or, more commonly, a class that derives from `CRequestHandlerT` or `IRequestHandlerImpl`) and is exposed via a handler map.

The *handler map* is simply a mapping between text strings and the name of a class. Because all HTML requests are text, ATL Server requires a way to convert a text string into a request for a specific class (i.e., the class that will handle this request or request handler). You can easily see the mapping in a simple example:

```
{{handler MyHandler.dll/Default}}
```

You need a way to get the string `Default` to map to an actual class in your request handler (which resides in MyHandler.dll). You can do this by using the appropriate macros as follows:

```
BEGIN_HANDLER_MAP()
  HANDLER_ENTRY("Default", CMyHandler)
END_HANDLER_MAP()
```

In this case, you see that the `CMyHandler` class will handle requests for this page. Thus, `CMyHandler` is the request handler for the given page.

Request handlers aren't limited to use via SRF files, however. Request handlers can be accessed directly via HTTP (by default), as is seen with ATL Server Web services.

Creating a Request Handler

In this section you'll create a request handler. You'll first examine what it looks like in traditional C++, and then you'll learn how it's implemented using the new Visual C++ attributes.

You can generate a basic request handler by using the ATL Server Project Wizard. Simply deselect the Generate Attributed Code option under the Developer Support Options tab to disable attributed code generation. For the time being, ignore the ISAPI project and focus strictly on the request handler project itself (application DLL).

Your request handler will reside in a DLL. In order to accomplish this, you'll require a certain minimal amount of plumbing code. If you open the .cpp file for your project, you'll see the code used to create the DllMain entry point. In addition to this code, you'll also see the handler map (which we discussed earlier). That's all that's required in the .cpp file. The real application logic infrastructure is waiting for you in the header file.

When you open the header file for your application DLL, the first thing you'll see is the `CMyHandler` class. This class derives from `CRequestHandlerT`, which provides some base functionality to your handler, such as SRF support.

In the `CMyHandler` class that follows you can see that there's a replacement method map. This is identical to your handler map, except that instead of mapping strings to classes, this map maps strings to methods in your class. In this case it maps the string `Hello` to the method `OnHello`. If you take a moment to look at the project's SRF file (in Visual Studio .NET you can switch to HTML view using the tabs at the bottom of the window to see the HTML; with the 2003 release it only works in this mode), things will begin to make sense.

Basically, you have an SRF file that looks something like this:

```
<html>
{{handler MyHandler.dll/Default}}
<body>
  This is a test: {{Hello}}
</body>
</html>
```

and a request handler map that looks something like this:

```
BEGIN_HANDLER_MAP()
  HANDLER_ENTRY("Default", CMyHandler);
END_HANDLER_MAP()
```

which combine with your actual request handler to form the following:

```
class CMyHandler : public CRequestHandlerT<CMyHandler>
{
public:
  BEGIN_REPLACEMENT_METHOD_MAP(CMyHandler)
    REPLACEMENT_METHOD_ENTRY("Hello", OnHello)
  END_REPLACEMENT_METHOD_MAP()
...
```

So MyHandler.dll is your application DLL. The `Default` string is mapped to the `CMyHandler` class, indicating that requests on the SRF page will be handled by methods in this class. Finally, you have the string `Hello` mapped to the method `OnHello`, indicating that whenever you see the tag `{{Hello}}` in the SRF file, you'll call the `OnHello()` method in the `CMyHandler` class.

The relationship among the SRF tags, the maps, and the various parts of the request handler should now be clear. To complete the picture, simply implement the `OnHello` method as follows:

```
HTTP_CODE OnHello(void)
{
  m_HttpResponse << "Hello World!";
  return HTTP_SUCCESS;
}
```

If you build this application (note that the build step will also deploy your application) and run it by navigating to `http://localhost/My/My.srf`, you'll see the following on the Web page:

```
This is a test: Hello World!
```

You can see that the `OnHello` method simply spits the string `Hello World!` into the response buffer returned to the client. Notice that if you use your browser's View Source command, no ATL Server tags are left in the data passed to the client. That's because they're all stripped by the stencil processor on the server side.

There's only one piece of information we still need to cover to help you understand the entire wizard-generated request handler, and that's the `ValidateAndExchange` method, which we've overlooked until now.

The `ValidateAndExchange` method is the method called before your page is rendered (before the stencil processor begins processing your page). This makes it the perfect place for any initialization code, as well as any processing of HTML form or query data (see Chapter 6 for more information on working with this data). In the case of the wizard code, you simply set the content type.

Now you understand the basic parts of an SRF file and a request handler. In the next section you'll learn how all this works with attributes.

Using Attributes

Visual C++ attributes represent a new philosophy in C++ development. Attributes are designed to allow developers to spend more time focusing on application logic (business logic) and a lot less time focusing on implementation. Attributes don't just help the initial implementer, they also make C++ code easier to read, manage, maintain, and consequently test.

Create a new default ATL Server project with the Project Wizard to see how attributes work. Let's begin again with the .cpp file.

This time you'll notice a few things. First, the handler map is missing. Second, some of the plumbing code that was previously required has been replaced. Instead, there are two uses of attributes. The attributes are marked with square brackets and (in our opinion) fit seamlessly into C++ code. In fact, it's very common that when people first look at the code they don't even realize that there's anything strange about it. The two attributes used are as follows:

```
[module(name="MyAttributedHandler", type="dll")]
...
[emitidl(restricted)];
```

The `module` attribute is used to generate the stub code that's required when creating a DLL (e.g., your DllMain function).

TIP *If you try to create your own DllMain (or other function generated by the* `module` *attribute) you'll receive build errors. To solve this problem, you should put this attribute on a class, and then override any of the functions you want by creating them in this class.*

The `emitidl` attribute is marked as restricted to indicate that IDL shouldn't be generated for this application (you aren't building a COM object!).

If you jump over to the header file, you'll see that things also look different. Your new header file (ignoring ValidateAndExchange, which remains the same) is of the following form:

```
[request_handler("Default")]
class CMyAttributedHandler
{
  [tag_name(name="Hello")]
  HTTP_CODE OnHello(void)
  {
    m_HttpResponse << "Hello World!";
    return HTTP_SUCCESS;
  }
};
```

The request_handler attribute replaces your handler map. You'll see that it takes the string Default as a parameter, and because it's "sitting" on the CMyAttributedHandler class, it maps the string to this class. It also ensures that the CMyAttributedHandler class derives from CRequestHandlerT, so the code to do this is no longer required.

The replacement method map is also missing. Again, attributes provide the replacement. This time the tag_name attribute, which takes a name parameter of Hello, will do the mapping between this string and its method (the OnHello method on which the attribute sits).

If you try the code, you'll see that it functions in exactly the same way as the previous example. In fact, if you go to the trouble of comparing the output of the compiler, you'll see that the attributed and unattributed applications are identical. So just what are these attributes and what do they do?

You can think of attributes as being like compile-time wizards. They basically generate C++ code for you at compile time. Unlike wizards, attributes can take advantage of knowledge gleaned from your code (from having the front-end of the compiler parse it), thereby making their code spits much more rich, powerful, and customized than those of traditional template-based wizards.

Basically, the compiler parses your code and calls into the attribute provider (unfortunately, for this release you can't write your own) when it sees an attribute. It informs the attribute provider of what attribute was seen and what its parameters were. Once the parser has reached the end of the appropriate block (e.g., the end of the handler class), it calls back into the attribute provider. The attribute provider can now use information the compiler learned about your class (such as class names, method names, and so on) to inject C++ code into your source. This isn't a template-based code injection—it's a programmatic-based code injection, which makes the code injection much richer and more powerful than those possible through traditional wizard templates.

You can always view the code generated by the attribute provider by using the `/Fx` compiler switch. Attributes aren't magic; they merely generate C++ source code (although sometimes the code they generate is extremely complex). This means that whenever you do something with attributes, it's always possible to do the same thing without attributes.

There are attributes designed to make it easier to work with ATL Server Web applications, ATL Server Web services, databases, Perfmon counters, and ATL COM. We touch on many of these attributes throughout the course of this book. The ATL COM attributes in particular may fascinate many ATL developers (but we don't cover them in this book). They're very powerful and flexible, and they enable developers to create a self-registering COM component with just a handful of lines of code.

For the rest of this chapter, you'll continue to use the attributes that you've seen demonstrated in this section.

Web Jukebox 1.0

In this section you'll begin using your knowledge of SRF files and request handlers to put together a basic online jukebox. To create your first online jukebox, simply create a Web page that displays all the songs available in the jukebox. When a user clicks a song, he or she will be prompted to download or open the associated file. (Depending on the user's browser settings, the file may actually play automatically.)

Rather than hard-coding the Web page with your list of songs, you'll use a simple Access database (.mdb file) to store your list of songs. For each song you'll need to maintain the name of the song; the musician, band, or composer of the song; and a brief description of the song. You'll also need to store the location of the song itself.

For purposes of simplicity, you'll keep the user interface for this application very simple. You'll use an HTML table with columns for each of the fields in which you're interested and a hyperlink to the file containing the song.

Getting Started

To create the skeleton for the online jukebox, launch the ATL Server Project Wizard, and name your project WebJukebox. Select File Cache, Datasource Cache, Predefined Performance Counters, and Session State (memory backed, not database backed) on the Server Options tab. Otherwise accept the defaults and create the application. Although you won't use all these functions in this example, you are encouraged to add the code required to use them as you continue through the book.

Start by opening the WebJukebox.srf file. You can work in either Design view or HTML view. (In the Visual Studio .NET 2003 release it is not possible to use Design View with SRF files. This functionality was removed to quick-fix some parser problems discovered very late in the ship cycle.) To begin, remove the comment tag at the beginning of the file. You should also remove `This is a test: {{Hello}}` from the document. If you're using Design view, you can use the Toolbox to drag and drop a table onto your page.

Create an HTML table with columns for each of your categories (name, musician/band/composer, and description). Use the Name field as a hyperlink to the file containing the song. You should end up with something that looks like this:

```
<table>
  <tr>
    <td><b>Name</b></td>
    <td><b>Musician / Band / Composer</b></td>
    <td><b>Description</b></td>
  </tr>
</table>
```

To generate your table from your database, you can use the power of the ATL Server `while` statement. This power is clear when you look at the following code:

```
<table>
  <tr>
    <td><b>Name</b></td>
    <td><b>Musician / Band / Composer</b></td>
    <td><b>Description</b></td>
  </tr>
  {{while MoreSongs}}
  <tr>
    <td><a href="{{Location}}">{{Name}}</a></td>
    <td>{{Musician}}</td>
    <td>{{Description}}</td>
  </tr>
  {{endwhile}}
</table>
```

Can you see what you've done here? You've inserted a `while` block around a second table row. What this means is that as long as the `MoreSongs` method returns `HTTP_SUCCESS`, you'll continue creating additional blocks of HTML that match those between the `while` and `endwhile` statements. That is, you'll keep creating additional rows in the table.

What data will go into these rows? Well, there are three entries (to match your three headings). The first entry is the name of the song. You use the `Name` method to return the name of each song. You use the power of HTML to make this value a hyperlink, and you use the `Location` method to determine the location of the hyperlink (i.e., the location of the song). Similarly, the `Musician` and `Description` methods will need to return the name of the musician and a description of the song, respectively.

If you now look at the WebJukebox.h file, you'll see that it contains a lot of code comments related to the implementation of the session state and the file cache. Simply remove these comments for the time being. You can also remove the `OnHello` method and replace it with skeletons for each of the methods we discussed previously. This should leave you with the following request handler:

```
 [ request_handler("Default") ]
class CWebJukeboxHandler
{
public:
     // Put public members here

     HTTP_CODE ValidateAndExchange()
     {
          // Set the content type
          m_HttpResponse.SetContentType("text/html");

          return HTTP_SUCCESS;
     }

protected:

     [ tag_name(name="MoreSongs") ]
     HTTP_CODE OnMoreSongs(void)
     {
          return HTTP_SUCCESS;
     }

      [ tag_name(name="Name") ]
     HTTP_CODE OnName(void)
     {
          return HTTP_SUCCESS;
     }

      [ tag_name(name="Location") ]
     HTTP_CODE OnLocation(void)
     {
          return HTTP_SUCCESS;
     }
```

```
    [ tag_name(name="Position") ]
    HTTP_CODE OnPosition(void)
    {
        return HTTP_SUCCESS;
    }

    [ tag_name(name="Description") ]
    HTTP_CODE OnDescription(void)
    {
        return HTTP_SUCCESS;
    }
}; // class CWebJukeboxHandler
```

Now you'll go ahead and implement each of these functions. First you need to connect to your database. To do this, you can use the OLE DB Consumer Wizard to connect to the WebJukebox.mdb file. Right-click the WebJukebox project in Solution Explorer and select Add ➤ Add Class to choose the ATL OLE DB Consumer Wizard. Open the wizard and use the Jet Provider to point to the WebJukebox.mdb file (which you can download from the Apress Web site, or create your own database using Access). Choose the Song List table and click OK twice on the dialog boxes that pop up.

The generated code will appear before you automatically. Remove the `#error` and the associated security warning. It's important to ensure that your database and database connections are secure. If you're using a modern database such as SQL, the best way to make it secure is to use a system such as Windows Authentication so you don't need to expose your credentials by sending them in the connection string. In this case you're storing data in a simple .mdb file, therefore you'll have all the information pass in the connection string. If we were using SQL Server or another fully featured database for this example, we would use proper Windows Authentication to protect our database, even for test code. Databases usually run as local system, and not protecting access to them is the equivalent of making normal users administrators on your machine.

If you're interested, you can examine the attributes used to make the database connection. Once you've finished, return to WebJukebox.h and `#include` the generated SongList.h file.

Now you can create a public member variable in your class of type `CSongList` to access the data from your database. Here's the code for implementing the rest of your functions:

```
[ request_handler("Default") ]
class CWebJukeboxHandler
{
public:
  // Put public members here
```

```
    CSongList m_songList;
    HRESULT hr;

    HTTP_CODE ValidateAndExchange()
    {
      // Set the content-type
      m_HttpResponse.SetContentType("text/html");
      hr = m_songList.OpenAll();
      if (hr != S_OK) return HTTP_S_FALSE;
      return HTTP_SUCCESS;
    }

  protected:

    [ tag_name(name="MoreSongs") ]
    HTTP_CODE OnMoreSongs(void)
    {
      hr = m_songList.MoveNext();
      if (hr != S_OK) return HTTP_S_FALSE;
      return HTTP_SUCCESS;
    }

     [ tag_name(name="Name") ]
    HTTP_CODE OnName(void)
    {
      m_HttpResponse << m_songList.m_Name;
      return HTTP_SUCCESS;
    }

     [ tag_name(name="Location") ]
    HTTP_CODE OnLocation(void)
    {
      m_HttpResponse << m_songList.m_Location;
      return HTTP_SUCCESS;
    }

     [ tag_name(name="Musician") ]
    HTTP_CODE OnMusician(void)
    {
      m_HttpResponse << m_songList.m_Musician;
      return HTTP_SUCCESS;
    }

     [ tag_name(name="Description") ]
```

```
  HTTP_CODE OnDescription(void)
  {
    m_HttpResponse << m_songList.m_Description;
    return HTTP_SUCCESS;
  }
}; // class CWebJukeboxHandler
```

The code is fairly self-explanatory. You initialize your database connection in the `ValidateAndExchange` method with the `OpenAll` call. Your `OnMoreSongs` method moves through the database entries and returns `HTTP_SUCCESS` as long as there's an entry to output. The outputting for each value is done by the other methods, which simply put information from the database into the HTML stream.

There you have it, your first ATL Server application!

Conclusion

By now you should have a good understanding of how basic Web applications work in the ATL Server framework. The relationship between SRF files and request handlers now should be easy to follow, and you should be able to begin creating your very own Web applications.

There's one final piece of the puzzle that remains hidden behind the scenes, but that should become clearer in the next chapter. If you're interested in more of the details of how request handlers work and how you can customize them for your own applications, you should take a look at Chapter 17. In that chapter we cover in depth the relationship between `IRequestHandlerImpl` and `CRequestHandlerT`, including when and why to use each of them and how to get the best out of your application.

CHAPTER 4

Introduction to ISAPI Services

So far we've treated the ISAPI DLL as a request dispatcher. Your ISAPI DLL receives requests and hands off the processing to the appropriate application DLL. Your ISAPI DLL is also the place to expose your ISAPI services.

ISAPI services allow developers to provide services to all their application DLLs. These might be global functions or shared global information such as session state, caches, or Perfmon counters. In this chapter we cover the basics of exposing an ISAPI service from your ISAPI DLL.

What to Put in Your ISAPI DLL

When your application is loaded by IIS, IIS locks your ISAPI DLL in memory. This makes ISAPI very efficient, but it adds some complexity to changing your ISAPI DLL. Changing your ISAPI DLL involves resetting IIS (which usually takes between 10 and 30 seconds) with an `iisreset` command.

The downside of changing your ISAPI DLL is that your server will be unable to process any incoming requests until the IIS service restarts and reloads your ISAPI. All requests that arrive before IIS is restarted will be completely lost. Therefore, it's recommended that you don't restart IIS often, which in turn means that you can't change your ISAPI DLL often.

For this reason, it makes sense to take advantage of ATL Server's separation between the application DLLs and the ISAPI DLL. The ISAPI DLL still has one unique advantage over the application DLLs. Application logic resides in the ATL Server thread pool in the form of worker threads. In this model, when a request comes in, the ISAPI DLL hands it off to an available worker thread. This thread processes the given request and then returns to the thread pool when it finishes processing. This means that data stored in your application DLL is *request specific.* Once a given request has been handled, the data in your thread will be reset.

The only way to store data that has the same lifetime as your application is to do so outside of the application DLL. The ISAPI DLL is perfect for many of these services.

TIP *It's also possible to use a Windows Service to store data that will have the same lifetime as your application, as you can see in the PerfPersist sample included with Visual Studio .NET.*

Designing Your ISAPI Services

The question that now arises is what services make sense for the ISAPI DLL. The answer is any service that stores some form of global state and is unlikely to change its functionality often. One good question to ask yourself is "Do I need to access/update this information over multiple requests?" If the answer is yes, then an ISAPI service may be the right solution for you.

Good examples of services that meet the criteria for exposing an ISAPI service include the following:

- *Caches:* Data in a Web application is usually cached based on global information. For example, you may want to cache the pages of your application that are hit most often, the most often used data source connections, or a commonly requested image or file. The information that determines, for example, what file is commonly requested relies on building up information over multiple requests. The file in question must also be returned to the user on various different requests.

- *Session state:* Session state is typically used to create state information over HTTP (a stateless protocol). You do this by finding a way to uniquely identify a given user (usually via cookies) and then accessing information specific to that user on each of the user's requests. Information such as what city the user lives in can be gathered on a single request, but it requires access on every request the user makes after that. Each of these requests can be handled by a different thread requiring a central storage mechanism.

- *Logging/Perfmon counters:* Usually you'll use Perfmon to track information that occurs over your application's lifetime. Similarly, logging is something you'll likely do based on information over time, as opposed to a specific request. Examples include counting how many purchases have been made on your site or logging what times of the day your application receives the most requests (and from what countries). You could even create a mechanism to log application errors and failures (e.g., failures to connect to the database).

Because the ISAPI DLL runs on a single thread, doesn't often get reset, and handles all incoming requests, it's capable of meeting all the requirements that these types of services demand. It also makes sense because these services are unlikely to change regularly. Session state is an example of a service that's designed into the application. Caching and logging are good examples of services that are honed during the develop-test cycle and therefore see little change once the application goes into production.

These are also all good reasons for why your ISAPI services should be some of the most carefully scrutinized code in your entire application. Services should be well designed so they provide the functionality required today and so they can be modified with minimal effort to extend that functionality in the future. Regularly called services are likely to be a bottleneck in your application, especially if they're processor intensive. You should examine the code carefully for security and reliability issues.

Code in your ISAPI DLL also falls into the category of being some of the only code in a Web application that needs to be thread-safe. Because you have multiple worker threads running, and all these threads are capable of calling your service at any time, you need to ensure that locking is carefully used on update commands and that information returned to callers is valid.

Creating an ISAPI Service

In this section you'll create an ISAPI service. The service will be very simple so you can focus on the service infrastructure and not concern yourself as much with the implementation details of a complex service. To fulfill these requirements, you'll create a simple page hit counter service. This service will simply count the number of requests the site has received over its lifetime and provide this number on demand.

NOTE *Normally for a page hit counter service, you're better off using a facility such as Perfmon, because it provides a lot of benefits in terms of accessibility, reliability, and logging. See Chapter 9 for more information on how to take advantage of this new feature.*

Creating a Simple Counter

Run through the ATL Server Project Wizard and make sure that all the options under the Server Options tab are unchecked (the default). This will ensure that you've disabled all the default ISAPI services that come with ATL Server.

You can open the .cpp file in your ISAPI project. Notice how little code it currently contains. All it basically does is expose the entry points required by IIS and delegate all the functionality to an instantiation of `CIsapiExtension`.

Add a new header file to this project. You'll put the code required for your counter there. Create a `CSimpleCounter` class that provides the functionality that you need. It should look something like Listing 4-1.

Listing 4-1. A Simple Counter

```
__interface ATL_NO_VTABLE __declspec(uuid("b3902ede-b647-4616-8ca4-1dcb98a015b0"))
ISimpleCounter : public IUnknown
{
  STDMETHOD (Set) ();
  STDMETHOD (Get) (long*);
};

class CSimpleCounter : public ISimpleCounter,
public CComObjectRootEx<CComGlobalsThreadModel>
{
  BEGIN_COM_MAP(CSimpleCounter)
    COM_INTERFACE_ENTRY(ISimpleCounter)
  END_COM_MAP()
protected:
    long m_Counter;
public:
  void Init(void)
  {
    m_Counter = 0;
  }

  STDMETHOD (Set)(void)
  {
    InterlockedIncrement(&m_Counter);
    return S_OK;
  }
  STDMETHOD (Get)(long *input)
  {
    *input = m_Counter;
```

```
    return S_OK;
  }
};
```

You can see that your class does everything you need: It initializes the counter to 0 when `Init` is called and it exposes a `Get` function and a `Set` function that allow you to either get the current value of the counter or increment the counter, respectively.

Now that you have the counter itself, you need to expose this counter as a service from your ISAPI DLL. We explain how to do this in the next section.

Exposing the Counter As a Service (from the ISAPI DLL)

Now you need to be able to expose the functionality provided by `CSimpleCounter` to the application DLL. The application DLL needs to be able to

1. Check if the service exists. This allows you to decouple the application DLL and ISAPI DLL somewhat, as opposed to tying the application to a specific instantiation of the counter.

2. Bind to the service if it exists. Obviously, if the service does exist, you want to get access to it.

3. Finally, you can actually use the service.

In order to do this, you need to create your own extension that extends the base `CIsapiExtension` by providing this new hit counter service. If you had selected any of the options on the Server Options tab of the Project Wizard, they would have already created this extension of `CIsapiExtension` for you (in order to expose their own functionality).

You'll start by modifying the `typedef` in the ISAPI .cpp. Currently, `ExtensionType` is a `CIsapiExtension`. In this case, you want to modify `ExtensionType` so that it's a `CMyIsapiExtension`. Go ahead and make the change so that

```
typedef CIsapiExtension<> ExtensionType;
```

becomes

```
typedef MyCIsapiExtension<> ExtensionType;
```

Now you'll create a `MyCIsapiExtension` header file where you'll define what `MyCIsapiExtension` really is. `CIsapiExtension` is templated on a thread pool class, a stat class, an error text provider, and worker traits. You need to template your `MyCIsapiExtension` on these same parameters so that you can pass them through. Thus, your definition of `MyCIsapiExtension` will look something like this:

```
template <class ThreadPoolClass=CThreadPool<CIsapiWorker>,
  class CStatClass=CNoRequestStats,
  class HttpUserErrorTextProvider=CDefaultErrorProvider,
  class WorkerThreadTraits=DefaultThreadTraits >
class MyCIsapiExtension :
  public CIsapiExtension<ThreadPoolClass,
    CStatClass,
    HttpUserErrorTextProvider,
    WorkerThreadTraits>
{
};
```

Now all you need to do to complete the service is implement the required methods in this class, as shown in Listing 4-2. This includes the `GetExtensionVersion` method that's called when the ISAPI is first loaded. It also includes an implementation for `QueryService` so that you can connect to your ISAPI service.

Listing 4-2. Making the Counter As a Service

```
#include "SimpleCounter.h"

template <class ThreadPoolClass=CThreadPool<CIsapiWorker>,
  class CStatClass=CNoRequestStats,
  class HttpUserErrorTextProvider=CDefaultErrorProvider,
  class WorkerThreadTraits=DefaultThreadTraits >
class CMyIsapiExtension : public CIsapiExtension<
          ThreadPoolClass,
          CStatClass,
          HttpUserErrorTextProvider,
          WorkerThreadTraits>
{
  typedef CIsapiExtension<ThreadPoolClass, CStatClass, HttpUserErrorTextProvider,
    WorkerThreadTraits> baseISAPI;

  CComObjectGlobal<CSimpleCounter> g_Counter;
public:
  BOOL GetExtensionVersion(HSE_VERSION_INFO* pVer)
  {
    if (!baseISAPI::GetExtensionVersion(pVer))
```

```
    {
      return FALSE;
    }
    if (GetCriticalIsapiError() != 0)
    {
      return TRUE;
    }
    g_Counter.Init();
    return TRUE;
  }

  HRESULT STDMETHODCALLTYPE QueryService(REFGUID guidService,
      REFIID riid, void** ppvObject)
  {
    if (InlineIsEqualGUID(guidService, __uuidof(ISimpleCounter)))
      return g_Counter.QueryInterface(riid, ppvObject);
    return baseISAPI::QueryService(guidService, riid, ppvObject);
  }
};
```

That's all there is to it—you have now exposed your counter as an ISAPI service. In the next section, you'll actually use your service from your application DLL by displaying a hit counter on your Web page.

Using the ISAPI Service

Start by opening up the main header file in your application DLL. It should contain the implementation of your wizard-generated "Hello World" request handler. Then `#include` CMyIsapiExtension.h, which is where your service resides. Take a look at the code in Listing 4-3.

Listing 4-3. Consuming the Service

```
#include "..\SimpleServiceIsapi\CMyIsapiExtension.h"
[ request_handler("Default") ]
class CSimpleServiceHandler
{
private:
  CComPtr<ISimpleCounter> m_SimpleCounter;
  long counter;
  public:
  HTTP_CODE ValidateAndExchange()
```

```
  {
    HRESULT hr = m_spServiceProvider->QueryService(
          __uuidof(ISimpleCounter),
          &m_SimpleCounter
          );
    if (FAILED(hr))
    {
      m_SimpleCounter = 0;
    }
    m_SimpleCounter->Set();
    m_HttpResponse.SetContentType("text/html");
    return HTTP_SUCCESS;
  }
protected:
  [ tag_name(name="Hello") ]
  HTTP_CODE OnHello(void)
  {
    m_HttpResponse << "Hello World!";
    return HTTP_SUCCESS;
  }
  [ tag_name(name="Counter") ]
  HTTP_CODE OnCounter(void)
  {
    m_SimpleCounter->Get(&counter);
    m_HttpResponse << counter;
    return HTTP_SUCCESS;
  }
}; // class CSimpleServiceHandler
```

You start by creating a `CComPtr` to your counter and a `long` to store the current hit value. You `QueryService` your ISAPI service in your `ValidateAndExchange` method and increment the counter. You then create the `OnCounter` method, which gets the value of the hit counter and outputs it.

Now all you need to do is modify the SRF file to include your new functionality. The following code will do the trick:

```
<html>
  {{handler SimpleService.dll/Default}}
  <body>
    This is a test: {{Hello}}<br>
    This page has been hit {{Counter}} times!<br>
  </body>
</html>
```

Now build and run the code. Keep refreshing the page and watch as your hit counter goes through the roof! Once you've read Chapter 6 you should try adding a button to this page that lets you reset the counter.

NOTE *You'll have to implement the functionality to expose this from the service. Currently the `Init` method isn't exposed.*

Conclusion

In this chapter you learned the basics of creating an ISAPI service. You also learned how you can use the service from your application. ATL Server provides a number of ISAPI services that you can use out of the box, and caches, session state, and Perfmon services are available to you from the ATL Server Project Wizard. All of these classes allow for easy exposure via ISAPI services.

ISAPI services provide an easy way to expose functionality to your entire application. They also allow you to maintain global state, and they're perfect for managing data that must survive the lifetime of the process.

It's important to remember, however, that changes to your ISAPI service will require that you reset IIS, so you should try to ensure that code exposed via ISAPI services isn't subject to constant change.

If a service you want to expose will require a lot of changes, you may want to consider exposing this functionality via a Windows Service instead. There's a sample that shows you how to do this included in the Visual C++ .NET product, under the ATL Server directory called PerfPersist.

So far we've concentrated on some of the core components that make up an ATL Server application. In the next chapter we examine the architecture of an ATL Server application as a whole at a high level.

CHAPTER 5

Inside the ATL Server Architecture

ATL Server applications are ISAPI extension applications. It's possible to build a simple, lightweight ISAPI extension application with ATL Server (i.e., by using `CIsapiExtension`). ATL Server provides myriad of features that you can use individually or bring together to form a rich framework. This framework provides a standard architecture for your application. You can pick and choose which parts of this architecture you want to use (for the most part), and you'll only pay for what you use.

We've already touched on parts of this architecture at a high level in previous chapters, and by now you know the basic components of an ATL Server application (handlers, application DLLs, SRFs, and ISAPIs) and the roles they play. However, do you really understand what happens when a request comes into your server?

In this chapter we drill down into the ATL Server architecture and examine step-by-step what happens when a request is received by the server. After you've read this chapter, you should have a good understanding of how a request is handled by ATL Server.

Key Components in ATL Server

One of the problems with creating ISAPI extensions from scratch is the basic infrastructure that you have to create before you can focus on your application logic. ATL Server is designed to solve this problem for you. It's still helpful, however, to look at what these different components are:

- *Thread pool:* You need to create a thread pool to handle requests. IIS has a limited number of threads with which to handle requests, and once all of these are used, new requests are rejected.

- *Buffers:* It's rare that your application will complete compiling its entire response straight away. To build up your response header, avoid expensive network calls, and enable keep-alive, you must build a buffering system to handle storing your response before it's sent.

- *Session state:* HTTP is a stateless protocol, but often you need to keep some information between requests. In a consumer Web application, this information is usually details about a given user. To accomplish this, you can use session state, which allows you to store key/value data in a "permanent system" (memory backed, database backed, or file backed by default).

- *Regular expressions:* Many Web applications need to process large amounts of text data, often from query or form variables. Regular expressions enable you to easily extract the information you need from strings. ATL Server regular expressions are based on the very popular Perl style.

- *Caches:* ATL Server provides a number of caches to help improve the performance of your application. Some of these caches work automatically in an application (e.g., the stencil cache for caching SRF pages). You can use other caches to make your code more efficient (e.g., the data source cache for caching database connections).

- *Security and cryptography:* ATL Server provides support for various security and cryptography functionality, such as Windows NT Challenge/Response (NTLM) and RSA Security's MD5. These security mechanisms can be useful in intranet and Internet situations.

- *Cookies:* To facilitate cookies, you need code to parse incoming cookies and format outgoing cookies correctly.

- *Query parameters:* Query parameters are often nontrivial, especially when you consider all the possible escape sequences. Every Web application needs to be able to parse these parameters.

- *Forms:* POSTed form data, multipart forms, and so on all must be parsed by the application. Many Web applications need to be able to handle posted data.

The preceding list covers some of the key components a Web application needs to be able to handle. Seem basic? Yes, they're all basic pieces of functionality. The problem is that they aren't provided by ISAPI, so every ISAPI extension developer needs to create this infrastructure over and over. ATL Server not only provides this basic functionality, but also allows developers to take advantage of more advanced Web functionality such as dynamic content, caching, and session state.

Processing an Incoming Request

In this section we take you through what happens to an incoming HTTP request. First, the client (e.g., Internet Explorer, Netscape Navigator, Opera, and so on) sends a request to your server. IIS receives this request and checks application mapping settings for the request. IIS keeps all this data in its metabase, and this data must be configured correctly for your Web application to work as desired. Both overmapping and undermapping settings can cause problems (security risks through overmapping and functionality breakage through undermapping).

If the request isn't mapped to an ATL Server ISAPI extension, then IIS will do whatever the extension mapping indicates. Let's assume that in this case it's an ATL Server request (because that's the scenario we're interested in).

If the request maps to your ISAPI extension, then your ISAPI extension will be invoked and it will check the incoming request to see what type of request it is. Typically you'll map SRF files and DLLs to your ISAPI extension, so we focus on these two mappings.

Say that the request is for an SRF file. Your ISAPI extension will open the SRF file to determine the name of the application DLL and the handler. The ISAPI extension will then check if the application DLL is in the cache. If the DLL isn't in the cache, then the ISAPI extension will load the application DLL and cache all the entry points.

Now the ISAPI extension will call into the entry point of your application DLL in order to obtain an instance of the appropriate handler. Once this has been done, `HandleRequest` can be called on the `IRequestHandler` interface of this handler.

The handler parses any query parameters and form variables that have been passed to it. It then calls `ValidateAndExchange`. If `ValidateAndExchange` fails, then the handler returns an error to your ISAPI extension. If `ValidateAndExchange` succeeds, the handler gets the name of the requested SRF file and queries the ISAPI extension to see if this SRF file is in the cache (stencil cache). If the stencil isn't in the cache, then the handler loads and parses this SRF file, and adds it to the cache. Once this is done, the handler can render the stencil.

Let's go back to the situation where your ISAPI extension received the request and checked what sort of request it was. In the previous case, we assumed that it was an SRF request, but what happens if it's a request for an application DLL directly? In this case the ISAPI extension checks if the application DLL is in the cache. If it isn't, the ISAPI loads it and caches the entry points. It will then call into the entry point and obtain an instance of the appropriate handler (designated by query parameters in the request). It proceeds by calling `HandleRequest` on the `IRequestHandler` interface.

This process may become clearer if you look at a diagram for a given request. Figure 5-1 shows the ISAPI flow control, and Figure 5-2 shows the application DLL flow control.

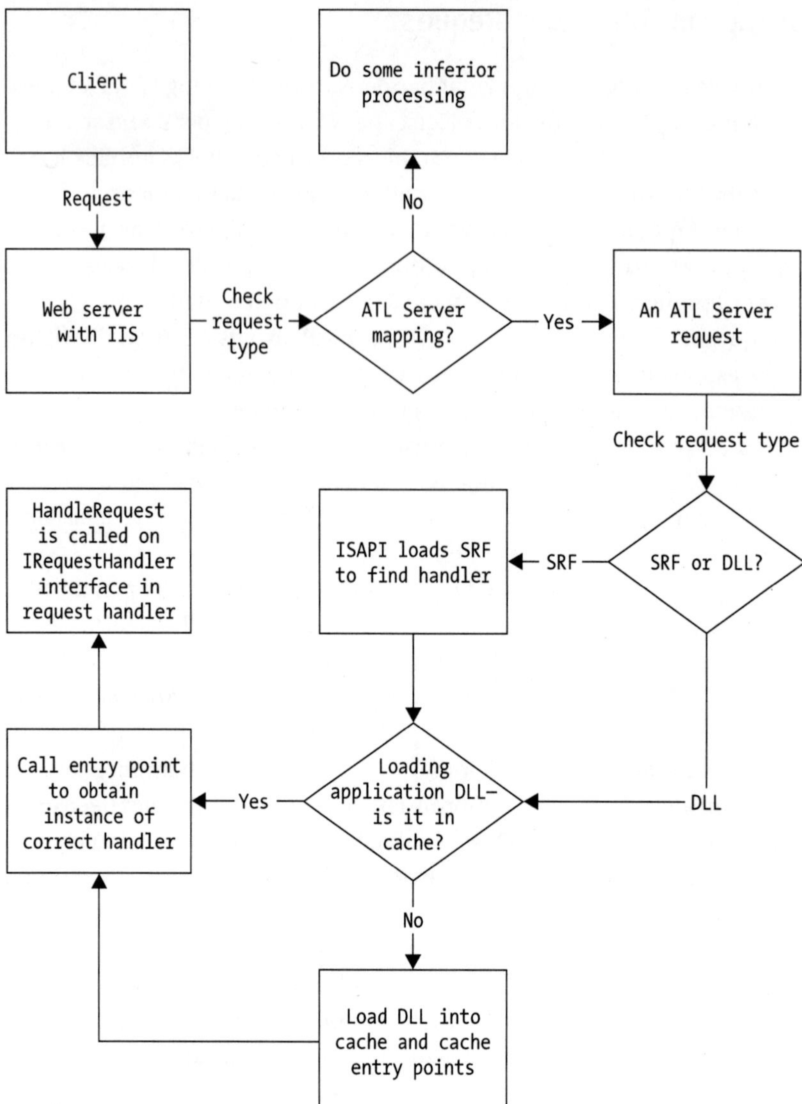

Figure 5-1. ISAPI flow control

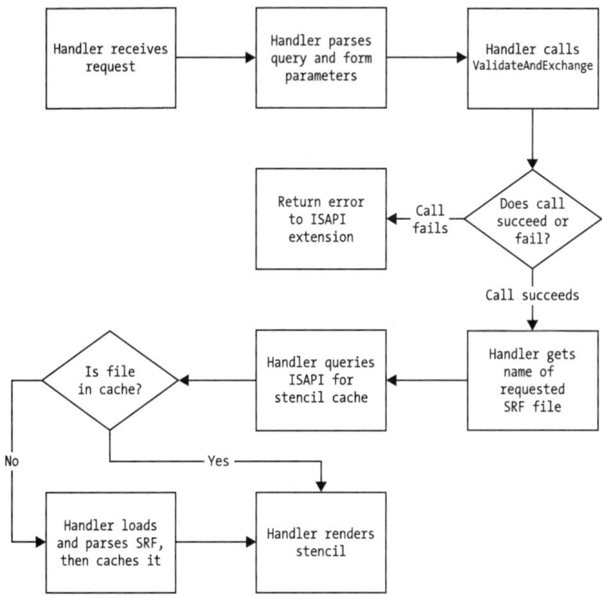

Figure 5-2. Application DLL (request handler) flow control

Key ATL Server Classes

In this section we briefly discuss some of the key ATL Server classes. These classes provide some of the core functionality in an ATL Server application. We begin by looking at the classes that play a key role in your ISAPI extension DLL, and then we cover the classes that are key to the success of your request handler (application DLL).

Key ISAPI Classes

The following classes play key roles in your ISAPI extension DLL:

- `CIsapiExtension` (atlisapi.h): As the main ISAPI extension implementation, this class forms the basis for your ISAPI extension class. It takes several template parameters that enable specification of the following: thread pool class, request statistic class, error text message class, page cache statistics, and stencil cache statistics. You'll see that it implements `HttpExtensionProc`, which is the entry point in IIS for a normal request. You can see it initializes data structures when a request arrives and places the request in the thread pool by calling `QueueRequest`.

- CThreadPool (atlutil.h): CThreadPool implements a simple I/O completion port–based thread pool. It's one of the classes that's useful outside of a Web application context, as I/O completion port–based thread pools are very efficient on Windows, and they're useful for many multithreaded applications. This class is templated on two parameters: the first is Worker, which is the class responsible for handling the requests that are queued on the thread pool, and the other is Traits, which implements a static CreateThread function that allows for overriding how threads are created. The SetSize and GetSize methods allow you to dynamically configure your thread pools. The Initialize function actually sets up the thread pool.

- CIsapiWorker (atlisapi.h): This is the default worker class that your CThreadPool is instantiated on. The Initialize and Execute methods provide the bulk of the functionality for this class. In particular, you'll notice that Execute makes a call to DispatchStencilCall.

- DispatchStencilCall (atlisapi.h): This isn't a class; rather, it's an important method in CIsapiExtension. This is the method that checks if the request is for an SRF file or a DLL (handler). It makes sure that the correct action is taken depending on the type of request. In the case of an SRF file, it will look at the handler, check if that handler is already in the cache, and call that handler. The parsing of the rest of the SRF file is done by your request handler.

Key Request Handler (Application DLL) Classes

The following classes play key roles in your request handler (application DLL):

- CRequestHandlerT (atlstencil.h): This class implements the major functionality of the request handler. It includes several initialization functions, but of the most interest is HandleRequest, which performs the default processing of HTTP requests. It includes steps to load, parse, and render the stencil (SRF file), and it flushes the information out. If you need to put in some custom initialization before a request is handled, or if you want to customize the way a request is handled, then you should override this function. CheckValidRequest, as its name implies, checks if the given HTTP request is valid, and it can be overridden if you have some custom requirements in this space.

- CHtmlTagReplacer (atlstencil.h): This class handles your stencil processing. It creates, stores, caches, initializes, loads, and parses CStencil-based objects. There's one instance of this class per request (typically), which is destroyed once the request is complete.

- `RenderStencil`, `Render`, `RenderToken`, and `RenderReplacement`: These functions all contribute to rendering a stencil in their own way. `RenderStencil` does some initialization, such as setting the code page, before handing off to `Render`. `Render` in turn calls recursively into `RenderToken`, which actually handles the rendering of the various tokens, using `RenderReplacement` to render the tags into the stream. `RenderReplacement` gets and calls a pointer to the member function. It gets this pointer by offsetting into the method replacement map.

These classes form the basis of an ATL Server application. Figure 5-3 illustrates the Web request class flow.

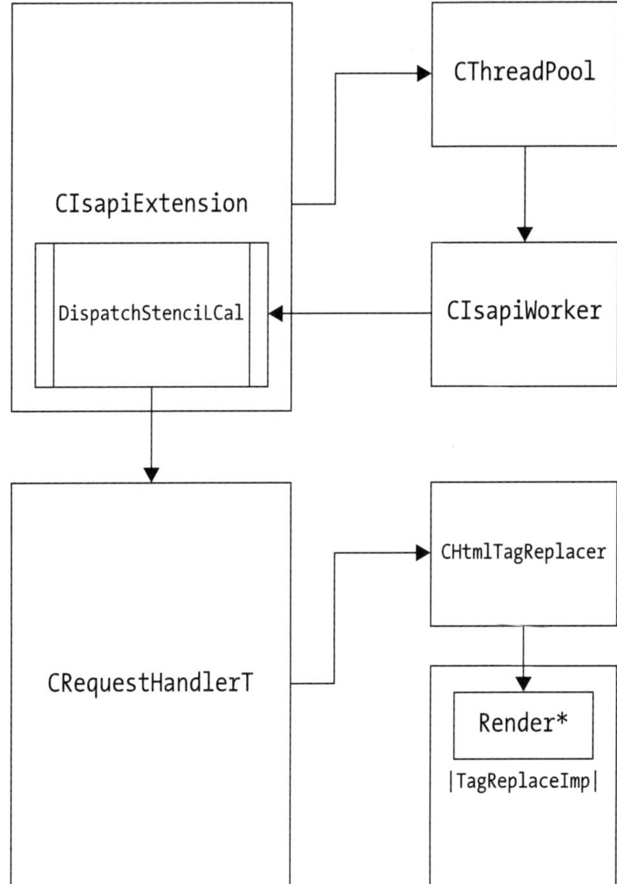

Figure 5-3. Web request class flow

There are many other classes and functions involved in a complete application, and ATL Server provides a very rich framework for a variety of tasks. The classes we described in this section represent some of the core functionality required to take an incoming request from IIS and get it to your handler methods in your request handler–derived class.

Key Classes in Web Service Requests

In this section we briefly discuss some of the classes and methods that are core to an ATL Server Web service request. We begin with the classes and methods that are important on the client, and then we look at the classes and methods that are important on the server.

Key Web Service Client Classes

The following classes play key roles in your ATL Server Web service client:

- `C`*`ProjectName`*`ServiceT`: This class is the sproxy-generated class that handles all the client-side communication for you in a Web service application. It includes atlsoap.h in order to provide its functionality. All the functionality discussed here refers to atlsoap.h or this class. This class uses the Microsoft XML Parser (MSXML) Simple API for XML (SAX) parser to parse XML packets (which means that COM is required and must be initialized in your client).

- `CSoapRootHandler` (atlsoap.h): You'll notice that `C`*`ProjectName`*`ServiceT` derives from `CSoapRootHandler`. This class is used on both the server and the client in ATL Server Web services. This class handles most of the work in a SOAP request. It does the parsing and marshaling for a request. It understands how to call any remote functions and what parameters need to be provided.

NOTE *Marshaling is the process through which types get converted. In the incoming request case, this is XML "types" being converted into real C++ types, and in the outgoing response case, this is C++ types being converted into XML.*

- `InitializeSOAP` (atlsoap.h): This function initializes the per-request heap and queries for the `ISAXXMLReader` interface.

- `GenerateResponse` (atlsoap.h): As its name implies, this function is responsible for generating the SOAP response for the client.

- `SendRequest` (atlsoap.h): Depending on which client you instantiate `C`*`ProjectName`*`ServiceT` on (`CSoapSocketClientT` by default) will decide which version of `SendRequest` gets called from the sproxy-generated file. This method is responsible for sending the request to the Web service and receiving the response. It's often useful to override `SendRequest` to provide custom functionality.

Key Web Service Server Classes

These classes play key roles in your ATL Server Web service:

- `CSoapRootHandler` (atlsoap.h): In case you missed it, this class is the workhorse in atlsoap.h. It's responsible for the majority of the SOAP work and is used in both the Web service client and server (see the `CSoapRootHandler` entry in the preceding section for more information).

- `CSoapHandler` (atlsoap.h): This class replaces the `CRequestHandlerT` class used in a normal ATL Server Web application request. This is done when you use the `soap_handler` attribute on your class. `CSoapHandler` derives from `CSoapRootHandler` and relies on this class to provide much of the SOAP-related functionality (parsing, marshaling, and so on). This class handles other functionality, such as initializing SOAP (SAX reader, per-request heap, and so on), initializing and setting SOAP headers correctly, receiving requests, and generating responses. It provides the required application logic around `CSoapRootHandler`.

These classes form the basis of an ATL Server Web service application (client or server). Figure 5-4 illustrates the Web service class flow.

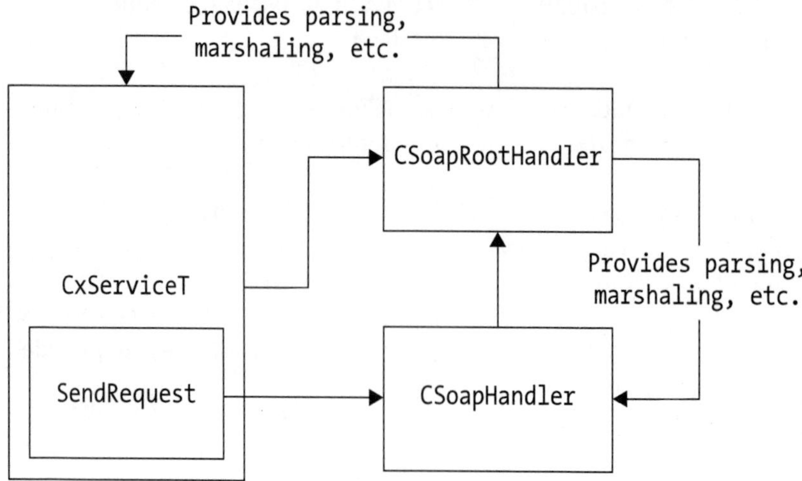

Figure 5-4. Web service class flow

The Web service framework relies heavily on the existing ATL Server infrastructure for many services, including the ISAPI extension DLL, thread pool, session state, caching, and so on. Other functions make up the ATL Server Web service framework, particularly in relation to customizing Web service behavior. The classes mentioned in this section, however, define the core functionality required to send and receive Web service requests.

Conclusion

In this chapter you looked at the architecture of a basic ATL Server application. You followed a request's journey from the user to your end application. You also examined some of the major classes and functions that ATL Server provides to make this model work. In addition, you looked at how an ATL Server Web service request is handled, including how a client puts its request together and how this is handled on the server (i.e., where a Web service request differs from any other Web request).

By now, you should have a good understanding of how you can architect an ATL Server application, and you should be familiar with how to use the ATL Server code base (e.g., where to find key classes and methods), some important overrides, and where to begin your source-code browsing.

Up until now we've focused heavily on the components and architecture of ATL Server. In the next chapter we move on to show you how to create applications that interact with the user.

CHAPTER 6

Getting User Input

WEB APPLICATIONS HAVE ADVANCED quite a bit in recent years. Although early attempts were purely informational (providing a magazine-style experience), modern Web applications are expected to be fully interactive. In fact, for many traditional, rich client applications where installation was difficult and time-consuming, distribution over the Web has become the perfect mechanism for reducing costs.

Therefore, it isn't surprising that simplifying the retrieval and usage of user input was a key design goal in ATL Server. To meet this goal, ATL Server provides an extensive framework that allows you to easily obtain, validate, and convert your user's input into specified data types. This framework is easily extensible, so you can customize it for your specific needs. Also, you can bypass the higher-level features of this framework, if necessary, and access your users' data in its raw format.

We start this chapter by looking at how the user will send data to your Web application.

Query Strings and Form Variables

Almost all input from a Web application that you build with ATL Server will be taken from query strings and/or form variables. In this section we discuss the differences between query strings and form variables. If you're already familiar with these concepts, feel free to skip to the next section, where we explain how ATL Server handles this data.

The input for a Web application is categorized as being all the values of the HTML tags that are inside a form (between the `<form></form>` tags) and have a `name` attribute specified. Consider the following example:

```
<input name="input1">Not part of input
<form>
  <input name="input2">Hello
  <text area name="input3">World!</textarea>
  <input name>Not part of input
</form>
```

In this example, only the values `Hello` and `World!` are considered as input values for this hypothetical Web application because they're the only elements that are both inside the form and have name attributes. This data is sent as follows:

```
input2="Hello"&input3="World!"
```

This data can be sent as a query string or as form variables. Query strings send the data appended to the URL of the request (very common in search engines), whereas form variables send the data by adding it as content to the HTTP request back that's sent to the server. The only difference between the two techniques is how the information is returned to your server, and you choose between the two by specifying the `METHOD` attribute in your form tag. If the `METHOD` attribute is specified as `POST`, then your data will be sent as form variables. If the `METHOD` attribute is `GET`, then your data will be sent as a query string. Consider the example in Listing 6-1.

Listing 6-1. Source for a Simple Server Response File (SRF)

```
{{handler userinput.dll/Default}}
<html>
  <body>
    <form method="post">
    <table border=1>
    <tr>
    <td colspan=2>
      Welcome to Ben's World of Fruit.
    </td>
    </tr>

    <tr>
    <td>Please select an item:</td>
    <td>
      <ul>
      <li><input type="radio" name="fruit" value="apple" ID="Radio1">Apple
      <li><input type="radio" name="fruit" value="peach" ID="Radio2">Peach
      <li><input type="radio" name="fruit" value="orange" ID="Radio3">Orange
      </ul>
    </td>
    </tr>

    <tr>
    <td>Type:</td>
    <td>
      <input type="radio" value=1 name="organic">Organic
      <input type="radio" value=0 name="organic">Conventional
    </td>
    </tr>

    <tr>
    <td>Quantity:</td>
```

```
        <td><input name="quantity"></td>
        </tr>

        <tr>
        <td colspan=2>
          <input type="submit" value="Go">
        </td>
        </tr>
        </table>
        </form>
    </body>
</html>
```

Because this example uses POST as the METHOD, the data will be sent as form variables. Using some hypothetical input as an example, the HTTP request sent to the server when this form is submitted would look like this:

```
POST /wof/bensworldoffruit.srf
.... (other HTTP headers omitted for brevity)
Content-Length:33
Fruit=apple&organic=1&quantity=1
```

If we had used GET, the input would be a query string, and our request would look like this:

```
GET /wof/bensworldoffruit.srf? Fruit=apple&organic=1&quantity=1
```

The main reason to choose POST over GET is that there are limitations on how long your query string can be. This limitation isn't standard between browsers. In practice, the limit of a GET request is roughly 1,000 characters. But, the main reason to choose GET over POST is that GET allows you to build a "canned" query for your Web application, for example:

```
<a href="/BensWorldOfFruit.srf?fruit=apple&organic=1&quantity=1>
Click here to buy an organic apple!<a/>
```

When your user clicks this link, the request will be sent as a query string to your ATL Server application as though the user had filled out the form and clicked Submit. We use this form as the basis for the rest of the examples in this chapter.

ISAPI developers will fondly remember having to handle and parse GET and POST requests themselves. This process was both tedious and error-prone. ATL Server provides a framework that handles most of this type of work for you.

The ValidateAndExchange Method

The first opportunity to access your user's input is in the `CRequestHandlerT::ValidateAndExchange` method. This method is called by ATL Server when a request is first received and before the stencil processor begins processing your SRF file. You should override this method and add logic to process your user's input. You'll look at two examples that use your request handler's `m_HttpRequest` member to access your user's input. First consider the example in Listing 6-2.

Listing 6-2. Display All Input Values in ValidateAndExchange

```
HTTP_CODE ValidateAndExchange()
{
  // Set the content-type
  m_HttpResponse.SetContentType("text/html");

  if (m_HttpRequest.GetMethod() == CHttpRequest::HTTP_METHOD::HTTP_METHOD_GET)
  {
    // we are using GET
    LPCSTR  name(NULL);
    LPCSTR  value(NULL);

    POSITION pos = m_HttpRequest.GetFirstQueryParam(&name, &value);
    while (pos)
    {
      m_HttpResponse << name << " = " << value << "<br>";
      pos = m_HttpRequest.GetNextQueryParam(pos, &name, &value);
    }
  }
  else
  {
    // we are using POST
    LPCSTR  name(NULL);
    LPCSTR  value(NULL);

    POSITION pos = m_HttpRequest.GetFirstFormVar(&name, &value);

    while (pos)
    {
     m_HttpResponse << name << " = " << value << "<br>";
     pos = m_HttpRequest.GetNextFormVar(pos, &name, &value);
```

```
31     }
32  }
33
34 return HTTP_SUCCESS;
35 }
```

This is an example of a trivial implementation of `ValidateAndExchange`. If you're using Visual Studio .NET, you'll notice that the Visual C++ ATL Server Project Wizard will generate a `ValidateAndExchange` method that's similar. Let's take a closer look at this example line-by-line:

- *Line 4:* This line isn't directly related to what we discuss in this chapter, but it's worthwhile having a quick look at it. Before sending any data back to your client, you have to set the content type. This tells the client how the client should display the data that you send. In this case, you're simply setting the content type to HTML text.

- *Line 7:* `GetMethod()` returns the method that was used to submit the data. You should recall that `POST` means that your data is in form variables, and `GET` means that your data is in a query string. You need this information so that you know where to look for your data. In practice, you should make sure that your application works with both `GET` and `POST`.

- *Lines 9 and 10:* Declare variables to hold the name and value of your input data. Recall that your user's input will be sent in name/value pairs (e.g., `fruit=apple`).

- *Line 12:* If you're using `GET`, you can get your first query string parameter by calling `GetFirstQueryStringParam()`. You can then use the return value of this method in subsequent calls to get other query string parameters.

- *Line 13:* `pos` will be `NULL` when there are no query string parameters.

- *Line 15:* You can use the `m_HttpResponse` member to send data back to your client. The >> operator for `CHttpRequest` is overloaded to handle most common data types and convert them to strings.

- *Line 16:* `GetNextQueryStringParam` will advance your iterator to the next query string parameter.

- *Lines 22 and 23:* Here you declare variables to hold the name and value of your input data. Recall that your user's input will be sent in name/value pairs (e.g., `input1=Hello World!`).

- *Line 25:* If you're using `POST`, you can get your first form variable by calling `GetFirstFormVar()`. You can then use the return value of this method in subsequent calls to get other form variables.
- *Line 29:* You can use the `m_HttpResponse` member to send data back to your client. The >> operator for `CHttpRequest` is overloaded to handle most common data types and convert them to strings.
- *Line 30:* `GetNextFormVar()` will advance your iterator to the next form variable.
- *Line 34:* You'll return success; this will tell ATL Server to process the SRF file. Returning an error (`HTTP_S_FALSE`) from `ValidateAndExchange` is the fastest way to tell ATL Server to stop processing the current request.

Now you've seen the easiest way to iterate over the values that your user has entered. Let's quickly look at another example in Listing 6-3.

Listing 6-3. Display a Specific Input Value in ValidateAndExchange

```
HTTP_CODE ValidateAndExchange()
{
    // set the content type
    m_HttpResponse.SetContentType("text/html");
    const CHttpRequestParams *requestParams(NULL);

   // determine what method our form is using
   if (m_HttpRequest.GetMethod() == CHttpRequest::HTTP_METHOD::HTTP_METHOD_POST)
    {
      // using POST
      requestParams = &(this->m_HttpRequest.GetFormVars());
    }
    else
    {
      // using GET
      requestParams = &(this->m_HttpRequest.GetQueryParams());
    }

    LPCSTR value(NULL);
    value = requestParams->Lookup("fruit");

```

```
22     if (value)
23     {
24       m_HttpResponse << "The fruit you chose was: " << value;
25     }
26     return HTTP_SUCCESS;
27 }
```

This example is very similar to the previous example, so we just focus on the differences in the following list, rather than looking at the code line-by-line:

- *Line 5:* You declare a pointer to your user's input. You don't know yet whether this data will be sent as a query string or as form variables, but in either case, this data will be exposed as a `CHttpRequestParams` object.
- *Line 11:* If you're using `POST`, then `GetFormVars` will return a pointer to your data.
- *Line 16:* If you're using `GET`, then `GetQueryParams` will return a pointer to your data.
- *Line 20:* Call `Lookup` to get the value of an input parameter named `fruit`.
- *Line 24:* If there's a value for the `fruit` parameter, then output its value using `m_HttpResponse`.

Now you've seen the first two basic ways of accessing your user's input. Either method is fine for this simple case, but you may have noticed that some functionality is lacking, for example:

- There's no way to set constraints on the values of your data.
- All the data is handled as strings—there's no data type conversion done for you.
- There's no way to keep track of which parameters are missing and which are valid.

Once again, ISAPI developers will probably be able to remember having to write tedious and error-prone code to implement this sort of functionality. In the next few sections, you'll look at how ATL Server addresses these issues and makes your life as a Web developer much easier.

Validating Input

You might have noticed that CHttpRequestParams derives from CValidateObject. There are two categories of methods that CHttpRequestParams inherits from: one category is a set of overloaded Validate methods, and the other category is a set of overloaded Exchange methods. These two sets of methods address the shortcomings that we listed in the previous section. The set of Validate methods allows you to determine if a specific input exists, and optionally whether that input fits into certain constraints, such as a minimum or maximum length. You'll examine this set of methods in detail in this section, and then you'll look at the Exchange methods in the next section. Consider the example in Listing 6-4.

Listing 6-4. Validating Input in ValidateAndExchange

```
HTTP_CODE ValidateAndExchange()
{
  const CHttpRequestParams *requestParams(NULL);

  // determine what method our form is using
  if (m_HttpRequest.GetMethod() == HttpRequest::HTTP_METHOD::HTTP_METHOD_POST)
  {
    // using POST
    requestParams = &(this->m_HttpRequest.GetFormVars());
  }
  else
  {
     // using GET
     requestParams = &(this->m_HttpRequest.GetQueryParams());
  }

 LPCSTR value;
 DWORD result = requestParams->Validate("fruit", &value, 5, 19, NULL);

 switch(result)
 {
   case VALIDATION_S_OK:
   {
     m_HttpResponse << "Ok, you chose a " << value;
     break;
   }
   case VALIDATION_E_LENGTHMIN:
   {
     m_HttpResponse << "Name of the fruit was not long enough.";
     break;
```

```
31      }
32      case VALIDATION_E_LENGTHMAX:
33      {
34        m_HttpResponse << "Name of the fruit was too long";
35        break;
36      }
37      case VALIDATION_S_EMPTY:
38      {
39        m_HttpResponse << "No fruit was selected";
40        break;
41      }
42      case VALIDATION_E_PARAMNOTFOUND:
43      {
44        m_HttpResponse << "input value was not found";
45        break;
46      }
47      case VALIDATION_E_INVALIDPARAM:
48      {
49        m_HttpResponse << "Invalid selection";
50        break;
51      }
52      case VALIDATION_E_FAIL:
53      {
54        m_HttpResponse << "unspecified error";
55        break;
56      }
57    }
58
59    return HTTP_SUCCESS;
60    }
```

Let's look at this example line-by-line:

- *Lines 1 through 16:* This is the same code that you've seen in previous examples to get a `CHttpRequestParams` object independent of whether you're using `POST` or `GET`.

- *Line 18:* You're trying to validate that the input parameter named `fruit` exists, and that it's between five and nine characters in length. This type of validation can help make your application more secure and robust. It helps you easily avoid buffer overruns by validating the length of your input before processing it. The last parameter is the validation context. You can ignore that for now and pass `NULL`; you'll look at validation contexts later on in this chapter.

- *Lines 20 through 56:* `Validate` will return a result as a `DWORD`. This value can be any of the following:

  - `VALIDATION_S_OK`: The named value was found and could be converted successfully.
  - `VALIDATION_S_EMPTY`: The name was present, but its value was empty.
  - `VALIDATION_E_PARAMNOTFOUND`: The named value was not found.
  - `VALIDATION_E_INVALIDPARAM`: The name specified was not found.
  - `VALIDATION_E_FAIL`: An unspecified error occurred.
  - `VALIDATION_E_LENGTHMAX`: The value exceeded the maximum length.
  - `VALIDATION_E_LENGTHMIN`: The value was less than the minimum length.

The validation features of ATL Server make it trivial to validate your input against a set of specified constraints. Doing this will add both robustness and security to your application. A lot of thought was put into designing this validation because this is an area in which many Web applications are prone to error.

There are also two overloads of `Validate` that do some basic data type conversion for you. You can validate your input for length as you saw previously and have the value returned as a `CString`. You can also validate your input for minimum and maximum values, and have the value returned as a `double`. We don't cover specific examples of these methods, as they're very similar to the example of `Validate` that we just presented.

Validation addresses the first shortcoming that we identified when you started looking at how to access your user's input. With validation, you can ensure that your input exists and conforms to a set of constraints that you've specified. We also touched on the fact that validation does some simple data type conversion for you. In the next section we expand on that idea and look at the `Exchange` functionality in ATL Server, which has extensive support for data type conversion.

Exchanging Data Types

The set of `Exchange` methods that `CHttpRequestParams` inherits from `CValidateObject` are designed to access the values inputted by the user and place them in variables in your code. These variables can be of a wide variety of data types. To correctly handle the data conversion required to do this (the user input is always of the type `string`); the exchange method is overloaded to handle the most common data types. Consider the following example (notice that some familiar code has been omitted for the sake of brevity):

```
bool value;
DWORD result = requestParams->Exchange("organic", &value, NULL);
```

This very simple example shows how you can automatically convert the value of an input parameter named `organic` into a `boolean` type. All the overloads of `Exchange` return the same `DWORD` values you saw for `Validate`. The only difference is that `Exchange` won't return `VALIDATE_E_LENGTHMIN` or `VALIDATE_E_LENGTHMAX`. Also note that you're passing in `NULL` as the last parameter; we'll continue to ignore the validation context for now as well.

As you can see, the `Exchange` method greatly simplifies the task of storing user data into variables in your code. The method has been designed to provide a wide range of support for many common types. `Exchange` is overloaded for each of the following types:

- `LPCSTR`
- `CString`
- `GUID`
- `bool`

One overload of `Exchange` is a template method. Use this overload to convert to any of the following types:

- `ULONGLONG`
- `LONGLONG`
- `double`
- `int`
- `long`
- `unsigned long`
- `short`
- `unsigned short`

The conversion routines that ATL Server uses are highly optimized, so you shouldn't worry about any performance degradation when you use them. Also, the set of data types was chosen very carefully so that they would be sufficient for almost every application. Of course, if you do need custom data types, then ATL Server is flexible enough to allow you to use them, and you can find more information about this later in the book.

So far, all the calls that you've made to `Validate` and `Exchange` have passed `NULL` as the validation context. In the next section you'll look at what the validation context is and how you can use it.

Using a Validation Context

Both the `Validate` and `Exchange` methods have an optional third parameter, which is of type `CValidateContext`. By passing an instance of a `CValidateContext`, you can keep track of which input elements couldn't be validated or couldn't be exchanged. Using a validation context makes it very easy to keep track of which input elements were incorrectly entered. One common use for the validation context is to highlight incorrectly entered information for the user so that he or she can easily identify these items and re-enter them.

The `CValidateContext` class takes ones optional `DWORD` parameter in its constructor. The `DWORD` input can be any combination of the following:

- `VALIDATION_S_OK`
- `VALIDATION_S_EMPTY`
- `VALIDATION_E_PARAMNOTFOUND`
- `VALIDATION_E_INVALIDPARAM`
- `VALIDATION_E_FAIL`

This parameter is used to specify what types of validation errors will constitute an actual error for a given call to exchange. The use of this parameter should become clearer as you continue building on your example application and use the combination of `VALIDATION_E_PARAMNOTFOUND|VALIDATION_S_EMPTY` to specify that you want missing or empty parameters to constitute an error. To do this, you'll need to keep track of these parameters:

```
// use a validation context object to keep track of our errors
CValidateContext validateContext(VALIDATION_E_PARAMNOTFOUND |
VALIDATION_S_EMPTY);
```

```
// get our value of 'fruit' as a CString
CString fruit;
requestParams->Exchange("fruit", &fruit, &validateContext);

// get the value of 'quantity' as an integer
int quantity;
requestParams->Exchange("quantity", &quantity, &validateContext);

// get the value of 'isorganic' as a boolean
bool isOrganic;
requestParams->Exchange("is_organic", &isOrganic, &validateContext);
```

The `CValidateContext::ParamsOK` method will return `true` if any of the parameters fell under the error criteria specified in your `DWORD` input. There are also a number of methods in the `CValidateContext` class to retrieve the number of results that had errors, as well as specific errors for specific variables.

To illustrate these uses, you'll continue to expand on your use of `CValidateContext` in the example. To begin, you'll make the `CValidateContext` object from the previous example a class member, and you'll add some replacement handlers to display errors beside each of the form elements that is incorrectly filled out.

Listing 6-5 is a complete listing of the sample that you started working on at the beginning of this chapter. This example should serve as a good review of everything that you've looked at in this chapter.

Listing 6-5. Using a Validation Context in ValidateAndExchange

```
[ request_handler("Default") ]
class CUserInputExample
{
private:
    CValidateContext m_validateContext;
    bool                       m_formHasBeenSubmitted;

public:
    HTTP_CODE ValidateAndExchange()
    {
        m_HttpResponse.SetContentType("text/html");

        const CHttpRequestParams *requestParams(NULL);
        if (m_HttpRequest.GetMethod() ==
            CHttpRequest::HTTP_METHOD::HTTP_METHOD_POST)
        {
```

```
            requestParams = &(this->m_HttpRequest.GetFormVars());
        }
        else
        {
            requestParams = &(this->m_HttpRequest.GetQueryParams());
        }

        m_formHasBeenSubmitted = (requestParams->GetCount() == 0) ?  false : true;

        if (!m_formHasBeenSubmitted)
        {
            return HTTP_SUCCESS;
        }

        m_validateContext.m_dwFlags = VALIDATION_S_EMPTY |
VALIDATION_E_PARAMNOTFOUND;

        CString fruit;
        requestParams->Exchange("fruit", &fruit, &m_validateContext);

        bool isOrganic;
        requestParams->Exchange("is_organic", &isOrganic, &m_validateContext);

        int quantity;
        requestParams->Exchange("quantity", &quantity, &m_validateContext);

        return HTTP_SUCCESS;
    }

protected:
    [tag_name("HasErrors")]
    HTTP_CODE OnHasErrors()
    {
        if (!m_formHasBeenSubmitted)
        {
            return HTTP_S_FALSE;
        }
        else
        {
            return (!m_validateContext.ParamsOK()) ? HTTP_SUCCESS : HTTP_S_FALSE;
        }
    }

    [tag_name("GetError")]
```

```
HTTP_CODE OnGetError(TCHAR *szName)
{
    if (!m_formHasBeenSubmitted)
    {
        return HTTP_SUCCESS;
    }

    DWORD errorType;
    if (!m_validateContext.GetResultAt(szName, errorType))
    {
        return HTTP_SUCCESS;
    }
    else
    {
        m_HttpResponse << "A value for " << szName;

        switch (errorType)
        {
            case VALIDATION_S_EMPTY:
                m_HttpResponse << " cannot be an empty value!";
                break;

            case VALIDATION_E_PARAMNOTFOUND:
                m_HttpResponse << " was not found!";
                break;

            case VALIDATION_E_INVALIDPARAM:
               m_HttpResponse << " was entered, but in an incorrect format!";
                break;

            default:
                m_HttpResponse << " was not a valid value!";
                break;
        }
    }

    return HTTP_SUCCESS;
}
};
```

Let's take a look at this example line-by-line:

- *Line 5:* This validation context object will be used by your replacement handlers to display errors.

- *Line 6:* This flag will determine whether or not the user has submitted the form. If the user hasn't submitted the form, then you don't want to do any validation.

- *Line 23:* Once you know how the form is being submitted, look at the number of request parameters being submitted. Even if the user didn't enter any values, the request parameters are submitted with empty values, so the number isn't 0. If the user hasn't submitted the form, you want to set your flag and return `HTTP_SUCCESS`. The flag will tell your tag replacement handlers not to do anything because the form hasn't been submitted. Returning `HTTP_SUCCESS` will allow the rest of your SRF file to be processed.

- *Line 30:* The `m_dwFlags` member in the `CValidateContext` class determines what types of validation results you want to specify as being invalid. In this example, you want to specify both empty and missing values as being errors. You don't necessarily need to specify both types, but we've done so for the purposes of this example.

- *Lines 32 through 39:* These lines are taken from the previous section. They get the value of `fruit` as a `CString`.

The SRF file corresponding to this application is shown in Listing 6-6.

Listing 6-6. Source for SRF That Requires Validation

```
{{handler userinput.dll/Default}}
<html>
  <body>
    <form method="post">
    <table border=1>

    <tr>
    <td colspan=2>
      Welcome to Ben's World of Fruit.
    </td>
    </tr>

    <tr>
    <td>Please select an item:</td>
    <td>
```

```
        <ul>
        <li><input type="radio" name="fruit" value="apple" ID="Radio1">Apple
        <li><input type="radio" name="fruit" value="peach" ID="Radio2">Peach
        <li><input type="radio" name="fruit" value="orange" ID="Radio3">Orange
        </ul>
        {{if HasErrors}}
          <br><font color="red">{{GetError(fruit)}}
        {{endif}}
      </td>
      </tr>

      <tr>
      <td>Type:</td>
      <td>
        <input type="radio" value=1 name="is_organic">Organic
        <input type="radio" value=0 name="is_organic">Conventional
        {{if HasErrors}}
          <br><font color="red">{{GetError(is_organic)}}</font>
        {{endif}}
      </td>
      </tr>

      <tr>
      <td>Quantity:</td>
      <td>
        <input name="quantity">
        {{if HasErrors}}
          <br><font color="red">{{GetError(quantity)}}</font>
        {{endif}}
      </td>
      </tr>

      <tr>
      <td colspan=2>
        <input type="submit" value="Go">
        {{if HasErrors}}
          <br><font color="red">Please correct your errors!</font>
        {{endif}}
      </td>

      </tr>
      </table>
      </form>
    </body>
</html>
```

As you can see from this example, using a validation context helps you quickly put together a user-friendly interface for your Web application.

Conclusion

To effectively interact with a Web application, either query strings or form data (or both) must be supported on the server side. Both of these techniques present the data in the same style (i.e., name/value pairs). However, this simplicity is hidden from developers due to the fact that all data is returned by IIS as one giant string that must be parsed.

ATL Server alleviates developers' problems by providing functionality that allows them to easily look through the data to find what they're looking for (either by looping through all the data or by looking up specific name/value pairs).

To make this data more usable, ATL Server provides additional functionality in the form of validation and exchange. The validation of the data ensures that it matches a given pattern and is of a given size. This helps quickly ensure that the data returned was valid, and it also helps prevent developers from suffering from buffer overruns caused by user input (the most dangerous kind of buffer overrun).

The exchange functionality is designed to make using the data returned by the user easy to process. To do this, the data must be copied into variables in the developer's code. This functionality and the appropriate data conversions are all provided by ATL Server.

Now that you have a good understanding about how to get input from your perspective users, in the next chapter you'll take a look at what you have to do to deploy your ATL Server application manually.

CHAPTER 7

Deploying an ATL Server Web Application

THIS CHAPTER FOCUSES ON deploying an ATL Server Web application (or Web service) on your development machine or testing area. Although this chapter contains information on automating deployment to multiple machines, this system isn't intended for deployment to production environments.

Deployment to production environments is a complex topic worthy of its own book. There are many tools available for developers of Web applications to deploy their finished product, and we recommend that readers who are interested in final deployment investigate these technologies (e.g., Microsoft's Application Center). Although these tools are designed to make machine replication and large-scale deployment much simpler, there's no reason why you can't use the deployment techniques outlined in this chapter for very small-scale production environments.

The other note about the deployment information in this chapter is that it's based on the Windows 2000 Internet Services Manager (ISM) system. This system does actually vary slightly from the systems provided in Windows NT 4.0, Windows XP, and Windows Server 2003; therefore, users should be aware of this when they work on these other systems.

Understanding the Administration Tool

The main tool for controlling your Web server is the ISM tool provided under the Administrative Tools menu on Windows machines with IIS. This tool allows you to connect to a local or remote machine to administer the Web site (use File ➤ Connect to administer a remote machine).

You should copy all the files you plan to use in your Web application (application DLL, ISAPI DLL, SRF files, HTML files, and any other files you might use) to a main folder and subfolders (you'll usually do this under a subfolder of Inetpub\wwwroot). You can then right-click your Web site in the ISM tool (usually Default Web Site) and create a new virtual directory (select New ➤ Virtual Directory). After you've named this virtual directory and pointed it at your actual directory (i.e., the root directory under which all your files have been copied, either directly or in subdirectories), you'll have a node for it under the Web site node in the tree under the Default Web Site node.

Right-clicking the node will allow you to select properties for that node. It's through these properties that you can correctly set up your virtual root (vroot).

Virtual Directory Tab

The first tab under these properties is the Virtual Directory tab. Among the path information, you'll notice that you can set up various configuration settings for this vroot.

You'll see that, by default, read permissions are enabled on the directory, as well as visit logging and indexing. Directory browsing is off by default, but for the development stage the ability to browse the files in a vroot (from your Web browser) can actually be very useful. For example, you can easily check if an image exists in the directory or if an .htm file is missing.

You'll need to set your execute permissions to Scripts and Executables, because ISAPI applications are executable applications (they execute x86 code directly on the server). The None setting will allow only static files to be retrieved, and the Scripts setting is designed to enable scripting technologies such as ASP.

Your Application Protection Level has three settings: Low, Medium, and High. In general, with Windows XP and below (IIS 5.0 and below) you'll want to run with Low application protection.[1]

The Low protection setting means that your application will run in the same process as your Web server (inetinfo.exe). Although this does open up some security vulnerabilities (e.g., crashes in your application will temporarily bring down the entire Web server) running out-of-process (i.e., outside of the Web server process) in IIS 5.0 and below means that your application will suffer a significant performance hit (usually above 40 percent). The Medium setting means that IIS will use the Distributed Component Object Model (DCOM) to communicate with your process, which will be loaded in a dllhost, where it's pooled with other Web applications. This means that your Web application will be capable of bringing down other applications, but not your Web server. And finally, you can place your application in a High protection environment, where IIS will communicate with it via DCOM, but your process will exist completely isolated from all other processes (i.e., each Web application will only be capable of crashing itself).

The next tab of interest is the Configuration button under this virtual directory setup. This is where you can map file extensions with the executable they'll be associated with, as well as the verbs that will be allowed to be passed to this executable. What this means is that if you map the file extension ".txt" with the executable "foo.exe", then all requests to this vroot for a file ending in .txt will be sent to foo.exe. The verb setting allows you to limit which requests will make it through. If you set ALL verbs, then `GET`, `HEAD`, `DEBUG`, `OPTIONS`, `PUT`, `DELETE`, `TRACE`, and

1. With Windows Server 2003 and IIS 6.0, Microsoft has made advancements that mean you no longer suffer a significant performance penalty from running outside of the Web server process, making the Medium and High options more appealing.

so on will be sent through to your executable. It's here that you'll map the fact that requests for SRF files and requests for DLLs (if you want to enable users to make requests directly to your application DLL for Web service requests, for example) should be handled by your ISAPI DLL.

You do this by clicking the Add button. In the field Executable, enter the location and name of your ISAPI DLL (e.g., **c:\inetpub\wwwroot\myapp\myisapi.dll**). Under Extension, type in the extension you wish to associate with this file (e.g., **.srf**). You are only able to associate one extension at a time with your executable. This means that you need to run through the Add procedure twice for most ATL Server Web applications: once to map SRF files to your ISAPI DLL and once to map DLL files to your ISAPI DLL.

You can then choose what verbs you'll allow. For ATL Server applications, it's generally wise to limit your application to `GET`, `HEAD`, `POST`, and `DEBUG`, although at application development time (on a development machine), it's generally perfectly OK to simply select ALL. Once you click OK, your mapping takes place.

In general, to install an ATL Server Web application, this is all that you need to do.

Other Tabs

The other tabs in the Properties page in the IIS tool are designed to allow you to set various settings for your vroot. This section briefly covers each of these tabs.

Documents Tab

The Documents tab is designed to allow you to set up your default documents and enable a document footer.

The Default Documents section basically allows you to set which files IIS should search for if a user types in a vroot and no specific file. The default settings are to open the default.htm page or the default.asp page (among others) if they exist. You can order the rules to set priorities, and you can add new files (e.g., default.srf). The rules work from a top-to-bottom ordering, and once a match is found all searching terminates.

The second section enables you to set a document footer. This allows you to specify an HTML-formatted footer to every document sent by your Web server. You could use this footer for a custom copyright or similar message at the end of each page served.

Directory Security Tab

The settings on the Directory Security tab allow you to view and modify some of the security settings for your vroot.

The "Anonymous access and authentication control" option allows you to configure your authentication and anonymous access features. You can use this control to confirm the identity of a user before that user is allowed to access your site (authenticated access), which includes support for Basic Authentication, Digest Authentication, or Integrated Windows Authentication. It uses the Windows user accounts to complete the authentication, or you can accept the default of not authenticating access to the vroot (anonymous access).

The IP Address and Domain Name restriction is available on Windows 2000 Server machines. It's designed to allow or prevent specific users, computers, groups, and domains from accessing the vroot. You do this by granting or denying access to IP addresses (with masks).

The Secure communications area allows you to create and view server certificates and requests for certificates (using the Certificate Wizard). This requires that you install a valid server certificate on your machine, which is required to set up Secure Sockets Layer (SSL). This is the same place that you would edit settings for your SSL setup.

HTTP Headers Tab

The HTTP Headers tab enables you to modify some of the header data being sent back to clients accessing your vroot.

The Enable Content Expiration setting lets you expire information on your server so that the browser knows to expire its cached data on the expiry date and recontact your server for new information.

The Custom HTTP Headers setting gives you the ability to add, edit, and remove custom HTTP header information to clients. This allows you to support instructions that aren't supported by the version of IIS that you have installed.

The Content Rating setting allows you to set information pertaining to the content of the material on your vroot. By setting ratings, you enable browsers such as Internet Explorer (3.0 and above) to flag potentially objectionable content to users, and you enable a number of filtering systems designed to protect children from objectionable Web content.

The MIME Map setting allows you to configure the additional file types that the Web server returns to browsers. The Windows File Types box lists the currently registered file types on the system, and the File Types box provides information on the file type extensions and the MIME mappings for this file.

Custom Errors Tab

You use the Custom Errors tab to set up custom HTTP errors for your site. This tab's settings determine what Web page will be returned to clients on various HTTP errors. You can use this tab to set up custom error files so that you return a custom error message on given HTTP errors. This tab also enables you to return to the default error if you make a mistake or change your mind.

Modifying Your ISAPI DLL

If your application is running in-process, then IIS locks your ISAPI DLL in memory. This means that you can't change your ISAPI DLL without stopping and restarting your Web server. You can stop and then start your Web server from the ISM tool using the toolbar buttons and menu commands provided, or by running the command-line tool(s) provided, or by manually stopping and starting the Web server service. Sometimes even if you aren't running in-process it's useful to reset IIS in order to have other settings take effect and to aid in debugging.

The main tool for stopping and restarting a Web server is iisreset.exe. This command-line utility will attempt to stop the Web server and then restart it (the inetinfo process).

To manually stop and restart the service, you'll want to use the `net stop` and `net start` commands on the w3svc service (`net stop w3svc` and `net start w3svc`). You could always use a front-end to these commands, such as Server Explorer, which is provided in the Visual Studio .NET shell.

You can set (on a project-by-project basis) whether or not you want to reset IIS in the project settings if you're developing in the Visual Studio .NET integrated development environment (IDE).

TIP *Often if you're having strange, unpredictable, and inexplicable problems with your Web server, stopping and restarting the IIS process can resolve them.*

Understanding the Visual Studio .NET Deployment Utility

For ATL Server projects in Visual Studio .NET, there is a small deployment utility that automates the tasks described in the previous section for you (on the local machine). The tasks required to deploy a Web application are as follows:

1. Use the ISM tool to create a virtual directory corresponding to a real directory on your machine.

2. Copy the files for your Web application to this virtual directory.

3. Configure the virtual directory (application mappings, protection level, and so on).

4. Restart IIS.

5. Modify the files, recopy them, and restart IIS if appropriate (repeatedly throughout development cycle).

These tasks can become repetitive. Although you need to configure your vroot only once, you do have to keep copying files to the appropriate directory, reset IIS if appropriate, and then launch your application, find any bugs, modify the appropriate files, and repeat this cycle. To simplify this task, the ATL Server team created a deployment utility that's exposed via the Properties page for a given project. To access this utility, right-click the project, select Properties, and look for the Web Deployment option at the bottom of the window.

The underlying command-line utility for this deployment system is the vcdeploy.exe tool located in the VC7\bin directory of your installation. This utility uses an XML configuration file to determine what files to deploy and what settings to enable (on the vroot) for this vroot.

The vcdeploy tool is capable of registering file extensions (to a given file) for a given vroot, copying files to a given vroot, and then stopping and restarting the w3svc service. In addition, it can perform many other common setup functions for deploying Web applications and configuring vroots.

Although the underlying XML schema for this utility may change, we provide examples of configuration scripts here so that you may better understand the working of the utility, perhaps customize it for your own use, or at the very least be more capable of creating functional deployment utilities yourself. Although the utility is limited to localhost through the IDE, there's no reason why it shouldn't work to deploy to a remote machine (assuming the user has a valid account with appropriate security permissions on the remote machine—usually as an administrator) if you change the machine from localhost to the name of the remote machine.

The first example schema in Listing 7-1 shows the creation of the vroot Postershop at the path d:\inetpub\wwwroot\mantaweb\postershop. The APPISOLATION setting allows the user to specify the application protection for the application (0=Low, 1=Medium, and 2=High). The APPFILEGROUP setting allows the developer to specify which source files to copy to which destination (relative to the vroot).

Listing 7-1. Example Vcdeploy XML Configuration File

```
<?xml version="1.0" encoding="Windows-1252"?>
<ATLSINSTSETTINGS>
  <WEBHOSTNAME>localhost</WEBHOSTNAME>
  <VIRTDIRNAME>Postershop</VIRTDIRNAME>
  <VIRTDIRFSPATH>d:\inetpub\wwwroot\MantaWeb\Postershop</VIRTDIRFSPATH>
  <APPISOLATION>0</APPISOLATION>

  <APPFILEGROUP>
    <APPFILENAME>
      <SRC>d:\projects\demo\Postershop\Postershop.srf</SRC>
      <DEST>Postershop.srf</DEST>
    </APPFILENAME>
    <APPFILENAME>
      <SRC>d:\projects\demo\Postershop\Debug\Postershop.dll</SRC>
      <DEST>Postershop.dll</DEST>
    </APPFILENAME>
  </APPFILEGROUP>
</ATLSINSTSETTINGS>
```

The second example in Listing 7-2 shows the deployment of the same application, but this time you're sending an ISAPI DLL (instead of the application DLL). This means you use the APPMAPPING tag to map the file extensions .srf and .dll to the ISAPI DLL that you're deploying. You also indicate which verbs you want to enable for these mappings (all other verbs will be disabled). By using the type="extension" parameter on the APPFILENAME tag, you ensure that the w3svc service will be stopped and then restarted after this file has been copied. Again, the destination directory is given relative to the root directory of the vroot.

Listing 7-2. Vcdeploy Configuration File for Sending an ISAPI DLL and Registering Against It

```
<?xml version="1.0" encoding="Windows-1252"?>
<ATLSINSTSETTINGS>
  <WEBHOSTNAME>localhost</WEBHOSTNAME>
  <VIRTDIRNAME>Postershop</VIRTDIRNAME>
  <VIRTDIRFSPATH>d:\inetpub\wwwroot\MantaWeb\Postershop</VIRTDIRFSPATH>
  <UNLOADBEFORECOPY>true</UNLOADBEFORECOPY>
  <APPISOLATION>0</APPISOLATION>

  <APPMAPPING fileext=".srf">
    <VERB>GET</VERB>
    <VERB>HEAD</VERB>
    <VERB>POST</VERB>
    <VERB>DEBUG</VERB>
  </APPMAPPING>

  <APPMAPPING fileext=".dll">
    <VERB>GET</VERB>
    <VERB>HEAD</VERB>
    <VERB>POST</VERB>
    <VERB>DEBUG</VERB>
  </APPMAPPING>

  <APPFILEGROUP>
    <APPFILENAME type="extension">
      <SRC>d:\projects\demo\PostershopIsapi\Debug\PostershopIsapi.dll</SRC>
      <DEST>PostershopIsapi.dll</DEST>
    </APPFILENAME>
  </APPFILEGROUP>
</ATLSINSTSETTINGS>
```

In addition to trying out deployment to remote machines, you could also use this configuration file to try automating deployment to multiple machines by offering multiple `WEBHOSTNAME`s.

To invoke the vcdeploy utility with a given configuration file (e.g., d:\config.xml) you would run this:

```
vcdeploy d:\config.xml
```

To silently run the utility (e.g., as part of a batch build) you would use the nologo option:

```
vcdeploy /nologo d:\config.xml
```

Of course, if your configuration file is in the directory that you're running the command from, there's no reason to give a path to the configuration file.

Conclusion

Although this chapter is by no means a comprehensive course in administering a Windows Web server, you should now have all the information you need to understand the basics of what's happening on your Web server and how to configure your server to run Web applications.

You should also now know how to go about manually deploying a Web application (or a Web service—you'll probably want to copy the .disco file instead of the .srf files) on your machine.

In this chapter you also looked at the vcdeploy command-line utility provided with Visual C++ .NET. Although this utility is definitely no replacement for the many professional tools for deploying production Web applications, it's very useful during the development cycle and for deploying simple test applications.

One of the problems with HTTP is that it's a stateless protocol. Without state it's virtually impossible to provide an interactive user experience, be it remembering items in a shopping cart or providing a personalized Web page to a user. To solve this problem, a feature known as *session state* has made its way into Web application programming. In the next chapter, you'll take a look at the flexible and extensible ATL Server session state functionality.

CHAPTER 8

Cookies and Session State

WEB APPLICATIONS ARE BY nature stateless because they communicate with users using HTTP, which is a stateless protocol. However, all but the most simplistic applications need to maintain some kind of state as users make requests. ATL Server provides two features for managing this information: session state and cookies.

Why do you need session state? *Session state* is the facility that enables you to store information about your users. A good example of session state is a customer's shopping cart and purchase information. Session state information is stored on the server (e.g., in a database); thus, the information isn't transmitted over the Web, making it perfect for sensitive information such as credit card numbers.

What about cookies? Well, *cookies* enable an application to maintain state by maintaining data on the user machine. Cookies send the data to the server on each request (as part of the header). This makes cookies unsuitable for sensitive information because all of the data that you've stored on your user's machine is sent with every request the user makes, no matter where the user makes those requests. So, any information that you store in a cookie should be as opaque as possible, as it's likely that it will be sent to other Web servers.

As you build more complex Web applications, you'll begin to appreciate the ability to store information between requests. In this chapter you'll start by looking at how you can add session state support to your ATL Server application.

Session State Service

Session state is exposed in ATL Server as a server service. By default, session state support isn't enabled, so you'll have to add the code to your ATL Server ISAPI extension yourself. As you become familiar with this code, you can use the ATL Server Project Wizard in Visual Studio .NET to generate this code for you.

`CSessionStateService` is the service provider that implements session state in ATL Server. To add session state support in ATL Server, you need to create and initialize an instance of this class in your ATL Server ISAPI extension class.

This is a common pattern that you'll notice about ATL Server. When you want to enable features such as session state or caching in ATL Server, you do so by adding code to your ATL Server ISAPI extension handler. You can add this code manually or use the ATL Server Project Wizard in Visual Studio .NET. ATL Server was designed to use this approach over a configuration file, registry settings, or some other dynamic format because the ultimate goal for ATL Server is to provide the highest level of flexibility and performance available in a server-side Web application framework.

ATL Server allows you to decide what features you want included in your application at the source code level, and it enables you to decide exactly how and when these features are initialized. At first, this approach might seem intimidating, but with practice you should see the performance and footprint advantages of this method. Also, please remember that you can automatically generate all of the configuration code that you'll examine in this chapter using the ATL Server Project Wizard in Visual Studio .NET.

Now that we've provided you with a bit of background about how ATL Server was designed, consider the example in Listing 8-1.

Listing 8-1. Declaration of an ATL Server ISAPI Extension Handler

```
template <class ThreadPoolClass=CThreadPool<CIsapiWorker>,
         class CStatClass=CNoRequestStats,
         class HttpUserErrorTextProvider=CDefaultErrorProvider,
         class WorkerThreadTraits=DefaultThreadTraits >
         class CsessionstateExtension :
public CIsapiExtension<ThreadPoolClass,
                       CStatClass,
                       HttpUserErrorTextProvider,
                       WorkerThreadTraits>
{
protected:
     typedef CIsapiExtension<ThreadPoolClass,
                             CStatClass,
                             HttpUserErrorTextProvider,
                             WorkerThreadTraits> baseISAPI;

    typedef CWorkerThread<WorkerThreadTraits> WorkerThreadClass;
    typedef CSessionStateService<WorkerThreadClass,
                                 CMemSessionServiceImpl>
                                 sessionSvcType;

    CComObjectGlobal<sessionSvcType> m_SessionStateSvc;

public:
    BOOL GetExtensionVersion(HSE_VERSION_INFO* pVer)
    {
        if (!baseISAPI::GetExtensionVersion(pVer))
```

```
        {
            return FALSE;
        }

        if (GetCriticalIsapiError() != 0)
        {
            return TRUE;
        }

        if (S_OK !=
         m_SessionStateSvc.Initialize(&m_WorkerThread,
                                 static_cast<IServiceProvider*>
                                 (this)))
        {
            ATLTRACE("Session service failed to initialize\n");
            TerminateExtension(0);

          return  SetCriticalIsapiError(IDS_ATLSRV_CRITICAL_SESSIONSTATEFAILED);
        }

        return TRUE;
    }

    BOOL TerminateExtension(DWORD dwFlags)
    {
        m_SessionStateSvc.Shutdown();
        BOOL bRet = baseISAPI::TerminateExtension(dwFlags);

        return bRet;
    }

    HRESULT STDMETHODCALLTYPE QueryService(REFGUID guidService,
                                           REFIID  riid,
                                           void**  ppvObject)
    {
        if (InlineIsEqualGUID(guidService,
                         uuidof(ISessionStateService)))

        return m_SessionStateSvc.QueryInterface(riid, ppvObject);

        return baseISAPI::QueryService(guidService, riid, ppvObject);
    }
};
```

Let's have a look at this code line-by-line:

- *Lines 1 through 9:* This code just declares your ATL Server ISAPI extension handler class, `CIsapiExtension`. This handler will use all of the ATL Server defaults.

- *Lines 12 through 19:* The `CSessionStateService` template takes two arguments. The first argument determines what class should handle expired sessions. You're using the `CWorkerThread` class to do this by default. You can also substitute your own class for this as well. For example, you might want to use a class that logs each expired session. The second argument determines how session state is actually implemented. The class that you pass in this argument will be responsible for creating, maintaining, and expiring sessions. ATL Server provides the `CMemSessionServiceImpl` and `CDBSessionServiceImpl` classes for you. These classes store session state in memory or in a SQL Server, respectively.

- *Line 21:* All ATL Server applications will share the same session service instance.

- *Lines 36 through 45:* Initialize your session state when the ISAPI extension is loaded.

- *Lines 50 through 56:* Shutting down your session state service will sweep any remaining sessions and clean up properly.

- *Lines 58 through 67:* `QueryService` is the generic way to get an interface pointer to any given service in an ATL Server ISAPI extension. This particular implementation will return the `ISessionStateService` interface if requested.

Configuring session state in the code may seem a bit awkward at first, but it follows the ATL Server philosophy of adding as little overhead as possible. If you don't plan on using session state services, you don't have the code in your built DLL, so you don't pay any overhead tax for it.

Now that you have your ATL Server ISAPI extension configured to expose session state, let's have a look at how you can use session state services in your ATL Server application.

Using Session State

ATL Server gives you more control over how you use session state in your application than most Web application programming frameworks. With ATL Server, you can choose the way session names are generated, where session state is stored, and how session IDs are sent to the user. `ValidateAndExchange` is typically the method where you initialize your session state. Listing 8-2 shows a sample ATL Server request handler class and its `ValidateAndExchange` method.

Listing 8-2. ValidateAndExchange Implementation

```
CComPtr<ISessionStateService> m_spSessionSvc;
CComPtr<ISession> m_spSession;

HTTP_CODE ValidateAndExchange()
{
    if (FAILED(m_spServiceProvider->QueryService(
                    __uuidof(ISessionStateService),
                    &m_spSessionSvc)))
    {
        return HTTP_FAIL;
    }

    const CCookie& sessionCookie = m_HttpRequest.Cookies("session");

    if (sessionCookie.IsEmpty())
    {
        CHAR  sessionName[CSessionNameGenerator::MIN_SESSION_KEY_LEN + 1];
        DWORD sessionLen = 0;

        if (FAILED(m_spSessionSvc->CreateNewSession(sessionName,
                                                    &sessionLen,
                                                    &m_spSession)))
        {
            return HTTP_S_FALSE;
        }
        sessionName[sessionLen - 1] = 0;

        m_HttpResponse.AppendCookie("session", sessionName);
    }
    else
    {
        CString sessionName;

        if (!sessionCookie.GetValue(sessionName))
        {
            return HTTP_S_FALSE;
        }

```

```
39         if (FAILED(m_spSessionSvc->GetSession(sessionName,
40                                                &m_spSession)))
41         {
42             return HTTP_S_FALSE;
43         }
44     }
45
46     return HTTP_SUCCESS;
47 }
```

This code may look unwieldy at first. Let's have a look at it line-by-line:

- *Lines 1 and 2:* Declare these as member variables in your request handler class.

- *Lines 6 through 8:* Get `ISessionStateService` from the ISAPI extension.

- *Line 13:* This example is sending the session ID as a cookie for the client to store. This is just one way of sending the session ID back to your user. If you're concerned that your user might not support cookies, you could store the session ID in your HTML form and have it sent back in a hidden input field.

- *Lines 17 through 28:* If there's no session cookie, then you have to create a new session. Calling `CreateSession` will create a newly named session for you. The name of the session is unique and will be generated by using the Microsoft Windows Crypto API. If the Crypto API isn't available, then `rand` will be used. You can also call `CreateSessionByName` to generate a session with a name of your choosing. You should, however, choose a name for your session wisely. It's a security risk if it's predictable how your session names are generated. If this is the case, hackers can create their own session names and trick your application into thinking that they're valid sessions. If you're generating your own session names or if you're using a platform that doesn't support the Crypto API (`rand` generates random, but predictable values) then you should exercise extreme caution to make sure your session names aren't predictable.

- *Lines 39 through 43:* Get your current session from the session state service. When you want to close this session, you should call `m_spSessionSvc->CloseSession`.

You get and set values in session state by calling `ISession::GetVariable()` and `ISession::SetVariable()`. All session values are set and retrieved as variants. The `ISession` interface also contains methods for enumerating the values in session state.

Using Database-Backed Session State

The last topic we cover in this chapter is how to store your session state in a database rather than in memory. Storing your session state in a database has numerous advantages. For example, if your Web service crashes, your session state will still be preserved. Also, using a database allows you to use session state in a Web farm scenario. In a Web farm, you can't guarantee that a set of requests in a given "session" will be processed by the same Web server. That means that the session state can't be stored in the memory of one Web server. If you use a central database, then your request can be processed by any of the Web servers in your Web farm.

As we mentioned before, ATL Server provides an implementation of a database-backed session state service. To use it, you only have to change the way you templatized the `CSessionStateService` class in your ATL Server ISAPI extension class.

The code in Listing 8-3 is necessary to use database-backed session state. This code may look daunting, but rest assured, it's completely generated for you by the ATL Server Project Wizard. You simply need to choose the OLE DB–backed session state services under the Server Options tab in the ATL Server Project Wizard.

Listing 8-3. Using Database-Backed Session State

```
#pragma once

#include <atlisapi.h>
#include <atldbcli.h>
#include <atlsession.h>
#define _DATASOURCE_CACHE 1

class CIsapiExtensionWorker : public CIsapiWorker
{
  typedef CDataSourceCache<>        ds_cache_type;
  CComObjectGlobal<ds_cache_type> m_dsCache;
```

```
public:
    CIsapiExtensionWorker()
    {}

~CIsapiExtensionWorker()
{}

virtual BOOL GetWorkerData(DWORD dwParam, void **ppvData)
{
    if (dwParam == _DATASOURCE_CACHE && ppvData)
    {
        *ppvData = (void *)&m_dsCache;
        m_dsCache.AddRef();
        return TRUE;
    }

    return FALSE;
}
};


template <class ThreadPoolClass=CThreadPool<CIsapiExtensionWorker>,
          class CStatClass=CNoRequestStats,
          class HttpUserErrorTextProvider=CDefaultErrorProvider,
          class WorkerThreadTraits=DefaultThreadTraits >
class CIsapiExtension :
    public CIsapiExtension<ThreadPoolClass,
                           CStatClass,
                           HttpUserErrorTextProvider,
                           WorkerThreadTraits>
{
protected:
    typedef CIsapiExtension<ThreadPoolClass,
                            CStatClass,
                            HttpUserErrorTextProvider,
                            WorkerThreadTraits> baseISAPI;
    typedef CWorkerThread<WorkerThreadTraits> WorkerThreadClass;
    typedef CSessionStateService<WorkerThreadClass,
                                 CDBSessionServiceImpl> sessionSvcType;
    CComObjectGlobal<sessionSvcType> m_SessionStateSvc;

public:
BOOL GetExtensionVersion(HSE_VERSION_INFO* pVer)
{
```

```
    if (!baseISAPI::GetExtensionVersion(pVer))
    {
        return FALSE;
    }

    if (GetCriticalIsapiError() != 0)
    {
        return TRUE;
    }

    if (S_OK != m_SessionStateSvc.Initialize(
                         &m_WorkerThread,
                         static_cast<IServiceProvider*>(this),
                         L"Provider=SQLOLEDB.1;\
                         Integrated Security=SSPI;\
                         Persist Security Info=False;\
                         Initial Catalog=pubs;\
                         Data Source=TestServer\\vsdotnet;\
                         Use Procedure for Prepare=1;\
                         Auto Translate=True;\
                         Packet Size=4096;\
                         Workstation ID=TestServer;\
                         Use Encryption for Data=False;\
                         Tag with column collation when possible=False",
                         ATL_SESSION_TIMEOUT))
    {
        ATLTRACE("Session service failed to initialize\n");
        TerminateExtension(0);

        return SetCriticalIsapiError(IDS_ATLSRV_CRITICAL_SESSIONSTATEFAILED);
    }

    return TRUE;
}

BOOL TerminateExtension(DWORD dwFlags)
{
    m_SessionStateSvc.Shutdown();
    BOOL bRet = baseISAPI::TerminateExtension(dwFlags);

    return bRet;
}

    HRESULT STDMETHODCALLTYPE QueryService(REFGUID guidService,
```

```
101                                        REFIID  riid,
102                                         void**  ppvObject)
103{
104    if (InlineIsEqualGUID(guidService,
105                          __uuidof(ISessionStateService)))
106    {
107        return m_SessionStateSvc.QueryInterface(riid, ppvObject);
108    }
109
110    if (InlineIsEqualGUID(guidService,
111                          __uuidof(IDataSourceCache)))
112    {
113        CIsapiWorker *pWorker = GetThreadWorker();
114        if (pWorker)
115        {
116            CDataSourceCache<> *pCache = NULL;
117            if (pWorker->GetWorkerData(_DATASOURCE_CACHE,
118                                       (void **)&pCache))
119            {
120                *ppvObject = static_cast<IDataSourceCache *>(pCache);
121
122                return S_OK;
123            }
124        }
125    }
126
127    return baseISAPI::QueryService(guidService, riid, ppvObject);
128 }
129
130virtual void OnThreadTerminate(DWORD /*dwThreadId*/)
131 {}
132 };
```

The difference between the code in Listing 8-3 and what you saw earlier is actually quite minimal. Let's look at these differences line-by-line:

- *Lines 8 through 11:* For every thread you have in your thread pool, you want to create and maintain one database connection. This will save you the overhead of connecting to the database each time you read or write to it. In many cases, especially when the amount of data being written is small (as it will likely be in this case), the time necessary to connect to the database is actually the dominant time. As usual, any time you want to do anything on a per-thread basis, you want to create a class that derives from `CIsapiWorker`.

- *Lines 34 through 42:* The only difference between this class declaration than what you've seen before is that you'll use your `CIsapiExtensionWorker` class instead of the default `CIsapiWorker` class.

- *Lines 50 and 51:* Earlier, you used the `CMemSessionServiceImpl` implementation class to create your session state service type. In order to use database-backed session state, you'll change the implementation to use `CDBSessionServiceImpl` instead.

- *Lines 67 through 81:* The initialization for your database-backed session state service is slightly different. You need to supply a connection string to the database that you're using. This connection string is built from the ATL Server Project Wizard. Keep in mind that for security reasons, you should always use Windows Integrated security instead of embedding credentials in the connection string.

Those are the only differences between using memory-backed session state and database-backed session state. The process of actually storing and retrieving values from either type of session state is identical.

One last important point: Before you can use the database-backed session state, you have to set up the database schema that it will use to store the session values. The schema that ATL Server requires can be created by executing the SessionServices.sql file located in the VC7\bin directory of your Visual Studio .NET installation. You can run this .sql file against any database that you deem suitable.

As we mentioned before, you use database-backed session state through the same `ISession` interface that you use any session state implementation in your ATL Server application. The only difference is that session variables aren't automatically removed from the database. So, when you're done with your session, you have to call `ISession::RemoveAllVariables` to remove the values of that session's variables.

Conclusion

Session state can be a powerful tool that you can use to build complex Web applications. As you learned in this chapter, ATL Server offers you this service with a degree of granularity and control that you can't find in any other Web application framework.

Now that you've looked a number of different features you can incorporate into your ATL Server applications, you'll spend the next chapter looking at various techniques to tune the performance of the ATL Server applications that you build.

CHAPTER 9

Perfmon

WINDOWS PERFORMANCE MONITOR (Perfmon) is a logging application distributed with the NT operating system (NT 3.1 and above) that allows users to log and monitor various aspects of their system. The Perfmon application (the front-end utility, not the underlying system) is designed for short-term, real-time monitoring of a system. The data is exposed as counters and graphs and may be viewed either locally or remotely.

Perfmon also provides a logging mechanism that enables users to collect data in a log file that they can export and view (as graphs or histograms) using the System Monitor. The logging mechanism is designed for extended monitoring of local or remote systems (or both).

The system is designed so you can determine how often to log data and how many counters to log. It even enables you to have multiple machines record data to a single log file (on a single administrator system) to enable easier maintenance of multiple machines (e.g., a Web farm). It's important to remember that excessive logging may lead to system slowdown and increased overhead for using logs and alerts. Excessive logging to a single system may also cause extensive network traffic.

The operating system provides a large number of base counters that are useful for monitoring generic system usage. These include counters that can be enabled for logging memory, processors, disks, and the network, among others. Many other applications, such as IIS, Exchange Server, and SQL Server, install additional counters that allow users to monitor application-specific functionality.

You can easily store Perfmon data in a database, which allows for long-term storage and backup of data, as well as the ability to make extensive and complex queries on the logged information. Perfmon is a stable system with a well-documented interface, so many tools are available to collect and analyze the data it stores.

Because many features, such as remote access, central logging, and graph and histogram generation are provided for free, Perfmon has several benefits over custom logging systems.

In the case of Web applications and ATL Server, you can use Perfmon to store and display information about your Web site. This information includes commonly used statistics such as the number of hits, bytes downloaded, pages visited, and so on.

Although Perfmon is perfectly suited to this task, it's also suitable for the real-time monitoring of any information on your system. You can use the ATL Server Perfmon helper classes for a wide variety of tasks, such as gathering and storing data from a remote sensor (in any sort of application, including non-Web applications).

Using Perfmon

Perfmon works by providing an infrastructure of objects, each of which can contain one or more counters. Thus, your application creates a new Perfmon object (this is the object that you can view from the Perfmon application) and then associates one or more counters with this object (the values of these counters are the values displayed by Perfmon).

The standard way to use Perfmon is to store your counters in your ISAPI DLL. Because this DLL is cross-application, it allows all areas of your application to update a common counter store. You should be careful of the consequences of putting a counter in your application DLL. If you put a counter in your application DLL, it will reset each time the DLL is unloaded (often after each request). This is rarely desirable.

ATL Server provides the following main classes for working with Perfmon:

- `CPerfObject`: This class represents a Perfmon "category." Examples include CPU, Processes, and Memory. Individual counters are defined via a map located in this class. It contains information such as the size of your object and an ID referring to your object, as well as a reference count and instance for your object. It also contains an offset from the beginning of the Perfmon object to the name of the instance.

- `CPerfMon`: This class represents a manager object that manages a collection of categories. Each category is represented by a `CPerfObject` class (as described in the previous bulleted point). This class includes functionality such as registration, unregistration, initialization, and uninitialization, as well as creating and releasing the instance of your object (`CreateInstance` and `ReleaseInstance`, respectively).

- This class also provides functionality to make using Perfmon counters easy, such as opening and closing the connection to your counter, as well as adding categories and counters and collecting data from existing counters.

ATL Server's Perfmon support is also simplified through the use of attributes. You'll see the attributed code that helps you work with Perfmon later in this chapter.

Out-of-the-Box Counters

ATL Server provides a number of common counters "out of the box." These counters are designed to give you an example of items that are very useful to monitor with a system such as Perfmon.

The ATL Server development team tried to provide many of the common examples of counters they thought Web application developers might find useful, but it's always possible to add your own custom counters, as you'll see in the next section. Here's a list of the counters provided:

- Active Threads
- Average Response Time
- Current Queued Requests
- Maximum Queued Requests
- Server Failed Requests
- Server Requests per Second
- Server Total Requests

NOTE *If you use the same ISAPI DLL for multiple applications (i.e., the same filename and the same directory), then your Perfmon statistics will be a combination of statistics for both applications. To avoid this, simply use a differently named ISAPI DLL or a different directory for the ISAPI DLL for each application you want to monitor.*

Understanding the Perfmon System

With Perfmon it's easy to start focusing on implementation details, which can lead you to quickly lose your understanding of what you're trying to accomplish. So now we'll just take a step back and look at this from a higher level.

You want to create a counter (or, more likely, a number of counters) to measure some arbitrary statistics for your application. Typically, you'll want to store your counter in your ISAPI DLL (because your ISAPI DLL handles every request and is common to all the application DLLs, it's the perfect place for storing "global variables"), and you'll want to update your counter from your application

DLL (your application DLL contains your application logic, therefore it contains the application-specific information you want to measure).

If you just wanted to read information from the global counter, then it could be this simple, but unfortunately you need to update it. Because you could be updating from one of any number of threads, you need to ensure that updating the counters is a thread-safe operation.

The Perfmon system is designed in a hierarchy that makes managing sets of counters as easy as possible from a user's point of view, but not necessarily from a developer's point of view. You can group one or more performance counters (which you can create with the ATL Performance Counter Wizard) into a performance category (which you can create with the ATL Performance Object Wizard). You can then manage one or more performance categories by using a Perfmon object manager.

TIP *When Visual Studio .NET and Visual Studio .NET 2003 were designed, the Perfmon categories were referred to as "objects," hence the fact that although we refer to Perfmon "categories," the associated class names, wizards, and so forth refer to Perfmon "objects." "Categories" is usually a better term to use and way to think about it, and the change from "objects" to "categories" may be made in a future version.*

When you add performance monitoring to your own application, you'll start from the top (the Perfmon object manager) and work your way down to the counters you want to use.

Creating a Perfmon Counter

In this section you'll create your first counter and the infrastructure necessary to have a counter. You'll set up a simple Web page that updates Perfmon with the number of hits that the page has received. You could easily modify this example counter to track the number of orders on a e-commerce site, the number of downloads of a particular application, or the number of times users click banners on your site.

To start, simply create a new ATL Server project and select Predefined Perfmon Counters from the Server Options tab. Create a new header file to hold your Perfmon information. As you saw in the previous section, you need to start with a performance monitor object manager.

You can do this by using the wizard (right-click the project you want to add the file to in Solution Explorer or Class view, select Add ➤ Add Class, and then select

ATL Performance Object Manager) or by writing the code by hand, either with or without attributes. For this example you'll first look at the code with attributes, and then you'll look at it without attributes.

Put this Perfmon code in a new header file in your ISAPI project. You then expose these counters to the application DLLs via a service from your ISAPI DLL. The performance object manager class looks like this:

```
[perfmon(name="MyMonitor", register=true)]
class MyMonitor
{
  public:

};
```

Now you need to create a performance object. Once again, there's a wizard to simplify this task (right-click the appropriate Perfmon object manager class in Class view and select Add ➤ Add Perfmon Object). Note that this code goes **before** the performance object manager class:

```
[perf_object(namestring="MyObject",
    helpstring="MyObject Helpstring",
    detail=PERF_DETAIL_NOVICE)]
class MyObject
{
  public:
};
```

Finally, add the counter itself. The wizard for doing so is again available from Class view (right-click the performance object class and select Add ➤ Add Perfmon Counter).

```
 [perf_object(namestring="MyObject",
    helpstring="MyObject Helpstring",
    detail=PERF_DETAIL_NOVICE)]
class MyObject
{
  public:
    [perf_counter(namestring="MyCounter",
        helpstring="MyCounter Helpstring",
        countertype=PERF_COUNTER_RAWCOUNT,
        defscale=0, detail=PERF_DETAIL_NOVICE)]
    ULONG Visits;
};
```

You can achieve the same results without using Visual C++ attributes. Again, start with the code for the ATL performance object manager:

```
class MyMonitor : public CPerfMon
{
  public:
    BEGIN_PERF_MAP(_T("MyMonitor"))
      CHAIN_PERF_OBJECT(MyObject)
    END_PERF_MAP()
};
```

If you look at the attributed example, you'll notice that the manager has a "register=true" parameter. This sets registration for your performance object manager, and because you aren't using attributes, you need to do this manually. You add the following code:

```
#define _ATL_PERF_REGISTER
PERFREG_ENTRY(MyMonitor);
```

Now you can add the Perfmon object:

```
class MyObject : public CPerfObject
{
  public:
    DECLARE_PERF_OBJECT(MyObject, 1, "MyObject", "MyObject Helpstring", -1);
};
```

And then you finish off by adding the counter. You'll notice that attributes greatly simplify this step by creating code that's easy to read and maintain:

```
class MyObject : public CPerfObject
{
  public:
    DECLARE_PERF_OBJECT(MyObject, 1, "MyObject", "MyObject Helpstring", -1);
    BEGIN_COUNTER_MAP(MyObject)
      DEFINE_COUNTER(Visits, "MyCounter",
                 "MyCounter Helpstring",
                  PERF_COUNTER_RAWCOUNT,
                  0)
    END_COUNTER_MAP();
    ULONG Visits;
};
```

To get your Perfmon counter to actually work, you have to instantiate your object manager and the Perfmon object itself. Open the main cpp file in your ISAPI project. You should already have the header file in which you defined the Perfmon object manager, object, and counter `#included`. Now create two global objects: one for the object manager and one as a pointer to the object itself:

```
MyMonitor g_Monitor;
MyObject *g_pObject;
```

Next, go to `GetExtensionVersion` to initialize Perfmon as follows:

```
g_Monitor.Initialize();
g_Monitor.CreateInstanceByName(L"My Monitor", &g_pObject);
```

Now build and deploy your code. You should run regsvr32 on your deployed ISAPI DLL at the command line (make sure to register the deployed ISAPI in your vroot, not the version under your project). Launch your browser and click the wizard-generated SRF file to actually load your application. You can now launch Perfmon from the command line or via the Start menu, and then click the plus sign (+) to add a counter. From the Performance Object drop-down list, select your performance object (e.g., "My Object"). From the Select Counters From list, you can choose your counter (e.g., "My Counter"). You could also change your performance object manager from the Instance selection.

You'll notice, however, that you currently have no way to access the performance counter from your application DLL. In the next section, you'll expose this counter to your application DLLs via a service. The only potential downfall with this scheme is if you expect to change your monitor code regularly, as changes to your monitor code will mean changing your ISAPI DLL, which in turn requires you to reset IIS. You can avoid this issue by exposing your perfmon counter as a windows service as seen in the PerfPersist sample shipped with Visual Studio.

Exposing a Perfmon Counter As an ISAPI Service

You'll continue learning about Perfmon throughout this chapter as you expose it via an ISAPI service. We recommend that you read Chapter 4 before continuing through this chapter.

Let's begin by taking the same simple counter application you created earlier and modifying it so that your Perfmon object is now exposed via an ISAPI service instead of from your ISAPI DLL.

To begin, you'll get rid of the global monitor and object that you created previously, as well as the code you added to `GetExtensionVersion`. You can also remove the #include for the header file, which contains your Perfmon class information. In this section we assume that you generated your ATL Server application from the wizard without choosing to expose any services from your ISAPI DLL (this is the default setting on the Server Options tab). If you did decide to expose some services from your ISAPI DLL, then don't worry, some of the code we present in this section will already have been generated for you.

Let's start in the .cpp file. By default, the wizard has generated a typedef for CIsapiExtension, which should look something like this:

```
typedef CIsapiExtension<> ExtensionType;
```

To expose your own services, you need to modify this code so that you provide your own IsapiExtension and a custom thread pool (so that you can initialize and expose all your services). To do this, modify the preceding code to look like the following:

```
typedef MyCIsapiExtension<> ExtensionType;
```

You should now create a header file where you define what MyCIsapiExtension actually is. Make sure to #include this header file in your .cpp file. You begin in the new header file by including <atlisapi.h>, which provides the base functionality off of which you'll create your application, as well as the header file in which you defined your Perfmon classes. You can now create your MyCIsapiExtension class derived from CIsapiExtension. Listing 9-1 presents the code for this class.

Listing 9-1. Custom ISAPI Extension Class

```
template <class ThreadPoolClass=CThreadPool<CIsapiWorker>,
  class CStatClass=CNoRequestStats,
  class HttpUserErrorTextProvider=CDefaultErrorProvider,
  class WorkerThreadTraits=DefaultThreadTraits >
class MyCIsapiExtension :
  public CIsapiExtension<ThreadPoolClass,
    CStatClass,
    HttpUserErrorTextProvider,
    WorkerThreadTraits>
{
protected:
  typedef CIsapiExtension<ThreadPoolClass, CStatClass, HttpUserErrorTextProvider,
      WorkerThreadTraits> baseISAPI;
  typedef CWorkerThread<WorkerThreadTraits> WorkerThreadClass;
public:
  BOOL GetExtensionVersion(HSE_VERSION_INFO* pVer)
  {
```

```
    if (!baseISAPI::GetExtensionVersion(pVer))
    {
      return FALSE;
    }
    if (GetCriticalIsapiError() != 0)
    {
      return TRUE;
    }
    return TRUE;
  }

  BOOL TerminateExtension(DWORD dwFlags)
  {
    BOOL bRet = baseISAPI::TerminateExtension(dwFlags);
    return bRet;
  }

  HRESULT STDMETHODCALLTYPE QueryService(REFGUID guidService,
      REFIID riid, void** ppvObject)
  {
    return baseISAPI::QueryService(guidService, riid, ppvObject);
  }

  virtual void OnThreadTerminate(DWORD /*dwThreadId*/)
  {
  }
};
```

Now you have a framework into which you can add your Perfmon objects that you'll expose via a service. Once you've finished creating the service, you'll consume it from your application DLL and use it as a page hit counter.

To create an interface that describes your hit counter interface, create a class that implements your hit counter. The code for this looks something like Listing 9-2.

Listing 9-2. Interface for a Simple Counter

```
__interface ATL_NO_VTABLE __declspec(uuid("A3B11C9C-C3B2-41ba-AA01-F086F4625B49"))
IHitCounter : public IUnknown
{
  HRESULT (IncrementCounter)();
};
class CHitCounter : public IHitCounter,
      public CComObjectRootEx<CComGlobalsThreadModel>
```

```
{
  BEGIN_COM_MAP(CHitCounter)
    COM_INTERFACE_ENTRY(IHitCounter)
  END_COM_MAP()
  MyObject *pObject;
  void InitCounter(MyObject *pIn)
  {
    pObject = pIn;
    pObject->Visits = 0;
  }
  HRESULT IncrementCounter()
  {
    InterlockedIncrement(reinterpret_cast<LONG *> (&pObject->Visits));
    return S_OK;
  }
};
```

You can now add in an instance of your Perfmon object manager and a pointer to an actual performance object to your class. You can also create an instance of `CHitCounter` and use it to initialize your counter, as shown in Listing 9-3 (remember to add this to your `MyCIsapiExtension` class). Adding this code means that you can remove your global object and monitor and also the initialization code from `GetExtensionVersion`.

Listing 9-3. Initializing the Counter

```
MyMonitor m_Monitor;
MyObject *m_pObject;
CComObjectGlobal<CHitCounter> m_Counter;
public:
BOOL GetExtensionVersion(HSE_VERSION_INFO* pVer)
{
  HRESULT hr = m_Monitor.Initialize();
  if (hr != S_OK)
  {
    return FALSE;
  }
    CPerfLock lock(&m_Monitor);
    hr = lock.GetStatus();
    if (FAILED(hr))
  {
    return FALSE;
  }
  hr = m_Monitor.CreateInstanceByName(1,
```

```
      L"Hit Counter",
      reinterpret_cast<CPerfObject**>(&m_pObject));
  if (FAILED(hr))
  {
    return FALSE;
  }
  m_Counter.InitCounter(m_pObject);
  if (FAILED(hr))
  {
    return FALSE;
  }
  if (!baseISAPI::GetExtensionVersion(pVer))
  {
    return FALSE;
  }

  if (GetCriticalIsapiError() != 0)
  {
    return TRUE;
  }
    return TRUE;
}
```

You also need to implement the QueryService method. Luckily, this is easy:

```
HRESULT STDMETHODCALLTYPE QueryService(REFGUID guidService,
         REFIID riid,
    void** ppvObject)
{
  if (InlineIsEqualGUID(guidService, __uuidof(IHitCounter)))
      return m_Counter.QueryInterface(riid, ppvObject);
  return baseISAPI::QueryService(guidService, riid, ppvObject);
}
```

Next, check that your service actually works by using it from your existing ValidateAndExchange method in your application DLL. First, find this method in the header file for your application DLL.

You'll need to #include your ISAPI header file where you have your CHitCounter code. Now you can use your hit counter to measure the hits to your page in Perfmon. The code looks like this (make sure if you remove the OnHello method that you remove the corresponding {{Hello}} tag from your SRF file):

```
[ request_handler("Default") ]
class CbkPerfmonCleanHandler
{
private:
  CComPtr<IHitCounter> m_HitCounter;
public:
  HTTP_CODE ValidateAndExchange()
  {
    // Set the content-type
    m_HttpResponse.SetContentType("text/html");
    HRESULT hr = m_spServiceProvider->QueryService(
          __uuidof(IHitCounter),
          &m_HitCounter);
    if (FAILED(hr))
    {
      m_HitCounter = 0;
      return HTTP_FAIL;
    }
    m_HitCounter->IncrementCounter();
    return HTTP_SUCCESS;
}
};
```

Now you should know how to expose a service from your ISAPI DLL and consume it from your application DLLs.

Some Other Types of Perfmon Counters

So far we've focused predominantly on the raw Perfmon counters. These counters basically allow you to store arbitrary data in Perfmon. Perfmon supports more than just raw data storage, however, and it provides a number of predefined counter types for many different situations. In this section, we cover the various styles of counter types and discuss some examples of where they're useful:

- `PERF_100NSEC TIMER`: This family of counters measures some data over time. The time measured is in 100-nanosecond increments. These counters help you measure the time that something is in use (or not in use). You might use these counters to tune your application by determining which functionality is most often in use and optimizing your application for these requests. Similarly, you might look for functionality that isn't often used and look for ways to remove it.

- PERF AVERAGE: These counters usually give some base data about your application. In particular, there are functions to calculate the average time per operation and the average bytes per operation. You can use these counters to measure things such as average response time or average request size.

- PERF COUNTER LARGE: These counters all have non-LARGE equivalents. The LARGE versions allow for 8 bytes of data, whereas the regular types only store 4 bytes. You can use these counters whenever your data is bigger than 4 bytes.

- PERF COUNTER MULTI: These counters have a non-MULTI counterpart. The MULTI versions allow you to track multiple items and provide you with an average. For example, whereas the TIMER tracks the time an item is in use, the MULTI_TIMER tracks the time a number of items are in use and then takes the average. These counters basically allow you to group data. For example, as opposed to wanting to know how much each individual cache is used, you may be more interested in comparing how often caching in general is used versus session state. MULTI counters allow you to average over all the cache timers.

- PERF RAW: These counters allow you to store some raw data. This is the type of the counter you just created, as well as many of the built-in ATL Server counters.

- PERF PRECISION: You should use these counters when the standard system timers aren't precise enough for accurate readings. The service providing the data for these counters needs to provide a timestamp. These counters are useful when monitoring short time-spans with high precision. For a Web application, these counters would be applicable for any server-side calculations—maybe measuring times for certain numerical computations.

- PERF SAMPLE: These counters allow a value of 1 or 0, and they track the number of 1s sampled. You can use a counter such as this to track an "on or off"–style sampling. For example, you could use these counters to monitor how often a cache is hit versus how often it's missed.

You can access these counters by using the `countertype` parameter in the `perf_counter` attribute (within your `perf_object`).

Conclusion

You should now have a good understanding of how you can use ATL Server Perfmon support to enhance your applications. We've covered not only the features that make Perfmon attractive, but also how to incorporate Perfmon usage into an ATL Server application by exposing it from your ISAPI DLL.

Perfmon is a general system for monitoring any applications, not just Web applications. Therefore, it's important to remember that you can use ATL Server's Perfmon support in any application that you create. Having seen the samples exposing Perfmon support from an ISAPI DLL in this chapter, it should be clear to you how to enable any existing application (or new application) with Perfmon functionality.

So far we've focused on ATL Server infrastructure and the Web application features of ATL Server. In the next chapter we'll introduce you to the ATL Server support for Web services. Web services enable your application to expose and consume method calls over the Internet.

CHAPTER 10

Web Services

***WEB SERVICES* REPRESENT A** new philosophy in application development and design. Based on standard protocols, Web services introduce a way of allowing applications to take advantage of Internet communication.

Web services enable applications to take advantage of the Internet by allowing them to make procedural calls and exchange data over the Web. By relying on Extensible Markup Language (XML) as the packaging, Web services allow communications between programs running all over the world, regardless of the underlying platform.

ATL Server has been designed to allow native C++ developers to easily create Web services on the Windows platform. The ATL Server Web service support has been extensively tested against Web services created using other tools and technologies (ASP.NET, Apache, and others) to ensure ease of use and interoperability.

In this chapter you'll examine what exactly Web services are, how they work, and how you can use ATL Server to take advantage of them in your own applications (or to migrate existing components forward). This chapter assumes you are somewhat familiar with XML and XML namespaces.

Introducing Web Services

The two main protocols in the ATL Server implementation of Web services are Simple Object Access Protocol (SOAP) and Web Services Description Language (WSDL). SOAP is the protocol for a Web service message, and WSDL is for defining the interface for a service being called.

In this section you'll also look at Universal Description, Discovery, and Integration (UDDI), a publishing service that allows developers to publish their Web services so that other developers may discover and use them. In addition, UDDI allows developers looking for Web services to find and consume those that they have access to.

For more information on SOAP and WSDL, please visit the following Web pages on the World Wide Web Consortium's (W3C's) site:

- Simple Object Access Protocol (SOAP): `http://www.w3.org/TR/SOAP/`
- Web Services Description Language (WSDL): `http://www.w3.org/TR/WSDL.html`
- XML Schema Part 0: Primer: `http://www.w3.org/TR/xmlschema-0/`

- XML Schema Part 1: Structures: `http://www.w3.org/TR/xmlschema-1/`
- XML Schema Part 2: Datatypes: `http://www.w3.org/TR/xmlschema-2/`

SOAP

SOAP is a protocol for the exchange of information in a distributed environment, which is achieved by the exchange of SOAP "messages." You'll see some examples of SOAP messages later in this section.

For many C++ developers, it's probably convenient to consider SOAP as a style of remote procedure call (RPC) using HTTP as the transport and XML as the data format or packaging. Although this definition is an oversimplification, it should provide a good sense of context. It's important to note, however, that neither SOAP nor the ATL Server SOAP support is limited to HTTP as the transport mechanism. Later on, you'll see how users can plug in their own transport mechanisms into the ATL Server SOAP support.

A SOAP message is an XML document with predefined elements that may have user-defined data as subelements. The basic format of a SOAP message as described in section 4 of the SOAP specification is as follows:

```
<SOAP:Envelope xmlns:SOAP="http://schemas.xmlsoap.org/soap/envelope/">
  <SOAP:Header>
    <!-- user data -->
  </SOAP:Header>
  <SOAP:Body>
    <!-- user data -->
  </SOAP:Body>
</SOAP:Envelope>
```

The `Header` element of the SOAP message is optional. The `Envelope` and `Body` elements are required in the SOAP message. You can find a full description of the SOAP message format in section 4 of the SOAP specification. Here's an example of a simple SOAP message:

```
<SOAP:Envelope xmlns:SOAP="http://schemas.xmlsoap.org/soap/envelope/">
  <SOAP:Body>
    <m:HelloWorld xmlns:m="Some-URI">
    <inputString>StringValue</inputString>
    </m:HelloWorld>
  </SOAP:Body>
</SOAP:Envelope>
```

Notice that the optional `Header` element has been omitted. The user data under the `Body` element is one possible encoding of a `Hello World` SOAP message. When viewed as an RPC message, the element `HelloWorld` is a wrapper element under `Body` that denotes the function name. `inputString` is a parameter to the function `HelloWorld` and has the value `StringValue`.

With that, let's continue on to the other major protocol in ATL Server Web services: WSDL.

WSDL

WSDL is an XML format for describing network services as a series of endpoints containing either document-oriented or procedure-oriented information. WSDL isn't specific to SOAP, but it has a predefined syntax for describing SOAP messages. For those familiar with COM, it may be convenient to think of WSDL as a Web service version of Interface Definition Language (IDL). Again, this is an oversimplification that should help provide some context.

A WSDL document is an XML document, and it uses XML Schemas to describe the format of the messages. (Extensible Schema Definition, or XSD, is described in the specifications you can find at the Web addresses we presented at the start of this section.) Listing 10-1 presents an example of a simple WSDL document.

Listing 10-1. A Simple WSDL Document

```
<?xml version="1.0"?>
<!-- ATL Server generated Web Service Description -->
<definitions
  xmlns:s="http://www.w3.org/2001/XMLSchema"
  xmlns:http="http://schemas.xmlsoap.org/wsdl/http/"
  xmlns:mime="http://schemas.xmlsoap.org/wsdl/mime/"
  xmlns:soap="http://schemas.xmlsoap.org/wsdl/soap/"
  xmlns:soapenc="http://schemas.xmlsoap.org/soap/encoding/"
  xmlns:s0="http://mynamespace"
  xmlns:wsdl="http://schemas.xmlsoap.org/wsdl/"
  xmlns:atls="http://tempuri.org/vc/atl/server/"
  targetNamespace="http://mynamespace"
  xmlns="http://schemas.xmlsoap.org/wsdl/"
>
  <types>
    <s:schema targetNamespace=http://mynamespace
 attributeFormDefault="qualified" elementFormDefault="qualified">
      <s:simpleType name="MyEnumeration">
        <s:restriction base="s:string">
```

```
          <s:enumeration value="Value1"/>
          <s:enumeration value="Value2"/>
          <s:enumeration value="Value3"/>
        </s:restriction>
      </s:simpleType>
      <s:complexType name="MyStruct">
        <s:sequence>
          <s:element name="EnumValue" type="s0:MyEnumeration"/>
          <s:element name="UIntValue" type="s:unsignedInt"/>
        </s:sequence>
      </s:complexType>
    </s:schema>
  </types>
  <message name="MyMethodIn">
    <part name="Parameter1" type="s0:MyStruct"/>
  </message>
  <message name="MyMethodOut">
    <part name="return" type="s0:MyStruct"/>
  </message>
  <portType name="MyServiceSoap">
    <operation name="MyMethod">
      <input message="s0:MyMethodIn"/>
      <output message="s0:MyMethodOut"/>
    </operation>
  </portType>
  <binding name="MyServiceSoap" type="s0:MyServiceSoap">
    <soap:binding transport="http://schemas.xmlsoap.org/soap/http" style="rpc"/>
    <operation name="MyMethod">
      <soap:operation soapAction="#MyMethod" style="rpc"/>
      <input>
        <soap:body use="encoded" namespace="http://mynamespace"
encodingStyle="http://schemas.xmlsoap.org/soap/encoding/"/>
      </input>
      <output>
        <soap:body use="encoded" namespace="http://mynamespace"
encodingStyle="http://schemas.xmlsoap.org/soap/encoding/"/>
      </output>
    </operation>
  </binding>
```

```
  <service name="MyService">
    <port name="MyServiceSoap" binding="s0:MyServiceSoap">
      <soap:address location="http://localhost/MyService.dll?Handler=MyService"/>
    </port>
  </service>
</definitions>
```

All WSDL documents begin with a `definitions` tag, which may also contain XML namespace declarations. The `definitions` tag is followed by the `types` tag, which in turn may contain `schema` tags, which contain XSD type definitions. In Listing 10-1, the `schema` element contains a `simpleType` element and a `complexType` element. The `simpleType` element in Listing 10-1 is used to define an enumeration named `MyEnumeration`, with the values `Value1`, `Value2`, and `Value3`. You may also use the `simpleType` element to extend or restrict other "primitive" types (e.g., to restrict the range of an `unsignedInt`). The `complexType` element in Listing 10-1 is used to define a struct named `MyStruct`, with the field `EnumValue`, which is of type `MyEnumeration`, and `UIntValue`, which is of type `unsignedInt`. You may also use the `complexType` element to define arrays, SOAP messages, and other types and elements. The `types` section is followed by a series of `message` elements, which are used to define the contents of a SOAP message. The `message` elements contain message `part` elements, which reference XSD types. The `message` elements are followed by one or more `portType` elements, which compose the individual messages into *operations*, which form a complete SOAP interaction (request/response). The `portType` element is in turn followed by a `binding` element, which references a `portType` element and its `operations` to `bind` the operations to specific SOAP protocols, namespaces, encoding styles, and so on. The final element is the `service` element, which references a `binding` element and provides a specific location URL at which the service can be invoked.

This is a very high-level view of WSDL. Listing 10-1 is an example of a WSDL document that is produced by the default configuration and settings of ATL Server Web services. A WSDL document will vary depending on the type of messages that are being passed, the encoding style, the transport mechanism, and other factors. WSDL provides an extensibility method that allows for custom elements to be inserted into WSDL documents. For more details on WSDL, consult the specifications noted previously.

Creating a Web Service

In this section you'll learn what's involved in creating a Web service and how ATL Server helps simplify many of the tasks involved in this process for you.

Creating a Web Service by Hand

To create a Web service by hand (without using any libraries or frameworks), you have to complete a number of tasks. The following steps outline the tasks you normally need to perform to correctly handle the reception of a SOAP message:

1. Determine the intended recipient of the message (e.g., the `HelloWorld` function).
2. Parse the XML of the message and marshal the parameters (e.g., `inputString`) into real C++ data types (e.g., a string).
3. Call the intended recipient of the message (`HelloWorld`) with the expected parameters (`inputString`).
4. After the function, take the output parameters and return value and generate a SOAP HTTP response message to send back to the client.

This doesn't even account for a situation where you intend the Web service to be callable from any client, in which case WSDL for the Web service also needs to be generated.

As you can clearly see, there's a lot of code involved in creating a Web service infrastructure, and most of this code actually needs to be duplicated for every exposed function. All of these issues must be resolved before you can focus on implementing your Web service functionality. Plus, all of this work only enables you to create Web service services—it doesn't include the infrastructure code required to create a Web service client!

Creating a Web Service with ATL Server

ATL Server is designed to solve the problems mentioned in the preceding section for you and make creating a Web service easy. ATL Server does this by allowing you to focus on implementing your application logic and not on the underlying infrastructure code.

Using the ATL Server Web Service Wizard

From the Visual Studio .NET New Project dialog box, choose the Visual C++ Projects folder, and then choose the ATL Server Web Service project.

You'll notice that the wizard dialog box that appears is nearly identical to that of the ATL Server Project Wizard described earlier. In fact, it's the same wizard, just with different default settings. The Application Options tab has the Create as Web Service box checked by default. Almost all the options and settings described earlier for ATL Server are available for ATL Server Web services. A few options are unavailable (they're grayed out). In the Application Options tab, the Validation Support and Stencil Processing Support options aren't available, because those options apply only to ATL Server projects that will handle Web page requests (i.e., SRF-based pages). Similarly, the locale and codepage options are unavailable because Web services don't use SRF files. On the Developer Support Options tab, the Attributed Code check box can't be unchecked, because ATL Server Web services require the use of attributes.

The ATL Server Web Service Wizard will generate the following Web service files (assuming that the project's name is MyProject):

- *MyProject.h:* Contains your Web service implementation
- *MyProject.disco:* The Web service .disco file
- *MyProject.htm:* A description of the Web service

The default Web service generated by the wizard is a simple "Hello World"–style Web service that shows how a basic ATL Server Web service works:

```
[
  uuid("989438E7-DC64-4C1E-9B7D-18AE00BA8EE2"),
  object
]
__interface IMyProjectService
{
  // HelloWorld is a sample ATL Server Web service method. It shows how to
  // declare a Web service method and its in-parameters and out-parameters
  [id(1)] HRESULT HelloWorld([in] BSTR bstrInput, [out, retval] BSTR *bstrOutput);
  // TODO: Add additional Web service methods here
};
```

First, embedded IDL is used to declare a COM interface that describes the Web service.

Through attributes, embedded IDL is now available to all COM developers and Web service developers. The COM-like syntax was chosen for a few very specific reasons. The benefit of choosing a COM-like syntax is that it enables COM developers to protect their existing investment. In terms of a similar coding style, it helps COM developers protect their existing investment in their knowledge of COM development. In terms of similar code (embedded IDL), it enables COM developers to easily protect their investment in existing code, making it easy for these developers to expose existing or new COM objects as Web services if they desire (with just a few lines of code).

The IDL attributes are used to specify the parameters of the Web service methods being exposed. In the wizard-generated code example, the `HelloWorld` method has two parameters, both of which are BSTRs: `bstrInput` and `bstrOutput` (in the next section we describe Web service types and their mappings to XSD). The IDL `in` attribute is used to specify that the `bstrInput` parameter is a part of the SOAP *request*, and the IDL `out` attribute is used to specify that the `bstrOutput` parameter is part of the SOAP *response* (in the next section we describe all the SOAP attributes in detail). Listing 10-2 shows the sample "Hello World" Web service.

Listing 10-2. "Hello World" Web Service

```
[
  request_handler(name="Default", sdl="GenProject1WSDL"),
  soap_handler(
    name="MyProjectService",
    namespace="urn:MyProjectService",
    protocol="soap"
  )
]
class CMyProjectService : public IMyProjectService
{
public:
// This is a sample Web service method that shows how to use the
// soap_method attribute to expose a method as a Web method
  [ soap_method ]
  HRESULT HelloWorld(/*[in]*/ BSTR bstrInput, /*[out, retval]*/ BSTR *bstrOutput)
  {
    CComBSTR bstrOut(L"Hello ");
    bstrOut += bstrInput;
    bstrOut += L"!";
    *bstrOutput = bstrOut.Detach();
    return S_OK;
  }
// TODO: Add additional Web service methods here
}; // class CMyProjectService
```

The `CMyProjectService` class implements the Web service described by the interface we examined previously.

The request_handler attribute (described earlier in the context of normal ATL Server Web applications) now has the additional sdl parameter, which specifies the handler name for retrieving the WSDL for the Web service. The soap_handler attribute specifies that the request handler is also a SOAP Web service (i.e., it will contain methods that will need to be able to decode incoming SOAP and encode outgoing messages as SOAP). The class inherits from the IMyProjectService interface and implements the HelloWorld method.

The soap_method attribute specifies which methods from the IMyProjectService interface are to be exposed via SOAP. The HelloWorld method is implemented as any COM method would be implemented, without any special processing required as a Web service method.

Consuming ATL Server Web Services

In this section we describe how to consume ATL Server Web services using Visual Studio .NET's Add Web Reference dialog box. You can use the options on this dialog box to consume any kind of Web service that exposes a WSDL description. The dialog box generates a proxy class that you can use to invoke a method on the Web service by simply calling the matching method in the proxy class. The dialog box generates an ATL Server native C++ proxy for C++ projects (in 2002), in 2003 managed C++ projects generate managed C++ proxies (native remains ATL Server).

In Solution Explorer, right-click the project to which you want to add the Web service proxy class and choose Add Web Reference. Enter the location of the Web service's WSDL for the address, for example, **http://localhost/MyProjectService/MyProjectService.dll?Handler=GetWSDL**. The Add Web Reference dialog box lists the WSDL that you've selected. You have the option of viewing the documentation for the Web service (if it exists). Click the Add Reference button to generate the proxy class. For example, if you're adding a Web reference to a Visual C++ project, an ATL Server proxy class will be generated using the sproxy.exe tool. The Build Output window should appear and show something like the following:

```
------ Build started: Project: Proxy1, Configuration: Debug Win32
Creating Web service proxy file...
/out:MyProjectService.h
Build log was saved at "file://c:\Code\Proxy\Debug\BuildLog.htm"
Proxy1 - 0 error(s), 0 warning(s)
--------------------- Done ----------------------
    Build: 1 succeeded, 0 failed, 0 skipped
```

As the output suggests, the Web service proxy class is generated in the file MyProjectService.h.

The generated proxy class will have methods that map to the methods in the Web service. In this example, there will be a `HelloWorld` method in the proxy class that can be called to invoke the `HelloWorld` method in the Web service:

```
HRESULT HelloWorld(
  BSTR bstrInput,
  BSTR* __retval
);
```

To invoke the method, create an instance of the proxy class and simply call the method as you would normally:

```
#include "MyProjectService.h"
int main()
{
  CoInitialize(NULL);
  {
    MyProjectService::CMyProjectService svc;
    CComBSTR bstrOut;
    svc.HelloWorld(CComBSTR(L"Joe"), &bstrOut);
    printf("%ws\n", bstrOut);
    return 0;
  }
  CoUninitialize();
}
```

When you run your program, it will output `Hello Joe!`.

You've covered the basics of creating and consuming ATL Server Web services in Visual Studio .NET. Now it's time to become more familiar with using ATL Server.

Using ATL Server Web Services

In this section you'll learn how to use ATL Server to create Web services. You'll begin by looking at the architecture of an ATL Server Web service and then see how a Web service request hooks into the ATL Server architecture.

Next, you'll investigate the SAX XML parser used to parse the XML of the incoming SOAP requests/responses. You'll move on to implement ATL Server Web services using attributes. You'll then see how common types are supported by ATL Server.

ATL Server Web Service Architecture

From ATL Server's point of view, a Web service is simply another request handler. The SOAP details are handled in the implementation of the request handler itself, which in turn dispatches to the user code once the XML has been marshaled to C++ types and marshals the returned C++ types back into XML for the response. Because the Web service is just another request handler, it can take advantage of all the services that a regular request handler can. It has access to all services that live in the ISAPI extension, and it can provide its own services as well. Figure 10-1 illustrates the lifetime of a typical request.

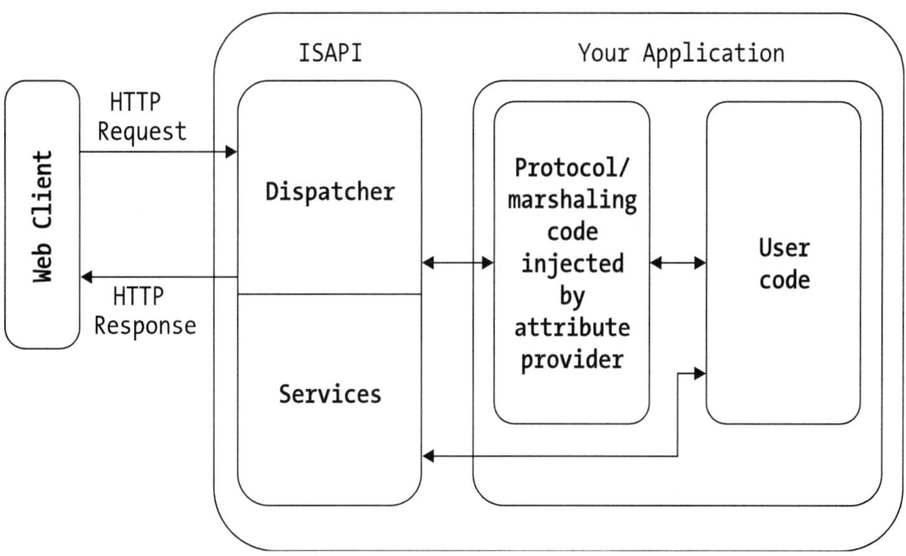

Figure 10-1. Application architecture for an ATL Server SOAP application

SAX

SOAP is based on XML, and the XML must be parsed somehow. ATL Server uses SAX to parse XML. The primary reasons SAX was chosen are performance and scalability. SAX is considerably faster than MSXML DOM for parsing, and it's considerably more lightweight as well—SAX uses significantly less memory and significantly fewer allocations than MSXML DOM.

Implementing Web Services

In the following sections you'll explore the various aspects of implementing ATL Server Web services. First, we cover the Visual C++ attributes that are provided by ATL Server for Web services. Then we cover the various types supported by ATL Server and how they map to XSD. We also describe how user-defined types, such as structs and enums, can be used with ATL Server. Finally, we cover how to use arrays in the Web service.

ATL Server Web Service Attributes

Just as ATL Server provides attributes to simplify the task of creating Web applications, it provides attributes to simplify the task of creating Web services. One important difference, however, is that while it's possible to create Web applications without the use of the `request_handler` and `tag_name` attributes, ATL Server Web services *require* the use of attributes. (Technically, it's possible to create Web services without attributes, because it's always possible to view the injected code; however, this won't be portable to future versions of ATL Server.)

ATL Server provides the following attributes for creating Web services: `soap_handler`, `soap_header`, and `soap_method`. Also, the `sdl` parameter of the `request_handler` attribute applies only when it's used in conjunction with the `soap_handler` attribute.

soap_handler

The `soap_handler` attribute applies to classes, and it designates that the class will handle SOAP requests. This ensures that the code to handle the marshaling of the XML gets injected by the attribute provider. Additionally, a different base class will be injected from the one that's normally injected by the `request_handler` attribute. The `soap_handler` attribute can appear only once per class.

The `soap_handler` attribute has five parameters: `name`, `namespace`, `protocol`, `style`, and `use`.

- `name`: This is the user-provided name for the Web service. This name appears in the WSDL as the name of the Web service and is used by sproxy.exe in generating the Web service proxy class. If this parameter isn't specified, the name of the class is used.

- `namespace`: This parameter is the user-provided namespace for the Web service, the XML namespace to which all user-defined types and methods will belong. It's the namespace that will be used to validate incoming SOAP messages. If this parameter isn't specified, the XML namespace will be based upon the name of the class. For example, if the class name is `CMyWebService`, the namespace will be `urn:CMyWebService`. Developers should choose a specific, unique namespace that properly distinguishes their Web service.

- `protocol`: This is a reserved parameter in the version of ATL Server that ships as part of Visual Studio .NET. The only permissible value is `soap`. In the future, other Web service protocols or extended SOAP protocols may be supported.

- `style`: This is the SOAP "style" to be used for the format of the SOAP messages. The permissible values are `rpc` and `document`; `rpc` is the default value. This parameter describes whether the SOAP messages are intended as remote procedure calls or XML documents.

- `use`: This is the SOAP "use" for the SOAP messages. The permissible values are `encoded` and `literal`; `encoded` is the default value. The `use` parameter indicates whether the SOAP messages are to be encoded using SOAP section 5 encoding rules, or whether they're describing the concrete XML schema of the message.

In the version of ATL Server that ships with Visual Studio .NET, the only permissible style/use combinations are `rpc/encoded` and `document/literal`.

CAUTION *When you use* `document/literal`*, multidimensional arrays aren't supported as SOAP headers or as parameters on a method exposed via SOAP.*

When the `soap_handler` attribute is used in conjunction with the `request_handler` attribute, its `sdl` parameter may be used to specify the handler name used to retrieve the WSDL for the Web service. If the handler name isn't specified, it defaults to a value based on the class name. For example, if the class name is `CMyWebService`, the `sdl` parameter defaults to `GenCMyWebServiceWSDL`.

soap_method

The `soap_method` attribute applies to methods, and it designates that the method on which it appears will be exposed via SOAP. The `soap_method` attribute can appear only once per method.

The `soap_method` attribute has one parameter: `name`.

- `name`: This parameter is the user-specified name for the exposed method. This is the name that will be used in the WSDL and that clients will need to use when invoking the Web service. If this parameter isn't specified, the name of the method will be used.

CAUTION *The method on which this attribute is placed must be an implementation of an interface method defined in an embedded IDL interface; otherwise, it will result in a compiler error. The reason for this is that unless the method is an interface method, the ATL Server framework can't determine which parameters are* `in` *parameters, which are* `out` *parameters, and if a return value is specified.*

soap_header

The `soap_header` attribute applies to methods, and it indicates that the method on which it appears will have the specified SOAP header in its SOAP message. Headers must be member variables. The `soap_header` attribute is optional and may appear one or more times per method. The `soap_header` attribute may appear only on methods that also have the `soap_method` attribute, although the `soap_method` attribute doesn't require the `soap_header` attribute.

The `soap_header` attribute has four parameters: `value`, `required`, `in`, and `out`.

- `value`: This is the name of the member variable that's being sent or received as a header. Variable size arrays may not be used as SOAP headers. The user must specify this parameter. There's no default value.

- `required`: This is a boolean parameter that indicates whether the specified header is optional or not. The default value for this parameter is `false`. If this parameter is set to `true`, the header will be sent as a SOAP `mustUnderstand` header, and the WSDL will indicate that the client should send the header as a mustUnderstand header. If a required header isn't received, ATL Server will return a SOAP fault.

- in: This is a boolean parameter that indicates whether the specified header is expected as part of a request. The default value is true.
- out: This is a boolean parameter that indicates whether the specified header should be sent as part of the response of the method. The default value is true.

CAUTION *When a* soap_header *attribute appears on a method, each instance must have a unique "value" parameter. That is, the same header can't appear as more than one SOAP header for a particular method.*

Types

In this section you'll look at the types supported by the ATL Server implementation of Web services. You'll see how C++ data types are mapped to XSD data types.

ATL Server supports all native C++ data types. It also defines a special type, ATLSOAP_BLOB, that's used to send binary data over SOAP. Table 10-1 shows the native types that are supported, along with their corresponding XSD data type mappings.

Table 10-1. ATL Server Data Types

C++ DATA TYPE	XSD DATA TYPE
bool	Boolean
char	Byte
_int8	Byte
unsigned char	unsignedByte
unsigned _int8	unsignedByte
short	Short

Table 10-1. ATL Server Data Types (Continued)

C++ DATA TYPE	XSD DATA TYPE
_int16	Short
unsigned short	unsignedShort
unsigned_int16	unsignedShort
wchar_t	unsignedShort
Int	int
_int32	int
long	int
unsigned int	unsignedInt
unsigned_int32	unsignedInt
unsigned long	unsignedInt
_int64	long
unsigned_int64	unsignedLong
double	double
float	dloat
BSTR	string
ATLSOAP_BLOB	base64Binary

ATL Server currently has no way to represent XSD types not listed in Table 10-1. You may use `typedef`s in place of direct references to native types. You must take care to ensure that the `typedef`s have the expected results. For example, in Visual C++ .NET, BSTR is the only type that ATL Server will map to string. If another string type is used, for example `LPCSTR`, it will be mapped to `const char *`, which ATL Server will attempt to map to an array of bytes, which isn't an efficient way to represent strings in SOAP. ATL Server will treat all pointer types as arrays. In these cases, the user is required to specify the size of the array by using the `size_is` attribute. The upcoming section on arrays describes arrays in detail.

ATL Server supports user-defined structs and enums, which we describe in detail in later sections of this chapter. ATL Server doesn't support unions in Visual C++ .NET. ATL Server doesn't support templatized types or template instantiations as SOAP types.

Arrays

ATL Server supports arrays in two forms: fixed-size arrays and variable-sized arrays. The arrays can contain any primitive or user-defined type that's supported by ATL Server. Fixed-size arrays are arrays of the form

```
int arr[5];
BSTR arr[2][3];
```

Variable-sized arrays are of the form

```
int *arr;
```

When you use variable-sized arrays, you must specify the size of the array with the `size_is` attribute. This is required to ensure that the array is marshaled correctly and safely. The `size_is` attribute references a parameter or struct field that specifies the size of the array. When the array is an `in`-only parameter, the `size_is` attribute is optional. If it appears for `in`-only parameters, the parameter specified in the `size_is` attribute will contain the number of array elements sent by client. The parameter referenced by the `size_is` attribute must have the same "in" and "out" attributes as the array to which it is applied. So a `size_is` parameter for an `out` array must also be an `out` parameter, a `size_is` parameter for an `in` array must also be an `in` parameter, and a `size_is` parameter for an `in/out` array must also be an `in/out` parameter. Listing 10-3 shows an example of this.

Listing 10-3. Sample Web Service Using Variable-Sized Arrays

```
[ uuid("643cd054-24b0-4f34-b4a1-642519836fe8"), object ]
__interface IRetArray
{
  [id(1)] HRESULT retArray(
[out] int *nSize,
[out, retval,
size_is(*nSize)] int **arrOut);
};
[
  request_handler(name="Default", sdl="retArraySDL"),
  soap_handler(name="RetArray",
  namespace="http://retArray ",
  protocol="soap")
]
class CRetArray : public IRetArray
{
public:
```

```
  [ soap_method ]
  HRESULT retArray(int *nSize, int **arrOut)
  {
    *nMax = 10;
    *arrOut = (int *)GetMemMgr()->Allocate(*nMax*sizeof(int));
    for (int i=0; i<*nMax; i++)
      (*arrOut)[i] = i;
    return S_OK;
  }
};
```

The `size_is` attribute appears in the IDL definition on the `arrOut` parameter and references the `nSize` parameter (we explain the call to `GetMemMgr()->Allocate` in detail in the section "Memory Management").

ATL Server doesn't support variable-length arrays of more than one dimension.

Fixed-size arrays don't require a `size_is` attribute, because the size of the array is part of its type. Fixed-size may also be multidimensional. Listing 10-4 shows an example of a Web service that uses multidimensional arrays.

Listing 10-4. Sample Web Service Using Multidimensional Arrays

```
[ uuid("643cd054-24b0-4f34-b4a1-642519836fe8"), object ]
__interface IRetArray
{
[id(1)] HRESULT retArray([out] int arrOut[3][3]);
};
[
  request_handler(name="Default", sdl="retArraySDL"),
  soap_handler(name="RetArray",
  namespace="http://retArray ",
  protocol="soap")
]
class CRetArray : public IRetArray
{
public:
  [ soap_method ]
  HRESULT retArray(int arrOut[3][3])
  {
    for (int i=0; i<3; i++)
   {
      for (int j=0; j<3; j++)
      {
        arrOut[i][j] = i*3+j;
```

```
      }
    }
  return S_OK;
  }
};
```

Structs

ATL Server supports user-defined structs. For most common structs, simply define and use the struct as you normally would. Listing 10-5 shows a sample Web service that uses structs.

Listing 10-5. Sample Web Service Using Structs

```
[ export ]
struct MyStruct
{
  BSTR strValue;
  int nValue;
};

// IStructService - Web service interface declaration
//
[
  uuid("4EA08537-12F7-4DC7-ABE5-483CFE0F4FE0"),
  object
]
__interface IStructService
{
  [id(1)] HRESULT StructTest([in] MyStruct tIn, [out, retval] MyStruct *tOut);
};

// StructService - Web service implementation
//
[
  request_handler(name="Default", sdl="GenStructWSDL"),
  soap_handler(
    name="StructService",
    namespace="urn:StructService",
    protocol="soap"
  )
]
class CStructService :
  public IStructService
```

```
{
public:
  [ soap_method ]
  HRESULT StructTest(/*[in]*/ MyStruct tIn, /*[out, retval]*/ MyStruct *tOut)
  {
    tOut->strValue = SysAllocString(tIn.strValue);
    tOut->nValue = tIn.nValue;
    return S_OK;
  }
}; // class CStructService
```

The export attribute is only necessary if you plan for your Web service to also be used as a COM object. If you don't plan on using your Web service as a COM object, it's completely harmless to leave it on your struct definition.

Structs can contain fields of nearly any type, including nested struct and enum fields. They can also contain array fields. You can use fixed-size arrays just as you would normally. When you use variable-length arrays, however, you must specify the array size, just as you do when you use a variable-length array as a parameter. Listing 10-6 shows a sample Web service that uses a struct that contains a variable-sized array.

Listing 10-6. Sample Web Service Using a Struct That Contains a Variable-Sized Array

```
[ export ]
struct MyStruct
{
  [size_is(nSize)] int *arr;
  int nSize;
};

// IStructService - Web service interface declaration
//
[
  uuid("4EA08537-12F7-4DC7-ABE5-483CFE0F4FE0"),
  object
]
__interface IStructService
{
  [id(1)] HRESULT StructTest([in] MyStruct tIn, [out, retval] MyStruct *tOut);
};


// StructService - Web service implementation
```

```
//
[
  request_handler(name="Default", sdl="GenStructWSDL"),
  soap_handler(
    name="StructService",
    namespace="urn:StructService",
    protocol="soap"
  )
]
class CStructService :
  public IStructService
{
public:
  [ soap_method ]
  HRESULT StructTest(/*[in]*/ MyStruct tIn, /*[out, retval]*/ MyStruct *tOut)
  {
    // set the size of the array
    // tIn.nSize will contain the number of array elements marshaled
    tOut->nSize = tIn.nSize;
    tOut->arr =
reinterpret_cast<int *>(GetMemMgr()->Allocate(
    tIn.nSize*sizeof(int)));
    if (!tOut->arr)
    {
      return E_OUTOFMEMORY;
    }
    for (int i=0; i<tIn.nSize; i++)
    {
      tOut->arr[i] = tIn.arr[i];
    }
    return S_OK;
  }
}; // class CStructService
```

Note that `tIn.nSize` will contain the number of array elements marshaled in, independent of the value that's sent in the client request. Thus, a malicious user can't spoof the number of array elements, which could otherwise result in walking past the end of an array. The `nSize` field of `tOut` will tell the ATL Server framework how many array elements to marshal back to the user.

Enums

ATL Server supports enums. You can use enums in ATL Server exactly as you would normally. Listing 10-7 shows a sample Web service that uses enums.

Listing 10-7. Sample Web Service Using Enums

```
[ export ]
enum MyEnum { Value1, Value2, Value3, Value4 };

// IEnumService - Web service interface declaration
//
[
  uuid("A745E7CB-AD49-41EB-B36C-D533B812EC64"),
  object
]
__interface IEnumService
{
  [id(1)] HRESULT TestEnum([in] MyEnum eIn, [out, retval] MyEnum *eOut);
};


// EnumService - Web service implementation
//
[
  request_handler(name="Default", sdl="GenEnumWSDL"),
  soap_handler(
    name="EnumService",
    namespace="urn:EnumService",
    protocol="soap"
  )
]
class CEnumService :
  public IEnumService
{
public:

  [ soap_method ]
  HRESULT TestEnum(/*[in]*/ MyEnum eIn, /*[out, retval]*/ MyEnum *eOut)
  {
    if (eIn == Value4)
    {
      *eOut = Value1;
    }
```

```
    else
    {
      *eOut = (MyEnum)(eIn+1);
    }
    return S_OK;
  }
}; // class CEnumService
```

Again, the export attribute on the enum declaration is only necessary when you plan for your Web service to also be used as a COM object. If you don't plan on using your Web service as a COM object, it's completely harmless to leave it on your enum definition.

BLOB Types

ATL Server supports BLOBs through the framework-defined ATLSOAP_BLOB struct. The definition of ATLSOAP_BLOB is as follows:

```
[ export ]
typedef struct _tagATLSOAP_BLOB
{
  unsigned long size;
  unsigned char *data;
} ATLSOAP_BLOB;
```

The data field is the raw bytes contained in the BLOB, and the size field indicates the number of bytes in the data field. The ATLSOAP_BLOB type maps to the XSD base64Binary type, hence the data is base64-encoded before being put on the wire. The memory for the data field is allocated in the same way arrays are allocated. Listing 10-8 shows a sample Web service using the ATLSOAP_BLOB type.

Listing 10-8. Sample Web Service Using ATLSOAP_BLOB

```
[
  uuid("41AF710A-EC7B-4FD5-B1C4-CBB58406AEF8"),
  object
]
__interface IBlobService
{
  [id(1)] HRESULT BlobTest(
[in] ATLSOAP_BLOB blobIn,
[out, retval] ATLSOAP_BLOB *blobOut);
};
```

```
// BlobService - Web service implementation
//
[
  request_handler(name="Default", sdl="GenBlobWSDL"),
  soap_handler(
    name="BlobService",
    namespace="urn:BlobService",
    protocol="soap"
  )
]
class CBlobService :
  public IBlobService
{
public:
  [ soap_method ]
  HRESULT BlobTest(
/*[in]*/ ATLSOAP_BLOB blobIn,
/*[out, retval]*/ ATLSOAP_BLOB *blobOut)
  {
    blobOut->size = blobIn.size;
    blobOut->data =
reinterpret_cast<unsigned char *>(GetMemMgr()->Allocate(
    blobIn.size));
    memcpy(blobOut->data, blobIn.data, blobIn.size);
    return S_OK;
  }
}; // class CBlobService
```

When sending binary data, you need to use the `ATLSOAP_BLOB` struct; otherwise, ATL Server won't treat the data as binary and won't perform the proper encodings to ensure correct transport.

Restricted Types

The only type restriction that ATL Server has is the use of variable-length multidimensional arrays. For example, the code in Listing 10-9 will result in a compiler error.

Listing 10-9. Illegal Input Header

```
[
  uuid("23E070EF-C8B5-4A0F-A299-FB50ABD6CD03"),
  object
]
__interface IRestrictedTypesService
{
  [id(1)] HRESULT Illegal([in] BSTR **arrInput);
};

 [
  request_handler(name="Default", sdl="GenRestrictedTypesWSDL"),
  soap_handler(
    name="RestrictedTypesService",
    namespace="urn:RestrictedTypesService",
    protocol="soap"
  )
]
class CRestrictedTypesService :
  public IRestrictedTypesService
{
public:

  [ soap_method ]
  HRESULT Illegal(/*[in]*/ BSTR **arrInput)
  {
    arrInput;
    return S_OK;
  }
}; // class CRestrictedTypesService
```

Listing 10-9 will result in the following compiler error message:

```
error C2338: soap_method
        Atl Attribute Provider : error ATL2213: "arrInput" parameter of method
"Illegal" has too many indirections. In parameters cannot have more than 1
indirection.
```

Variable-length multidimensional arrays aren't allowed as `in` parameters, `out` parameters, struct fields, or SOAP headers. The restriction is due to implementation details relating to memory management.

SOAP Headers

In this section you'll look at how SOAP headers are defined and used. As described earlier, SOAP headers are defined using the `soap_header` attribute. SOAP headers designate member variables of the class to be sent or received as SOAP headers on a per-method basis. Listing 10-10 shows a sample Web service that uses SOAP headers.

Listing 10-10. Sample Web Service Using SOAP Headers

```
[
  uuid("E8F59246-F4CB-4B8D-8F09-1F8C79F5A825"),
  object
]
__interface IHeader1Service
{
  [id(1)] HRESULT HeaderMethod([out, retval] BSTR *ReturnValue);
};

[
  request_handler(name="Default", sdl="GenHeader1WSDL"),
  soap_handler(
    name="Header1Service",
    namespace="urn:Header1Service",
    protocol="soap"
  )
]
class CHeader1Service :
  public IHeader1Service
{
public:

  BSTR HeaderValue;

  [ soap_method ]
  [ soap_header(value="HeaderValue", required=false, in=true, out=false) ]
  HRESULT HeaderMethod(/*[out, retval]*/ BSTR *ReturnValue)
  {
    if (HeaderValue != NULL)
    {
      *ReturnValue = SysAllocString(HeaderValue);
    }
```

```
    else
    {
      *ReturnValue = NULL;
    }

    return S_OK;
  }

}; // class CHeader1Service
```

In Listing 10-10, the `HeaderMethod` SOAP method declares that the `HeaderValue` member variable be used as a SOAP header for the method. The `soap_header` attribute's parameters declare that the header isn't a required header, which means that its absence won't result in an error; that the header is an `in` header, which means it's expected as part of the SOAP request packet; and that the header isn't an `out` header, which means that it won't be sent back to the client as part of the SOAP response packet. If the `required` parameter to the `soap_header` attribute is set to `true`, the header *must* be present if it's an `in` header. If the header isn't present, the ATL Server framework will return an error to the client. Required headers also impact the WSDL that's generated for the Web service by making the header a `mustUnderstand` header. Any `mustUnderstand` headers must be recognized by the SOAP processor; if they aren't, they're required to return an error.

SOAP headers must be public member variables. If a private or protected member variable is used, it will result in a compiler error. Again, this is due to implementation details of the ATL Server framework. In future versions, protected or private members might be permitted.

Any type that's supported by ATL Server may be used as a SOAP header, with the exception of variable-length arrays. ATL Server has no way to retrieve marshaling information about the size of the arrays as it can with the `size_is` attribute in IDL interface and struct definitions, hence it can't marshal and clean up the array. You may still use variable-length arrays inside of structs that are used as SOAP headers, however—you just can't use them directly as SOAP headers.

SOAP headers are automatically cleaned up by the ATL Server framework; however, users must initialize the values themselves, as they would with any other member variable. If custom cleanup is required for a SOAP header, users should override the `CleanupHeaders` function in their `soap_handler` class (see Chapter 19 for more details on custom handling).

SOAP Faults

In this section you'll look at how ATL Server handles SOAP faults. *SOAP faults* are the way Web services convey error and status information to a client. A SOAP fault is a special type of message, and it defines four subelements (see section 4.4 of the SOAP 1.1 specification): `faultcode`, `faultstring`, `faultactor`, and `detail`.

- `faultcode`: The `faultcode` element is intended to provide an algorithmic mechanism for identifying the fault. SOAP defines four default fault codes:
    - `VersionMismatch` means the SOAP processor found an invalid namespace for the SOAP envelope element.
    - `MustUnderstand` means that the SOAP processor encountered a header marked as `mustUnderstand`, which it didn't recognize.
    - `Client` means the client request is incorrect.
    - `Server` means that the error occurred on the server, rather than for some reason relating to the client request.
- `faultstring`: The `faultstring` element is intended to provide a human-readable description of the error.
- `faultactor`: The `faultactor` element is intended to provide information about who caused the fault within a message path.
- `detail`: The `detail` element is intended to provide application-specific error information.

ATL Server represents SOAP faults through the `CSoapFault` class, which has member variables to represent each of the preceding subelements. We describe how to retrieve fault information from the client later in the "ATL Server Web Service Client" section. For now, we'll explain how to return custom SOAP faults from the Web service.

ATL Server will automatically return faults for errors that occur while marshaling the SOAP request. This includes VersionMismatch, MustUnderstand, Server, and Client faults. Users can return custom SOAP faults by calling the `SoapFault()` function. Listing 10-11 shows a sample Web service that returns a custom SOAP fault.

Listing 10-11. Sample Web Service Using a Custom SOAP Fault

```
[
  uuid("31F30250-D5BB-4022-B6E2-CEA65EC7B06D"),
  object
]
__interface IFault1Service
{
  [id(1)] HRESULT FaultTest([in] BSTR bstrInput);
};


 [
  request_handler(name="Default", sdl="GenFault1WSDL"),
  soap_handler(
    name="Fault1Service",
    namespace="urn:Fault1Service",
    protocol="soap"
  )
]
class CFault1Service :
  public IFault1Service
{
private:

  bool IsInvalidArg(BSTR bstrInput)
  {
    bstrInput;
    return true;
  }

public:
  [ soap_method ]
  HRESULT FaultTest(/*[in]*/ BSTR bstrInput)
  {
    if (IsInvalidArg(bstrInput))
    {
      SoapFault(SOAP_E_CLIENT, L"Invalid Argument", sizeof("Invalid Argument")-1);
      return E_INVALIDARG;
    }

    return S_OK;
  }
}; // class CFault1Service
```

In Listing 10-11, the FaultTest method checks the input to ensure it's a valid value; if it isn't, it returns a SOAP fault with a custom error message. Additionally, ATL Server will attempt to find an appropriate error message for an HRESULT error using the FormatMessage API. In Listing 10-11, FaultTest could have also returned E_INVALIDARG, and ATL Server would have loaded the appropriate error message using FormatMessage.

Users can also use the CSoapFault class directly by filling in the fields that represent the subelements and then calling the GenerateFault method with a class derived from IWriteStream. Listing 10-12 shows a sample Web service that uses the GenerateFault method to return a custom SOAP fault.

Listing 10-12. Sample Web Service Using the GenerateFault Method to Return a SOAP Fault

```
[
  uuid("2E55C132-0E5A-4EE9-9CAA-0B4824738D6B"),
  object
]
__interface IFault2Service
{
  [id(1)] HRESULT FaultTest([in] BSTR bstrInput);
};

 [
  request_handler(name="Default", sdl="GenFault2WSDL"),
  soap_handler(
    name="Fault2Service",
    namespace="urn:Fault2Service",
    protocol="soap"
  )
]
class CFault2Service :
  public IFault2Service
{
private:

  bool IsInvalidArg(BSTR bstrInput)
  {
    bstrInput;

    return true;
  }

public:
```

```
  [ soap_method ]
  HRESULT FaultTest(/*[in]*/ BSTR bstrInput)
  {
    if (IsInvalidArg(bstrInput))
    {
      CSoapFault fault;
      fault.m_soapErrCode = SOAP_E_CLIENT;
      fault.m_strDetail = L"Invalid Argument";
      fault.GenerateFault(m_pHttpResponse);

      return E_INVALIDARG;
    }
    return S_OK;
  }
}; // class CFault2Service
```

Memory Management

In this section you'll look at how memory is managed in an ATL Server Web service. In general, users will never have to free memory themselves, provided they allocate the memory in the way required by the ATL Server framework.

ATL Server follows COM rules with respect to memory allocation: `out` parameters must be NULL or must be able to be deallocated. For `in/out` parameters, users should free the memory before assigning into it; otherwise, the same rules as for `out` parameters apply. There are three cases when users will have to manage memory: when dealing with strings, when dealing with variable-length arrays, and when dealing with `ATLSOAP_BLOB`s.

When dealing with strings (BSTRs), you should allocate memory using `SysAllocString*` and free memory with `SysFreeString`. In other words, you allocate and free memory in the same way you would normally when dealing with BSTRs.

For variable-length arrays and `ATLSOAP_BLOB`s, you should allocate memory as explained in "Types" section previously, using the `IAtlMemMgr` interface that's returned from the `GetMemMgr()` method. The `IAtlMemMgr` interface is defined as follows:

```
__interface __declspec(uuid("654F7EF5-CFDF-4df9-A450-6C6A13C622C0")) IAtlMemMgr
{
public:
  void* Allocate( size_t nBytes ) throw();
  void Free( void* p ) throw();
  void* Reallocate( void* p, size_t nBytes ) throw();
  size_t GetSize( void* p ) throw();
};
```

By default, ATL Server uses a per-thread heap for its allocations. Users can provide their own `IAtlMemMgr` using the `SetMemMgr` method. After calling `SetMemMgr`, ATL Server will use the passed-in `IAtlMemMgr` for all its allocations, and it will also be returned from the `GetMemMgr()` method. Users should set a different memory manager when they are using asynchronous Web services (see Chapter 19 for more details).

The ATL Server framework will automatically handle the cleanup of memory after the processing of a Web service request. ATL Server Web service clients, however, will have to manage the memory after a Web service proxy method invocation themselves. We describe this process further in the next section.

ATL Server Web Service Clients

In this section you'll look at ATL Server Web service clients in more detail. You'll examine how they differ from ATL Server Web services and how they're similar. First, you'll look at the type support in ATL Server Web service clients.

Types

Table 10-2 shows how the ATL Server Web service proxy class generated by sproxy.exe maps XSD types to C++ data types.

Table 10-2. XML Data Type to C++ Data Type Mapping

XML SCHEMA DATA TYPE	C++ DATA TYPE (SPROXY)
boolean	bool
byte	char
unsignedByte	unsigned char
short	short
unsignedShort	unsigned short
int	int
unsignedInt	unsigned int
long	__int64
integer	__int64
nonPositiveInteger	__int64
negativeInteger	__int64

Table 10-2. XML Data Type to C++ Data Type Mapping (Continued)

XML SCHEMA DATA TYPE	C++ DATA TYPE (SPROXY)
unsignedLong	unsigned __int64
nonNegativeInteger	unsigned __int64
positiveInteger	unsigned __int64
decimal	double
double	double
float	float
string	BSTR
hexBinary	ATLSOAP_BLOB
base64Binary	ATLSOAP_BLOB
dateTime	BSTR
time	BSTR
date	BSTR
gMonth	BSTR
gYearMonth	BSTR
gYear	BSTR
gMonthDay	BSTR
gDay	BSTR
duration	BSTR
anyURI	BSTR
ENTITIES	BSTR
ENTITY	BSTR
ID	BSTR
IDREF	BSTR
IDREFS	BSTR
language	BSTR
Name	BSTR
NCName	BSTR
NMTOKEN	BSTR

Table 10-2. XML Data Type to C++ Data Type Mapping (Continued)

XML SCHEMA DATA TYPE	C++ DATA TYPE (SPROXY)
NMTOKENS	BSTR
normalizedString	BSTR
NOTATION	BSTR
QName	BSTR
token	BSTR

The mapping is the reverse of the mapping from C++ types to XSD types on the Web service side. Types that aren't directly supported, such as `normalizedString`, are represented as strings (BSTRs).

User-defined types, such as structs and enums, are also extracted from the XSD and appropriate definitions are emitted by sproxy.exe. When sproxy.exe emits the definition for a function that has a variable-length array as input or output, or when it encounters a struct that has a variable-length array field, it will emit a parameter or field that's used as the `size_is` for that array. The name of the parameter or field will be of the form `__[`*`parameter or field name`*`]_nSizeIs`. For `in` parameters, users are required to pass in the number of elements in the array so that the ATL Server framework knows how many elements to marshal. For `out` parameters, ATL Server will fill in this value with the number of elements that were marshaled. The `size_is` parameter/field will appear directly after the array parameter/field to which it applies in the function/struct definition. We present examples of this in the next section.

Memory Management

In this section you'll examine memory management in ATL Server Web service clients. Unlike ATL Server Web services, where ATL Server controls the full lifetime of the request and hence the data for the request, ATL Server controls neither the lifetime of the input parameter nor the output parameters on the client side. Users must manage much of the memory on the client side themselves; however, ATL Server provides several helper functions to make the job easier.

Strings on the client are managed just as they are on the server (i.e., using the `SysAllocString*` and `SysFreeString` functions). `CComBSTR` or `_bstr_t` can be used to simplify the task.

Arrays are allocated as they are on the server (i.e., using the proxy class's `GetMemMgr()` method to get the `IAtlMemMgr` interface and then invoking the `Allocate()` method to allocate the memory). Arrays can then be freed using `IAtlMemMgr`'s `Free()` method function provided by ATL Server. Listing 10-13 shows how array memory should be managed on the client.

Listing 10-13. Managing Array Memory on the Client

```
CWebServiceProxy proxy;
int *pArrInput = proxy.GetMemMgr()->Allocate(10*sizeof(int));
for (int i=0; i<10; i++)
{
  pArrInput[i] = i;
}
int *pArrOutput;
int nSize = 0;
HRESULT hr = proxy.EchoArray(pArrInput, 10, &pArrOutput, &nSize);
if (SUCCEEDED(hr))
{
  proxy.GetMemMgr()->Free(pArrOutput);
}
proxy.GetMemMgr()->Free(pArrInput);
```

Note the use of the `size_is` fields in Listing 10-13. The "10" represents the number of elements in the input array to marshal, and the `nSize` parameter is used to return the number of elements marshaled by the framework.

Structs can be cleaned up using the `AtlCleanupValueEx` template function. This function ensures that all struct fields, including strings, arrays, and nested structs, are cleaned up properly. Listing 10-14 shows how to manage struct memory on the client.

Listing 10-14. Managing Struct Memory on the Client

```
CWebServiceProxy proxy;
WebServiceStruct wsStruct;
wsStruct.s = SysAllocString(L"string");
wsStruct.arr = proxy.GetMemMgr()->Allocate(10*sizeof(int));
wsStruct.__arr_nSizeIs = 10;
for (int i=0; i<10; i++)
{
  wsStruct.arr[i] = i;
}
WebServiceStruct wsStructOut;
HRESULT hr = proxy.EchoStruct(wsStruct, &wsStructOut);
if (SUCCEEDED(hr))
{
  AtlCleanupValueEx(&wsStructOut, proxy.GetMemMgr());
}
AtlCleanupValueEx(&wsStruct, proxy.GetMemMgr());
```

Note the use of the `size_is` field for the preceding struct. This is used for the same marshaling purposes as in the previous array example.

Cleanup of arrays of structs can also be simplified using the `AtlCleanupArrayEx` or `AtlCleanupArrayMDEx` template function. The latter function handles cleanup of multidimensional arrays. Listing 10-15 shows how to manage the memory of arrays of structs on the client.

Listing 10-15. Cleaning Up Arrays of Structs

```
CWebServiceProxy proxy;
WebServiceStruct *pArrInput =
proxy.GetMemMgr()->Allocate(
    10*sizeof(WebServiceStruct));
for (int i=0; i<10; i++)
{
  pArrInput[i].s = SysAllocString(L"String");
  pArrInput[i].arr = proxy.GetMemMgr()->Allocate(10*sizeof(int));
  for (int j=0; j<10; j++)
  {
    pArrInput[i].arr[j] = j;
  }
pArrInput[i].__arr_nSizeIs = 10;
}
WebServiceStruct *pArrOutput;
int nSize = 0;
HRESULT hr = proxy.EchoStructArray(pArrInput, 10, &pArrOutput, &nSize);
if (SUCCEEDED(hr))
{
  AtlCleanupArrayEx(pArrOutput, nSize, proxy.GetMemMgr());
  proxy.GetMemMgr()->Free(pArrOutput);
}
AtlCleanupArrayEx(pArrOutput, 10, proxy.GetMemMgr());
proxy.GetMemMgr()->Free(pArrInput);
```

NOTE *Users must still free the top-level array manually.*

Multidimensional arrays can be cleaned up using the `AtlCleanupArrayMDEx` template function. The only difference between this function and the `AtlCleanupArrayEx` function is that instead of taking a count of the elements, it takes an array containing information about the dimensions of the array. For example:

```
WebServiceStruct arrInput[2][3];
// Web service calls
int arrInputSize[] = {2, 2, 3};
AtlCleanpuArrayMDEx(&arrInput, arrInputSize, proxy.GetMemMgr());
```

The `arrInputSize` array indicates that this is a two-dimensional array (first element). The remaining elements describe each dimension's size.

Error Handling

In this section you'll look at how errors are reported and handled in ATL Server Web service clients.

When a SOAP request fails, the proxy class will set an error state that can be retrieved using the `GetClientError()` function. This function returns a `SOAPCLIENT_ERROR` enum value that describes the type of error. The enum is defined as follows:

```
// client error states
enum SOAPCLIENT_ERROR
{
  SOAPCLIENT_SUCCESS=0,            // everything succeeded
  SOAPCLIENT_INITIALIZE_ERROR,     // initialization failed - most
                                   // likely an MSXML installation
                                   // problem
  SOAPCLIENT_OUTOFMEMORY,          // out of memory
  SOAPCLIENT_GENERATE_ERROR,       // failed in generating the response
  SOAPCLIENT_CONNECT_ERROR,        // failed connecting to server
  SOAPCLIENT_SEND_ERROR,           // failed in sending message
  SOAPCLIENT_SERVER_ERROR,         // server error
  SOAPCLIENT_SOAPFAULT,            // a SOAP Fault was returned by the server
  SOAPCLIENT_PARSEFAULT_ERROR,     // failed in parsing SOAP fault
  SOAPCLIENT_READ_ERROR,           // failed in reading response
  SOAPCLIENT_PARSE_ERROR           // failed in parsing response
};
```

The errors are essentially as described in the comments next to the enum values. The most relevant error is probably the `SOAPCLIENT_SOAPFAULT` error. The `SOAPCLIENT_SOAPFAULT` error is returned when the Web service being invoked returns a SOAP fault. Information about the SOAP fault can be retrieved using the proxy class's `m_fault` member variable, which is a `CSoapFault`. The same fields that we described in the earlier section on SOAP faults will be filled in according to the information returned by the Web service. Listing 10-16 shows how to retrieve error information from the proxy class.

Listing 10-16. Using SOAP Fault Information on the Client

```
HRESULT hr = proxy.WebMethod();
if (FAILED(hr))
{
  SOAPCLIENT_ERROR soapErr = proxy.GetClientError();
  switch(soapErr)
  {
    case SOAPCLIENT_INITIALIZE_ERROR :
      printf("initialization failed: check MSXML installation\n");
      break;
    case SOAPCLIENT_OUTOFMEMORY :
      printf("out of memory\n");
      break;
    case SOAPCLIENT_GENERATE_ERROR :
      printf("failed while generating request\n");
      break;
    case SOAPCLIENT_CONNECT_ERROR :
      printf("failed to connect to server\n");
      break;
    case SOAPCLIENT_SEND_ERROR :
      printf("failed while sending SOAP request\n");
      break;
    case SOAPCLIENT_SERVER_ERROR :
      printf("server error : %d\n", proxy.GetStatusCode());
      break;
    case SOAPCLIENT_PARSEFAULT_ERROR :
      printf("failed in parsing fault\n");
      break;
    case SOAPCLIENT_READ_ERROR :
      printf("failed while reading response\n");
      break;
    case SOAPCLIENT_PARSE_ERROR :
      printf("failed while parsing response\n");
      break;
    case SOAPCLIENT_SOAPFAULT :
      printf("SOAP Fault:\n"
             "fault code : %ws\n"
             "fault string : %ws\n"
             "fault detail : %ws\n",
```

```
                proxy.m_fault.m_strFaultCode,
                proxy.m_fault.m_strFaultString,
                proxy.m_fault.m_strDetail);
        break;
      default:
        printf("unknown error\n");
    }
}
```

Note the use of the proxy class's `GetStatusCode` method. This method retrieves the HTTP code that is returned by the server.

Conclusion

In this chapter you explored the basic uses and functionality of the ATL Server Web service support. You examined how to create Web services. You saw how to use user-defined types, such as structs and enums, in Web services. You also saw how arrays can be used within the ATL Server Web service framework. You learned how memory is managed in Web services and how to use and create SOAP faults from within a Web service. In addition, you examined the client side of all of these areas. You should now be able to create basic Web services using ATL Server.

One of the great things about ATL Server is that many of the classes are useful on applications other than Web applications and Web services. In the next chapter we examine how you can take advantage of some of the core ATL Server classes to solve problems you may face in many of your non-Web applications.

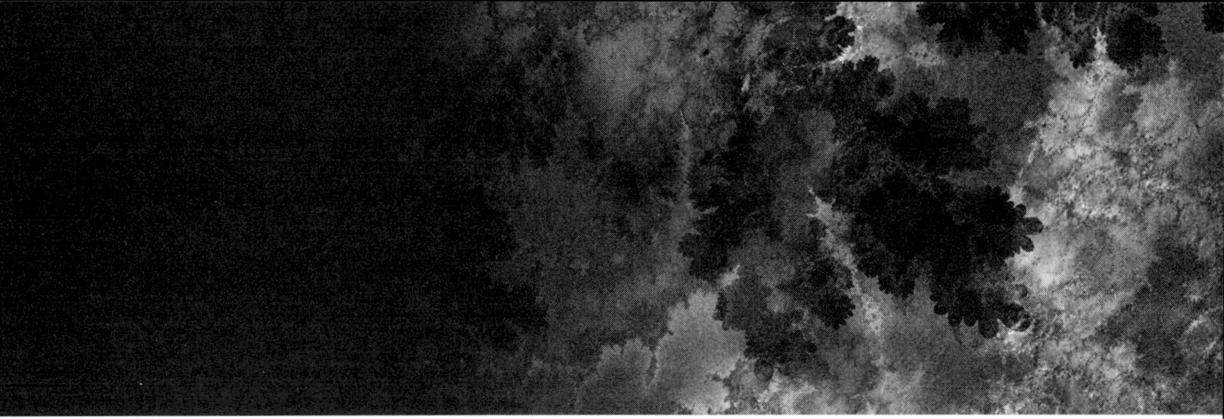

Part Two
Advanced Concepts and Techniques

CHAPTER 11

Using ATL Server Components in Stand-Alone Applications

MANY OF THE CHALLENGES you'll face while developing a Web application are challenges you'll encounter in other applications as well. This chapter deals with reusing ATL Server components in the context of non-Web applications.

The ATL Server framework was designed for high-performing and very scalable Web applications. However, flexibility and modularity were always a priority. Therefore, you are able to use some powerful components of ATL Server out of the Web context. In this chapter we demonstrate this with two of the most useful components: the ATL Server thread pool and the stencil processor.

Reusing the ATL Server Thread Pool

Many of today's applications require multithreading. The most common scenario is a server application that will process multiple requests from multiple clients at the same time. This approach is particularly useful when processing a request involves *idle* time, which is time when the processor isn't used, such as waiting for a database server to return the response to a query or for a timeout to occur. Using multithreading, the total waiting time (which is the sum of the wait time for all the clients) is dramatically reduced.

Multithreading can be very useful in client applications as well as on server applications. Consider the following scenario, for example: A desktop application is used to query information about customers. The user could send the query and then wait for the response for each customer, or the user could use the wait time to send new requests. Of course, the second approach is more productive. This scenario is implemented as this section's sample (available in the `StandaloneThreadpool` sample).

General Considerations

A simple approach to the multithreading problem is to spawn a thread for each job that starts. This might work very well for a desktop application, assuming that the user won't enter the information required to start a new job very fast and that the average waiting time for completing the jobs isn't too long. However, if the application is on a server, if the user is an exceptionally fast typist (or can batch commands), or if completing a job takes a very long time, this approach won't work very well. The reason for this is that many threads mean, at the operating system level, many context switches (as well as the added overhead of creating and deleting many threads), a rather time-consuming operation. So, instead of the performance increasing, the overall performance might very well stay the same or even drop.

This is where a thread pool proves useful. A *thread pool* is a mechanism that's able to queue a large number of jobs for execution on a limited number of threads, and then process the jobs on a first-come, first-serve basis as the working threads become available. A thread pool usually provides an interface for the following operations:

- Initialization (usually by specifying the number of threads to be created in the thread pool)
- Posting a job
- Resizing the thread pool (possibly while running)
- Shutting down the thread pool

By using a thread pool, the system won't get overwhelmed by the number of spawned threads and the jobs are still executed in a synchronous manner. The user doesn't even need to know that some of his or her requests are queued and processed later.

The ATL Server Thread Pool Class

In this section we discuss how the ATL Server thread pool works. This thread pool is based on I/O completion ports, and it's defined in the file atlutil.h as follows:

```
template <class Worker, class ThreadTraits=DefaultThreadTraits>
class CThreadPool : public IThreadPoolConfig
```

NOTE *For details on the I/O completion ports mechanism, or for the* `ThreadTraits` *template parameter, please see the MSDN documentation* (`ms-help://MS.VSCC/MS.MSDNVS/fileio/filesio_4z1v.htm` *and* `ms-help://MS.VSCC/MS.MSDNVS/vclib/html/vclrfCThreadPool.htm`).

Here you'll focus on the worker template parameter (aka the archetype). The thread pool class will create an object of this type for each thread in the thread pool. This object "knows" how to deal with the specific needs of the application. The `CThreadPool` class can only deal with this kind of object, so it doesn't need to care about the application's specifics.

First of all, the implementation of the worker archetype has to define a type for `RequestType`. `RequestType` is a token of information that can be posted to the thread pool and that's enough to identify a job once the thread pool has found an available thread for it. Due to the I/O completion ports–based implementation of the `CThreadPool` class, this token has to be of a type that can be safely casted to (and from) `ULONG_PTR`.

Happily, `ULONG_PTR` is a type perfectly compatible with a pointer type (actually, it's intended for casting a pointer to an `unsigned long` for pointer arithmetic) and, even more happily, all the pointers are the same size. Therefore, the worker implementation can easily define `RequestType` to be *any* pointer, even a pointer to whatever struct or class you use to contain a job description. This is what the default ATL Server usage of `CThreadPool` does in the `CIsapiWorker` class (`RequestType` is an `AtlServerRequest*`) and also what the `StandaloneThreadpool` sample does (which we discuss later in this chapter). Just one note before going further: Although a pointer is a very convenient underlying type for `RequestType`, the type *doesn't have to be a pointer.* For example, it could very well be the ordinal index of the job in an array of jobs.

Once the `RequestType` is defined, the worker class should implement the following methods:

```
BOOL Initialize(void* pvWorkerParam);
void Execute(
                RequestType request,  void* pvWorkerParam,
                OVERLAPPED* pOverlapped );
void Terminate(void* pvWorkerParam);
```

Whenever a thread is idle, the thread pool class will fetch a job description token (`RequestType`) from the queue and pass it to the worker object of the idle thread by invoking `Execute` with the job description token as parameter.

NOTE `pvWorkerParam` *is a global parameter that can be passed in during the initialization of the* `CThreadPool` *class and will be forwarded to all the calls to the worker objects for all the threads in the thread pool. This parameter could be a pointer denoting some global configuration object or some global service provider object necessary during job processing, but it could be* `NULL` *if it isn't needed.*

Now, to use the `CThreadPool` class in any application, you have to perform the following steps:

1. Define the data structure that identifies a job to be processed asynchronously.
2. Implement the worker archetype and perform the real job execution in the `Execute` method of the implementation.
3. Instantiate a `CThreadPool` specialization based on the worker class just defined.
4. Start using this specialized instance.

This is exactly what the sample code does. In the next section you'll take a step-by-step look at how the steps we just described are performed.

ATL Server Thread Pool Class Sample

The scenario is the following: In order to better help its customers, a customer support center needs an application that allows retrieval of customer-related information from a database (once the customer has identified him- or herself). Assuming that the database retrieval takes a few seconds, maybe minutes, the operator could help one customer while looking up the information for another.

Overall, the application will take the name of the customer as input (say, "Suzy Q") and return information about Suzy, as follows:

```
Lookup for Suzy Q SUCCEEDED:
        Age: 56
        Location: Redmond, WA
        Product: Sport shoes
-----------------
```

A lookup job can be described by the name of the customer to look for. Once the lookup is completed, you need a way to notify the main application thread of the completion so that the results can be displayed to the operator. Therefore, the job can be described by a structure defined as follows:

```
struct stJobDescriptor
{
      CStringA        strUserName;
      JOB_COMPLETION_CALLBACK        pfnCompletionCallback;
};
```

Also, a way of storing the lookup results would help:

```
struct stResultDescriptor
{
      CStringA      strUserName;
      int           nAge;
      CStringA      strLocation;
      CStringA      strProduct;
};
```

pfnCompletionCallback is the completion notification mechanism. It's a pointer to a routine defined as follows:

```
typedef void (*JOB_COMPLETION_CALLBACK)(HRESULT hRet, stResultDescriptor& result);
```

Whenever a job is complete, the completion routine associated with the job will be invoked with the return code and the results of the lookup (hRet and result) as parameters.

Once the job description is complete, you move to step 2, which is implementing the worker archetype. (Please see the WorkingThreadPool.h file in the sample's directory for the code discussed here.)

The worker implementation (CSampleDatabaseWorker) will start by defining RequestType:

```
public:
    typedef stJobDescriptor* RequestType;
```

As the CThreadPool class uses Worker::RequestType in the implementation, it's mandatory that this definition appears at public scope.

For this simple case, there's no need for initialization or termination code, so the Initialize and Terminate implementations won't do anything. However, these functions are called as a thread in the thread pool is created or terminated, respectively. They're *not* invoked for each job. Therefore, these functions are the best place to instantiate/release some per-thread cached objects (as an ISAXXMLReader pointer, see the CIsapiWorker class in atlisapi.h, or a database connection object) that will be used during job processing.

Now, the main job processing routine: Execute. It takes as a parameter a Worker::RequestType object, and therefore it can be safely implemented as follows:

```
void Execute(stJobDescriptor* pRequestInfo, void* pvParam,
                              OVERLAPPED *pOverlapped)
```

because in this implementation RequestType is a pointer to a stJobDescriptor structure.

This sample code simulates a time-consuming database call by sleeping for 10 seconds, then picking up some random results from a predefined set. To increase the realism of the simulation, some calls will fail.

The important part comes after the database call simulation, at the end of the Execute implementation:

```
if( pRequestInfo->pfnCompletionCallback )
{
pRequestInfo->pfnCompletionCallback(hrPseudoDBResult, result);
}
```

The callback routine for displaying the search results is invoked, taking as parameters the lookup return code and the results of search, if any.

Now that the implementation of the worker archetype is complete, you can move to steps 3 and 4, instantiating the thread pool and using it. To clarify the code, use the following definition:

```
typedef CThreadPool<CSampleDatabaseWorker>    CSampleProcessingPool;
```

Then you perform the instantiation of the thread pool and the usage in the StandaloneThreadpool.cpp file in the main function, as shown here:

```
CSampleProcessingPool    threadPool;
// Initialize the thread pool to 4 threads per CPU
threadPool.Initialize(0, -4);
...
// Queuing a new request
if( !threadPool.QueueRequest(pJobDesc) )
...
// Shutting down the thread pool
threadPool.Shutdown();
```

Results and Conclusions

After running the sample application with a few "customer names," the screen looks like this:

```
Enter customer name, then <ENTER> to lookup, or 'Q' to quit:John Doe
Lookup job started...
Enter customer name, then <ENTER> to lookup, or 'Q' to quit:Suzy Q
Lookup job started...
Enter customer name, then <ENTER> to lookup, or 'Q' to quit:PRANISH KUMAR
Lookup job started...
Enter customer name, then <ENTER> to lookup, or 'Q' to quit:
Lookup for John Doe SUCCEEDED:
        Age: 11
        Location: Boise, ID
        Product: Sport shoes
------------------

Lookup for Suzy Q SUCCEEDED:
        Age: 56
        Location: Redmond, CA
        Product: Sport shoes
------------------

Lookup for PRANISH KUMAR FAILED:
------------------
```

This should show pretty clearly that the jobs were simultaneously executed.

What isn't shown on the output screen but can be easily verified is the time difference between this solution and the serialized one (the one-by-one execution of the jobs). By serializing these calls, the total processing time would have been ~30 seconds (because you know that each call takes ~10 seconds to be processed). Using the thread pool, the total processing time is around 12 seconds.

Of course, this result isn't typical for a database client. The real result depends a lot on the application specifics. If the job processing has a long idle time (e.g., interrogating a database server), then more threads in the thread pool might be helpful. On the other hand, if the job processing is CPU-intensive and contains many computations, then a large number of threads in the pool might actually hurt the performance.

Here's a summary of what you've learned in this section:

- ATL Server provides a very flexible thread pool class that you can easily use in generic applications.
- The model for using this thread pool requires an implementation of the worker archetype, an instance of which will live in each of the threads in the pool.
- This per-thread instance will perform the actual job processing.
- The worker implementation is also a good place to store per-thread processing helpers, as an `ISAXXMLReader` pointer or a database connection object.
- The developer is responsible for collecting the job processing results (either by using them during processing or by saving them at the end of the `Execute` method).

Reusing the ATL Server Stencil Processor

The *stencil processor* is the feature of ATL Server that allows content generation (usually an HTML response) based on the stencil SRF files. This mechanism allows separating the static part of the response from the dynamic content. For example, the HTML payload required to describe a table and the font and the background color of the cells is completely separated in the SRF files from the actual values inside those table cells. This separation offers the following benefits:

- The response format can be easily changed. The response page can be changed to have a different look and feel as the whole site gets updated, while the processing code that fills in the actual information doesn't need to be touched.
- Localization of the response is now an easy task. It doesn't involve touching the code base—only the static part of the SRF has to be modified. Alternately, different localized versions of the same SRF file can be stored on the server to generate responses in different languages.
- The developers of the static part (the GUI) and those of the processing part (the engine) can focus on their specific areas without worrying much about how their work will affect the other side.

Now, these advantages, although particularly significant in the context of a Web application, can't be ignored in other applications either. Just consider the large class of desktop applications that generates reports or must, somehow, generate formatted output. `printf` or `CString::Format` are pretty powerful formatters, but you can't use them to render 1,000 records coming from a local database. This section shows how you can use the ATL Server stencil processor to generate some completely non-HTML output in a stand-alone application.

How the ATL Server Stencil Processor Works

First, although we're talking about "the stencil processor," ATL Server actually provides two stencil processors. The MSDN documentation for SRF files (see `ms-help://MS.VSCC/MS.MSDNVS/vccore/html/vcconATLServerServerResponseFileDefined.htm`) distinguishes between stencil files and SRF files. There's a basic stencil processor that implements the basic processing code for "stencil files," and there's an HTML stencil processor for "SRF files."

The HTML stencil processor is tightly integrated with the HTTP ISAPI extension architecture of ATL Server. This section deals with the basic stencil processor, so we'll just say a few words on the HTML stencil processor and then we'll focus on the basic one. The HTML stencil processor inherits from the basic stencil processor and adds some functionality that's very useful in the context of generating HTML response. Among these extensions are

- The `{{handler}}` element, which you use to indicate which application DLL should be associated with the current stencil file

- The `{{subhandler}}` element, which allows you to use content-generating code from a different source (i.e., a different application DLL)

- The `{{include}}` element, which allows you to include external content sources (HTML documents, ATL Server application DLLs, or other SRF files) inside the document being generated

A good reason for enumerating the features in the preceding list is that they are *not* supported in the basic stencil generator. Of course, you could implement them in another processor inheriting from the basic one, following the model of the HTML stencil.

So, let's see what the basic stencil processor can do. It implements the basic mechanism of content generation:

- It supports the replacement tags. For example, you can use it to associate the element `{{Name}}` with some custom `OnName` function to have the function called whenever the element is encountered.

- It supports elements with parameters. For example, you could associate the `{{Person}}` element with the `OnPerson(LPSTR strParam)` function and have `OnPerson("Name")` called whenever `{{Person(Name)}}` is encountered.

- It supports the basic processing directives: `{{if…}}`, `{{else}}`, `{{endif}}`, `{{while}}`, and `{{endwhile}}`.

The stencil processing mechanism is implemented in the `CStencil` class (defined in the atlstencil.h file). This class can take care of loading a stencil document from a file, from a resource, or from a string, and parsing the stencil. Provided with an object that contains replacement methods, it can also walk the parsed stencil document and call into the replacement methods.

To interoperate with the `CStencil` class, an object containing replacement methods has to implement the `ITagReplacer` interface. This interface is used in two moments of the stencil processing. First, some of its methods (such as `FindReplacementOffset`) are called during parsing of the stencil to make sure that all the replacement elements have an associated replacement method. This is to ensure that the `{{Name}}` element (for example) has the `OnName` method associated with it. Then, during the actual rendering, the `RenderReplacement` method is called to actually invoke the replacement method.

It's easy to realize that by implementing `ITagReplacer` directly, you'll end up with a big "switch" block that returns a function address or calls a function after comparing an input string (the element name) with a set of hard-coded values (the replacement elements supported by the implementation).

To help the implementers, ATL Server provides the `ITagReplacerImpl` template class, which hides all the implementation details behind macros such as

```
BEGIN_REPLACEMENT_METHOD_MAP(Replacer)
    REPLACEMENT_METHOD_ENTRY("Name", OnName)
    …
END_REPLACEMENT_METHOD_MAP
```

This macro system is far more readable and maintainable.

So, instead of implementing the ITagReplacer interface, the developer of a class containing the replacement methods faces the far more reasonable challenge of inheriting from the ITagReplacerImpl<> base class and focuses on his or her replacement handlers, as follows:

```
class CMyReplacementMethodsHolder:
        public ITagReplacerImpl< CMyReplacementMethodsHolder>
```

Now you can use the CStencil class to both parse and render the stencils. Next, you'll look at what you have to do to use the CStencil processor outside the regular HTML rendering context.

The next question that arises is "Where is the content rendered?" If you look at the definition of the CStencil class, you notice the Render method which, as you may expect, will render the actual content. Render is defined as follows:

```
    virtual HTTP_CODE Render(
        ITagReplacer *pReplacer,
        IWriteStream *pWriteStream,
        CStencilState* pState = NULL)
```

The first parameter is the ITagReplacer implementation, which contains the replacement methods, as we've already discussed. The second parameter is an IWriteStream implementation, an interface defined as follows:

```
__interface IWriteStream
{
    HRESULT WriteStream(LPCSTR szOut, int nLen, DWORD *pdwWritten);
    HRESULT FlushStream();
};
```

You can implement this interface to write in almost any media. You could write by using an EXTENSION_CONTROL_BLOCK function (in the ISAPI context), or you could write into a socket, a pipe, a file, or the standard output.

The last parameter of the Render function is a CStencilState structure pointer. CStencilState is used to provide state information useful in the ISAPI context. As we don't cover the ISAPI context here, and the parameter is defaulted to NULL, we ignore it in this section.

We use the same approach in this section as we did in the previous section, meaning we present a sequence of steps to be performed to support stencil rendering in a non-Web application and then demonstrate each step in the sample provided for this section.

To use the stencil processor outside of the HTTP context, an application should

1. Provide an implementation of the `IWriteStream` interface that will render the content to the desired media.
2. Provide an implementation of the `ITagReplacer` interface, most likely by deriving a class from the `ITagReplacerImpl` helper class, and put into this class the handling methods for the stencil's replacement tags.
3. Instantiate a `CStencil` object.
4. Parse/render the stencil.

In the next section we analyze these steps in the associated sample, `StanaloneStencilProc`.

Stencil Processor Sample

As we stated in the beginning of this chapter, we show you how to use the stencil in a completely non-HTML-related way. For this purpose, the sample is a wizard for authoring SOAP servers and clients. The application allows users to design a Web service through some (hopefully) clear and intuitive mouse actions, and then it generates the code for the SOAP server and for the client. It goes the extra mile in helping (or annoying) the developer by generating valid code and providing suggestions on how/where the SOAP parameters should be used, allocated, or freed.

The sample builds an in-memory list of all the functions of the Web service, each function containing the list of parameters. Then it uses this list to generate the code for the client and for the server. To make the code more readable, the Microsoft Foundation Classes (MFC) interface is almost completely separated from the actual file rendering code. The only files that are involved in rendering are ContentGenerator.h and SoapWizard.h.

The stencils used for rendering the server and client files are in the sample's Templates subfolder. The code for the actual server and client is rendered based on the files having one of the following extensions: .cpp.srf or .h.srf. The sample also generates a Visual Studio .NET solution file and two project files, but they might not be valid in upcoming versions of Visual Studio.

Let's start by looking at the stencil files in the Templates subfolder. The important code resides in TemplateClient\TemplateClient.cpp.srf and in TemplateServer\TemplateServer.srf. The other files aren't very important and don't contain many replacement tags.

Why Are the Stencil Replacement Tags So Poorly Indented?

The replacement tags indentation often looks weird or just plain ugly. For example, the following fragment

```
{{while SelectNextParam}}
{{if Param(IsIn)}}        {{Param(Name)}};
{{endif}}{{endwhile}}
```

would be so much better looking and readable if it was indented like this:

```
{{while SelectNextParam}}
        {{if Param(IsIn)}}
                {Param(Name)}};
        {{endif}}
{{endwhile}}
```

Well, the reason for this indenting scheme is to ensure that the result code will be good looking. For a function like the following:

```
HRESULT DoSomething([in]int a, [out]int* pb, [in]int c)
```

the first stencil fragment will render this:

```
    a;
    c;
```

while the second will render the following code (empty lines are intentional here):

```
            a;






        c;
```

NOTE *A* {{while}}...{{endwhile}} *block will render each and every character between these two replacement tags, including the new lines and white spaces. The same applies to an* {{if}}...{{endif}} *statement.*

The main stencil processor code lies in the ContentGenerator.h file. It starts with the CWriteStreamOnFile class, an implementation of the IWriteStream interface that allows content rendering into a file using the C++ streams.

Besides the required WriteStream and Flush methods, it provides operator << implementations for some very common types such as LPCTSTR, CString&, and unsigned int, which are widely used in the replacement handler implementation.

The second component is the CSAHandler class (the StandAlone replacement handler), which implements the ITagReplacer interface by inheriting from ITagReplacerImpl. The class holds a pointer to the stream to render to and contains a *replacement map*, a set of REPLACEMENT_METHOD_ENTRY macros that map internal methods to replacement tags that can occur inside a stencil.

In this particular implementation, CSAHandler also controls the CStencil object. It provides a single entry-point for rendering (the renderFile method) that executes steps 3 and 4 in the algorithm described previously for supporting stencil processing in non-Web applications.

The main code path (with error checking removed for clarity) for what renderFile does is as follows:

```
CStencil    stencil;
hRet    =   stencil.LoadFromFile(szSRFFile);
bRet    =   stencil.ParseReplacements(this);
stencil.FinishParseReplacements();
hRet    =   stencil.Render(this, pStream);
```

The function calls perform the following actions:

- LoadFromFile loads the stencil. It could be replaced with LoadFromResource or LoadFromString.

- ParseReplacements maps the replacement tags inside the stencil to actual methods inside the ITagReplacer object passed as parameter (in this case, the CSAHandler object itself).

- FinishParseReplacements ensures the correctness of the parsed stencil (it ensures that all of the {{if}} tags are matched by {{endif}} tags and so forth).

- `Render` starts rendering the content into the specified `pStream` parameter using the `ITagReplacer` object passed as the first parameter (the `CSAHandler` object) as the provider of replacement methods.

The last class in the file, `CContentGenerator`, does the management work. It creates the destination folder, instantiates a `CSAHandler` object, and calls `renderFile` for all the files that are part of the combined client/server solution.

After you execute the sample, you have to open and build the generated project in Visual Studio through these steps:

1. Build the server project.

2. Right-click the WSDL file in the client and select Update Web Reference. This is to run the sproxy tool and generate the proxy header file.

3. Build and run the client application.

The servers (and clients) generated by this sample don't completely cover the SOAP support provided by ATL Server. The wizard doesn't support compound types inside the SOAP methods (structs and arrays), and it doesn't allow specifying SOAP headers. The reason for this limitation is to keep the stencils as simple as possible.

Conclusion

In this chapter you learned that the ATL Server stencil processor provides a very flexible way of generating text content to any kind of media. You can easily use the stencil processor in any application by implementing the `IWriteStream` interface and creating a replacement handler class.

The `CStencil` class, which you can use outside of the ISAPI context of ATL Server, doesn't support a few replacement tags that may appear in the HTML projects. You can implement most of the unsupported replacement elements either by using tags with parameters or by inheriting from the `CStencil` object and enriching the stencil grammar.

One of the great things about ATL Server is that it was designed from the beginning to create high performance Web applications. There are, however, many things that a development team can do to ensure that their application will perform as they require. In the next chapter we take a high-level look at some of the performance tuning tips and tricks that the ATL Server team learned as they worked with internal and external development teams using ATL Server.

CHAPTER 12

Caching

ATL SERVER PROVIDES EXTENSIVE and versatile caching support that you can use from within ATL Server Web applications and Web services, or independently in applications unrelated to the Web. Caching is a useful way to improve the performance of your application. By caching data that would be prohibitively expensive to retrieve or compute on every request, you can significantly enhance the performance of a Web application or Web service.

In this chapter, we examine the different types of caches offered by the ATL Server framework. We also discuss how to customize the caches for specific data types and how to override default values for timeouts.

Types of Caches

ATL Server offers several different types of caches, each with its own intended purpose, customization, and benefits. You'll cover these cache types in detail in this section.

CMemoryCacheBase

`CMemoryCacheBase` is the base class for `CMemoryCache`, `CStencilCache`, and `CFileCache`. This class provides the basic functionality of caching data items in memory and implements the basic flushing and culling capabilities of the derived caches.

CMemoryCache

This cache stores cache data items in memory. When you add items to this cache, it's possible to pass in an `HINSTANCE` to the DLL in which the data lives. The cache will increment the reference count of that DLL (i.e., it will add-ref it) to ensure the DLL isn't unloaded while the data is still active in the cache. To use this functionality, you need to pass in a valid `IServiceProvider` to the `Initialize` function of the cache. That `IServiceProvider` must have `IDllCache` as one of its services.

CBlobCache

This cache stores cache data items in memory. This class inherits from CMemoryCache. When you add items to this cache, the cache will ensure that adding the entry won't cause the cache to exceed the limits set for cache memory allocation size and maximum entry count.

CDllCache

This cache caches DLLs and deals with the loading and unloading of DLLs in the cache based on reference counts.

CStencilCache

This is a cache specific to ATL Server. It's unlikely users will use this class independently. You use CStencilCache to cache preprocessed stencils for request handler processing, thus saving you the cost of parsing the stencil on every request.

CFileCache

This cache keeps track of files. Even though this cache is derived from CMemoryCacheBase, the files aren't cached in memory—only the filenames are cached. When a file cache entry expires or is removed from the cache for any reason, it's deleted from disk.

CDataSourceCache

This cache stores open database connection in memory. This cache is somewhat different from the other ATL Server caches in that it's very specific, very simple, and assumes synchronous access. That's why when you choose the "Data source cache" option in the ATL Server Project Wizard, the cache is added as a per-thread service.

All of the caches (with the exception of CDataSourceCache) have flushing and culling capability. *Flushing* removes items from the cache based on criteria such as "least recently used" or "least often used." *Culling* removes items from the cache based on data expiration and data lifetimes.

When to Use Caching

You can use caching whenever you have the need to store long-lived, static (or relatively static) data. An application can also cache data that would be too expensive to retrieve or compute every time there's a need for it. By caching long-lived or expensive-to-compute data, an application can greatly enhance its performance.

The ATL Server framework makes use of various types of caching in its Web application request and Web service request processing. ATL Server makes use of the stencil cache to store preprocessed stencil files, thus avoiding the cost of parsing them every time they're needed. The framework also makes use of the DLL cache to manage the loading and unloading of request handler DLLs, which eliminates the cost of loading and unloading these DLLs every time they're needed. The file cache is also used to manage caching pages generated by Web requests. Page caching can be used whenever a page contains dynamic content that changes infrequently.

Caching Support Example

In this section you'll look at a basic example of using the ATL Server caching support by creating a Web application that uses the BLOB cache.

From the ATL Server Project Wizard, go to the Server Options tab and check the "Blob cache" option under the "Additional support options" section. This generates an ATL Server ISAPI DLL with a BLOB cache built in as an ISAPI service exposed through the `IServiceProvider` interface. It also generates commented-out skeleton code to access the BLOB cache from within the request handler. Listing 12-1 shows the program for the ISAPI extension.

Listing 12-1. BLOB Cache Extension

```
// CBlobCacheExtension - the ISAPI extension class
template <class ThreadPoolClass=CThreadPool<CIsapiWorker>,
    class CStatClass=CNoRequestStats,
    class HttpUserErrorTextProvider=CDefaultErrorProvider,
    class WorkerThreadTraits=DefaultThreadTraits >
class CBlobCacheExtension :
    public CIsapiExtension<ThreadPoolClass,
        CStatClass,
        HttpUserErrorTextProvider,
        WorkerThreadTraits>
{
```

```
protected:

    typedef CIsapiExtension<ThreadPoolClass,
        CStatClass, HttpUserErrorTextProvider,
        WorkerThreadTraits> baseISAPI;
    typedef CWorkerThread<WorkerThreadTraits> WorkerThreadClass;

    // blob cache support
    CBlobCache<WorkerThreadClass, CStdStatClass > m_BlobCache;

public:

    BOOL GetExtensionVersion(HSE_VERSION_INFO* pVer)
    {
        if (!baseISAPI::GetExtensionVersion(pVer))
        {
            return FALSE;
        }

        if (GetCriticalIsapiError() != 0)
        {
            return TRUE;
        }


        if (S_OK != m_BlobCache.Initialize(
            static_cast<IServiceProvider*>(this), &m_WorkerThread))
        {
            ATLTRACE("Blob cache service failed to initialize\n");
            TerminateExtension(0);
            return SetCriticalIsapiError(IDS_ATLSRV_CRITICAL_BLOBCACHEFAILED);
        }

        return TRUE;
    }

    BOOL TerminateExtension(DWORD dwFlags)
    {
        m_BlobCache.Uninitialize();
        BOOL bRet = baseISAPI::TerminateExtension(dwFlags);
        return bRet;
    }

    HRESULT STDMETHODCALLTYPE QueryService(REFGUID guidService,
```

```
            REFIID riid, void** ppvObject)
    {
        if (InlineIsEqualGUID(guidService, IID_IMemoryCache))
            return m_BlobCache.QueryInterface(riid, ppvObject);
        return baseISAPI::QueryService(guidService, riid, ppvObject);
    }
}; // class CblobCacheExtension
```

You'll modify the code for the request handler to retrieve weather information from the cache (and cache it if it doesn't exist yet). Listing 12-2 presents the code for the memory cache client, which handles the freeing of data.

Listing 12-2. Weather Data Memory Cache Client

```
class CMemoryCacheClient :
    public IMemoryCacheClient
{
public:

    // IMemoryCacheClient
    STDMETHOD(QueryInterface)(REFIID riid, void **ppv)
    {
        if (!ppv)
            return E_POINTER;

        if (InlineIsEqualGUID(riid, __uuidof(IUnknown)) ||
            InlineIsEqualGUID(riid, __uuidof(IMemoryCacheClient)))
        {
            *ppv = static_cast<IMemoryCacheClient*>(this);
            return S_OK;
        }
        return E_NOINTERFACE;
    }

    STDMETHOD_(ULONG, AddRef)()
    {
        return 1;
    }

    STDMETHOD_(ULONG, Release)()
    {
        return 1;
    }
```

```
    STDMETHOD(Free)(const void *pData)
    {
        if (!pData)
            return E_POINTER;

        free(*((void **) pData));

        return S_OK;
    }
};
CMemoryCacheClient g_MemoryCacheClient;
```

Listing 12-3 shows the modified request handler code.

Listing 12-3. Modified Request Handler

```
[ request_handler("Default") ]
class CBlobCacheHandler
{
private:
    // Put private members here
    // uncomment the service declaration(s) if you want to use
    // a service that was generated with your ISAPI extension

    // Blob cache support
    CComPtr<IMemoryCache> m_spBlobCache;

    const char * m_szWeather;
    DWORD m_dwSize;

protected:
    // Put protected members here

public:
    // Put public members here

    HTTP_CODE ValidateAndExchange()
    {
        // TODO: Put all initialization and validation code here

        // Set the content-type
        m_HttpResponse.SetContentType("text/html");

        // uncomment the service initialization(s) if you want to use
```

```
        // a service that was generated with your ISAPI extension


        // Get the IMemoryCache service from the ISAPI extension
        if (FAILED(m_spServiceProvider->QueryService(__uuidof(IMemoryCache),
                        &m_spBlobCache)))
            return HTTP_FAIL;

        HCACHEITEM hEntry = NULL;

        // attempt to look up the entry
        HRESULT hr = m_spBlobCache->LookupEntry("Weather_Today", &hEntry);
        if (FAILED(hr) || !hEntry)
        {

            // attempt to add the entry (just make it static data)
            static const char * const s_szWeather =
                "Sunny, 78 degrees F, No rain, Light wind";
            size_t nLen = strlen(s_szWeather);

            // allocate the data even though it's static, just to show how it would
            // be done if it were being retrieved dynamically
            char * szData = (char *)malloc(nLen+1);
            if (!szData)
                return HTTP_ERROR(500, ISE_SUBERR_OUTOFMEM);
            strcpy(szData, s_szWeather);

            // create the expires time (just make it 24 hours from now)
            CFileTime cftExpires = CFileTime::GetCurrentTime() + CFileTime::Day;
            hr = m_spBlobCache->Add(
                "Weather_Today",        // the key for the data
                szData,                 // the data
                (DWORD)nLen+1,            // the size of the data
                &cftExpires,            // the expiration time of the data
// the DLL of the handler where the data lives (so the DLL will not be unloaded)
                m_hInstHandler,
// the out parameter that points to the added data
                &hEntry,
// the IMemoryCacheClient that will be used to free the data
                &g_MemoryCacheClient);
            if (FAILED(hr) || !hEntry)
                return HTTP_FAIL;
        }
```

```
        hr = m_spBlobCache->GetData(hEntry, (void **)&m_szWeather, &m_dwSize);
        if (FAILED(hr) || !m_szWeather || m_dwSize == 0)
            return HTTP_FAIL;

        return HTTP_SUCCESS;
    }

protected:
    // Here's an example of how to use a replacement tag with the stencil processor
    [ tag_name(name="Hello") ]
    HTTP_CODE OnHello(void)
    {
        m_HttpResponse << "Hello World! <br>"
                          "Today's weather is : ";
        m_HttpResponse.WriteLen(m_szWeather, m_dwSize-1);

        return HTTP_SUCCESS;
    }
}; // class CBlobCacheHandler
```

You retrieve (or add and then retrieve) the weather information in the `ValidateAndExchange` function and then display it to the user as part of the `OnHello` tag method.

The `CMemoryCacheClient` class implements the `IMemoryCacheClient` interface, which frees data from the cache. In this instance you're just using `malloc` and `free`, but it's possible to do more complicated allocation schemes (as is used with `CStencilCache`, where the stencil frees itself upon removal from the cache). In this example, you just used static data, but of course you could retrieve the weather information from a database or through a Web service call.

Key Types and Data Types

In the preceding example, you used the BLOB cache, which always takes and stores a `void*` type as its entry data and a `LPCSTR` type as its entry key. But by using the lower-level caches, it's possible to customize the key types and data types to achieve better type-safety and ease of use by avoiding casting.

Let's modify the previous example by using the `CMemoryCache` directly to store the data in a more useful fashion. Again, you'll use the ATL Server Project Wizard with the "Blob cache" option checked on the Server Options tab. However, you'll modify the ISAPI extension to use a custom cache derived from `CMemoryCache` instead of using `CBlobCache` directly. You'll call the new cache `CBlobCacheEx`, and in it you'll store a `CWeatherData` struct that contains information about the weather, such as the temperature, rain conditions, and wind conditions. You'll also need to define a new IMemoryCacheEx interface because you've changed the types of the key and the data. The key is now an integer that refers to the day of the week, and the data is now the CWeatherData struct. Listing 12-4 shows the program for the modified ISAPI extension.

Listing 12-4. Definition of CBlobCacheEx

```
enum WIND_CONDITION { wcNone = 0, wcLight, wcBreezy, wcHurricane };
enum RAIN_CONDITION { rcNone = 0, rcLight, rcShowers, rcTorrential };

struct CWeatherData
{
    int nTemp;
    WIND_CONDITION eWind;
    RAIN_CONDITION eRain;
};

__interface ATL_NO_VTABLE __declspec(uuid("a69dda6f-59da-4ba3-84f8-38b8db65201c"))
    IMemoryCacheEx : public IUnknown
{
    // IMemoryCache Methods
    STDMETHOD(Add)(int Key, CWeatherData* Data, DWORD dwSize,
                FILETIME *pftExpireTime,
                HINSTANCE hInstClient, HCACHEITEM *phEntry,
                IMemoryCacheClient *pClient);

    STDMETHOD(LookupEntry)(int szKey, HCACHEITEM * phEntry);
    STDMETHOD(GetData)(const HCACHEITEM hEntry, CWeatherData **ppData,
        DWORD *pdwSize) const;
    STDMETHOD(ReleaseEntry)(const HCACHEITEM hEntry);
    STDMETHOD(RemoveEntry)(const HCACHEITEM hEntry);
    STDMETHOD(RemoveEntryByKey)(int Key);

    STDMETHOD(Flush)();
};

template <
        class MonitorClass,
        class StatClass=CStdStatClass,
        class SyncObj=CComCriticalSection,
        class FlushClass=COldFlusher,
        class CullClass=CExpireCuller >
class CBlobCacheEx : public CMemoryCache<CWeatherData*,
```

```
        StatClass, FlushClass, int,
        CElementTraits<int>, SyncObj, CullClass>,
        public IMemoryCacheEx,
        public IMemoryCacheControl,
        public IMemoryCacheStats,
        public IWorkerThreadClient
    {
        typedef CMemoryCache<CWeatherData*, StatClass, FlushClass, int,
            CElementTraits<int>, SyncObj, CullClass> cacheBase;

        MonitorClass m_Monitor;

    protected:
        HANDLE m_hTimer;

    public:
        CBlobCacheEx() : m_hTimer(NULL)
        {
        }

        HRESULT Initialize(IServiceProvider *pProv)
        {
            HRESULT hr = cacheBase::Initialize(pProv);
            if (FAILED(hr))
                return hr;
            hr = m_Monitor.Initialize();
            if (FAILED(hr))
                return hr;
            return m_Monitor.AddTimer(ATL_BLOB_CACHE_TIMEOUT,
                static_cast<IWorkerThreadClient*>(this),
                (DWORD_PTR) this, &m_hTimer);
        }

        template <class ThreadTraits>
        HRESULT Initialize(IServiceProvider *pProv,
            CWorkerThread<ThreadTraits> *pWorkerThread)
        {
            ATLASSERT(pWorkerThread);

            HRESULT hr = cacheBase::Initialize(pProv);
            if (FAILED(hr))
                return hr;
```

```
    hr = m_Monitor.Initialize(pWorkerThread);
    if (FAILED(hr))
        return hr;

    return m_Monitor.AddTimer(ATL_BLOB_CACHE_TIMEOUT,
        static_cast<IWorkerThreadClient*>(this),
        (DWORD_PTR) this, &m_hTimer);
}

HRESULT Execute(DWORD_PTR dwParam, HANDLE /*hObject*/)
{
    CBlobCacheEx* pCache = (CBlobCacheEx*)dwParam;

    if (pCache)
        pCache->Flush();
    return S_OK;
}

HRESULT CloseHandle(HANDLE hObject)
{
    ATLASSERT(m_hTimer == hObject);
    m_hTimer = NULL;
    ::CloseHandle(hObject);
    return S_OK;
}

~CBlobCacheEx()
{
    if (m_hTimer)
        m_Monitor.RemoveHandle(m_hTimer);
}

HRESULT Uninitialize()
{
    if (m_hTimer)
    {
        m_Monitor.RemoveHandle(m_hTimer);
        m_hTimer = NULL;
    }
    m_Monitor.Shutdown();
    return cacheBase::Uninitialize();
}
```

```
// IUnknown methods
HRESULT STDMETHODCALLTYPE QueryInterface(REFIID riid, void **ppv)
{
    HRESULT hr = E_NOINTERFACE;
    if (!ppv)
        hr = E_POINTER;
    else
    {
        if (InlineIsEqualGUID(riid, __uuidof(IUnknown)) ||
            InlineIsEqualGUID(riid, __uuidof(IMemoryCacheEx)))
        {
            *ppv = (IUnknown *) (IMemoryCacheEx *) this;
            AddRef();
            hr = S_OK;
        }
        if (InlineIsEqualGUID(riid, __uuidof(IMemoryCacheStats)))
        {
            *ppv = (IUnknown *) (IMemoryCacheStats*)this;
            AddRef();
            hr = S_OK;
        }
        if (InlineIsEqualGUID(riid, __uuidof(IMemoryCacheControl)))
        {
            *ppv = (IUnknown *) (IMemoryCacheControl*)this;
            AddRef();
            hr = S_OK;
        }

    }
    return hr;
}

ULONG STDMETHODCALLTYPE AddRef()
{
    return 1;
}

ULONG STDMETHODCALLTYPE Release()
{
    return 1;
}
```

```
    // IMemoryCache Methods
    HRESULT STDMETHODCALLTYPE Add(int Key, CWeatherData *Data, DWORD dwSize,
        FILETIME *pftExpireTime,
        HINSTANCE hInstClient,
        HCACHEITEM *phEntry,
        IMemoryCacheClient *pClient)
    {
        HRESULT hr = E_FAIL;
        //if it's a multithreaded cache monitor we'll let the monitor
        //take care of cleaning up the cache so we don't overflow
        // our configuration settings. if it's not a threaded cache monitor,
        // we need to make sure we don't overflow the configuration settings
        // by adding a new element
        if (m_Monitor.GetThreadHandle()==NULL)
        {
            if (!cacheBase::CanAddEntry(dwSize))
            {
                //flush the entries and check again to see if we
                // can add
                cacheBase::FlushEntries();
                if (!cacheBase::CanAddEntry(dwSize))
                    return E_OUTOFMEMORY;
            }
        }
        _ATLTRY
        {
            hr = cacheBase::AddEntry(Key, Data, dwSize,
                pftExpireTime, hInstClient, pClient, phEntry);
            return hr;
        }
        _ATLCATCHALL()
        {
            return E_FAIL;
        }
    }

    // omitted .- all other methods delegate to CacheBase or m_statObj

}; // CBlobCacheEx
```

Listing 12-5 shows the modified ISAPI extension that uses the newly defined cache.

Listing 12-5. Modified ISAPI Extension

```
// CMemoryCacheExtension - the ISAPI extension class
template <class ThreadPoolClass=CThreadPool<CIsapiWorker>,
    class CStatClass=CNoRequestStats,
    class HttpUserErrorTextProvider=CDefaultErrorProvider,
    class WorkerThreadTraits=DefaultThreadTraits >
class CMemoryCacheExtension :
    public CIsapiExtension<ThreadPoolClass,
        CStatClass,
        HttpUserErrorTextProvider,
        WorkerThreadTraits>
{

protected:

    typedef CIsapiExtension<ThreadPoolClass, CStatClass,
        HttpUserErrorTextProvider,
        WorkerThreadTraits> baseISAPI;
    typedef CWorkerThread<WorkerThreadTraits> WorkerThreadClass;

    // blob cache support
    CBlobCacheEx<WorkerThreadClass, CStdStatClass > m_BlobCache;

public:

    BOOL GetExtensionVersion(HSE_VERSION_INFO* pVer)
    {
        if (!baseISAPI::GetExtensionVersion(pVer))
        {
            return FALSE;
        }

        if (GetCriticalIsapiError() != 0)
        {
            return TRUE;
        }


        if (S_OK != m_BlobCache.Initialize(
            static_cast<IServiceProvider*>(this), &m_WorkerThread))
        {
            ATLTRACE("Blob cache service failed to initialize\n");
            TerminateExtension(0);
```

```
            return SetCriticalIsapiError(IDS_ATLSRV_CRITICAL_BLOBCACHEFAILED);
        }

        return TRUE;
    }

    BOOL TerminateExtension(DWORD dwFlags)
    {
        m_BlobCache.Uninitialize();
        BOOL bRet = baseISAPI::TerminateExtension(dwFlags);
        return bRet;
    }

    HRESULT STDMETHODCALLTYPE QueryService(REFGUID guidService,
            REFIID riid, void** ppvObject)
    {
        if (InlineIsEqualGUID(guidService, __uuidof(IMemoryCacheEx)))
            return m_BlobCache.QueryInterface(riid, ppvObject);
        return baseISAPI::QueryService(guidService, riid, ppvObject);
    }
}; // class CMemoryCacheExtension
```

Listing 12-5 defines the `CMemoryCacheClient` class, the `CWeatherData` struct, and the new `CBlobCacheEx` cache class. It also defines the `IMemoryCacheEx` interface and makes the appropriate modifications to the `CIsapiExtension`-derived class so that it uses `CBlobCacheEx`.

Now you'll modify the request handler to use this new cache. You'll need to `QueryService` for the `IMemoryCacheEx` interface instead of the `IMemoryCache` interface, and you'll need to retrieve and add the data using the `CWeatherData` struct and the integer that represents the day of the week. And, of course, you'll need to modify the way you display the data in the tag method. Listing 12-6 is the program for the modified request handler.

Listing 12-6. Modified Request Handler Using the New Cache

```
// MemoryCache.h : Defines the ATL Server request handler class
//
#pragma once

#include "..\memorycacheisapi\memorycacheextension.h"

[ request_handler("Default") ]
class CMemoryCacheHandler
```

```
{
private:
    // Put private members here
    // uncomment the service declaration(s) if you want to use
    // a service that was generated with your ISAPI extension

    // Blob cache support
    CComPtr<IMemoryCacheEx> m_spBlobCache;
    CWeatherData *m_pData;
    DWORD m_dwSize;

protected:
    // Put protected members here

public:
    // Put public members here

    HTTP_CODE ValidateAndExchange()
    {
        // TODO: Put all initialization and validation code here

        // Set the content-type
        m_HttpResponse.SetContentType("text/html");

        // uncomment the service initialization(s) if you want to use
        // a service that was generated with your ISAPI extension


        // Get the IMemoryCacheEx service from the ISAPI extension
        if (FAILED(m_spServiceProvider->QueryService(__uuidof(IMemoryCacheEx),
                    &m_spBlobCache)))
            return HTTP_FAIL;

        SYSTEMTIME st;
        GetSystemTime(&st);

        HCACHEITEM hEntry = NULL;
        // attempt to look up the entry
        HRESULT hr = m_spBlobCache->LookupEntry(st.wDayOfWeek, &hEntry);
        if (FAILED(hr) || !hEntry)
        {
            // attempt to add the entry (just make it static data)

            // array of day-of-week to weather struct mappings
```

```
            static const CWeatherData s_arrWeather[] =
            {
                { 78, wcNone, rcShowers },
                { 81, wcLight, rcNone },
                { 65, wcBreezy, rcLight },
                { 85, wcHurricane, rcTorrential },
                { 72, wcLight, rcLight},
                { 60, wcNone, rcNone},
                { 100, wcBreezy, rcShowers }
            };

            // allocate the data even though it's static,
            // just to show how it would
            // be done if it were being retrieved dynamically
            CWeatherData *pData = (CWeatherData *)malloc(sizeof(CWeatherData));
            if (!pData)
                return HTTP_ERROR(500, ISE_SUBERR_OUTOFMEM);
            *pData = s_arrWeather[st.wDayOfWeek];

            // create the expires time (just make it 24 hours from now)
            CFileTime cftExpires = CFileTime::GetCurrentTime() + CFileTime::Day;
            hr = m_spBlobCache->Add(
                st.wDayOfWeek,
                pData,
                (DWORD)sizeof(CWeatherData),
                &cftExpires,
                m_hInstHandler,
                &hEntry,
                &g_MemoryCacheClient);

            if (FAILED(hr) || !hEntry)
                return HTTP_FAIL;
        }

        hr = m_spBlobCache->GetData(hEntry, &m_pData, &m_dwSize);
        if (FAILED(hr) || !m_pData|| m_dwSize == 0)
            return HTTP_FAIL;

        return HTTP_SUCCESS;
    }

protected:
    // Here is an example of how to use a replacement
    // tag with the stencil processor
```

```
    [ tag_name(name="Hello") ]
    HTTP_CODE OnHello(void)
    {
        static const char * const s_szWind[] =
            {"None", "Light", "Breezy", "Hurricane" };
        static const char * const s_szRain[] =
            {"None", "Light", "Showers", "Torrential" };
        m_HttpResponse << "Hello World! <br>"
                          "Today's weather is :<br>"
                          "Wind: " << s_szWind[m_pData->eWind] << "<br>"
                          "Rain: " << s_szRain[m_pData->eRain] << "<br>"
                          "Temp: " << m_pData->nTemp;

        return HTTP_SUCCESS;
    }
}; // class CmemoryCacheHandler
```

Timeouts

There are various timeouts used for the different caches. These timeouts are generally handled using preprocessor macros that can be overridden by the user. You use the timeouts to determine when automatic flushing and culling of the cache will occur. Here are the preprocessor macros you use for each of the caches:

- `ATL_BLOB_CACHE_TIMEOUT`: Timeout used by the BLOB cache for flushing and culling.
- `ATL_DLL_CACHE_TIMEOUT`: Timeout used by the DLL cache for flushing.
- `ATL_FILE_CACHE_TIMEOUT`: Timeout used by the file cache for flushing and culling.
- `ATL_STENCIL_CACHE_TIMEOUT`: Timeout used by the stencil cache for flushing and culling.
- `ATL_STENCIL_CHECK_TIMEOUT`: Timeout used by the stencil cache to check against the base SRF file from which it was parsed.
- `ATL_STENCIL_LIFESPAN`: The lifespan of a stencil in the stencil cache, which is independent of other flushing and culling parameters. That is, when a stencil's lifespan has expired it will be removed, regardless of other factors.

Cache Parameters

The caches can be tuned in various ways. The BLOB cache has the following functions that allow tuning how large the cache can grow in terms of memory allocation and total entries (these functions are supported underneath by the `CMemoryCacheBase` class). Any `CMemoryCacheBase`-derived class can use these functions provided the correct parameters are passed in when entries are added to the cache for the size of the data.

- `SetMaxAllowedSize`: This function sets the maximum allowable size of the data that's stored in the cache. If a cache reaches its limit while adding an entry, an attempt will be made to flush the cache before failing to ensure there are no stale entries taking up space.

- `GetMaxAllowedSize`: This function retrieves the maximum allowable size of the data stored in the cache.

- `SetMaxAllowedEntries`: This function sets the maximum number of entries in the cache (independent of the size of the entries). If a cache reaches its limit while adding an entry, an attempt will be made to flush the cache before failing to ensure there are no stale entries taking up space.

- `GetMaxAllowedEntries`: This function retrieves the maximum allowable entry count for a cache.

Cache Statistics

The caches (with the exceptions of the DLL cache and the data source cache) support retrieving cache statistics such as cache hits and misses, current allocation size and entry count, and the maximum allocation size and entry count. These cache statistics can be integrated with Perfmon (ATL Server has built-in Perfmon support for the caches). You can turn these statistics on and off by using the `StatClass` template parameter for the caches that support them.

By default, all the caches use `CStdStatClass`, which maintains cache statistics for each of the caches but doesn't integrate with Perfmon. For Perfmon integration, the template parameter should be changed to `CPerfStatClass`. If no cache statistics are desired, you can use `CNoStatClass` to no-op the statistics operations in the caches. There's one important caveat: Due to a limitation/bug in the VC7 version of ATL Server, there can be only one cache statistics instance per module. That is, if you have a BLOB cache and a file cache, each using `CPerfStatClass`, you can't get independent cache statistics for these caches, because they'll both go through the same instance of `CPerfStatObject`. You'll need to define your own

`CPerfStatClass` to get independent cache statistics. This is simply a matter of cutting and pasting, and then renaming `CPerfStatClass` for each independent cache.

Conclusion

The caching options provided by ATL Server are powerful and versatile. They make the task of caching data very simple, and they also allow you a great deal of flexibility when you need to customize the cache.

In this chapter you examined the basic usage of the ATL Server caching support and you saw how you can customize it to provide greater type-safety and ease of use. You also learned how you can tune the caches by setting limits on their allocation size and entry counts. In addition, you saw how you can integrate the caches with Perfmon to provide performance information such as cache hits and misses.

However, there's also a great deal of advanced customization you can do with the caches that we didn't discuss in this chapter. For example, the DLL cache and the file cache have cache peer support. A *peer* class is one that's called back when entries are added and removed from the cache. These classes can provide even more powerful customization support by acting as a kind of trigger for these cache operations. For more information on peer classes, consult the MSDN documentation.

One of the main reasons for choosing ATL Server as a technology is to create a high-performance application. ATL Server allows you to get as close to the underlying technologies as you desire, and though this ensures that maximum performance is attainable, it also means that the development team is responsible for ensuring that its application performs well. In the next chapter you'll take a look at some of the application tuning tips and tricks that the ATL Server team learned while working with both internal and external groups

CHAPTER 13

Application Tuning: Real World Tips and Tricks

AS YOU'VE SEEN, THE ATL Server library provides a large set of powerful building blocks for developing high-end Web applications and Web services. These building blocks enable developers to create fast, efficient, and small applications, but it's this same power and control that helps developers shoot themselves in the foot.

In this chapter we present tips and tricks for tuning your application, including some of the common mistakes that developers make and how to design your application so that you avoid these mistakes. We also cover best practices for identifying problems in your application early, so that you can fix them as they occur.

The main areas of discussion for this chapter are performance, security, scalability, and reliability for your application. We start the chapter by looking at some issues with COM.

COM

There are two extremes that developers can go to with COM. The first is the developer who wants to use COM for everything, and the other is the developer who wants to avoid COM no matter what.

There are many good reasons for using COM in your application—just make sure that you have some before you use COM in your application. Good reasons for using COM are as follows:

- You have existing, well-designed, tested COM objects.
- You want a componentized application design.
- You want to take advantage of COM+ services.

This is by no means a comprehensive list, but it helps emphasize the importance of good early design in your application. There are, however, a number of problems that you can run into if you decide to use COM in your application. (In fact, you can run into some of these issues even if you don't use COM, but they're more common for COM developers.) We discuss these issues in the sections that follow.

OLE Automation Types

One of the first issues that the ATL Server team often finds with real-world applications is an abuse of OLE Automation types (e.g., BSTRs). The OLE Automation types are designed and optimized for communicating over COM interfaces. They can, however, lead to scalability and performance problems if you abuse them in your applications.

How do you know if you are "abusing" OLE Automation types? Examine their use in your application. Are you keeping their use almost exclusively to COM communication code? Or are you using them throughout your application? It's not uncommon for the ATL Server team to see examples of applications where, even though COM isn't being used, OLE Automation types are used extensively. Though it's obviously not a problem to perform one or two simple operations on these types, are you passing them through to other functions? Because of the limitations of these types, the ATL Server team often sees cases where developers are converting from OLE Automation types to richer types (e.g., BSTRs to `CStrings`), and then back to OLE Automation types to pass to another function, which then converts to a richer type, and so on. This cycle of constant type conversions is unwieldy, unnecessary, and very inefficient.

Marshaling

One of the keys to making efficient use of COM in your application is understanding marshaling of COM interfaces. This involves not only understanding the concepts of marshaling (which are beyond the scope of this book), but also understanding which marshaler you're using (yes, you have a choice).

The main point we want to get across in this section is that you do have a choice of marshaler, and for almost all applications the default marshaler is going to be inefficient. Examples of other marshalers that may be more efficient are the ATL Wizard–generated marshaler and the COM+ lightweight marshaler (if you're using COM+). Another way to go is to create a custom marshaler, but there are issues with this.

Most of the issues with custom marshaling revolve around ensuring that your custom marshaler is efficient for the application in which you're going to use it. Again, it can be easy to try and reuse a previously created custom marshaler or to make use of a companywide custom marshaler that was designed to be very efficient for a different application.

Security and Process Model

Another important issue if you're going to use COM is that you need to understand the security and process model of COM. These are issues that you need to keep in mind when designing your application, ensuring that you keep the pros and cons of different options in mind and choose the one that best suits your particular application.

The COM process model enables developers to use an object in-process or from an external process. There are advantages to using each of these models. Running from within your application's process (or IIS) enables very efficient communication with the object, but it does pose some risks. These risks include isolation (crashes in the COM object will now bring down your application), application size (your application will increase in size, making for less efficient use of processor caches), and separation (updating the component won't be as easy).

Running from outside of your application's process (or IIS) protects you from these risks, but you now pay a cross-process marshaling penalty whenever you try to access your object.

The COM security model enables you to ensure your objects are correctly secured. There are two risks you face here. The first (less severe) risk is that your objects become inaccessible to your application. The second (more severe) risk is that your objects are now accessible to unauthorized users. This is a problem particularly if your object is processing sensitive information.

COM+

COM+ development issues run exactly the same as the COM development issues: Either developers use COM+ without requiring any of its features and add unnecessary overhead and complexity to their applications, or they avoid COM+ like the plague and end up implementing the same functionality in a less efficient and more bug-prone way.

Why would you want to use COM+? Do you need COM+ functionality? COM+ functionality includes the following:

- *Transaction support:* Transactions are a very complex area of computer science. COM+ provides one of the best transactional implementations under Windows, so if you need transaction support in your application, use COM+.
- *Object pooling:* Object pooling allows your application to be more efficient by having a preinstantiated pool of objects to which you make requests. If you want object pooling, consider using COM+.
- *Context management:* Context management allows your application to keep information about its execution environment, such as the identity of the object's creator and the transaction encompassing the work of the object.
- *Security:* COM+ provides its own security system that enables you to make the most of object isolation and how your objects interact with each other.

Need this or other COM+ functionality? Then don't reinvent the wheel—just use COM+!

Databases

Almost all Web applications require extensive use of a database. Web applications and services tend to rely heavily on gathering data from a database and presenting it to the user. Databases represent an entire field of study, which is beyond the scope of this book, but we present some tips and tricks in this section that can really help you get the most out of your Web application.

Picking the right database and database access story can make a huge difference in the performance of your application. First, you should gather trial developer databases from different vendors and try them out in your production environment (or a simulation of your production environment) to get a feel for the performance of each database.

Investigate through articles, benchmarks, and experimentation which data access story is going to be best. There are many factors here, but foremost are performance and ease of use. Different database versions can easily see 10 percent or 20 percent changes in comparative performance of data access types. Older databases might provide very efficient ODBC communication, newer databases might be better accessed through OLE DB, or you may need the productivity of ADO despite the performance hit.

The database might be one of the most expensive pieces of your application. It may also be one of the easiest ways to improve performance, so a 20 percent performance improvement is usually going to be worth an extra $10,000.00 or $20,000.00 investment (be it in database hardware or software) on the server.

Once you've picked the right data access story for your application, the next step is to make sure that you make good use of your database. Modern databases provide extensive functionality, and they provide this functionality in a very efficient manner. What sorts of functionality should you take advantage of?

- *Transactions:* Although COM+ provides great transactions for the middle tier, transactions on the database are best handled by the database's own transaction facility.

- *Stored procedures:* Stored procedures are a great mechanism for accessing your database. Your database probably optimizes data to make your stored procedures efficient, and you limit your network bandwidth usage by calling functions (instead of sending long SQL statements). On top of all this, you can easily debug and maintain stored procedures, which makes working with them far easier than hard-coded strings in your application.

- *Clustering and load balancing:* Modern database servers usually provide many of the functions required to use them in large server farms. Good examples are clustering and load balancing technologies, which are often provided by the databases themselves or via auxiliary tools.

If you're going to spend a lot of time in the database, then this is a good place to look for making performance improvements in your application.

Using the Right Tools

Designing applications for the server poses a number of interesting problems that don't occur in client-side application development. Several advantages compensate for these problems, however, one of the largest advantages being the ability to tune your application for the hardware and environment on which it will run.

It's extremely important that development teams set up a laboratory system that mimics their production environment as closely as possible. This laboratory is useful right from the start of application development, as it allows for continuous gathering of application data, which when stored as metrics provides a measurable system for monitoring an application.

It's critical that data on performance, scalability, and reliability be monitored throughout application development. There are many benefits to developing software with this sort of infrastructure:

- Problems can be detected early (right after introduction), making debugging easier (smaller code path).
- Environmental issues (especially in terms of performance and scalability) can be better understood, and the application can be better tuned for environmental specifics from the start.
- The team has very good ideas on the "maximums" for the system. The best performance, scalability, and reliability in the production environment can be determined and used as ideal goals for the final application.

An important part of gathering these metrics is using the right tools to measure them and using the right tools to help you quickly find and fix problems in your application. In the following sections you'll look at just some of the tools that will help you get the most out of your application.

Profiler

A *profiler* allows the your team to understand where the application is spending most of its time. In the development of ATL Server, profilers were used constantly on test applications in order to understand bottlenecks, so that performance tuning could be tailored to where it was most needed.

Numerous times, the ATL Server design team saw situations where developers (of end applications) would try to fix perceived performance issues without ever using a profiler. Occasionally, the developers had picked the worst area of their applications, and sometimes they were completely off track. The one fact that always bore true was that developers would get at least a 10 percent performance improvement by running a profiler and spending a week or two examining and acting on the results.

Although performance must be designed into an application, it's important to use a profiler often to ensure that silly coding mistakes, or unknown side effects of APIs or third-party libraries, aren't greatly degrading performance of an application.

Profilers can also help identify if the problem isn't in the application itself, but in your data access or network communication.

Perfmon

ATL 7.0 ships with some new Perfmon utility classes that make using the NT Perfmon system easy. In Chapter 9 we spent some time reviewing the ATL Server support for Perfmon. This functionality can be very useful to help monitor your application performance during the development cycle.

Perfmon data is very easily to collect and store, and it has the advantage of being viewable from remote locations. Thus, whether you're gathering Perfmon data from your development machines or from your laboratory setup, it's always easy to quickly get and analyze the data that you're interested in.

In particular, you should use Perfmon to measure metrics of concern, such as CPU utilization, memory utilization, use of resources, or time spent using resource such as files, handles, and so on. You should be sure to analyze this data (you can use the many tools available for analyzing Perfmon data or you can generate your own) to look for unusual behavior in your application.

Task Manager

Often overlooked by developers, Windows Task Manager is often the fastest way to discover problems in your latest coding changes. Task Manager is capable of viewing numerous pieces of data in real time on your application, including CPU utilization, memory utilization, and utilization of other resources such as handles.

With Task Manager, you should look for real-time, telltale signs of poor application coding. Good examples include erratic CPU utilization and resource leaks. Major resource leaks in particular are easily picked up with Task Manager. You can easily watch the memory utilization for your application increase over time or the number of handles your application has open slowly increase with each incoming request. In your laboratory setup, you can use Task Manager to quickly detect these mainline problems. Task Manager is not 100 percent accurate; instead, use it to gauge obvious trends (i.e., leaks), as opposed to using it for reliable metrics (i.e., working set).

Web Stress Tool

A Web stress tool such as Microsoft Application Center Test (ACT) is also a must-have in your arsenal of tools. This type of tool is designed to stress Web applications over long periods of time and allow for analysis of performance and other data during these runs.

A Web stress tool will help you best simulate how your application will respond in a real-world environment (especially if you run the tool on your application in a controlled laboratory environment). Can your application handle the number of clients that it's supposed to? Is your application quickly becoming database or network bound under stress? Is your high CPU utilization indicative of unnecessary locks in your code?

The performance numbers from this kind of tool are more meaningful than simple closed-network or (even worse) localhost testing. They're realistic (if your laboratory is realistic) and can show problems in your application at high loads.

A Web stress tool is also designed for testing the reliability of your application, and you should ensure that you leave the tool pounding your server for several days at a time. With these long stress runs, you should look for signs of trouble such as your application returning error pages. It's in these long runs that you'll discover the smaller memory and other resource leaks in your application. Once again, Perfmon is your good friend in recording the data required to find these problems.

A Web stress tool is a great way to find serious problems in your server application, particularly in terms of reliability and performance under realistic (or heavy) loads. By completing these tests in your laboratory, you'll get a feel for how your application will work in the real world. Also, because many problems manifest themselves only under these stressful conditions, you'll have a great environment to debug reliability and performance problems in your application. It sure beats having to debug them on a production server!

Putting It All Together

By using all these tools in conjunction, you'll be able to gather and record specific metrics for your application. When you keep a constant measure of these metrics, you can quickly diagnose and resolve many problems such as the following in your application:

- Sudden drops in performance (remembering that in a server application, even a 10 percent performance hit can kill an application's response time) can be quickly found and solved.
- Newly introduced memory or handle leaks are much easier to track down when the team knows the new code path(s) introduced in which the leaks must occur.
- Changes in database performance and response time can be identified and correctly attributed to changes in the application or in the layout/structure of the database itself.

Recording and monitoring the metrics of your application is also the best way to determine which hardware configuration best suits your application. Maybe there are problems that you didn't expect to have, such as a very high load on your internal communications (lots of internal data exchange) or poor scalability from your application.

The laboratory environment and the use of these tools also allow you to discover how your application should be tuned for the production environment. You should fine-tune thread pools, buffer sizes, and the like in the laboratory environment to ensure that your application will run at its best.

Common Symptoms and the Problems That Cause Them

Several main symptoms can arise when you monitor an application, and each is indicative of different problems that may occur. We describe these symptoms in the following sections.

It's important to remember that your application may be suffering from more than one of these problems at the same time. This points to the importance of continuous measurement of metrics, which really is the only way you'll recognize unusual and unexpected behaviors in your application.

Low CPU, Low Requests per Second

This problem is commonly representative of an application that's taking unnecessary locks. Remember that some APIs or libraries may take locks that you aren't aware of. A good way of identifying the problem is using a profiler. This should make it easy for you to pinpoint exactly where your threads are getting blocked.

High CPU, Low Requests per Second

This problem is usually caused by inefficient code (e.g., infinite loops). However, it's also possible that this problem is occurring because your application simply requires more CPU power (i.e., it's a processor-intensive application). The difference between the two scenarios is best seen from the results of regular testing. Did your last change involve significant changes in processing, or was it supposed to be just a bug fix?

Low Requests per Second, High Network Usage

This problem usually indicates that your network is incapable of handling the load. In some cases, it might indicate inefficient network usage. It's important that you try to simulate the network traffic expected in the production environment to get a feel for how your application will perform (particularly if it isn't the only application using the network).

Low Requests per Second, High Database Usage

This problem usually indicates that your database is incapable of handling the load or that your application is accessing the database in an inefficient manner. Again, regular testing is required to easily tell the difference. It's important that you have a database expert examine your database queries and table structure to ensure that they're efficient. It's also important that you choose a database system capable of handling the expected load.

Low CPU, High Requests per Second

This isn't usually a serious problem, especially if you haven't completed the processing code for your application or you're expecting rapid expansion in your application's capabilities. You should check that your application is working as expected (it may be that the application is just returning errors, hence the excellent performance). Also, before you lower your system requirements, be sure to check that your application doesn't require the extra processing power for processing unusual requests (there are many types of applications that have very high-burst CPU requirements, although their average requirements are very low).

Conclusion

This chapter was designed to give you a feel for some of the tools available to you as a Web developer, how to take advantage of these tools, and some of the common problems to look out for. Though much of this chapter's advice may have seemed obvious, it's important that when you find performance problems in the development cycle, your team develops a structured approach to identifying the causes.

By keeping the information discussed here in the back of your mind, you should be able to shave off a lot of time when developing high-end applications. The chapter stressed the importance of constant measuring to make identifying problems easy.

Although problems are easy to detect and isolate on their own, we all know what it's like to make some major revisions to a production application and suddenly find that the application is running abnormally (too slowly, with random crashes, or behaving strangely under load). In these situations it can be extremely difficult to pinpoint the problem unless you take a systematic and constructive approach. This technique is aided not only by the many tools available, but also through the use of constant testing, which allows isolation of the problem (or the cause of the problem) to a reduced number of code paths.

In Chapter 4 we covered some of the basics of your ISAPI DLL and in Chapter 9 we showed how to expose your Perfmon counters as a service from your ISAPI DLL. In the next chapter, we take a closer look at ISAPI services, what services ATL Server provides, what sorts of services you should expose, and how they work.

CHAPTER 14

ISAPI Extensions As Service Providers

In the ATL Server architecture, the ISAPI extension module acts as an invariant from the moment the Web application is initialized until it's unloaded or the server is shut down. That is, the ISAPI extension doesn't get unloaded or reloaded for each request. It is, therefore, the appropriate place to store state information and reusable objects.

ATL Server features such as the cache engines and the pools (the database connection pool and the thread pool) are stored inside the ISAPI module because they rely on this invariance property. Packages of functions that contain reusable code or allow access to persistent information are grouped in COM-like interfaces and exposed as services by the ISAPI module.

In this chapter we discuss dealing with such ISAPI services. Based on how the actual service implementation is stored, we distinguish three categories of such services and then discuss their properties, together with examples of ATL Server features implemented in this manner and sample code.

A Simple ISAPI Service

Rather than defining a new mechanism for exposing reusable information or code, the ATL Server team decided to use a standard COM interface, `IServiceProvider`, to allow access from the request handlers to the reusable pieces of code or data that reside in the ISAPI module. The `IServiceProvider` interface provides a way of obtaining a COM interface pointer (therefore, a callable object) without any other detailed knowledge about where or how the object is stored. This way, any object that exposes a COM interface can be contained in the ISAPI module and reused by the request handler, with the only requirement being that both the ISAPI and the consumer know about the interface exposed by that object.

The actual functionality of the service doesn't change the way it's exposed by the ISAPI module or the way it's used by the request handlers. This section covers how to implement and use a very simple service that only adds two integers and returns the result. The service functionality consists of a single function:

```
HRESULT AddTwoNumbers( int inA, int inB, int* pOutRet);
```

As specified previously, all the functionality of the service has to be packaged in a COM-like interface to be exposed by the ISAPI module. So, for this particular service, you'll create a new header file with the following content:

```
#pragma once
// IGenericService.
__interface __declspec(uuid("5BC416A1-CBA5-4769-9DEB-75E673E229FF"))
IGenericService : public IUnknown
{
    HRESULT AddTwoNumbers(int  inA, int  inB, int* pOutRet);
};
```

This header file contains the definition of the service. It has to be visible for both the ISAPI module (which will expose it) and the request handler (which will use it).

NOTE *Please note that a service doesn't have to implement a newly declared interface. It can very well be a COM interface already implemented in some external component. For example, ATL Server uses a predefined interface (*`ISAXXMLReader`*), and its implementation that comes with MSXML, in exposing a SAX reader service.*

As you just declared the interface (as opposed to using a predefined one), let's move to the implementation of this simple service. (For the purposes of this sample, the implementation will appear in the ISAPI module itself.)

```
#include "..\GenericService\CommonServiceDefinition.h"
class  CGenericService : public IGenericService
{
public:
        ULONG        STDMETHODCALLTYPE  AddRef()         {return 1;}
        ULONG        STDMETHODCALLTYPE Release()         {return 1;}
        HRESULT STDMETHODCALLTYPE QueryInterface(REFIID riid, void** ppvObject)
        {
                if( !ppvObject )
                        return E_POINTER;
                if( IsEqualIID( riid, IID_IUnknown))
                        *ppvObject = static_cast<IUnknown*>(this);
                else if( IsEqualIID( riid, __uuidof(IGenericService)))
                        *ppvObject = static_cast<IGenericService*>(this);
                else
```

```
                return E_NOINTERFACE;
            AddRef();
            return S_OK;
        }
        HRESULT AddTwoNumbers(int inA, int inB, int* pOutRet)
        {
            if( !pOutRet )
                return E_POINTER;
            *pOutRet  = inA + inB;
            return S_OK;
        }
};
```

By now, you have a service implementation (`CGenericService`) and its interface (`IGenericService`). Let's see how this service can be exposed by the ISAPI extension module.

As mentioned previously, the `CIsapiExtension` class (the base class for all the ISAPI extension modules in ATL Server) implements the standard COM `IServiceProvider` interface. The `IServiceProvider` interface exposes the `QueryService` method defined as follows:

```
virtual HRESULT STDMETHODCALLTYPE QueryService(
        /* [in] */ REFGUID guidService,
        /* [in] */ REFIID riid, /* [out] */ void ** ppvObject);
```

The `guidService` parameter identifies the service to be returned, and `riid` describes the interface that's requested from that service. On success, `ppvObject` will contain the returned interface.

To expose the new service (`CGenericService`) in the ISAPI extension, you must override `CIsapiExtension`'s `QueryService` method. This means that the default implementation for `CIsapiExtension` is no longer enough, so you should move from the code generated by the wizard, which looks like this:

```
typedef CIsapiExtension<> ExtensionType;
ExtensionType   theExtension;
```

to a new class, defined as follows:

```
class CMyExtension : public CIsapiExtension<>
{
};
CMyExtension theExtension;
```

The newly created class will contain a protected member, `m_internalGenericSvc`, of type `CGenericService`. This member is the actual service. All you have to do now is override the `QueryService` method:

```
virtual HRESULT STDMETHODCALLTYPE QueryService(
        REFGUID guidService, REFIID riid, void **ppvObject)
{
if( IsEqualIID(guidService, __uuidof(IGenericService))   &&
     IsEqualIID(riid, __uuidof(IGenericService)) )
      return m_internalGenericSvc.QueryInterface( riid, ppvObject);
else
     return CIsapiExtension<>::QueryService( guidService, riid, ppvObject);
}
```

You exploit here the fact that your service implements a single interface (`IGenericService`). You don't have to use a distinct GUID for the service, so you can use the same GUID of the interface.

Let's move now to consuming the service. In the request handler, you'll need an `IServiceProvider` pointer to query for your just-implemented service. Conveniently, a base class for all the request handlers (`IRequestHandlerT`) contains a pointer to the `IServiceProvider` interface implemented by the ISAPI module. That pointer is stored in the `IRequestHandlerT::m_spServiceProvider` member and can be used directly.

It's important that the service interface definition is visible in the request handler, so you'll include the definition header here (CommonServiceDefinition.h).

The code for retrieving the service from the ISAPI module and using it looks like the following (with error handling removed for clarity):

```
m_HttpResponse   <<   "Result (10 + 20 ) = ";
CComPtr<IGenericService>   spGenSvc;
hRet = m_spServiceProvider->QueryService(
                              __uuidof(IGenericService), &spGenSvc);

if( SUCCEEDED(hRet) )
{
        hRet  =  spGenSvc->AddTwoNumbers(10, 20, &iRet);
}
m_HttpResponse  <<  iRet;
```

When you place this code in a tag replacement method (say, in the `OnHello` method generated by the wizard), it will get the `IGenericService` pointer from the ISAPI module and then invoke `AddTwoNumbers` on the service and display the results.

So far, we've explained how a service can be defined, exposed by the ISAPI module, and then reused from a request handler. The consumer part will remain the same for all the ISAPI services. In the following sections we discuss differences in how you can store services in the ISAPI module and the impact of these differences on service behavior.

Built-in Global ISAPI Services

The simplest case of a service is a stateless package of reusable functions. You can easily implement such a service as a class with no members. The `IGenericService` package described in the previous section is a good example of this type of service.

As the service is stateless, no problems will occur from simultaneously using it from multiple threads. (ATL Server processes multiple requests on multiple threads, so it's possible—even likely—that the service will be used by multiple threads at the same time.) This raises some problems if the service contains some persistent data (such as a cache service) that's to be shared by multiple threads. You have to use a synchronization mechanism to ensure thread safety of the persistent data. This is the solution used by the BLOB cache and file cache services in ATL Server.

Examples of commonly used functionalities that you can easily implement using global ISAPI services are as follows:

- *Basic authentication service:* Use such a service to validate a user based on login name and password.

- *Counter service:* Use such a service to display the number of hits on the Web application.

Here follows some analysis of a hypothetical counter service, as it has a few particularities that make it a good case study for global services. Such a service would increment (in a thread-safe manner; for instance, with the `InterlockedIncrement` API) a counter whenever a page (therefore, a request handler) is hit by an HTTP request. In addition, the service would provide an interface for retrieving the current number of hits to display it on pages. The service would also be responsible for persisting to a selected medium (usually the hard drive or a database) the current counter value, to preserve it while the Web application is shut down.

You can implement a simple version of the counter service by modifying the previous generic service to make it expose methods for incrementing, serializing, and retrieving the counter. Then, each request handler would be responsible for incrementing the counter and asking for a serialization of the value (or the increment functionality would also ensure that the value is persisted).

A more refined implementation would take advantage of the behavior of the ISAPI extensions. You can do this by overriding the following functions in the `CIsapiExtension` derivative:

- First, override the `HttpExtensionProc` function. This function is invoked anytime an HTTP request is processed by the ISAPI extension; therefore, it's a very good place for incrementing the counter value. The function has to call the base class's implementation to actually handle the request.

```
DWORD HttpExtensionProc(LPEXTENSION_CONTROL_BLOCK lpECB)
{
        // add Counter incrementing code here,
        // then call the default implementation>
        return __super::HttpExtensionProc(lpECB);
}
```

- Override the `TerminateExtension` function. This function is invoked anytime an ISAPI extension is unloaded; therefore, it's a good place to ensure that the counter value is persisted.

```
BOOL TerminateExtension(DWORD dwFlags)
{
        // add code here for saving the Counter value
        //  to the persistence medium
        return __super:: TerminateExtension (dwFlags)
}
```

- Override the `GetExtensionVersion` function. This function is invoked anytime an ISAPI extension is loaded; therefore, it's a good place to ensure that the counter value is loaded from the persistence storage.

```
BOOL GetExtensionVersion(HSE_VERSION_INFO* pVer)
{
        // add code here for loading the Counter value
        // from the persistence medium
        return __super:: GetExtensionVersion(pVer)
}
```

By using these overrides, the request handlers don't have to worry anymore about incrementing the request counter and, therefore, you can use precompiled application DLLs (containing request handlers) and the page counter will be incremented for those as well.

In conclusion, the global ISAPI services are a flexible mechanism for shared functionalities that involve little or no contention. If the service is stateless, then the only thing to do (besides actually implementing the service) is to expose it by overriding the ISAPI extension class's `QueryService` method. If the service has a state and that state has to be persisted, then the `GetExtensionVersion` and `TerminateExtension` methods of the ISAPI extension class are very good opportunities for saving and restoring the state of the service. Also, for services with state, the routines that might change the state have to be thread-safe.

Built-in per-Thread ISAPI Services

You've already seen how a job that will be frequently executed from various request handlers (such as incrementing a hit counter) can be stored in a service in the ISAPI application. Also, we've suggested a way of solving thread contention issues (by using NT synchronization mechanisms). Now, if the job to be thread-safe is atomic (such as incrementing a hit counter), the Interlocked APIs will solve most of the problems. If the job isn't atomic, but you can reasonably assume that it will take a small number of CPU cycles to be executed, you can use more powerful APIs. ATL Server provides a set of wrappers for objects such as mutexes and critical sections.

What if the job to be executed is supposed to take a long time? Assume that your Web application fetches some information from a Web service and then displays that information in a human-friendly form on a Web page. Each request to your Web application would generate one or more requests to the Web service. All these requests will be executed through a proxy class (generated, of course, with sproxy).

Using per-Thread Services

Now, you could create a proxy class every time you have to send a request. This is pretty expensive: A proxy class has to `CoCreateInstance` for `ISAXXMLReader`, which is a time-consuming operation. So you need to somehow reuse one existing proxy object (or a limited number thereof).

This "cache" of proxy objects fits very well in an ISAPI service: All the request handlers will use them and they have to not be destroyed for the lifetime of the Web application. But when multiple threads (request handlers) attempt to use the proxy objects, you'll need a way to ensure that contention is avoided.

The jobs to be synchronized are taking a long time to complete. You could have a small pool of objects, and then spend time waiting for one of them to be free, or you could have a large number of objects, and then waste memory and resources while they aren't used.

The optimal number of pooled proxy objects for this scenario is exactly as many proxy objects as threads. This way, each thread will have a proxy available whenever necessary, and no memory will be wasted with extra proxies, but still some time will be wasted in finding the free proxy object when necessary for a given thread (although you know now for sure that there's at least one).

In the next section, you'll learn how you can expose the proxy objects in the preceding case as per-thread instances of ISAPI services and use them without any need for synchronization.

How to Implement the Actual Service

We start with a brief note on the ATL Server threading model: Each request is executed by a request handler in a single thread. The thread is part of the ISAPI thread pool. Each thread in the thread pool has an instance of a worker object. The worker object class is passed as a template parameter to the ISAPI extension class. The worker instance exists for the lifetime of the respective thread; therefore, it will be shared in a thread-safe way by all the requests to be executed on that thread.

You'll wrap the access to the proxy object in an ISAPI service, and then you'll have an instance of the ISAPI service living inside each worker object. Eventually, you'll modify the ISAPI extension so that `QueryService`, if invoked with the service ID of the proxy object, will return the one in the current thread.

The remote Web service to be accessed by all the Web application requests is available as the Services\PerThreadSvc\RemoteWeatherService sample. It provides the following interface:

```
[id(1)] HRESULT GetCityList([out, retval] int*        pnSize,
                            [out, size_is(*pnSize)] BSTR **arCityList);
[id(2)] HRESULT GetCityForecast([in] BSTR        bstrCity,
                        [out, retval] double *dForecastTemperature);
```

You wrap it into an ISAPI service defined as follows:

```
// IPerThreadSvc.
__interface __declspec(uuid("5BC416A1-CBA5-4769-9DEB-75E673E229FF"))
        IPerThreadWeatherSvc : public IUnknown
{
        // Gets the list of cities
        HRESULT GetCityList(int* pCount, BSTR**        arCities);
        HRESULT GetCityForecast(BSTR bstrCity, double* pdRet);
        HRESULT CleanupCityList(BSTR* arCities, int nCount);
};
```

This way, a request handler (like the sample one, Services\PerThreadSvc\PerThreadSvc) can use it as soon as you make it available in the ISAPI extension.

How to Make a Service per-Thread

In the ISAPI extension, Services\PerThreadSvc\PerThreadSvcIsapi, you'll start by creating a class (`CPerThreadWeatherSvc` in PerThreadSvcIsapi.cpp) that implements the `IPerThreadWeatherSvc` service interface. The class will contain a proxy client object for the weather Web service discussed previously. That proxy client object is based on the class generated by sproxy and is defined as follows:

```
RemoteWeatherService::CRemoteWeatherService        *m_pSvc;
```

The service implementation class also defines two methods, `Initialize` and `Uninitialize`, that will create and destroy the proxy object, respectively.

So far, you have an ISAPI service implementation that exposes the functionality of the remote weather Web service and can be used by the request handlers. Now you'll create an instance of this service implementation object in each worker, thus in each ISAPI worker thread. You'll do this by creating a new class, `CExtendedIsapiWorker`, that extends the existing `CIsapiWorker` class. This new class will contain a `CPerThreadWeatherSvc` object that implements the ISAPI service:

```
class CExtendedIsapiWorker : public CIsapiWorker
{
public:
        CPerThreadWeatherSvc                m_WeatherSvc;
```

The base class (`CIsapiWorker`) provides two virtual methods, `Initialize` and `Terminate`, that are invoked by the working thread when it starts (the worker object has just been created) and ends (the worker object is about to be destroyed). You'll override these virtuals to invoke the `CPerThreadWeatherSvc` object's `Initialize` and `Uninitialize` methods.

The next steps are pretty straightforward:

1. Declare an ISAPI extension derivative that uses the `CExtendedIsapiWorker` class:

```
class CIsapiEx : public CIsapiExtension<CThreadPool<CExtendedIsapiWorker> >
```

2. Override the new ISAPI class's `QueryService` method to support the `PerThreadWeather` service:

```
        virtual HRESULT STDMETHODCALLTYPE QueryService(
                REFGUID guidService,
                REFIID riid,
                void **ppvObject)
{
        if (!ppvObject)
                return E_POINTER;
        if (InlineIsEqualGUID(guidService,
                        __uuidof(IPerThreadWeatherSvc)))
   {
           CExtendedIsapiWorker *p =
           (CExtendedIsapiWorker*)GetThreadWorker();
          ATLASSERT( p != NULL );
        return p->m_WeatherSvc.QueryInterface(riid, ppvObject);
    }
        // otherwise look it up in the base class
        return __super::QueryService(guidService, riid, ppvObject);
}
```

3. Instantiate an ISAPI extension object from the newly defined class instead of the original `CIsapiExtension`. Replace

```
ExtensionType theExtension;
```

4. with

```
CIsapiEx theExtension;
```

Now the application is ready to compile and work. Each request handler can access the service via the ISAPI `QueryService` interface, and the returned service is the instance dedicated to the current thread, which you can use without worrying about possible contention and without waiting for it to become available.

Optimization

The original ISAPI worker object, `CIsapiWorker`, contains some objects that may prove useful in your proxy class service: an `ISAXXMLReader` object and a heap to be used in thread-specific allocations. You can reuse these objects in the proxy object as well. As you can see in the actual sample code, they're passed from the worker object to the ISAPI service implementation via the `Initialize` method and then used to initialize the SOAP proxy class and to set the memory manager to be used by that proxy class.

This way, the thread will use a dedicated heap (eliminating heap contention), and a single `ISAXXMLReader` object (saving the cost of `CoCreateInstance`-ing a new one for the proxy).

Per-Thread ISAPI Services Conclusion

The per-thread ISAPI services provide a powerful mechanism for avoiding the cost of synchronization primitives. Although this mechanism requires some more development effort than a regular ISAPI service, the results are worth the effort.

This mechanism is used by the ATL Server framework to provide the following functionality (some of the functionality is optional and selectable in the ATL Server Project Wizard in Visual Studio):

- The `ISAXXMLReader` service provided by all the ISAPI extensions (if the user doesn't choose to explicitly disable it by defining the `ATL_NO_SOAP` constant)
- The optional database connection service, which provides a thread-dedicated database connection
- The optional browser capabilities service

Dynamically Adding Services to the ISAPI Application

So far, we've discussed services that are built into the Web application—that is, services that are "known" by the ISAPI extension class at compile time. This is necessary for the `QueryService` implementation, which has to know how to map a service GUID to an existing object.

In this section we describe a more flexible way of adding services at runtime, meaning after the Web application (and, most important, the ISAPI DLL) has been loaded and is already receiving requests. We cover a set of functions, namely `AddService` and `RemoveService`, that are part of the `IIsapiExtension` interface, an interface implemented by all the `CIsapiExtension` derivatives and therefore by all the ISAPI extension classes in ATL Server.

The functions are defined as follows:

```
HRESULT AddService(
   REFGUID guidService,
   REFIID riid,
   IUnknown* punk,
   HINSTANCE hInstance);
```

```
HRESULT RemoveService(
   REFGUID guidService,
   REFIID riid);
```

AddService makes a service available through the IServiceProvider:: QueryService method of the CIsapiExtension class. That is, once AddService was invoked for a given service (let's call it DynamicService), any request handler can use that service through the regular mechanism described in the first section of this chapter (i.e., the QueryService method).

AddService takes as parameters a service GUID (the guidService parameter) and an interface GUID (the riid parameter). These parameters are enough to identify a given service inside the QueryService implementation. The IUnknown pointer is the actual implementation of the service to be returned by QueryService to any request for this specific service.

The last parameter, hInstance, although not used in the QueryService architecture, plays an important role. It's the instance handle of the DLL containing the dynamically added service, and passing it to AddService ensures that the DLL will be kept loaded as long as the service might be in use.

Once a service is no longer in use, it can be unloaded through a call to RemoveService. RemoveService takes as parameters the GUIDs of the service and the interface. A call to RemoveService will make the service unavailable through QueryService and also will decrement the reference count for the instance handle of the DLL containing the service. If this reference count reaches zero, the DLL will soon be unloaded (as soon as the DLL cache maintenance thread gets a chance to do this). As a consequence, you can safely invoke RemoveService from a request handler different from the one that actually added the service—even from a different application DLL, or from the ISAPI DLL itself.

The Services\DynamicServices sample proves the dynamically added services concept. It assumes (a rather simplistic approach, but good enough for a sample's sake) that all the DLLs in the virtual directory, except the RequestHandler DLL and the ISAPI DLL, are DLLs containing dynamic services. Furthermore, it assumes that sending a simple HTTP request to those DLLs will register the service they contain.

The Web application invokes various arithmetical operations that take two double parameters and then display the result. The actual arithmetical operation code is implemented in a dynamic service. For instance, you would have to load the service contained in the Add.dll to sum two numbers.

Conclusion

The ISAPI services provide a way of sharing data and functionality between different request handlers. The data preserved in these services will be available for the lifetime of the Web application or until the service is removed (for dynamic services).

If some simple stateless functionality is to be shared between request handlers, a global ISAPI service is the easiest design choice. If data has to be shared between request handlers, a global ISAPI service should again be the design of choice, but the access to data has to be synchronized using NT synchronization primitives, like Interlocked functions, or critical section or mutex objects. ATL provides handy wrappers for most of the synchronization objects.

If some functionality that relies on state information has to be shared by multiple request handlers (as long as data *is not* to be shared), then a per-thread service design will meet the requirements. This is a useful choice also for functionalities that can benefit (usually in performance) from removing the thread synchronization code. They won't be thread-safe, but they don't need to be as they'll be visible only from the current thread.

Plug-in kind of functionalities can be exposed as dynamic ISAPI services. This design choice provides a reliable mechanism for swapping objects that implement the same interface (the service interface) without worrying about the lifetime of the objects, as the ISAPI framework takes care of this.

A major task that every development team must face is debugging its Web application. In the next chapter we take a closer look at debugging ATL Server applications and present some useful tips and tricks.

CHAPTER 15

Debugging ATL Server Applications

THE MSDN DOCUMENTATION for ATL Server contains several articles on debugging ATL Server applications. They explain how to set a breakpoint in an ISAPI Web application or in a Web service, how to attach the debugger to the IIS process running a specific Web application, and how to trace debug information in a server-safe manner (i.e., using the WebDbg sample that comes with Visual Studio .NET to avoid blocking pop-up assertion dialog boxes).

This chapter assumes that you're already familiar with the debugging information presented in MSDN. Our purpose in this chapter is to enable a knowledgeable developer who has already mastered the Web debugging features offered by Visual Studio .NET to get as close as possible to the source of the problem he or she is tracking.

Server-Side Debugging

This section offers hints for tracking problems in server applications, based on where these problems seem to occur.

ISAPI Initialization

According to the ISAPI specification, each DLL has to expose three functions to be called by IIS. `GetExtensionVersion` and `TerminateExtension` are invoked by IIS when the ISAPI DLL is loaded and unloaded, respectively. Then `HttpExtensionProc` is invoked for processing each HTTP request. In this section we cover the initialization of an ISAPI application, so we focus on the `GetExtensionVersion` implementation.

The typical ATL Server ISAPI DLL instantiates a `CIsapiExtension` derivative, a class that provides implementations for the three methods described previously. The exported `GetExtensionVersion` function calls into the `GetExtensionVersion` method of the `CIsapiExtension` derivative. The code in this method is initializes the internal components of the ISAPI extension: the DLL cache, the stencil cache, and the thread pool.

An error in the initialization of these components is fatal for the ATL Server application (the `GetExtensionVersion` function will return a failure code to IIS, which will unload the ISAPI DLL and all subsequent requests will fail). Such an error is reported to the client just as an HTTP 500 error ("Internal Server Error"), with no details about what happened.

Furthermore, the errors in the `GetExtensionVersion` function are particularly difficult to debug. Whenever an error occurs in, say, a request handler, pressing F5 (or whatever the preferred keystroke is for launching the debugger) helps a lot in solving the problem. The usual "F5 debugging" doesn't work for this function because of the way F5 debugging works: Visual Studio sends a DEBUG request to the IIS server, which loads the ATL Server ISAPI DLL. The application is responsible for sending back to the client (Visual Studio, in this case) the debug session ID as well as the process ID for the process that loaded the ISAPI DLL. After receiving this information, Visual Studio attaches the debugger to that process, and the user can walk through the code. Now, if the initialization code fails (i.e., `GetExtensionVersion` returns `FALSE`), the ISAPI DLL isn't loaded and it can't handle the DEBUG request, so the F5 debugging attempt will fail.

NOTE *For complete details on F5 debugging support, please see the implementation of the* `ProcessDebug` *function in atlisapi.h.*

So, you end up with an initialization function that, on failure, breaks not only the application but also the usual debugging methodology. We'll discuss now how you can handle such a failure.

First, let's see how you can detect such a failure. If you check the implementation of `CIsapiExtension::GetExtensionVersion`, you'll notice that any potential failure generates a call like this:

```
return SetCriticalIsapiError(IDS_ATLSRV_CRITICAL_DLLCACHEFAILED);
```

`SetCriticalIsapiError` has two implementations in atlisapi.h. Using `#defines`, only one of them will be compiled into the ISAPI DLL.

The default implementation will log an error description into the system's application event log. For instance, the preceding line will log an error like this: "A critical error has occurred initializing the ISAPI extension: DLL cache initialization failed." So, if an ATL Server application fails to load, checking the application log will let you know whether the problem occurred in the initialization or elsewhere.

After that, the `SetCriticalIsapiError` function, according to the ISAPI specification, *should* return `FALSE`, so that the error is propagated to IIS. Oddly enough, the function returns `TRUE` (i.e., it doesn't signal the loading error to the IIS). It also sets an internal variable (`m_dwCriticalIsapiError`) to contain the error code just signaled. The reason for this behavior is that ATL Server wants to enable sending the error information to the client. By returning `TRUE` here, IIS doesn't unload the ISAPI DLL and continues with the request processing, and the `HttpExtensionProc` function will be invoked. The first lines of `HttpExtensionProc` will check for the value of the `m_dwCriticalIsapiError` internal variable and, if this contains an error, it will send the error message to the user (the same error message that got logged in the event handler). This way, a client will receive the information about the failing DLL cache initialization rather than a generic "Internal Server Error" message.

Sending the error information to the user can be controlled via conditional compiling. If the `ATL_CRITICAL_ISAPI_ERROR_LOGONLY` constant is defined at compile time, then the error will be logged into the event log, but the details *will not* be sent to the client. Instead, a generic "A server error has occurred" message will be sent.

NOTE *The default wizard-generated application will send error information to the user in Debug mode and will only log the error in the event log for the Release build.*

You can change the behavior described previously by defining `ATL_NO_CRITICAL_ISAPI_ERROR` at compile time. This way, the second implementation of `SetCriticalIsapiError` is compiled. The second implementation does nothing, but it returns `FALSE`, forcing IIS to unload the ISAPI DLL.

Assuming that you want to get the combined behavior of both implementations (logging the error in the event log, but also returning `FALSE` to IIS to force unloading the DLL), you would have to modify the exported `GetExtensionVersion` function's code as follows:

```
...
BOOL bRet    = theExtension.GetExtensionVersion(pVer);
if(bRet && theExtension.GetCriticalIsapiError() != 0)
{
    return FALSE;
}
```

Debugging a problem based on the errors in the application error log is very helpful if you don't have direct access to the server where the product is deployed, or it isn't possible to debug the application there.

If you can install a debugger on the server, you can use a more effective approach. We should mention again that the main debugging issue is that F5 debugging won't work for the initialization code. If the debugger is *already* attached to the process that loads the ISAPI DLL, then you can investigate the cause of the failure.

For the wizard-generated ATL Server applications, the deployment tool sets the application protection to Low (IIS process). That means the application is loaded in IIS. The IIS process is usually well known (it's inetinfo.exe for IIS 5.*x*, Windows 2000, and Windows XP). So, all you have to do is attach the debugger to the inetinfo.exe process *before* your first attempt to launch the failing ISAPI extension. If you've already made an attempt to launch the application, then you can reset IIS (from the command line by using either the `iisreset` command or the `net stop w3svc/net start w3svc` commands). Then, just attempting to load the ISAPI application in the browser will hit the breakpoint set in `GetExtensionVersion`.

For custom deployed applications (which don't necessarily run in the IIS process), you have to identify the loader process first. For Medium application protection, IIS will load all the ISAPI DLLs into a separate process, usually dllhost.exe. For Isolated mode, IIS will spawn a separate process for each ISAPI application.

In this case, the following code snippet will help you in identifying the process to attach the debugger to (the modified body of the `GetExtensionVersion` function is presented):

```
extern "C" BOOL WINAPI GetExtensionVersion(HSE_VERSION_INFO* pVer)
{
    DWORD     dwProcId = ::GetCurrentProcessId();
    TCHAR     szChar[MAX_PATH];
    _stprintf(szChar, _T("Attach to: %d"), dwProcId);
    ::MessageBox( NULL, szChar, _T("ATL Server Debugging"),
MB_OK | MB_SERVICE_NOTIFICATION);
    return theExtension.GetExtensionVersion(pVer);
}
```

NOTE *You will need to enable the World Wide Web Publishing Service to interact with the desktop in order to see the message. To do this, open the properties of the service from the service administration snap-in and select the checkbox that enables this functionality under the Log On tab.*

Once you launch the application in the browser, a message box will appear that includes text similar to the following:

```
---------------------------
ATL Server Debugging
---------------------------
Attach to: 288
---------------------------
OK
---------------------------
```

You should attach the debugger to the specified process ID, set a breakpoint right after the MessageBox call in the preceding code snippet, and then click OK on the message box. The breakpoint should be hit immediately, allowing debugging of the initialization code.

Request Loading and Processing

We mentioned the HttpExtensionProc function, invoked for processing each request, in the previous section. In this section we explain how to track down problems that appear between the moment when the request is accepted by the ISAPI extension and the moment when the application DLL takes control over the request (i.e., when HandleRequest is invoked). During this time, the request is managed by the internals of ATL Server, and finding a bug requires a good understanding of what's happening.

The HttpExtensionProc implementation posts the request in the thread pool queue. Whenever a working thread is free, it picks the first work item in the queue and executes that work item. As shown in previous chapters, the execution is performed by the per-thread worker class. By default, this worker class is CIsapiWorker. Whenever a new work item is fetched from the queue, it's passed to CIsapiWorker's Execute method.

There the actual execution of the request starts. Also, it's very important to realize that it's there that any exception from the execution is caught.

The code for CIsapiWorker::Execute looks like this (error handling and ATL-specific macros aside):

```
try
{
    (static_cast<IIsapiExtension*>(pvParam))->DispatchStencilCall(pRequestInfo);
}
catch(...)
{
    ATLASSERT(FALSE);
}
```

NOTE *While you develop an ATL Server request handler, it's possible that some requests pop up an assertion dialog box on the screen with a message like this: "...\inetinfo.exe: Assertion failed in atlisapi.h, line 663". This problem (which we also describe in Chapter 27) means that an exception occurred in the handling of the request. To find the source of the exception, just set a breakpoint on the line below the one that invokes* `DispatchStencilCall`. *Then, in the Visual Studio Debug menu, select Exceptions and select "Break into the debugger" for all types of exceptions.*

`DispatchStencilCall` parses the request's URL and determines the handler that has to be invoked for handling the request based on the extension of the URL object. Then, the actual handler interface is obtained by calling either `LoadDispatchFile` (for SRF files) or `LoadDllHandler` (for DLLs without stencil support).

NOTE *If the URL's object (the object requested by the HTTP client) is an SRF file, that file is loaded and parsed until the* `{{handler ..}}` *replacement tag is encountered. This replacement tag describes the DLL containing the main request handler, as well as the name of that handler. For instance, SRF file content such as*

```
{{handler MyApp.dll/SomeHandler}}
```

actually means

```
"Load the MyApp.dll library and look for a handler called SomeHandler"
```

The same request handler can be described in an URL like this:

```
http://localhost/MyTestApp/MyApp.dll?Handler=SomeHandler
```

Any ATL Server application DLL (i.e., a DLL that contains at least a request handler) exports a set of methods for handling those request handlers. To find those handlers, just go in a command prompt in the same directory where the DLL is stored and execute the following:

```
C:\MyFolder>dumpbin /EXPORTS SomeApp.dll
```

The output will contain something like this:

```
3     5 00033374 _GetAtlHandlerByName@12
4     6 0003333D _InitializeAtlHandlers@8
5     7 00033C02 _UninitializeAtlHandlers@0
```

which means that the respective methods are exported by the DLL.

The ordinals, as well as the addresses of the exported functions, may differ between applications, but you can't use a DLL as a request handler if these methods (at least `_GetAtlHandlerByName`) aren't exported.

The actual implementation of these exported functions is usually hidden by either the macros or the attributes used in developing the request handler DLL:

```
[request_handler("Default")]
```

or

```
HANDLE_ENTRY("Default", CSomeAppHandler)
```

NOTE *You can understand the actual implementation by using the wizard to generate an ATL Server project (without an ISAPI application), disabling the Attributed code option in the Developer support pane, and then inspecting the* `HANDLE_ENTRY` *macro's usage in the .cpp file generated by the wizard, as well as its implementation in atlisapi.h.*

It's important to remember the following points:

- `InitializeAtlHandlers` initializes all the handlers contained in the request handler.
- `UninitializeAtlHandlers` uninitializes the handlers.
- `GetAtlHandlerByName` loads a handler by its name.
- `InitializeAtlHandlers` and `_UnitializeAtlHandlers`, if implemented (if found in the application DLL), are invoked when the DLL is loaded and unloaded, respectively.
- `GetAtlHandlerByName` provides the ISAPI code with the actual request handler implementation that's supposed to handle the requests for that named

handler. In the preceding example, `_GetAtlHandlerByName` returns the address of a `CSomeAppHandler` instance.

Once the handler has been identified, it's cast to an `IRequestHandler` pointer, the base class for all the request handlers supported by ATL Server. Among other functions, this interface provides the `HandleRequest` method, which transfers control from the ISAPI extension to the request handler. `HandleRequest` is a method you can override in your request handler class to gain more control over the behavior of the Web application.

The preceding details, although not directly related to the purpose of this chapter (to provide debugging hints for ATL Server applications), will hopefully simplify the process of finding the location of bugs while handling the request for you. `DispatchStencilCall` is responsible for caching the result of an invocation and also for deciding when a request has to be executed and when the cached result of a previous execution can be returned.

Finding Errors in SRF Files

In this section you'll focus on identifying problems with parsing SRF files. The most common errors in SRF files are generated by misspelled replacement tag names. We use a simple scenario to show how to find these kinds of problems.

You'll start by creating a wizard-generated ATL Server application that contains an ISAPI extension and a request handler. Then, in the wizard-generated SRF file, just modify the `{{Hello}}` replacement tag to be `{{Helo}}` (a misspelled version of the replacement tag name) and launch the application in the browser. The response looks like the following:

```
Server Error
SRF file could not be loaded.
```

This is hardly enough information to help you find the problem. The reason this information isn't more detailed is that the Web application's clients aren't supposed to accidentally get access to the internal structure of the application (information such as replacement handler names, request handler names, and so forth shouldn't be exposed to clients—not even in case of an error).

As a developer, however, you have a way to get extended information. Just go into the stdafx.h file of the application DLL generated earlier and add the following line *before* `#include` <atlstencil.h>:

```
#define ATL_DEBUG_STENCILS
```

After you rebuild and launch the application, the browser returns the following:

```
<html>
<head>
</head>
<body>
This is a test: {{Helo}}<br>
</body>
</html>
```

When `ATL_DEBUG_STENCILS` is defined, ATL Server simply copies the request handlers it doesn't understand into the output buffer, so curly braces will describe the place where the error occurred (in this case, the misspelled `{{Helo}}` replacement tag, which should actually be `{{Hello}}`).

Let's see how you can find this error without using the `ATL_DEBUG_STENCILS` symbol. Once the stencil file is loaded, it's preparsed (i.e., the replacement tags are identified and kept in an array of tokens, with each token containing the name of the replacement tag). After preparsing, the array of tokenized replacement tags is "resolved"—that is, the method to be called is determined for each of the tags. This happens in the `CStencil::FinishParseReplacements` method, in atlstencil.h.

The code for `FinishParseReplacements` iterates through the vector of tokenized replacement tags and, whenever one of them can't be resolved, invokes either the `AddError` method (for syntax errors in the SRF) or the `AddReplacementError` method (for replacement handlers that can't be resolved). So, by setting a breakpoint in both functions, you'll catch the SRF file error.

NOTE *To find* `AddError` *and* `AddReplacementError` *in atlstencil.h, just look for the strings* `AddError(UINT` *or* `AddReplacementError(LPCSTR`. *They occur less often than the actual call to functions.*

After you set the breakpoints, if you load the application in the browser again the breakpoints are hit. You have just to go one step back in the call stack (in `FinishParseReplacements`) and inspect the values of the following local variables in the debugger:

```
+    token.szMethodName    0x01c3fea1 "Helo"
+    token.pStart         0x0163a78a "{{ Helo}}<br></body></html>
```

This not only shows you the misspelled tag (the method name), but also gives you an idea of where in the SRF file the error occurred.

`FinishParseReplacements` will also generate an error whenever an `{{if}}`/`{{else}}`/`{{while}}` block isn't correctly closed, so understanding the implementation of this function will help with most of the SRF syntax problems that you may encounter.

So far, we've discussed ways of finding syntactical errors in SRF files. Assuming that an SRF file is correct, its rendering may still generate an error if one of the replacement methods fails. In the next section we analyze how to identify a failing replacement method.

Identifying a Failing Replacement Method

First, let's see what kind of failures require special effort to locate. A failure that throws an exception needs no extra work: The debugger can catch an exception as it's thrown and break the code execution exactly at the point where the exception is thrown. We described in the "Request Loading and Processing" section how to catch an exception in the request handler.

A replacement method may also fail by returning an unsuccessful HTTP error code. You can't catch such a failure in the way we described earlier, as no exception is thrown. We discuss in this section a way of identifying this kind of failing replacement method.

To demonstrate, in the test application you built in the previous section, you'll change the implementation of the replacement method for `{{Hello}}` and make it return `HTTP_FAIL` instead of `HTTP_SUCCESS`, as generated by the wizard. The following response is generated when the page is loaded in the browser:

```
<html><head><title>Server Error</title></head>
<body>Server Error</body></html><html>
<head>
</head>
<body>
This is a test: Hello World!
```

The `Server Error` part of the response is generated by the failing method. Now you'll try to debug the Web application to find the failing invocation.

The replacement method is invoked during stencil processing. The method invocation is performed by a `CStencil` method called `RenderReplacement`. If you search for this method in atlstencil.h, you'll find the implementation. The implementation identifies the method to be invoked and then calls that method with the following code if the replacement tag has no parameters:

```
if (pfn)
{
    hcErr = (pT->*pfn)();
}
```

It calls that method with the following code if the replacement tag has parameters:

```
if (pfn)
{
    hcErr = (pT->*pfn)(pvParam);
}
```

In the preceding code snippets, `pfn` is a pointer to the replacement method. Assuming you can somehow break the execution of the program here when a method fails, stepping into the `(pT->*pfn)` call in the preceding code will debug exactly the failing replacement method.

To break the execution when a replacement method fails, you can set a conditional breakpoint at the last line of the function. That line returns the result of the invocation:

```
return hcErr;
```

In the ATL Server version that comes with Visual Studio .NET 2003, that line is 379 in atlstencil.h.

The conditional breakpoint should get hit whenever `hcErr` represents an error. Now, an HTTP error code is built with a macro like this:

```
#define HTTP_ERROR(err, sub) \
   ((HTTP_CODE)(DWORD_PTR)MAKELONG((WORD)err, (WORD)sub))
```

Particularly, `HTTP_SUCCESS` is defined as `HTTP_ERROR(0,0)`, whereas `HTTP_FAIL` is defined as `HTTP_ERROR(500, SUBERR_NONE)`. The HTTP error codes are built using the error 500 and some suberror code. Therefore, you want the conditional breakpoint to get hit whenever the error code is 500 or more. The condition for the breakpoint could be described as "have the `LOWORD` part greater or equal to 500," or

```
(hcErr & 0xffff) >= 500
```

NOTE *To set a conditional breakpoint, just set the breakpoint, then right-click the red button inserted in the source code and select Breakpoint Properties. In the Breakpoint Properties dialog box, select Condition, which will allow you to enter the condition.*

Now, with the conditional breakpoint in place, you can start the application again in the debugger. Whenever the breakpoint is hit, you know that a replacement method just failed. To know exactly which method failed, you can re-execute the `RenderReplacement` function. To do so, just scroll up to the beginning of the function, right-click, and select Set Next Statement. When you execute the code into the debugger, you'll then get exactly the failing method to be called again when stepping into the `(pT->*pfn)` invocation described previously.

Client-Side SOAP Debugging

In this section we describe problems you may encounter in a Web service client and ways to fix them. However, we cover only some general troubleshooting issues. You'll need a good understanding of the ATL Server SOAP framework and the HTTP client code to debug more serious SOAP problems.

The first step in writing a Web service client is, usually, getting a proxy file for the Web service. The proxy file is generated by the sproxy tool that comes with ATL Server. You can invoke sproxy from the command line or by selecting the Add Web Reference menu item in Visual Studio .NET.

The result of running the sproxy tool is a header file that contains a class generated especially for the service indicated as parameter for the sproxy tool. You must then include the header in your application and invoke the methods of the proxy class. The code that accomplishes this looks very much like the following:

```
#include "TWSService.h"
int SoapInvocation()
{
    TWSService::CTWSService svc;
    BSTR bstrIn, bstrOut;
    bstrIn    =    ::SysAllocString(L"Test");
    HRESULT    hr = svc.HelloWorld(bstrIn, &bstrOut);
    printf("RetCode %d\n", hr);
    if( SUCCEEDED(hr))
```

```
    {
        printf("%ls\n", bstrOut);
        return 0;
}
    return 1;
 }
```

Any failure in invoking the Web service will be signaled by the return value from the method of the proxy class. The SOAP infrastructure used in the proxy class will return simply `E_FAIL` if any problem occurs, and details are provided using a different mechanism that we describe a little bit later. This means that any failure that isn't `E_FAIL` is related to something other than the SOAP infrastructure, and you should try to figure out what the problem is.

A common non-`E_FAIL` code returned by a SOAP method is

```
hr    0x800401f0 CoInitialize has not been called.
```

This error code means that the COM library wasn't initialized. The solution is to call `CoInitialize(NULL)` (or any of the similar functions: `CoInitializeEx`, `AfxOleInit`, and so forth) in the executing thread before the first SOAP call is made.

COM is used in the proxy class to create an instance of `ISAXXMLReader`, the SAX parser used in handling SOAP payloads. If the user already has a SAX XML reader that isn't using COM, that reader can be passed as a parameter to the constructor of the proxy class and the COM initialization isn't required anymore (assuming, of course, that the available reader isn't a COM object itself).

After the initialization succeeds, the SOAP infrastructure will signal any error by setting the client error member of the proxy class. You can access this error flag with code such as the following:

```
SOAPCLIENT_ERROR    err = svc.GetClientError();
```

The possible values of the `SOAPCLIENT_ERROR` enumeration are described in the MSDN documentation. A line of code like the preceding will always make a developer's life easier, so it's strongly recommended that you have it in the error-checking code. Chapters 19 and 25 should provide enough details for you to debug the causes of most of the error codes in this enumeration.

In this chapter we discuss only the `SOAPCLIENT_PARSE_ERROR` flag, which signals an error in the response payload. To be able to debug this kind of problem, you need to see the XML payload returned by the server. You can do this by defining the `_ATLSOAP_TRACE_XML` constant *before* including atlsoap.h. That means either in the stdafx.h header or right before including the sproxy-generated header file. You can also do this by setting the compiler command-line flag `/D _ATLSOAP_TRACE_XML`.

With the newly built application, when a Web service method is invoked, both the request's and the response's XML payloads are going to be traced by the application and can be captured for investigation of the parsing problem.

Debugging Helper: The ISAPI WebDbg Tool

ATL Server comes with a very helpful tool, ISAPI WebDbg (webdbg.exe). This tool allows you to read the trace generated by an ATL Server (debug) application without attaching the Visual Studio debugger to the IIS process.

ATL Server creates a named pipe where all the trace messages are pushed. WebDbg opens the other end of the named pipe and displays all the traces and assertions from the ATL Server application. Even more helpful, WebDbg can access the ATL Server trace pipe on a different machine.

You can launch webdbg.exe from the Program Files menu in the Visual Studio .NET Tools submenu. Alternately, you can launch it from the command line as webdbg.exe (assuming that the VS Tools directory is in the path).

Now you'll see how you can use the tool with a new wizard-generated ATL Server application. Just add the following line in the `OnHello` replacement method (or any replacement method, if you decide to use an existing application):

```
ATLTRACE("Executing HelloWorld\n");
```

Then launch the WebDbg application and also launch the application in the browser. As the replacement method is executed, the message is displayed in the text area of the tool. In the File menu of the WebDbg tool, select Select Pipe to use the following pipe name to connect to the ATL Server pipe on another machine:

```
\\<server_name>\pipe\AtlsDbgPipe
```

(You can use "." for the server name to point to the local machine.)

WebDbg provides some other helpful features, such as filtering a message based on the prefix or based on ATL Server regular expressions. In addition, you can break the application in the debugger whenever a particular message is traced. To do so, in the Filter dialog box select the "Break on message" option.

Conclusion

Because of its server-side nature, ATL Server debugging is slightly more complex than a regular console application. You'll need a good understanding of the ATL Server code and Web development issues to successfully troubleshoot problems.

It's our hope that with the hints we provided in this chapter and with use of the WebDbg tool, your life as a developer will be made much easier.

The role of many Web applications is to present information to a user or to take and store information from the user. This data might include online catalogs, online ordering information, or today's weather. Regardless of the kind of data you're working with, you'll need to access a database. In the next chapter we take a look at accessing databases with ATL Server.

CHAPTER 16

Database Access with ATL Server

IF YOU'RE WRITING WEB applications with ATL Server, accessing a database is probably one of the most common tasks you'll perform. If your Web application is going to access a database, in many cases, the dominant factor in determining the performance of your Web application in general will be the time it takes to make a connection to the database. Because of this, ATL Server provides a data source cache that you can use to store database connections. In this chapter you'll focus on using this cache.

The data source cache in ATL Server is geared toward working with OLE DB Consumer Templates. Before we examine the data source cache directly, we'll take a quick look at OLE DB Consumer Templates.

Using OLE DB Consumer Templates

The OLE DB Consumer Templates library does an excellent job of catering to developers with both sophisticated and simple database access needs. Visual C++ also has a wizard that makes generating OLE DB Consumer Template classes for your particular database very easy. Unless you have specific needs not addressed by OLE DB Consumer Templates, you should consider making this library your preferred way of accessing databases.

Let's take a quick look at how you can use the Visual C++ ATL OLE DB Consumer Wizard to generate code to access databases in your application. You should consult the Microsoft Developer Network (MSDN) documentation for a complete overview of OLE DB Consumer Templates.

If you're using Microsoft Visual C++ .NET, you can run the OLE DB Consumer Wizard from any type of project by choosing the ATL OLE DB Consumer icon from the dialog box shown in Figure 16-1 (assuming you're working in a new or existing ATL Server project).

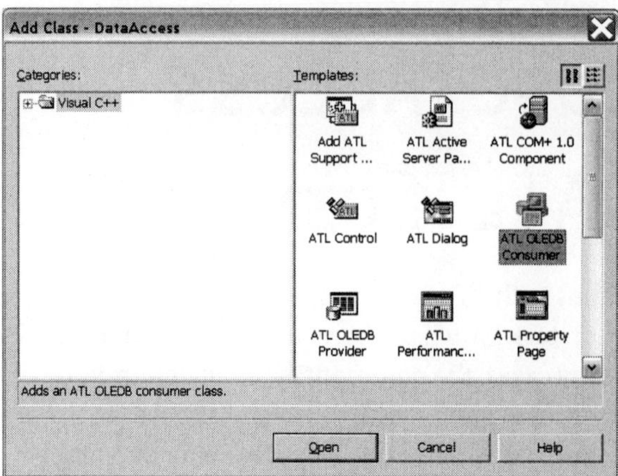

Figure 16-1. Selecting the ATL OLE DB Consumer icon

In this section we'll walk you through this wizard and look at its options. First, you'll see the wizard's Welcome screen, as shown in Figure 16-2.

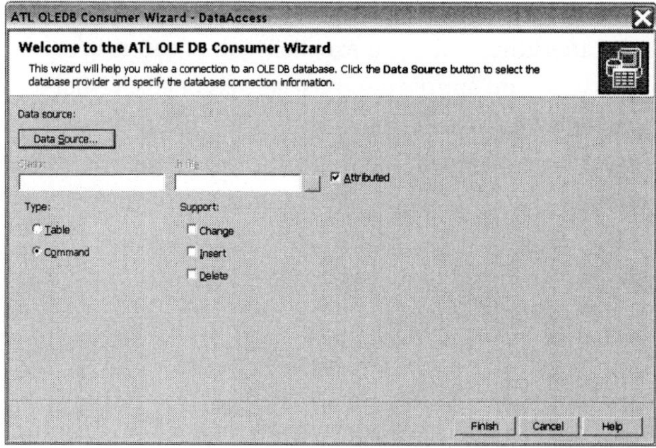

Figure 16-2. The Welcome screen of the ATL OLE DB Consumer Wizard

The Attributed option is checked by default. Attributes are new in Visual C++ .NET and are used to keep the generated code clean and easy to read.

The type of template you'll generate for this example is a table, so select the Table radio button in the Type section. You're accessing your database by table only in this example; in a production application, you'll most likely use the Command option to generate a template that will allow you to access a stored procedure.

Next, click the Data Source button to select the database your template will target. Doing so brings up the Data Link Properties dialog box, as shown in Figure 16-3.

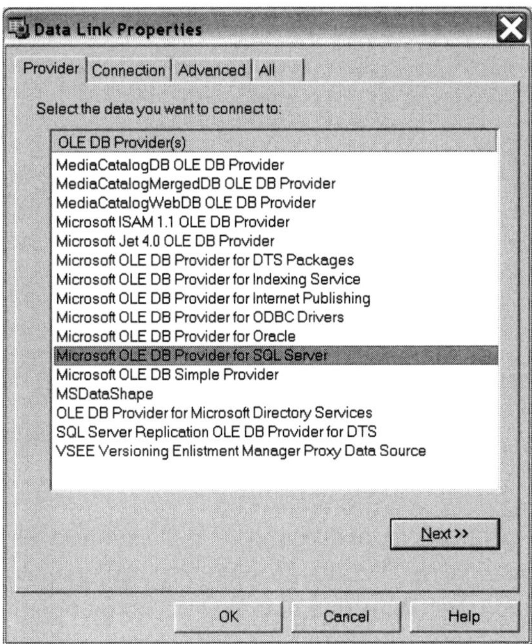

Figure 16-3. The Data Link Properties dialog box

In this example, you'll access a SQL Server, so choose the Microsoft OLE DB Provider for SQL Server option. As you can see, OLE DB allows you to access a wide range of data formats. Each format is called an "OLE DB Provider." Click the Next button to continue once you've chosen your OLE DB provider.

The Data Link Properties dialog box enables you to specify the database you want to access and how to authenticate with it. For this example, you'll access the Northwind example database, as shown in Figure 16-4.

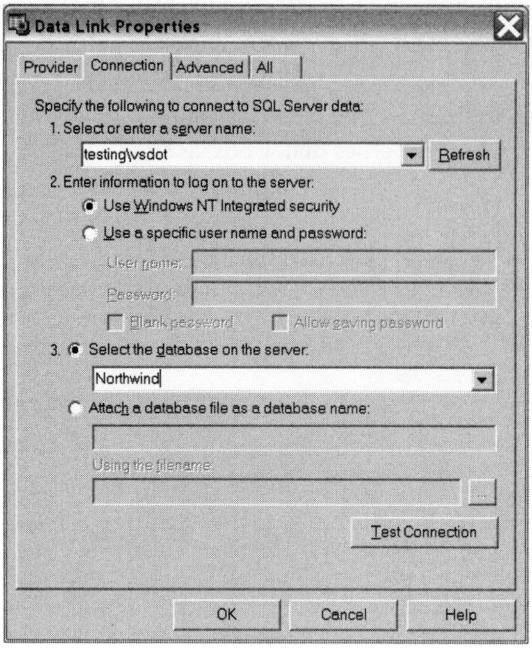

Figure 16-4. Selecting the Northwind database

For security reasons, you should always try to design your application so that you can use Windows NT Integrated security for authentication, so make to sure to select that radio button. Clicking the Test Connection button at the bottom of the dialog box will allow you to determine if the authentication information you've provided is valid.

Once you've entered a database and the proper authentication information, click the OK button to move on to the Select Database Object dialog box, as shown in Figure 16-5.

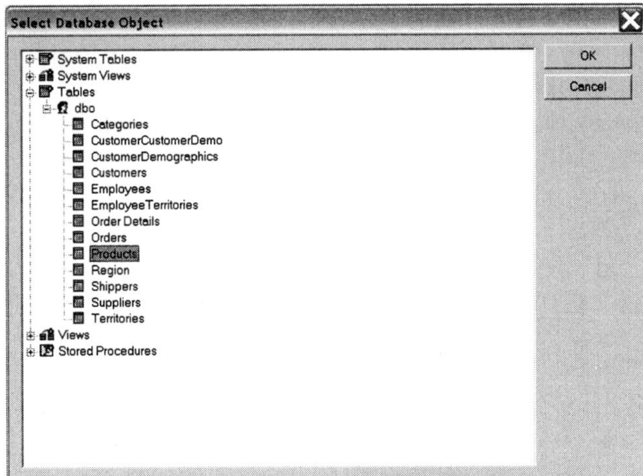

Figure 16-5. The Select Database Object dialog box

This dialog box allows you to choose the database object your template will access. In this example, you'll access the Products table. Click OK and you're taken back to the original dialog box (see Figure 16-6).

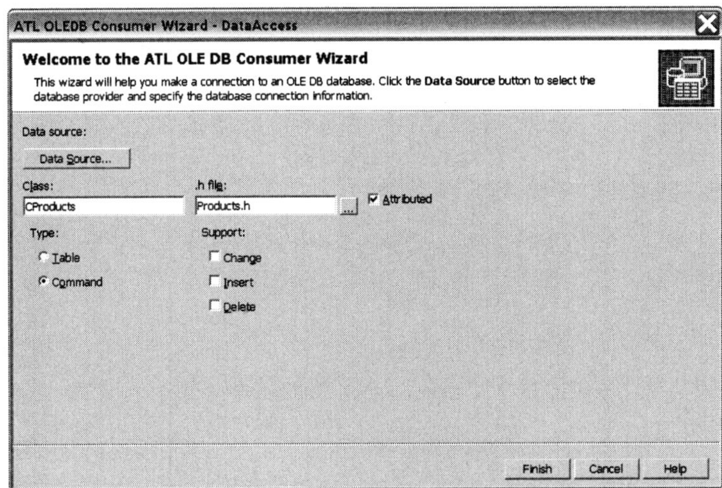

Figure 16-6. Returning to the Welcome screen

The wizard now has all of the information it needs to generate your OLE DB Consumer Template. Feel free to change the class name and/or filename to suit your taste. Click Finish to generate your template.

The new file, Products.h, will be added automatically to your project. Listing 16-1 presents this file.

Listing 16-1. The Products.h File

```
#pragma once

[
#error Security Issue: The connection string may contain a password
// The connection string below may contain plain text passwords and/or
// other sensitive information. Please remove the #error after reviewing
// the connection string for any security related issues. You may want to
// store the password in some other form or use a different user authentication.
 db_source(L"Provider=SQLOLEDB.1;\
            Integrated Security=SSPI;\
            Persist Security Info=False;\
            Initial Catalog=Northwind;\
            Data Source=testing\\vsdotnet;\
            Use Procedure for Prepare=1;\
            Auto Translate=True;Packet Size=4096;\
            Workstation ID=TestMachine;\
            Use Encryption for Data=False"),
 db_table(L"dbo.Products")
 ]
 class CProducts
 {
 public:
     [ db_column(1,
                status=m_dwProductIDStatus,
                length=m_dwProductIDLength) ] LONG m_ProductID;
     [ db_column(2,
                status=m_dwProductNameStatus,
                length=m_dwProductNameLength) ] TCHAR m_ProductName[41];
     [ db_column(3,
                status=m_dwSupplierIDStatus,
                length=m_dwSupplierIDLength) ] LONG m_SupplierID;
     [ db_column(4,
                status=m_dwCategoryIDStatus,
                length=m_dwCategoryIDLength) ] LONG m_CategoryID;
     [ db_column(5,
                status=m_dwQuantityPerUnitStatus,
```

```
            length=m_dwQuantityPerUnitLength) ]
            TCHAR m_QuantityPerUnit[21];
[ db_column(6,
            status=m_dwUnitPriceStatus,
            length=m_dwUnitPriceLength) ] CURRENCY m_UnitPrice;
[ db_column(7,
            status=m_dwUnitsInStockStatus,
            length=m_dwUnitsInStockLength) ] SHORT m_UnitsInStock;
[ db_column(8,
            status=m_dwUnitsOnOrderStatus,
            length=m_dwUnitsOnOrderLength) ] SHORT m_UnitsOnOrder;
[ db_column(9,
            status=m_dwReorderLevelStatus,
            length=m_dwReorderLevelLength) ] SHORT m_ReorderLevel;
[ db_column(10,
            status=m_dwDiscontinuedStatus,
            length=m_dwDiscontinuedLength) ] VARIANT_BOOL m_Discontinued;

// The following wizard-generated data members contain status
// values for the corresponding fields. You
// can use these values to hold NULL values that the database
// returns or to hold error information when the compiler returns
// errors. See Field Status Data Members in Wizard-Generated
// Accessors in the Visual C++ documentation for more information
// on using these fields.
// NOTE: You must initialize these fields before setting/inserting data!

DBSTATUS m_dwProductIDStatus;
DBSTATUS m_dwProductNameStatus;
DBSTATUS m_dwSupplierIDStatus;
DBSTATUS m_dwCategoryIDStatus;
DBSTATUS m_dwQuantityPerUnitStatus;
DBSTATUS m_dwUnitPriceStatus;
DBSTATUS m_dwUnitsInStockStatus;
DBSTATUS m_dwUnitsOnOrderStatus;
DBSTATUS m_dwReorderLevelStatus;
DBSTATUS m_dwDiscontinuedStatus;

// The following wizard-generated data members contain length
// values for the corresponding fields.
// NOTE: For variable-length columns, you must initialize these
//       fields before setting/inserting data!

DBLENGTH m_dwProductIDLength;
```

```
81.     DBLENGTH m_dwProductNameLength;
82.     DBLENGTH m_dwSupplierIDLength;
83.     DBLENGTH m_dwCategoryIDLength;
84.     DBLENGTH m_dwQuantityPerUnitLength;
85.     DBLENGTH m_dwUnitPriceLength;
86.     DBLENGTH m_dwUnitsInStockLength;
87.     DBLENGTH m_dwUnitsOnOrderLength;
88.     DBLENGTH m_dwReorderLevelLength;
89.     DBLENGTH m_dwDiscontinuedLength;
90.
91.
92.     void GetRowsetProperties(CDBPropSet* pPropSet)
93.     {
94.         pPropSet->AddProperty(DBPROP_CANFETCHBACKWARDS,
95.                               true,
96.                               DBPROPOPTIONS_OPTIONAL);
97.         pPropSet->AddProperty(DBPROP_CANSCROLLBACKWARDS,
98.                               true,
99.                               DBPROPOPTIONS_OPTIONAL);
100.    }
101.};
```

Let's take a look at this code line-by-line:

- *Lines 9 through 17:* As mentioned earlier, you should always try to use Windows NT Integrated security as your authentication mechanism. If you choose SQL Server authentication, the username and password that you enter will show up in clear text in this file. Because of this possibility, the OLE DB Consumer Wizard will generate this `#error` directive by default. You have to remove it manually in order for this file to compile.

- In line 9, the `db_source` attribute generates code behind-the-scenes to create instances of `CDataSource` and `CSession`. Attributes are essentially mechanisms introduced in Visual C++ .NET to generate code. In the next section you'll look at how you can modify this code to use a data source from the cache that ATL Server provides.

- *Line 18:* The `db_table` attribute generates code behind-the-scenes to create an instance of `CTable` for accessing the specified table.

- *Lines 23 through 51:* These `db_column` attributes are used to determine which columns in the database table to associate with which members in the class. For example, the first column in the table is associated with, or bound to, the `m_productID` member variable.

Before you modify the code in Listing 16-1, you'll look at what you need to do to expose the data source cache to an ATL Server application in the next section.

Using the ATL Server Data Source Cache

The data source cache is available to the ATL Server application as a service by the ATL Server ISAPI extension. Recall that the ATL Server ISAPI extension is the code that routes requests to your ATL Server application. In many cases, you'll build one ATL Server ISAPI extension that can be used by numerous ATL Server applications.

You can add the data source cache service to your ATL Server ISAPI extension by simply choosing it as an option in the ATL Server Project Wizard, as shown in Figure 16-7.

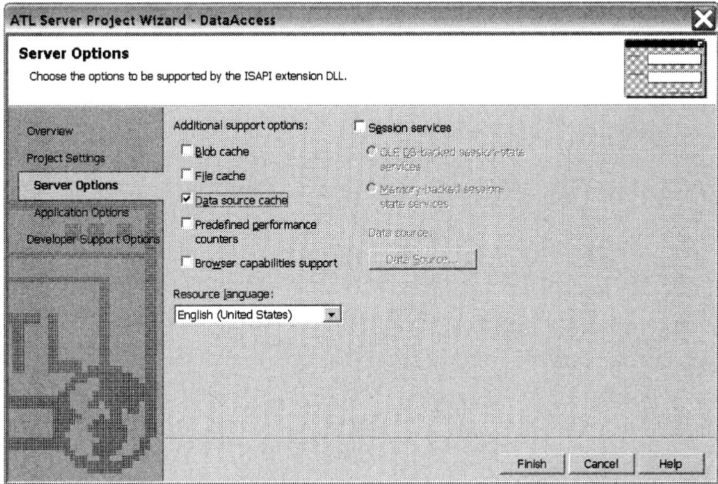

Figure 16-7. Adding the data source cache service in the ATL Server Project Wizard

Alternately, you can incorporate the code that you'll walk through in this chapter into your existing ATL Server ISAPI extension.

When you choose the data source cache option, the ATL Server Project Wizard generates the code in Listing 16-2.

Listing 16-2. Using the ATL Server Data Source Cache

```
#pragma once

#include <atlisapi.h>
#define _DATASOURCE_CACHE 1
// CDataAccessExtensionWorker - custom thread worker class
```

```
// for per-thread services

class CDataAccessExtensionWorker : public CIsapiWorker
{
    // per thread data source cache
    typedef CDataSourceCache<>      ds_cache_type;
    CComObjectGlobal<ds_cache_type> m_dsCache;

public:

    CDataAccessExtensionWorker()
    {
    }

    ~CDataAccessExtensionWorker()
    {
    }


    virtual BOOL GetWorkerData(DWORD dwParam, void **ppvData)
    {
        if (dwParam == _DATASOURCE_CACHE && ppvData)
        {
            *ppvData = (void *)&m_dsCache;
            m_dsCache.AddRef();
            return TRUE;
        }
        return FALSE;
    }
}; // class CDataAccessExtensionWorker

// CDataAccessExtension - the ISAPI extension class
template <class ThreadPoolClass=CThreadPool<CDataAccessExtensionWorker>,
          class CStatClass=CNoRequestStats,
          class HttpUserErrorTextProvider=CDefaultErrorProvider,
          class WorkerThreadTraits=DefaultThreadTraits >
          class CDataAccessExtension :
    public  CIsapiExtension<ThreadPoolClass,
            CStatClass,
            HttpUserErrorTextProvider,
            WorkerThreadTraits>
{

protected:
```

```

    typedef CIsapiExtension<ThreadPoolClass,
                            CStatClass,
                            HttpUserErrorTextProvider,
                            WorkerThreadTraits> baseISAPI;
    typedef CWorkerThread<WorkerThreadTraits> WorkerThreadClass;

public:

     BOOL GetExtensionVersion(HSE_VERSION_INFO* pVer)
     {
         if (!baseISAPI::GetExtensionVersion(pVer))
         {
             return FALSE;
         }
     }

     if (GetCriticalIsapiError() != 0)
     {
       return TRUE;
     }

     return TRUE;
    }

    BOOL TerminateExtension(DWORD dwFlags)
    {
        BOOL bRet = baseISAPI::TerminateExtension(dwFlags);
        return bRet;
    }

    HRESULT STDMETHODCALLTYPE QueryService(REFGUID guidService,
                                           REFIID  riid,
                                           void**  ppvObject)
    {
        if (InlineIsEqualGUID(guidService,
            __uuidof(IDataSourceCache)))
        {
            CIsapiWorker *pWorker = GetThreadWorker();
            if (pWorker)
            {
                CDataSourceCache<> *pCache = NULL;
                if (pWorker->GetWorkerData(_DATASOURCE_CACHE,
                                           (void **)&pCache))
```

```
94.              {
95.                  *ppvObject = static_cast<IDataSourceCache *>(pCache);
96.                  return S_OK;
97.              }
98.          }
99.      }
100.     return baseISAPI::QueryService(guidService,
101.                                    riid,
102.                                    ppvObject);
103. }
104.
105. virtual void OnThreadTerminate(DWORD /*dwThreadId*/)
106. {
107. }
108. }
```

Let's take a look at this code line-by-line:

- *Line 11:* The data source cache is implemented by the `CDataSourceCache` class. This class is actually a template; by default it doesn't do synchronization. If you want to use this class from multiple threads in the same request handler, then you should specify `CComCriticalSection` as a template parameter.

- *Line 12:* You'll make your instance of `CDataSourceCache` global to the application.

- *Lines 25 through 33:* The `GetWorkerData` method is called once for each worker thread. You want to increment the reference count so that it's in synch with the number of worker threads in the thread pool maintained by ATL Server.

- *Line 38:* You're using the `CDataAccessExtensionWorker` class in the thread pool instead of the default thread worker class.

- *Lines 81 through 103:* The `QueryService` method is how all services are exposed by an ATL Server ISAPI extension. Line 82 determines whether the service being queried is the data source cache service. If it is, you "get" the reference to the data source cache from the worker thread by calling `GetWorkerData` and returning that interface to the caller. This `if` statement contains a clause for each service your extension supports.

Now that you understand how a service is exposed by the ATL Server ISAPI extension, in the next section you'll look at how your ATL Server application can use this service.

Using the Data Source Cache Service

Using the data source cache in an ATL Server application is extremely simple. You can call the `GetDataSource` function (defined in atlcache.h) to get a pointer to a `CDataConnection` class as follows:

```
CDataConnection dc;
GetDataSource( m_spServiceProvider,
               _T("connection_string "),
               _T("connection_string"),
               &dc ))
```

This method will either return a `CDataConnection` object that was cached or create one and add it to the cache. The second parameter is the name given to the data source connection, and the third parameter is the connection string that the data source should use. For convenience, you should consider using the same value in both cases. That way, you can just use the connection string to reference the data source you're interested in.

In the next section you'll put everything you looked at in this chapter together and learn to use ATL Server's data source cache with OLE DB Consumer Templates and generate some HTML based on the data in your database.

Putting It All Together

You'll build a simple ATL Server application that displays some of the data in the Products table in the Northwind sample database provided by Microsoft.

The first step is to change your OLE DB Consumer Template so that it can be used with the ATL Server data source cache. You can do this by simply removing the `db_source` attribute. You'll want to do this so that your OLE DB Consumer Template won't create a data source on its own; rather, you want it to use the data source you provide. Your Products.h file now looks like Listing 16-3.

Listing 16-3. Modifications to the Generated OLE DB Consumer Template Code

```
#pragma once
[db_table(L"dbo.Products")]
class CProducts
{
public:
```

```
[ db_column(1,
          status=m_dwProductIDStatus,
          length=m_dwProductIDLength) ]   LONG m_ProductID;
[ db_column(2,
          status=m_dwProductNameStatus,
          length=m_dwProductNameLength) ] TCHAR m_ProductName[41];
[ db_column(3,
          status=m_dwSupplierIDStatus,
          length=m_dwSupplierIDLength) ] LONG m_SupplierID;
[ db_column(4,
          status=m_dwCategoryIDStatus,
          length=m_dwCategoryIDLength) ] LONG m_CategoryID;
[ db_column(5,
          status=m_dwQuantityPerUnitStatus,
          length=m_dwQuantityPerUnitLength) ]
          TCHAR m_QuantityPerUnit[21];
[ db_column(6,
          status=m_dwUnitPriceStatus,
          length=m_dwUnitPriceLength) ] CURRENCY m_UnitPrice;
[ db_column(7,
          status=m_dwUnitsInStockStatus,
          length=m_dwUnitsInStockLength) ] SHORT m_UnitsInStock;
[ db_column(8,
          status=m_dwUnitsOnOrderStatus,
          length=m_dwUnitsOnOrderLength) ] SHORT m_UnitsOnOrder;
[ db_column(9,
          status=m_dwReorderLevelStatus,
          length=m_dwReorderLevelLength) ] SHORT m_ReorderLevel;
[ db_column(10,
          status=m_dwDiscontinuedStatus,
          length=m_dwDiscontinuedLength) ]
          VARIANT_BOOL m_Discontinued;

// The following wizard-generated data members contain status
// values for the corresponding fields. You
// can use these values to hold NULL values that the database
// returns or to hold error information when the compiler returns
// errors. See Field Status Data Members in Wizard-Generated
// Accessors in the Visual C++ documentation for more information
// on using these fields.


DBSTATUS m_dwProductIDStatus;
DBSTATUS m_dwProductNameStatus;
```

```
    DBSTATUS m_dwSupplierIDStatus;
    DBSTATUS m_dwCategoryIDStatus;
    DBSTATUS m_dwQuantityPerUnitStatus;
    DBSTATUS m_dwUnitPriceStatus;
    DBSTATUS m_dwUnitsInStockStatus;
    DBSTATUS m_dwUnitsOnOrderStatus;
    DBSTATUS m_dwReorderLevelStatus;
    DBSTATUS m_dwDiscontinuedStatus;

    // The following wizard-generated data members contain length
    // values for the corresponding fields.
    // NOTE: For variable-length columns, you must initialize these
    //       fields before setting/inserting data!

    DBLENGTH m_dwProductIDLength;
    DBLENGTH m_dwProductNameLength;
    DBLENGTH m_dwSupplierIDLength;
    DBLENGTH m_dwCategoryIDLength;
    DBLENGTH m_dwQuantityPerUnitLength;
    DBLENGTH m_dwUnitPriceLength;
    DBLENGTH m_dwUnitsInStockLength;
    DBLENGTH m_dwUnitsOnOrderLength;
    DBLENGTH m_dwReorderLevelLength;
    DBLENGTH m_dwDiscontinuedLength;


    void GetRowsetProperties(CDBPropSet* pPropSet)
    {
        pPropSet->AddProperty(DBPROP_CANFETCHBACKWARDS,
                              true,
                              DBPROPOPTIONS_OPTIONAL);
        pPropSet->AddProperty(DBPROP_CANSCROLLBACKWARDS,
                              true,
                              DBPROPOPTIONS_OPTIONAL);
    }
};
```

The next step is to instantiate CProducts with a data source that you get from the ATL Server data source cache. You can do this in the ValidateAndExchange method in your ATL Server application request handler class. The code for your ATL Server application so far looks like Listing 16-4.

Listing 16-4. Reading Data from the Data Source

```
#pragma once

#define CONNECTION_STRINGW L"Provider=SQLOLEDB.1;\
                            Integrated Security=SSPI;\
                            Persist Security Info=False;\
                            Initial Catalog=Northwind;\
                            Data Source=testing\\vsdotnet;\
                            Use Procedure for Prepare=1;\
                            Auto Translate=True;\
                            Packet Size=4096;\
                            Workstation ID=TestMachine;\
                            Use Encryption for Data=False;

#define CONNECTION_STRINGT _T("Provider=SQLOLEDB.1;\
                             Integrated Security=SSPI;\
                             Persist Security Info=False;\
                             Initial Catalog=Northwind;\
                             Data Source=testing\\vsdotnet;\
                             Use Procedure for Prepare=1;\
                             Auto Translate=True;\
                             Packet Size=4096;\
                             Workstation ID=TestMachine;\
                             Use Encryption for Data=False;

[ request_handler("Default") ]
class CDataAccessHandler
{
private:
    CProducts m_products;

public:
    HTTP_CODE ValidateAndExchange()
    {
        m_HttpResponse.SetContentType("text/html");

        CDataConnection dataConnection;
        if( FAILED( GetDataSource( m_spServiceProvider,
                                   CONNECTION_STRINGT,
                                   CONNECTION_STRINGW,
                                   &dataConnection ) ) )
        {
            return HTTP_S_FALSE;
```

```
        }

        if( FAILED( m_products.Open( dataConnection ) ) )
        {
            return HTTP_S_FALSE;
        }

        if( FAILED( m_products.MoveFirst() ) )
        {
            return HTTP_S_FALSE;
        }

        return HTTP_SUCCESS;
    }
};
```

Most of this code has been assembled from what you've looked at throughout this chapter. At this point, if you haven't run into any errors, your ATL Server application will have a member, `m_products`, that will use a data connection from your cache and provide you access to the database specified by the `CONNECTION_STRINGT` connection string. This access will be made using a cached connection. The first time you access this ATL Server application, you'll create the connection and cache it. Subsequent requests to this application will use the cached data connection and not establish a new one. Thus, you suffer the overhead of connecting to a database only once.

Now that you have access to your database, you'll look at one way of displaying data from that connection. ATL Server's SRF syntax gives you a very convenient way of iterating over data.

The first tag that you add will determine whether or not you have data to display. Define the tag as follows and add it to your ATL Server application:

```
[tag_name( "HasMoreData" )]
HTTP_CODE OnHasMoreProducts()
{
    if( m_products.MoveNext() == DB_S_ENDOFROWSET )
    {
        return HTTP_SUCCESS;
    }
    else
    {
        return HTTP_S_FALSE;
    }
}
```

Let's look at this code line-by-line:

- *Line 1:* This attribute associates the SRF tag {{HasMoreData}} with this method. You can use this method in a {{while}} {{endwhile}} loop that will keep executing as long as you have rows in the database table.

- *Line 4:* The MoveNext method is used to iterate over the rows in a given result set. In this case, you're iterating over the rows in the Products table in your Northwind database. In your application, you may be iterating over the results returned by a stored procedure. In any case, this method will return DB_S_ENDOFROWSET when there are no more results. As long as there are more results, you want to return HTTP_SUCCESS.

In your SRF file, you can use this tag as follows:

```
{{while HasMoreResults}}
{{endwhile}}
```

This loop will allow you to iterate over each row in your table. This isn't very interesting yet because you haven't displayed any data from your table. Now introduce the following two methods into your ATL Server application:

```
[tag_name( "ProductName" )]
HTTP_CODE OnProductName()
{
    m_HttpResponse << m_products.m_ProductName;

    return HTTP_SUCCESS;
}

[tag_name( "ProductPrice" )]
HTTP_CODE OnProductPrice()
{
    m_HttpResponse << m_products.m_UnitPrice;

    return HTTP_SUCCESS;
}
```

These two methods demonstrate the power and simplicity of OLE DB Consumer Templates. Recall that the db_column attributes in the definition of the CProducts class determine which database columns are bound to which members.

In this case, the `m_ProductName` and `m_UnitPrice` members contain the product name and unit price of the current row in the Products table. When you call `m_products.MoveNext()`, the values of these member variables will be automatically updated to the values of the columns in the next row in your table. All of the work of binding these variables to these values is done by the OLE DB Consumer Templates library.

By putting each value in its own tag, you have a great deal of flexibility in the SRF file to decide how you want to display the data. For example, you can display your data in a table with the following SRF syntax:

```
<table border=1>
{{while HasMoreResults}}
    <tr><td>{{ProductName}}</td><td>${{UnitPrice}}</td></tr>
{{endwhile}}
</table>
```

This produces output that looks like that shown in Figure 16-8.

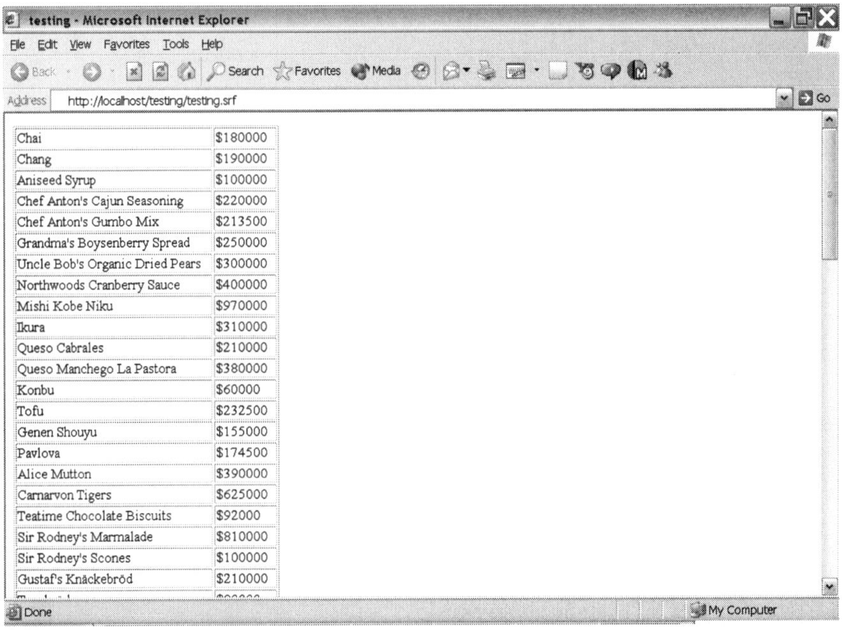
testing - Microsoft Internet Explorer
File Edit View Favorites Tools Help
Back Search Favorites Media
Address http://localhost/testing/testing.srf
Go
Chai $180000
Chang $190000
Aniseed Syrup $100000
Chef Anton's Cajun Seasoning $220000
Chef Anton's Gumbo Mix $213500
Grandma's Boysenberry Spread $250000
Uncle Bob's Organic Dried Pears $300000
Northwoods Cranberry Sauce $400000
Mishi Kobe Niku $970000
Ikura $310000
Queso Cabrales $210000
Queso Manchego La Pastora $380000
Konbu $60000
Tofu $232500
Genen Shouyu $155000
Pavlova $174500
Alice Mutton $390000
Carnarvon Tigers $625000
Teatime Chocolate Biscuits $92000
Sir Rodney's Marmalade $810000
Sir Rodney's Scones $100000
Gustaf's Knäckebröd $210000
Done
My Computer

Figure 16-8. Displaying data using SRF

Without changing any code, you can use the following SRF syntax to display your data in a list:

```
<ul>
{{while HasMoreResults}}
    <li>{{ProductName}}( ${{UnitPrice}} )
{{endwhile}}
</ul>
```

This code produces output that looks like that shown in Figure 16-9.

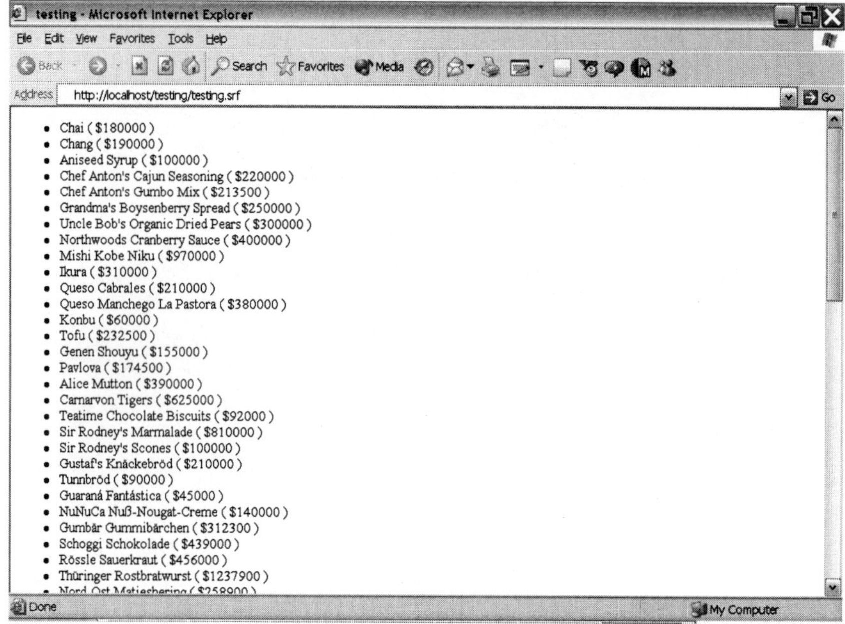

Figure 16-9. Sample output in a list

Breaking out each column value into its own SRF tag gives you the freedom to display your data in a number of ways without having to change code. In the real world, doing this allows you to give your Web designers a great deal of artistic freedom without having to change any code.

Conclusion

As you've seen, OLE DB Consumer Templates make it very easy and clean to access databases, and the wizard provided by Visual C++ .NET makes generating these templates trivial. With only minor changes, you can use these templates with the ATL Server data cache. Using this cache reduces the number of database connections your application needs to create, which is likely one of the most expensive operations your application will perform. Finally, the use of SRF tags allows you to display the data from your data source in a flexible manner. This combination of OLE DB Consumer Templates, SRF tags, and the ATL Server data source cache gives you an easy way to build data-driven Web applications that perform well under high loads.

By now you should have a pretty good understanding of how to build basic ATL Server applications. In the next chapter, you'll look at some of the inner workings of the ATL Server library and see how you can leverage and customize it to suit more advanced needs.

CHAPTER 17

Advanced SRF

NOW THAT WE'VE COVERED the basics of ATL Server SRF files and request handlers, we can examine more advanced areas; in particular, extending the stencil syntax for custom tags. Familiarity with the ATL Server stencil extensibility mechanisms will provide you with the tools to work around many of the issues and limitations you may encounter in writing your Web applications.

Extending Stencil Syntax

In this section we examine how to extend the ATL Server stencil syntax by adding custom tags and modifying the way existing tags work. We show you how to add several new control-flow tokens to demonstrate how you can override and extend the stencil syntax. You'll add the following control-flow tags:

- `if_and`: Same as the `if` tag, but the `if` block is entered only if *all* the statements in the conditional are `true` (hence `and`)
- `if_or`: Same as the `if` tag, but the `if` block is entered if *any* of the statements in the conditional are `true` (hence `or`)
- `if_not`: Same as the `if` tag, but the `if` block is entered only if the statement in the conditional is *not* `true`

Additionally, you'll add support to the `if_and` and `if_or` tags for `not` statements using the `!` syntax. That is, `{{if_and !tag1 tag2}}` evaluates to `true` only if `tag1` is *not* `true` and `tag2` is `true`. You'll also extend the `else` and `endif` tags to support the new conditional tags.

The ATL Server framework breaks up stencil processing into two parts: parsing the stencil and rendering the stencil. As we explained earlier, this parse-once model avoids the costs of parsing the stencil on every page hit. The top-level parsing method is `CStencil::ParseReplacements`, which in turn calls `CStencil::ParseToken` for each stencil tag that's encountered. You'll override `ParseToken` to handle your new tags and extend the `else` and `endif` tags. You'll also need to override `CStencil::FinishParseReplacements` to check for unclosed `if` blocks and other errors in the same way as the base `CStencil` class does.

The rendering of the stencil is handled in the `CStencil::Render` function, which in turn calls `CStencil::RenderToken` for each stencil token. You'll override `RenderToken` to handle the rendering of your new tags.

The first thing you need to do is define constants to represent your new tags:

```
#define STENCIL_ANDSTART        (STENCIL_USER_TOKEN_BASE + 0x00000001)
#define STENCIL_ANDPART         (STENCIL_USER_TOKEN_BASE + 0x00000002)
#define STENCIL_ORSTART         (STENCIL_USER_TOKEN_BASE + 0x00000003)
#define STENCIL_ORPART          (STENCIL_USER_TOKEN_BASE + 0x00000004)
#define STENCIL_IFNOT           (STENCIL_USER_TOKEN_BASE + 0x00000005)
```

Note that all the tags are based from `STENCIL_USER_TOKEN_BASE`, which is defined by the ATL Server framework and is meant to be used as a base for custom tags.

The next thing you need to do is derive a class from `CStencil` to handle your new tags. Because by default ATL Server request handlers derive from `CHtmlStencil` (which in turn derives from `CStencil`), you'll derive from `CHtmlStencil`. You'll call your new class `CCustomStencil`.

```
class CCustomStencil : public CHtmlStencil
{
public:

    CCustomStencil(IAtlMemMgr *pMemMgr) throw()
        :CHtmlStencil(pMemMgr)
    {
    }

       // omitted...
};
```

Then you need to override `ParseToken` to understand your new tags and override the behavior of the `endif` and `else` tags. You'll use the ATL Server support functions `SkipSpace` and `CheckTag` to verify your tags, as shown in Listing 17-1. If the token doesn't match one of your new tags or the tags you need to override, you'll delegate to the base class.

Listing 17-1. Overridden ParseToken Method

```
virtual PARSE_TOKEN_RESULT ParseToken(LPSTR szTokenStart,
        LPSTR szTokenEnd, DWORD *pBlockStack, DWORD *pdwTop) throw()
    {
        LPCSTR pStart = szTokenStart;
        pStart += 2; //skip curlies
        pStart = SkipSpace(pStart, GetCodePage());
        DWORD dwLen = (DWORD)(szTokenEnd - szTokenStart);
```

```
        int nIndex = -1;

        if (CheckTag("if_and", sizeof("if_and")-1, pStart, dwLen))
            nIndex = ParseAnd(szTokenStart, szTokenEnd, pBlockStack, pdwTop);
        else if (CheckTag("if_or", sizeof("if_or")-1, pStart, dwLen))
            nIndex = ParseOr(szTokenStart, szTokenEnd, pBlockStack, pdwTop);
        else if (CheckTag("endif", sizeof("endif")-1, pStart, dwLen))
            nIndex = ParseEndEx(szTokenStart, szTokenEnd, pBlockStack, pdwTop);
        else if (CheckTag("else", sizeof("else")-1, pStart, dwLen))
            nIndex = ParseElseEx(szTokenStart, szTokenEnd, pBlockStack, pdwTop);
        else if (CheckTag("if_not", sizeof("if_not")-1, pStart, dwLen))
            nIndex = ParseIfNot(szTokenStart, szTokenEnd, pBlockStack, pdwTop);
        else
        {
            // delegate to base class
            return __super::ParseToken(szTokenStart, szTokenEnd,
                pBlockStack, pdwTop);
        }

        if (nIndex < 0)
            return INVALID_TOKEN;
        return RESERVED_TOKEN;
    }
```

Now let's look at what you need to do implement one of these new tags in more detail. You'll take the simplest example first: `if_not`. All you need to do in this case is delegate to the ATL Server support function `ParseReplacement` with your custom token type `STENCIL_IFNOT`, as shown in Listing 17-2.

Listing 17-2. Overridden FinishParseReplacements Method

```
bool FinishParseReplacements() throw()
    {
        DWORD dwSize = GetTokenCount();

        // iterate over the tokens
        for (DWORD dwIndex = 0; dwIndex < dwSize; dwIndex++)
        {
            StencilToken& token = *(GetToken(dwIndex));

            // only modify the new tags
            bool bModify = (token.type == STENCIL_ANDPART ||
                token.type == STENCIL_ORPART ||
                token.type == STENCIL_IFNOT ||
```

```
        token.type == STENCIL_ANDSTART ||
        token.type == STENCIL_ORSTART);

    // unclosed blocks are conditional start
    // tags with the dwLoopIndex == STENCIL_INVALIDOFFSET
    bool bUnclosedBlock =
        ((token.type == STENCIL_ANDSTART ||
        token.type == STENCIL_ORSTART ||
        token.type == STENCIL_IFNOT)
        && token.dwLoopIndex == STENCIL_INVALIDOFFSET);

    if (bModify && token.szMethodName[0] &&
        (token.dwFnOffset == STENCIL_INVALIDOFFSET || bUnclosedBlock))
    {
        // if it is an unclosed block or if we cannot resolve the
        // replacement method, convert to text tags
        if (bUnclosedBlock ||
            m_pReplacer->FindReplacementOffset(
                token.szMethodName, &token.dwFnOffset,
                token.szHandlerName, &token.dwObjOffset,
                &token.dwMap,
                (void **)&token.dwData, m_pMemMgr) != HTTP_SUCCESS)
        {
            DWORD dwStartIndex = dwIndex;

            // if the token is STENCIL_ANDPART or STENCIL_ORPART,
            // find the start of the block
            if (token.type == STENCIL_ANDPART ||
                token.type == STENCIL_ORPART)
            {
                DWORD dwStartType =
                    (token.type == STENCIL_ANDPART ?
                    STENCIL_ANDSTART : STENCIL_ORSTART);
                DWORD dwStartIndex = dwIndex-1;

                while (IsValidIndex(dwStartIndex) &&
                    GetToken(dwStartIndex)->type != dwStartType)
                {
                    --dwStartIndex;
                }

                if (GetToken(dwStartIndex)->type != dwStartType)
                    dwStartIndex = dwIndex;
            }
```

```
        DWORD dwLoopIndex = GetToken(dwStartIndex)->dwLoopIndex;

        // if STENCIL_ANDSTART or STENCIL_ORSTART,
        // convert component tokens to STENCIL_CONDITIONALEND,
        // so they are skipped during rendering and set
        // szMethodName to an empty string, so it is ignored by
        // the base class's FinishParseReplacements
        if (GetToken(dwStartIndex)->type == STENCIL_ANDSTART ||
            GetToken(dwStartIndex)->type == STENCIL_ORSTART)
        {
            DWORD dwNextToken = dwIndex+1;
            while (dwNextToken != dwLoopIndex &&
                dwNextToken != STENCIL_INVALIDINDEX)
            {
                if (GetToken(dwNextToken)->type
                        == STENCIL_ANDPART ||
                    GetToken(dwNextToken)->type
                        == STENCIL_ORPART)
                {
                    GetToken(dwNextToken)->type =
                        STENCIL_CONDITIONALEND;
                    GetToken(dwNextToken)->szMethodName[0] = 0;
                }

                dwNextToken++;
            }
        }

        // unresolved replacement, convert it to a text token
        GetToken(dwStartIndex)->type = STENCIL_TEXTTAG;
        GetToken(dwStartIndex)->szMethodName[0] = 0;

        // convert all linked tokens to text tokens as well
        // this includes: endif, else, endwhile
        while (dwLoopIndex != dwIndex &&
            dwLoopIndex != STENCIL_INVALIDINDEX)
        {
            GetToken(dwLoopIndex)->type = STENCIL_TEXTTAG;
            GetToken(dwLoopIndex)->szMethodName[0] = 0;
            dwLoopIndex = GetToken(dwLoopIndex)->dwLoopIndex;
        }
    }
}
```

```
    }

    // call the base FinishParseReplacements to handle other tags
    return __super::FinishParseReplacements();
}
```

To render the new tags, override the RenderToken function, as shown in Listing 17-3. This function will check the token type and then delegate to RenderAnd, RenderOr, and RenderIfNot. If the token type isn't one of your new tokens, delegate to the base class implementation.

Listing 17-3. Overridden RenderToken Method

```
DWORD RenderToken(
        DWORD dwIndex,
        ITagReplacer* pReplacer,
        IWriteStream *pWriteStream,
        DWORD *pdwErrorCode,
        void* pState = NULL) const throw()
    {
        DWORD dwNextToken = STENCIL_INVALIDINDEX;
        DWORD dwErrorCode = HTTP_SUCCESS;
        const StencilToken* ptoken = GetToken(dwIndex);
        if (ptoken)
        {
            switch(ptoken->type)
            {
            case STENCIL_ANDSTART:
                // render the {{if_and ...}} tag
                dwNextToken = RenderAnd(dwIndex, pReplacer, &dwErrorCode);
                break;
            case STENCIL_ORSTART:
                // render the {{if_or ...}} tag
                dwNextToken = RenderOr(dwIndex, pReplacer, &dwErrorCode);
                break;
            case STENCIL_IFNOT:
                // render the {{if_not ...}} tag
                dwNextToken = RenderIfNot(dwIndex, pReplacer, &dwErrorCode);
                break;
            default:
                // delegate to the base class
                dwNextToken = __super::RenderToken(dwIndex, pReplacer,
                        pWriteStream, &dwErrorCode, (CStencilState *)pState);
                break;
```

```
        }
    }

    if (pdwErrorCode)
        *pdwErrorCode = dwErrorCode;

    return dwNextToken;
}
```

Note that even though you override the parsing of the `endif` and `else` tags, you don't need to override their runtime behavior.

The `RenderIfNot` function is effectively the same as rendering normal `if` blocks with the exception of the evaluation of the condition that determines if the block is entered (see Listing 17-4).

Listing 17-4. Rendering the if_not Tag

```
DWORD RenderIfNot(
        DWORD dwIndex,
        ITagReplacer *pReplacer,
        DWORD *pdwErrorCode) const throw()
    {
        const StencilToken* ptoken = GetToken(dwIndex);
        DWORD dwNextToken = STENCIL_INVALIDINDEX;
        DWORD dwErrorCode = HTTP_SUCCESS;

        if (!ptoken)
            return STENCIL_INVALIDINDEX;

        // ensure the function is valid
        if (ptoken->type == STENCIL_IFNOT &&
            ptoken->dwFnOffset == STENCIL_INVALIDINDEX)
        {
            dwErrorCode =
                HTTP_ERROR(500, ISE_SUBERR_STENCIL_INVALIDFUNCOFFSET);
        }
        else
        {
            // ensure that we end with an {{endif}} or an {{else}}
            if (ptoken->dwLoopIndex == STENCIL_INVALIDINDEX)
            {
                dwErrorCode =
                    HTTP_ERROR(500, ISE_SUBERR_STENCIL_MISMATCHIF);
            }
```

```
            else
            {
                // points to the end of the loop
                DWORD dwLoopIndex = ptoken->dwLoopIndex;

                // Call the replacement method.
                // If it returns HTTP_S_FALSE, we render everything up to
                //  the end of the conditional.
                // if it returns HTTP_SUCCESS, the condition is not met
                // and we render the else part if it exists or jump past
                // the endif otherwise
                DWORD dwErr = pReplacer->RenderReplacement(ptoken->dwFnOffset,
                    ptoken->dwObjOffset, ptoken->dwMap, (void *)ptoken->dwData);

                if (dwErr == HTTP_S_FALSE)
                {
                    // if the method returns false, execute the block
                    dwNextToken = dwIndex+1;
                    dwErrorCode = HTTP_SUCCESS;
                }
                else if (dwErr == HTTP_SUCCESS)
                {
                    // if the method returns true,
                    // jump to the end of the block
                    dwNextToken = dwLoopIndex+1;
                    dwErrorCode = HTTP_SUCCESS;
                }
                else
                {
                    // otherwise, an error occurred
                    dwNextToken = STENCIL_INVALIDINDEX;
                    dwErrorCode = dwErr;
                }
            }
        }

        if (pdwErrorCode)
            *pdwErrorCode = dwErrorCode;

        return dwNextToken;
    }
```

For rendering `if_and` and `if_or`, you need to handle the multiple statements in the conditional as well as potential `!` (not) conditions in the statement. You simply loop over the statements and call the replacement methods, as shown in Listing 17-5. Depending on whether it's an `and` or an `or`, you short-circuit on first success or first failure.

Listing 17-5. Rendering the if_and Tag

```
DWORD RenderAnd(
        DWORD dwIndex,
        ITagReplacer *pReplacer,
        DWORD *pdwErrorCode) const throw()
    {
        const StencilToken* ptoken = GetToken(dwIndex);
        DWORD dwNextToken = STENCIL_INVALIDINDEX;
        DWORD dwErrorCode = HTTP_SUCCESS;

        if (!ptoken)
            return STENCIL_INVALIDINDEX;

        // ensure that the function offset is valid
        if (ptoken->type == STENCIL_ANDSTART &&
            ptoken->dwFnOffset == STENCIL_INVALIDINDEX)
        {
            dwErrorCode =
                HTTP_ERROR(500, ISE_SUBERR_STENCIL_INVALIDFUNCOFFSET);
        }
        else
        {
            // ensure that we end with and {{endif}} or and {{else}}
            if (ptoken->dwLoopIndex == STENCIL_INVALIDINDEX)
            {
                dwErrorCode = HTTP_ERROR(500, ISE_SUBERR_STENCIL_MISMATCHIF);
            }
            else
            {
                // points to the end of the loop
                DWORD dwLoopIndex = ptoken->dwLoopIndex;
                DWORD dwErr;

                // loop over the components of the if_and
                do
                {
                    // call the replacement method
```

```
        dwErr = pReplacer->RenderReplacement(ptoken->dwFnOffset,
            ptoken->dwObjOffset,
            ptoken->dwMap,
            (void *)ptoken->dwData);

        // check if it is '! <method_name>' call
        if (ptoken->dwData)
        {
            // invert the return code
            if (dwErr == HTTP_S_FALSE)
                dwErr = HTTP_SUCCESS;
            else if (dwErr == HTTP_SUCCESS)
                dwErr = HTTP_S_FALSE;
        }

        // short-circuit on failure
        if (dwErr)
            break;

        // go to the next token
        dwIndex++;

        // ensure that the token is valid
        if (STENCIL_SUCCESS == (dwErrorCode = IsValidIndex(dwIndex)))
        {
            ptoken = GetToken(dwIndex);
        }
        else
        {
            dwErr = dwErrorCode;
            break;
        }

        // loop until we reach the end of the {{if_and ...}} methods
    } while (ptoken->type == STENCIL_ANDPART);

    if (!dwErr)
    {
        // if successful, dwIndex is the index of the
        // first token inside the {{if_and ...}} block
        dwNextToken = dwIndex;
        dwErrorCode = HTTP_SUCCESS;
    }
```

```
            else if (dwErr == HTTP_S_FALSE)
            {
                // if we failed, jump to the end of the block
                // ({{else}} or {{endif}})
                // and increment by one
                dwNextToken = dwLoopIndex+1;
                dwErrorCode = HTTP_SUCCESS;
            }
            else
            {
                // an error has occurred
                dwNextToken = STENCIL_INVALIDINDEX;
                dwErrorCode = dwErr;
            }
        }
    }

    if (pdwErrorCode)
        *pdwErrorCode = dwErrorCode;

    return dwNextToken;
}
```

You have now successfully added all the code necessary to parse and render your new tags. To use the new tags in an ATL Server request handler, you need to specify the stencil type, as shown in Listing 17-6.

Listing 17-6. Overriding the StencilType Template Parameter

```
class CMyHandler :
    public CRequestHandlerT<
        CMyHandler,
        CComSingleThreadModel,
        CHtmlTagReplacer<CMyHandler, CCustomStencil> >
{
// normal request handler code...

}; // class CMyHandler
```

Now `CMyHandler` can use the new tags in all SRF files that refer to it.

Overriding File Extensions

In many cases, it's desirable to use a file extension other than .srf for your server response files. The ATL Server framework makes this easy to do. All that you need to do is override the ATL_DEFAULT_STENCIL_EXTENSION macro. There are certain constraints, however. You must override it directly to a string and not to a variable. That is,

```
#define ATL_DEFAULT_STENCIL_EXTENSION ".myext"
```

is acceptable, whereas

```
#define ATL_DEFAULT_STENCIL_EXTENSION s_szExt
```

is not acceptable (where s_szExt is a string variable).

Additionally, you must override the ATL_DEFAULT_STENCIL_EXTENSION macro consistently. That is, all request handler and ISAPI projects must contain this #define, or else inconsistent behavior will occur.

Similarly, you can override the .dll extension using the ATL_DEFAULT_DLL_EXTENSION macro. The same rules that apply to the .srf extension also apply to the .dll extension.

Conclusion

In this chapter, you learned how to customize SRF files. You saw how it's possible to extend and modify the stencil syntax to handle custom tags. You also saw how it's possible to modify the extensions that are accepted by the ATL Server framework for .srf files and .dll files. Familiarity with these techniques can help you overcome obstacles you may encounter due to limitations in the default framework support.

In this chapter you took a close look at some of the advanced features that the SRF model provides. In the next chapter you'll take a similar look at request handlers. In particular you'll examine the classes that ATL Server provides and how you can extend them to customize your request handlers to handle any task.

CHAPTER 18

Advanced Request Handlers

THE ATL SERVER INFRASTRUCTURE is designed so that you can easily choose the level of complexity that's suited to your needs or that you're comfortable working with. In this chapter, we explore ways of increasing this level of complexity and illustrate how doing so can help you develop your application.

The classes that make up ATL Server's infrastructure generally use a combination of template parameters and interfaces to allow you to configure them. By providing a class that follows the archetype of a given template parameter, you as an ATL Server developer can easily extend the functionality of ATL Server. By obtaining pointers to various interfaces that ATL Server exposes, you can obtain information about your application as it's running. The Visual Studio and MSDN documentation for ATL Server does an excellent job of detailing these template parameter archetypes and interfaces.

In this chapter, we focus on an example that illustrates how you can use these archetypes and interfaces to add richer functionality to your ATL Server application. The ATL Server infrastructure processes requests using a thread pool. The default implementation of this thread pool uses a static number of threads that wait on an I/O completion port. The example we present in this chapter follows this model, but the thread pool will increase the number of threads dynamically based on the load of the server.

This example isn't intended to be a comprehensive illustration of the different ways you can extend ATL Server, nor is it intended to meet production-level comprehensiveness and quality. The example dynamic thread pool is just meant to introduce and illustrate some techniques that you can apply to your own ATL Server applications. Let's take a look at how you can implement this example.

Creating a Thread Pool

The thread pool for this example will size itself based on the following conditions when a request is received:

- If the CPU utilization is less than 20 percent and there are no free threads, then add another thread before adding the request to the queue. This will keep the CPU busy processing as many requests as possible.

- If the CPU utilization is equal to or greater than 80 percent, shut down a thread before adding the request to the queue. This will slow down the number of requests that you process (causing more to be queued) and hopefully give the CPU more time to concentrate on finishing the requests it's already processing.

This is a pretty basic algorithm, but it presents a good opportunity to illustrate how you can add and remove threads from the thread pool as well as obtain information about a running ATL Server application.

To implement this dynamic thread pool, you're going to have to be able to do the following:

- You need to determine the maximum number of threads that your dynamic thread pool can support at any given time.

- You need to be able to determine how many threads are being used to process requests at any given time.

- You need to be able to determine what the CPU utilization is at any given moment.

- You need to be able to add or subtract threads from your thread pool.

Luckily, you have the `CThreadPool` class to derive from to save you the work necessary to set up a thread pool. This lets you concentrate on implementing the preceding items. The code that you'll look at as you move through each of these sections has comments and error checking removed. This keeps the code shorter and easier to read. Please see the end of this section for a complete listing of the example.

Let's take a look at how you'll declare your thread pool class:

```
template <class Worker = CIsapiWorker,
        class ThreadTraits = DefaultThreadTraits >
class CDynamicThreadPool :
    public CThreadPool< Worker, ThreadTraits >
{
}
```

As you can see, the template signature matches that of the `CThreadPool` class. This makes it very easy to drop in your new thread pool class where you previously used `CThreadPool`.

The `CThreadPool` class has an initialization method declared as follows:

```
HRESULT Initialize(void      *pvWorkerParam=NULL,
                   int       nNumThreads=0,
                   DWORD     dwStackSize=0,
                   HANDLE    hCompletion=INVALID_HANDLE_VALUE)
                   throw()
```

You'll override this method to insert some initialization code. For this example, you'll use this method to initialize the code that you need to dynamically size your thread pool.

Runtime ATL Server Information

As we previously discussed, in order to decide whether you need to add or remove threads from your thread pool, you need to know whether or not there are any free threads in the pool. This information, as well as other pieces of information, is available from the `IRequestStats` interface. This information is defined as follows:

```
IRequestStats : public IUnknown
{
    long GetTotalRequests();
    long GetFailedRequests();
    long GetAvgResponseTime();
    long GetCurrWaiting();
    long GetMaxWaiting();
    long GetActiveThreads();
};
```

You'll call the `GetActiveThreads()` method to determine how many threads are occupied with requests.

In order to get a pointer to the `IRequestStats` interface, you first need a pointer to the `IIsapiExtension` interface. Luckily, a pointer to this interface is passed as the first parameter to the `CThreadPool::Initialize` method. This `IIsapiExtension` pointer is passed as a `void*`, so you'll have to cast it first. After that, you just need to call `QueryInterface` to get a pointer to `IRequestStats`. You'll store the pointer to this interface as a class member so you can use it when you're processing requests to the thread pool. The code for all of this is as follows (with error checking omitted for conciseness):

```
IIsapiExtension *isapiExtension = NULL;
isapiExtension = static_cast<IIsapiExtension*> (pvWorkerParam);

isapiExtension->QueryInterface(__uuidof(IRequestStats),
        (void**)&m_requestStats)));
```

You don't want to indiscriminately add threads as requests come in, so your next step is to determine how many threads the server that you're running on can support. You'll use a simple formula to determine this value. The maximum number of threads your pool can support will be 25 threads per CPU. You can determine the number of processors your server has using a call to `GetSystemInfo`. The code for doing so is as follows:

```
SYSTEM_INFO systemInfo;
ZeroMemory(&systemInfo, sizeof(SYSTEM_INFO));

GetSystemInfo(&systemInfo);
m_maxThreads =  systemInfo.dwNumberOfProcessors * CPU_MAX_THREADS;
```

The final piece of initialization code that you need is code to read the CPU utilization of your server. You'll use the performance counter API to read the `% Processor Time` performance counter to determine the CPU utilization of your server at any given time. Here's the code necessary to initialize the performance counter API:

```
PDH_STATUS pdhStatus = PdhOpenQuery(NULL, NULL, &m_pdhQuery);

PDH_COUNTER_PATH_ELEMENTS pdhPathElements[1];
pdhPathElements[0].dwInstanceIndex  = (DWORD)-1;
pdhPathElements[0].szCounterName    = TEXT("% Processor Time");
pdhPathElements[0].szInstanceName   = TEXT("_Total");
pdhPathElements[0].szMachineName    = NULL;
pdhPathElements[0].szObjectName     = TEXT("Processor");
pdhPathElements[0].szParentInstance = NULL;

DWORD counterPathSize = 0;
pdhStatus = PdhMakeCounterPath(pdhPathElements,
                               NULL,
                               &counterPathSize,
                               NULL);
```

```
TCHAR *counterPath = NULL;
counterPath = new TCHAR[counterPathSize];

pdhStatus = PdhMakeCounterPath(pdhPathElements,
                               counterPath,
                               &counterPathSize,
                               NULL);
m_pdhCounter = NULL;
pdhStatus = PdhAddCounter(m_pdhQuery,
                          counterPath,
                          NULL,
                          &m_pdhCounter);
```

You still want the default implementation of CThreadPool::Initialize, to be called, so finish by calling the base implementation and returning:

```
return __super::Initialize(pvWorkerParam, nNumThreads, dwStackSize, hCompletion);
```

With your initialization out of the way, you only need to implement the logic necessary for adding or removing threads from your pool. You can make this decision as each request comes in.

Dynamically Sizing a Thread Pool

The CThreadPool::QueueRequest method is called to queue requests into the thread pool. You'll overload this method to insert your dynamic sizing code. This method is defined as follows:

```
BOOL QueueRequest(Worker::RequestType request) throw()

// Implementing our logic to determine whether
// to add or remove threads from our pool is actually quite simple:

LONG processorTime = GetProcessorTime();
if (processorTime >= CPU_UPPER_THRESHOLD)
{
    int numThreads = 0;
    if (SUCCEEDED(GetSize(&numThreads)) && numThreads > 1)
    {
        SetSize(numThreads - 1 );
    }
```

```
    }
    else if (processorTime <= CPU_LOWER_THRESHOLD)
    {
        int numThreads = 0;
        if ( SUCCEEDED(GetSize(&numThreads)) &&
             m_requestStats->GetActiveThreads() == numThreads &&
             numThreads < m_maxThreads)
        {
            SetSize(numThreads + 1);
        }
    }
```

You first get the CPU utilization. If that utilization is equal to or greater than your upper threshold, which is determined to be 80 percent, then you want to reduce the number of threads that you have by one. You do, however, always want to have at least one thread in your pool.

If the CPU utilization is less than or equal to your lower threshold, which is determined to be 20 percent, and there are no free threads, then you want to increment the number of threads in your pool by one. Of course, you do this only if you haven't exceeded the maximum number of threads that you've set for yourself.

No matter if you've added or removed threads, you want to finish by calling the base implementation of `QueueRequest` to actually queue the request:

```
return __super::QueueRequest( request );
```

That's all the code necessary to implement a dynamic thread pool class in ATL Server. Listing 18-1 shows the complete example.

Listing 18-1. Implementing a Dynamic Thread Pool Class

```
#pragma once

#include <atlisapi.h>
#include <atlutil.h>
#include <windows.h>
#include <pdh.h>

//
// Remove one thread per request if CPU usage is equal to or higher
// than this value.
//
#define CPU_UPPER_THRESHOLD 80
```

```
//
// Add one thread per request if CPU usage is equal to or lower than
// this value.
//
#define CPU_LOWER_THRESHOLD 20

//
// Limit the maximum number of threads per CPU to this value.
//
#define CPU_MAX_THREADS     25

/////////////////////////////////////////////////////////////////
// CDynamicThreadPool - This class extends the functionality
// of CThreadPool by dynamically resizing itself when it
// receives a request based on the following criteria:
//
//       - If the CPU usage is less than or equal to a certain
//         CPU usage percentage (CPU_LOWER_THRESHOLD),
//         there are no free threads, and we have not reached
//         our maximum (CPU_MAX_THREADS), add another thread
//         to the pool before queuing the request.
//
//       - If the CPU usage is equal to or higher than a certain
//         CPU usage percentage (CPU_UPPER_THRESHOLD), then
//         remove 1 thread from the pool before queuing the
//         request.
/////////////////////////////////////////////////////////////////
template <class Worker       = CIsapiWorker,
          class ThreadTraits = DefaultThreadTraits >
          class CDynamicThreadPool :
        public CThreadPool< Worker, ThreadTraits >
{
private:
    PDH_HQUERY             m_pdhQuery;
    PDH_HCOUNTER           m_pdhCounter;
    int                    m_maxThreads;
    CComPtr<IRequestStats> m_requestStats;

public:
    CDynamicThreadPool() :
        m_pdhQuery(NULL),
        m_pdhCounter(NULL),
        m_maxThreads(0),
        CThreadPool< Worker, ThreadTraits>()
```

```
{
}

//
// We need to do the following types of additional
// initialization:
//
// 1. Get and keep a pointer to IRequestStats from
//    pvWorkerParam.
// 2. Set the maximum number of threads we can create
//    based on the number of CPUs.
// 3. Set up PDH handles so that we can query the
//    processor time performance object.
//
// No matter what, always return the base implementation
// of Initialize
//
HRESULT Initialize(void      *pvWorkerParam=NULL,
                   int       nNumThreads=0,
                   DWORD     dwStackSize=0,
                   HANDLE    hCompletion=INVALID_HANDLE_VALUE)
                   throw()
{
    //
    // 1. Get and keep a pointer to IRequestStats from
    //    pvWorkerParam.
    //
    if (!pvWorkerParam)
    {
        //
        // If we can't get the IRequestStats pointer, don't
        // bother doing the rest of the initialization.
        //
        goto error;
    }

    IIsapiExtension *isapiExtension = NULL;
    isapiExtension = static_cast<IIsapiExtension*> (pvWorkerParam);

    if (FAILED(isapiExtension->QueryInterface(__uuidof(IRequestStats),
                                              (void**)&m_requestStats)))
    {
        //
        // If we can't get the IRequestStats pointer, don't bother
```

```
        // doing the rest of the initialization.
        //
        goto error;
    }

    //
    // 2. Set the maximum number of threads we can create based on the
    //    number of CPUs.
    //
    SYSTEM_INFO systemInfo;
    ZeroMemory(&systemInfo, sizeof(SYSTEM_INFO));

    GetSystemInfo(&systemInfo);
    m_maxThreads = systemInfo.dwNumberOfProcessors * CPU_MAX_THREADS;

    //
    // 3. Set up PDH handles so that we can query the processor time
    //    performance object.
    //

    //
    // Clean PDH handles just in case.
    //
    CleanPdh();

    PDH_STATUS pdhStatus = PdhOpenQuery(NULL, NULL, &m_pdhQuery);
    if (pdhStatus !=  ERROR_SUCCESS)
    {
        goto error;
    }

    //
    // Build a path to the processor time performance object.
    //
    PDH_COUNTER_PATH_ELEMENTS pdhPathElements[1];

    pdhPathElements[0].dwInstanceIndex  = (DWORD)-1;
    pdhPathElements[0].szCounterName    = TEXT("% Processor Time");
    pdhPathElements[0].szInstanceName   = TEXT("_Total");
    pdhPathElements[0].szMachineName    = NULL;
    pdhPathElements[0].szObjectName     = TEXT("Processor");
    pdhPathElements[0].szParentInstance = NULL;

    //
```

```
// Get the size of the path.
//
DWORD counterPathSize = 0;
pdhStatus = PdhMakeCounterPath(pdhPathElements,
                               NULL,
                               &counterPathSize,
                               NULL);
if (pdhStatus !=  ERROR_SUCCESS)
{
    goto error;
}

//
// Allocate room for the counter path.
//
TCHAR *counterPath = NULL;
counterPath = new TCHAR[counterPathSize];
if (!counterPath)
{
    goto error;
}

//
// Get the counter path.
//
pdhStatus = PdhMakeCounterPath(pdhPathElements,
                               counterPath,
                               &counterPathSize,
                               NULL);
if (pdhStatus !=  ERROR_SUCCESS)
{
    goto error;
}

//
// Add the processor time counter to our query.
//
m_pdhCounter = NULL;
pdhStatus = PdhAddCounter(m_pdhQuery,
                          counterPath,
                          NULL,
                          &m_pdhCounter);
if (pdhStatus !=  ERROR_SUCCESS)
{
```

```
            goto error;
        }

        //
        // If we got here, we were successful
        //
        goto success;
error:
        //
        // If we failed, clean up our handles.
        //
        CleanPdh();

success:
        if (counterPath)
        {
            delete[] counterPath;
            counterPath = NULL;
        }

        //
        // Return the base initialization.
        //
        return __super::Initialize(pvWorkerParam,
                                   nNumThreads,
                                   dwStackSize,
                                   hCompletion);
    }

    virtual ~CDynamicThreadPool()
    {
        CleanPdh();
    }

    //
    // Override QueueRequest function to include dynamic size analysis.
    //
    BOOL QueueRequest(Worker::RequestType request) throw()
    {
        //
        // Get our current CPU utilization
        //
        LONG processorTime = GetProcessorTime();
```

```
        if (processorTime >= CPU_UPPER_THRESHOLD)
        {
            //
            // If we match our upper CPU utilization, shut down a thread
            // before queuing this request. This will hopefully slow
            // down the number of requests we are processing, which will
            // give the CPU a chance to recover and process the currently
            // executing requests.
            //
            int numThreads = 0;
            if (SUCCEEDED(GetSize(&numThreads)) && numThreads > 1)
            {
                SetSize(numThreads - 1 );
            }
        }
        else if (processorTime <= CPU_LOWER_THRESHOLD)
        {
            //
            // Otherwise, if we match the lower CPU utilization boundary,
            // look at the number of active threads.
            // If there are no free threads and we have not reached our
            // maximum number of threads, add another thread to the pool
            // before queuing this current request.
            //
            int numThreads = 0;
            if (SUCCEEDED(GetSize(&numThreads))                  &&
                m_requestStats->GetActiveThreads() == numThreads &&
                numThreads < m_maxThreads)
            {
                SetSize(numThreads + 1);
            }
        }

        return __super::QueueRequest( request );
    }

private:
    LONG GetProcessorTime()
    {
        LONG                 processorTime = 0;
        PDH_FMT_COUNTERVALUE pdhCounterValue;
        ZeroMemory(&pdhCounterValue, sizeof(PDH_FMT_COUNTERVALUE));

        if (PdhCollectQueryData(m_pdhQuery) == ERROR_SUCCESS)
```

```
        {
            if (PdhGetFormattedCounterValue(m_pdhCounter,
                                            PDH_FMT_LONG,
                                            NULL,
                                            &pdhCounterValue))
            {
                processorTime = pdhCounterValue.longValue;
            }
        }

        return processorTime;
    }

    void CleanPdh()
    {
        if (m_pdhCounter != NULL)
        {
            PdhRemoveCounter(m_pdhCounter);
        }

        if (m_pdhQuery != NULL)
        {
            PdhCloseQuery(m_pdhQuery);
        }
    }
};
```

Conclusion

The small example that you've looked at in this chapter is only one extension of ATL Server. You should be able to apply the techniques we've covered here in your applications to suit your needs. Even if you have no need to extend ATL Server, the `IRequestStats` interface is a good, nonintrusive way of obtaining information about your application as it's running—one more way that ATL Server helps you build high-performance, high-availability applications.

In Chapter 10 we presented an overview of the ATL Server Web service support, and as you might have expected, ATL Server provides a lot more power and flexibility. In the next chapter we take a more advanced look at Web services and drill down into some of the more powerful functionality the library provides.

CHAPTER 19

Advanced Web Services

NOW THAT YOU'VE COVERED the basics of ATL Server Web services, you can examine more advanced areas, such as integrating Web services and COM, Web service interoperability issues, custom transports, extensibility mechanisms, and implementation internals. Familiarity with these advanced techniques and implementation details will provide you with tools to take advantage of the flexibility and power of ATL Server Web services to work around almost any of the issues you'll undoubtedly come across in writing new Web services or taking advantage of Web services in existing code.

ATL Server and COM

In this section you'll examine how you can integrate ATL Server Web services with COM. The examples and techniques described in this section apply when you're moving existing COM objects to take advantage of Web services, or when you're writing new objects that function both as COM objects and Web services.

COM Attributes

In addition to the ATL Server attributes described in earlier chapters, Visual C++ .NET provides attributes that simplify the task of creating COM objects. As with the ATL Server attributes, under the covers the COM attributes inject C++ code for the COM objects. You can view the injected code the same way you can view the ATL Server attributed injected code: by using the `/Fx` switch on the compiler or by going to Project ➤ Properties ➤ C/C++ ➤ Output Files and choosing Yes for Expand Attributed Source.

Listing 19-1 shows a simple attributed ATL COM object.

Listing 19-1. An Attributed COM Object

```
// HelloWorld.h : Defines the ATL Server request handler class
//
#pragma once
[ emitidl(true) ];

// disable warning about IRequestHandler not being emitted to IDL
#pragma warning(disable:4096)
```

```
[
    uuid("14FC0AE5-0900-4D88-AB69-D721B13F5479"),
    object,

    // Add the following attributes
    dual
]
__interface IHelloWorldService
{
   [id(1)] HRESULT HelloWorld([in] BSTR bstrInput, [out, retval] BSTR *bstrOutput);
};

[
    request_handler(name="Default", sdl="GenHelloWorld1WSDL"),
    soap_handler(
        name="HelloWorld1Service",
        namespace="urn:HelloWorld1Service",
        protocol="soap"
    ),

    // Add the following attributes
    coclass,
    progid("HelloWordService.1"),
    uuid("8C9D14D0-A82E-424F-9A61-6293AAE11EF0")
]
class CHelloWorldService :
    public IHelloWorldService
{
public:

    DECLARE_PROTECT_FINAL_CONSTRUCT()

    HRESULT FinalConstruct()
    {
        return S_OK;
    }

    void FinalRelease()
    {
    }

    [ soap_method ]
   HRESULT HelloWorld(/*[in]*/ BSTR bstrInput, /*[out, retval]*/ BSTR *bstrOutput)
    {
```

```
        CComBSTR bstrOut(L"Hello ");
        bstrOut += bstrInput;
        bstrOut += L"!";
        *bstrOutput = bstrOut.Detach();

        return S_OK;
    }
};


// HelloWorld.cpp : Defines the entry point for the DLL application.
//

#include "stdafx.h"
// For custom assert and trace handling with WebDbg.exe
#ifdef _DEBUG
CDebugReportHook g_ReportHook;
#endif

#include "HelloWorld.h"

[ module(
         name="MyHelloWorld",
         type="dll",

         // add the following parameters
         uuid = "{7BC54312-5149-4D14-9562-0618DA510BC9}",
         helpstring = "HelloWorld 1.0 Type Library"
         ),
]
class CDllMainOverride
{
public:
    BOOL WINAPI DllMain(DWORD dwReason, LPVOID lpReserved)
    {
#if defined(_M_IX86)
        if (dwReason == DLL_PROCESS_ATTACH)
        {
            // stack overflow handler
            _set_security_error_handler( AtlsSecErrHandlerFunc );
        }
#endif
        return __super::DllMain(dwReason, lpReserved);
    }
};
```

We created Listing 19-1 as a normal ATL Server Web service named "HelloWorld" and made the following modifications:

- Stdafx.h was modified to remove the `_ATL_NO_COM_SUPPORT` macro, as you'll be using COM.
- `[ emitidl(restricted) ];` was removed from HelloWorld.h (it appears after the class definition).
- `[ emitidl(true) ];` was added to the top of HelloWorld.h.
- The `dual` attribute was added to the interface definition.
- The `coclass`, `progid`, and `uuid` attributes were added to the class definition.
- The `uuid` and `helpstring` parameters were added to the `module` attribute.

As with the ATL Server SOAP attributes, the COM attributes make use of embedded IDL and are broken up into interface definition and class implementation. Adding Web service support to the example in Listing 19-1 would simply be a matter of adding the `soap_handler` and `request_handler` attributes to the class definition and adding `soap_method` attributes to the methods that are to be exposed via SOAP. You'll examine that technique in more detail in later sections of this chapter, but first we present a brief overview of the COM attributes used in the example:

- `emitidl`: This attribute controls whether all attributes following its declaration will be included in the compiler-generated IDL file. atlsoap.h defaults to `[emitidl(restricted)];` which can subsequently be overridden to true or false; once an `emitidl` with true or false has been declared, it can't be overridden.
- `dual`: The compiler will include the interface on which this attribute appears in the library block of its generated IDL file.
- `coclass`: This attribute marks the class on which it appears as a COM object.
- `progid`: This attribute specifies the programmatic identifier (ProgID) for the COM object defined by the class on which it appears.
- `uuid`: This attribute defines the universal unique identifier (UUID) for the COM object defined by the class on which it appears or, in the case of the `module` attribute, for the type library for the DLL.

There are additional attributes for version-independent ProgIDs, control of the threading model, and other functionality. We don't go into further detail on the COM attributes here because they don't apply to the interaction between Web services and COM. Consult the Visual Studio .NET documentation for more information.

All you need to do to add COM support to an ATL Server Web service is add the previously listed attributes. It's also just as easy to add Web service support to an attributed ATL COM object. After you create an ATL project and add a simple ATL object to it using the Add Class Wizard, simply add the `soap_handler` and `request_handler` attributes to the coclass definition. Listing 19-2 presents an example.

Listing 19-2. A Dual COM Object and Web Service

```
// MyObject.h : Declaration of the CMyObject

#pragma once
#include "resource.h"       // main symbols
#include <atlsoap.h>
[ emitidl(true) ];


// IMyObject
[
    object,
    uuid("0CA838BD-9423-4B78-8B3A-1E4B9698525B"),
    dual,    helpstring("IMyObject Interface"),
    pointer_default(unique)
]
__interface IMyObject : IDispatch
{
    [id(1)] HRESULT HelloWorld([in] BSTR bstrIn, [out, retval] BSTR *bstrOut);
};



// CMyObject

[
    coclass,
    threading("apartment"),
    vi_progid("BasicCOM.MyObject"),
    progid("BasicCOM.MyObject.1"),
```

```
    version(1.0),
    uuid("D958904B-F324-496A-9DB9-016F01D5BAF3"),
    helpstring("MyObject Class"),

    // Add these additional attributes
    request_handler(name="Default", sdl="GenWSDL"),
    soap_handler(name="MyObject")
]
class ATL_NO_VTABLE CMyObject :
    public IMyObject
{
public:
    CMyObject()
    {
    }


    DECLARE_PROTECT_FINAL_CONSTRUCT()

    HRESULT FinalConstruct()
    {
        return S_OK;
    }

    void FinalRelease()
    {
    }

    // add the soap_method attribute to the interface method implementation
    [ soap_method ]
    HRESULT HelloWorld(BSTR bstrIn, BSTR *bstrOut)
    {
        CComBSTR bstrRet = L"Hello ";
        bstrRet+= bstrIn;
        bstrRet+= "!";

        *bstrOut = bstrRet.Detach();

        return S_OK;
    }

public:

};
```

The project in Listing 19-2 was generated using the ATL Server Project Wizard and then using the Add Class Wizard to add an ATL simple object named `MyObject`. To add Web service support, the `request_handler` and `soap_handler` attributes were added.

You can now invoke the object through COM:

```
Dim obj
set obj = WScript.CreateObject( "BasicCOM.MyObject" )
strRet = obj.HelloWorld("Joe")
WScript.Echo(strRet)
```

And you can invoke it through SOAP:

```
#define _WIN32_WINNT 0x0500
#include <stdio.h>
#include "MyObject.h"

int main()
{
    CoInitialize(NULL);
    {
        MyObject::CMyObject obj;
        CComBSTR bstrRet;
        HRESULT hr = obj.HelloWorld(CComBSTR("Joe"), &bstrRet);
        if (SUCCEEDED(hr))
        {
            printf("%ws\n", bstrRet);
        }
    }
    CoUninitialize();
}
```

Objects that expose user-defined data types have a little more work to do. You'll examine this in next section.

User-Defined Types

The same type limitations on ATL Server Web services described in the earlier chapters still apply. When you use user-defined types (UDTs), you need to add the `export` attribute to the type definition if you want the type to be visible in the type library. In Listing 19-3, the enumeration `MyEnumeration` used by the COM object has the `export` attribute so that `MyEnumeration` will appear in the type library.

Listing 19-3. Web Service Using an Enumeration

```
// EnumObject.h : Declaration of the CEnumObject

#pragma once
#include "resource.h"       // main symbols
#include <atlsoap.h>
[ emitidl(true) ];

[ export ]
enum MyEnumeration
{
    Value1,
    Value2,
    Value3
};


// IEnumObject
[
    object,
    uuid("F3AF9E86-98ED-4B2F-8A5B-7439745ED7E9"),
    dual,    helpstring("IEnumObject Interface"),
    pointer_default(unique)
]
__interface IEnumObject : IDispatch
{
    [id(1)] HRESULT EnumTest(
        [in] MyEnumeration eIn,
        [out, retval] MyEnumeration *eOut);
};

// CEnumObject

[
    coclass,
    threading("apartment"),
    vi_progid("EnumExample.EnumObject"),
    progid("EnumExample.EnumObject.1"),
    version(1.0),
    uuid("CADF04A4-6023-490A-827D-7E35F069FEFA"),
    helpstring("EnumObject Class"),
```

```
    request_handler(name="Default", sdl="GenWSDL"),
    soap_handler(name="EnumObject")
]
class ATL_NO_VTABLE CEnumObject :
    public IEnumObject
{
public:
    CEnumObject()
    {
    }


    DECLARE_PROTECT_FINAL_CONSTRUCT()

    HRESULT FinalConstruct()
    {
        return S_OK;
    }

    void FinalRelease()
    {
    }

    [ soap_method ]
    HRESULT EnumTest(MyEnumeration eIn, MyEnumeration *eOut)
    {
        *eOut = eIn;
        return S_OK;
    }

public:

};
```

Similarly, structs used in the COM object should have the `export` attribute if they're to appear in the type library. In Listing 19-4, the struct `MyStruct` used by the COM object has the `export` attribute.

Listing 19-4. Web Service Using Structs

```
// StructObject.h : Declaration of the CStructObject

#pragma once
#include "resource.h"       // main symbols
#include <atlsoap.h>
[ emitidl(true) ];

[ export ]
struct MyStruct
{
    int n;
    BSTR s;
};

// IStructObject
[
    object,
    uuid("4933C2D4-EA9A-4988-A163-E19BA560AE16"),
    dual,    helpstring("IStructObject Interface"),
    pointer_default(unique)
]
__interface IStructObject : IDispatch
{
    [id(1)] HRESULT StructTest(
        [in] MyStruct tIn,
        [out, retval] MyStruct *tOut);
};

// CStructObject

[
    coclass,
    threading("apartment"),
    vi_progid("StructExample.StructObject"),
    progid("StructExample.StructObject.1"),
    version(1.0),
    uuid("CD55DAD9-597B-4652-BAC7-2E8CD5AA7BB0"),
    helpstring("StructObject Class"),
    request_handler(name="Default", sdl="GetWSDL"),
```

```
    soap_handler(name="StructObject")
]
class ATL_NO_VTABLE CStructObject :
    public IStructObject
{
public:
    CStructObject()
    {
    }


    DECLARE_PROTECT_FINAL_CONSTRUCT()

    HRESULT FinalConstruct()
    {
        return S_OK;
    }

    void FinalRelease()
    {
    }

    [ soap_method ]
    HRESULT StructTest(MyStruct tIn, MyStruct *tOut)
    {
        tOut->n = tIn.n;
        tOut->s = tIn.s ? SysAllocString(tIn.s) : NULL;

        return S_OK;
    }

public:

};
```

IDispatch Types

The majority of `IDispatch` types are supported; however, common types such as `VARIANT`, `IDispatch*`, `IUnknown*`, and `SAFEARRAY`s aren't supported, as they fall into one of the categories of unsupported types described in earlier chapters. It's best to deal with `VARIANT` and `SAFEARRAY` in the same way you do other unsupported data types: Try to convert them into a supported data type for the SOAP interface. For

IDispatch* and IUnknown*, there's no general workaround. When the IDispatch object is effectively a data object (such as a scripting data object), it can be converted into a supported type (such as a struct) before making the call to SOAP.

In Listings 19-5 and 19-6, the fields of MyStruct are converted from the properties of the passed-in IDispatch object before being passed to the exposed SOAP method. They're then converted back into an IDispatch object with the appropriate properties.

Listing 19-5. Web Service Functioning as a Scriptable Object in JScript

```
// test.js

function MyStruct(n, s)
{
    this.s = s;
    this.n = n;
}

var obj = WScript.CreateObject("DispExample.DispWrapperObject");

var tIn = new MyStruct(1, "Joe");
var tOut = obj.DispTest(tIn);

WScript.Echo( tOut.n + ", " + tOut.s )
```

Listing 19-6. Web Service Functioning as a Scriptable Object

```
// DispWrapperObject.h : Declaration of the CDispWrapperObject

#pragma once
#include "resource.h"       // main symbols
#include <atlsoap.h>
[ emitidl(true) ];

[ export ]
struct MyStruct
{
    int n;
    BSTR s;
};


// IDispWrapperObject
[
```

```
    object,
    uuid("879E3783-0AF9-43D2-85C3-66AF07CFC4BD"),
    dual,    helpstring("IDispWrapperObject Interface"),
    pointer_default(unique)
]
__interface IDispWrapperObject : IDispatch
{
    [id(1)] HRESULT StructTest(
        [in] MyStruct tIn,
        [out, retval] MyStruct *tOut);
    [id(2)] HRESULT DispTest(
        [in] IDispatch *tIn,
        [out, retval] IDispatch **tOut);
};



// CDispWrapperObject

inline HRESULT GetDispProperty(
    IDispatch *pDispatch,
    LPCWSTR wszName,
    VARIANT *pvOut)
{
    HRESULT hr;

    if (!pDispatch || !wszName)
        return E_INVALIDARG;

    if (!pvOut)
        return E_POINTER;

    DISPID dispid;
    hr = pDispatch->GetIDsOfNames(
        IID_NULL, (LPOLESTR *)&wszName, 1, NULL, &dispid);
    if (FAILED(hr))
        return hr;

    DISPPARAMS EmptyParams;
    EmptyParams.cArgs = 0;
    EmptyParams.cNamedArgs = 0;
    EmptyParams.rgdispidNamedArgs = NULL;
    EmptyParams.rgvarg = NULL;
    hr = pDispatch->Invoke(
```

```
        dispid, IID_NULL, NULL, DISPATCH_PROPERTYGET,
        &EmptyParams, pvOut, NULL, NULL);
    if (FAILED(hr))
        return hr;

    return S_OK;
}

class CDispatchBag : public IDispatch, public CComObjectRoot
{
private:

    struct CProp
    {
        int m_nCnt;
        CComVariant m_var;
        CStringW m_str;

        CProp(LPCWSTR wsz, int nCnt)
            : m_str(wsz), m_nCnt(nCnt)
        {
        }
    };

    CAtlArray<CProp> m_props;

public:

    BEGIN_COM_MAP(CDispatchBag)
        COM_INTERFACE_ENTRY(IDispatch)
    END_COM_MAP()

    VARIANT * AddProperty(LPCWSTR wszName)
    {
        VARIANT *pRet = NULL;
        _ATLTRY
        {
            size_t nCount = m_props.GetCount();
            CProp prop(wszName, (int) nCount);
            size_t nIndex = m_props.Add(prop);
            if (nCount < m_props.GetCount())
            {
                pRet = &(m_props[nIndex].m_var);
            }
```

```
    }
    _ATLCATCH( e )
    {
        e;
    }

    return pRet;
}

virtual HRESULT STDMETHODCALLTYPE GetTypeInfoCount(
    UINT *pctinfo)
{
    if (!pctinfo)
        return E_INVALIDARG;

    *pctinfo = 0;
    return S_OK;
}

virtual HRESULT STDMETHODCALLTYPE GetTypeInfo(
    UINT iTInfo,
    LCID lcid,
    ITypeInfo **ppTInfo)
{
    if (!ppTInfo)
        return E_INVALIDARG;

    *ppTInfo = NULL;

    return DISP_E_BADINDEX;
}

virtual HRESULT STDMETHODCALLTYPE GetIDsOfNames(
    REFIID riid,
    LPOLESTR *rgszNames,
    UINT cNames,
    LCID lcid,
    DISPID *rgDispId)
{
    HRESULT hr = S_OK;

    for (UINT i=0; i<cNames; i++)
    {
        bool bFound = false;
```

```
                for (size_t nIndex=0; nIndex<m_props.GetCount(); nIndex++)
                {
                    if (m_props[nIndex].m_str == rgszNames[i])
                    {
                        rgDispId[i] = (DISPID)nIndex;
                        bFound = true;
                        break;
                    }
                }
                if (!bFound)
                {
                    rgDispId[i] = DISPID_UNKNOWN;
                    hr = DISP_E_UNKNOWNNAME;
                }
            }

            return hr;
        }

        virtual HRESULT STDMETHODCALLTYPE Invoke(
            DISPID dispIdMember,
            REFIID riid,
            LCID lcid,
            WORD wFlags,
            DISPPARAMS *pDispParams,
            VARIANT *pVarResult,
            EXCEPINFO *pExcepInfo,
            UINT *puArgErr)
        {
            if (dispIdMember < 0 || dispIdMember > (long)m_props.GetCount())
                return DISP_E_MEMBERNOTFOUND;

            if (wFlags != DISPATCH_PROPERTYGET)
                return DISP_E_MEMBERNOTFOUND;

            if (!pVarResult || !pDispParams)
                return E_INVALIDARG;

            return VariantCopy(pVarResult, &m_props[dispIdMember].m_var);
        }
    }; // class CDispatchBag

    [
        coclass,
```

```
    threading("apartment"),
    vi_progid("DispExample.DispWrapperObject"),
    progid("DispExample.DispWrapperObject.1"),
    version(1.0),
    uuid("99843466-E53E-49C3-9191-0E41A3D427DF"),
    helpstring("DispWrapperObject Class")
]
class ATL_NO_VTABLE CDispWrapperObject :
    public IDispWrapperObject
{
public:
    CDispWrapperObject()
    {
    }


    DECLARE_PROTECT_FINAL_CONSTRUCT()

    HRESULT FinalConstruct()
    {
        return S_OK;
    }

    void FinalRelease()
    {
    }


    [ soap_method ]
    HRESULT StructTest(MyStruct tIn, MyStruct *tOut)
    {
        tOut->n = tIn.n;
        tOut->s = tIn.s ? SysAllocString(tIn.s) : NULL;

        return S_OK;
    }

    // NOTE: the soap_method attribute is omitted here
    //       so this method is not exposed via SOAP
    HRESULT DispTest(IDispatch *tIn, IDispatch **tOut)
    {
        CComVariant vInt;
        CComVariant vStr;
        MyStruct structIn;
```

```
MyStruct structOut;
*tOut = NULL;

HRESULT hr = GetDispProperty(tIn, L"n", &vInt);
if (FAILED(hr))
    return hr;
if (vInt.vt != VT_INT && vInt.vt != VT_UI1 &&
    vInt.vt != VT_I2 && vInt.vt != VT_I4 &&
    vInt.vt != VT_UI2 && vInt.vt != VT_UI4 &&
    vInt.vt != VT_UINT)
    return E_INVALIDARG;

structIn.n = vInt.intVal;

hr = GetDispProperty(tIn, L"s", &vStr);
if (FAILED(hr))
    return hr;
if (vStr.vt != VT_BSTR)
    return E_INVALIDARG;

structIn.s = vStr.bstrVal;

hr = StructTest(structIn, &structOut);
if (FAILED(hr))
    return hr;

CComObject<CDispatchBag> *pDispBag = new CComObject<CDispatchBag>;
if (pDispBag)
{
    pDispBag->AddRef();
    VARIANT *pVar = pDispBag->AddProperty(L"n");
    if (pVar)
    {
        pVar->vt = VT_INT;
        pVar->intVal = structOut.n;
        pVar = pDispBag->AddProperty(L"s");
        if (pVar)
        {
            pVar->vt = VT_BSTR;
            pVar->bstrVal = structOut.s;
            *tOut = static_cast<IDispatch*>(pDispBag);
            return S_OK;
        }
    }
```

```
            pDispBag->Release();
        }

        if (structOut.s)
            SysFreeString(structOut.s);

        return E_OUTOFMEMORY;
    }

public:

};
```

Allocation

Earlier, you learned the proper way to allocate data for Web services using the `GetMemMgr()->Allocate` function. When it's invoked through SOAP, `GetMemMgr()->Allocate` will allocate data using a per-thread heap provided by the ATL Server ISAPI infrastructure. However, when an object is invoked through COM, data needs to be allocated differently. COM allocations must be done through the COM allocator functions: `CoTaskMemAlloc`, `CoTaskMemFree`, and `CoTaskMemRealloc`. Luckily, no special-case code is required to make this work. ATL Server defaults to using the COM allocator functions and only changes to the ATL Server ISAPI per-thread heap when explicitly invoked through SOAP. Users should continue to use the `GetMemMgr()->Allocate` and `GetMemMgr()->Free` functions for memory management, and ATL Server will ensure the correct allocator is used for each invocation method.

This brings up the issue of how ATL Server determines whether an object is being invoked through COM or whether it's being invoked through SOAP. We address this issue in the next section.

Determining Whether an Object Is Invoked As COM or As SOAP

In general, when you write an object that supports both SOAP and COM, it's preferable to avoid having to write code for special-case situations for a particular invocation method. However, there are situations when this may be necessary, and it's necessary to determine how the object was invoked.

As we mentioned in the previous section, ATL Server defaults to assuming COM invocation and only switches to using the ATL Server ISAPI-provided per-thread allocator when invoked through SOAP. You can use the same method to provide a convenient way to retrieve the information about the object's invocation method. Listing 19-7 shows how to encapsulate this functionality in a base class.

Listing 19-7. Determining the Method of Invocation

```
// WhichInvoke.h : Declaration of the CWhichInvoke

#pragma once
#include "resource.h"       // main symbols
#include <atlsoap.h>
[ emitidl(true) ];


// IWhichInvoke
[
    object,
    uuid("D15E83BF-35BB-496F-9BE9-E0260443A292"),
    dual,    helpstring("IWhichInvoke Interface"),
    pointer_default(unique)
]
__interface IWhichInvoke : IDispatch
{
    [id(1)] HRESULT Test([out, retval] BSTR *InvokeType);
};



// CWhichInvoke

[
    coclass,
    threading("apartment"),
    vi_progid("COM_OR_SOAP.WhichInvoke"),
    progid("COM_OR_SOAP.WhichInvoke.1"),
    version(1.0),
    uuid("8777423D-7594-4116-94B9-70CCEE66DE27"),
    helpstring("WhichInvoke Class"),

    request_handler(name="Default", sdl="GenWSDL"),
    soap_handler(name="WhichInvoke")
]
```

```
class ATL_NO_VTABLE CWhichInvoke :
    public IWhichInvoke
{
private:

    BOOL m_fCOMInvoke;

public:
    CWhichInvoke()
    {
        // default to COM
        m_fCOMInvoke = TRUE;
    }

    // override InitializeHandler
    HTTP_CODE InitializeHandler(
        AtlServerRequest *pRequestInfo,
        IServiceProvider *pProvider)
    {
        HTTP_CODE hcErr = __super::InitializeHandler(pRequestInfo, pProvider);
        if (hcErr == HTTP_SUCCESS)
        {
            m_fCOMInvoke = FALSE;
        }

        return hcErr;
    }


    DECLARE_PROTECT_FINAL_CONSTRUCT()

    HRESULT FinalConstruct()
    {
        return S_OK;
    }

    void FinalRelease()
    {
    }

    [ soap_method ]
    HRESULT Test(BSTR *InvokeType)
```

```
    {
        if (m_fCOMInvoke)
            *InvokeType = SysAllocString(L"COM!");
        else
            *InvokeType = SysAllocString(L"SOAP!");

        return S_OK;
    }

public:

};
```

In Listings 19-8 and 19-9, the boolean variable `m_fCOMInvoke` defaults to `TRUE`. The ATL Server `InitializeHandler` method is overridden to set `m_fCOMInvoke` to `FALSE`, as the `InitializeHandler` method will only be called if the object is being invoked through SOAP. The member function `IsCOMInvoke` accesses the `m_fCOMInvoke` member.

Listing 19-8. Demonstration of Determining the Method of Invocation in COM

```
// test.js

var obj = WScript.CreateObject("COM_OR_SOAP.WhichInvoke");

var strInvoke = obj.Test();
WScript.Echo(strInvoke);
```

Listing 19-9. Demonstration of Determining the Method of Invocation in SOAP

```
// test.cpp

#define _WIN32_WINNT 0x0500
#include "WhichInvoke.h"

int main()
{
    CoInitialize(NULL);
    {
        WhichInvoke::CWhichInvoke obj;
        CComBSTR bstrInvoke;
```

```
        HRESULT hr = obj.Test(&bstrInvoke);
        if (SUCCEEDED(hr))
            printf("%ws\n", bstrInvoke);

    }
    CoUninitialize();
}
```

Running test.js will output "COM!" and running test.cpp will output "SOAP!"

SOAP Faults and IErrorInfo

Earlier you learned how to return custom SOAP faults from ATL Server Web services. COM has its own error-reporting mechanisms, however, and it isn't possible to directly return SOAP faults through COM. In this section you'll examine how to combine custom SOAP fault generation with COM's `IErrorInfo` error reporting mechanism.

You can accomplish combining SOAP faults and COM errors by adding `ISupportErrorInfo` to your COM object using the `support_error_info` attribute. You can then call `AtlReportError` when generating errors to provide custom error text. To generate SOAP faults based on this custom error text, you override the `GenerateAppError` method for `CSoapHandler`, which then uses the `IErrorInfo` object to retrieve the custom error information and inserts it into the SOAP fault. Listing 19-10 shows how to return a custom COM error using IErrorInfo.

Listing 19-10. Returning a Custom Error Using IErrorInfo

```
// ErrorExample.h : Declaration of the CErrorExample

#pragma once
#include "resource.h"       // main symbols
#include <atlsoap.h>
[ emitidl(true) ];


// IErrorExample
[
    object,
    uuid("CB3722F0-D016-409C-81F8-804520B9AB1D"),
    dual,    helpstring("IErrorExample Interface"),
    pointer_default(unique)
]
```

```
__interface IErrorExample : IDispatch
{
    [id(1)] HRESULT ReturnError();
};



// CErrorExample

[
    coclass,
    threading("apartment"),
    vi_progid("ErrorFault.ErrorExample"),
    progid("ErrorFault.ErrorExample.1"),
    version(1.0),
    uuid("C1457735-C0FD-4858-9A2D-42B60A4A93DE"),
    helpstring("ErrorExample Class"),

    support_error_info("IErrorExample"),
    request_handler(name="Default", sdl="GenWSDL"),
    soap_handler(name="ErrorExample")
]
class ATL_NO_VTABLE CErrorExample :
    public IErrorExample
{
public:
    CErrorExample()
    {
    }


    DECLARE_PROTECT_FINAL_CONSTRUCT()

    HRESULT FinalConstruct()
    {
        return S_OK;
    }

    void FinalRelease()
    {
    }
```

```
    void GenerateError(HRESULT hr, LPCWSTR wszErr)
    {
        AtlReportError(GUID_NULL, wszErr);
    }

    // override GenerateAppError
    HRESULT
    GenerateAppError(
        IWriteStream *pStream,
        HRESULT hr
        )
    {
        CComPtr<IErrorInfo> spErr;
        HRESULT hrInternal = GetErrorInfo(0, &spErr);
        if (SUCCEEDED(hrInternal))
        {
            CComBSTR bstrErr;
            hrInternal = spErr->GetDescription(&bstrErr);
            if (SUCCEEDED(hrInternal) && bstrErr.m_str)
            {
                return SoapFault(SOAP_E_SERVER, bstrErr, bstrErr.Length());
            }
        }

        return SoapFault(
            SOAP_E_SERVER,
            L"Unexpected Error",
            sizeof("Unexpected Error")-1);
    }

    [ soap_method ]
    HRESULT ReturnError()
    {
        GenerateError(0x80040200, L"Custom Failure Text");
        return 0x80040200;
    }

public:

};
```

Listing 19-11 shows an example of how to retrieve the information from a SOAP client.

Listing 19-11. Retrieving Custom Error Information from IErrorInfo

```
// test.cpp

#define _WIN32_WINNT 0x0500
#include "ErrorExample.h"

int main()
{
    CoInitialize(NULL);
    {
        ErrorExample::CErrorExample obj;
        HRESULT hr = obj.ReturnError();
        if (FAILED(hr))
            printf("%ws\n", obj.m_fault.m_strDetail);

    }
    CoUninitialize();
}
```

When called, the program will output "Custom Failure Text."

ATL Server Web Service Internals

By now you may be wondering how ATL Server Web services really work and what goes on under the covers of attributes, XML, and marshaling. You may also be wondering why ATL Server has the limitations it has or how it's able to achieve the performance it does. In this section you'll examine the inner workings of attributes and ATL Server Web services with the goal of answering some of these questions. In the process of answering these questions, you'll expand upon the set of tools and techniques you've learned in order to leverage the flexibility of ATL Server so you can take full advantage of the power of ATL Server Web services. We aim to show that there's no great magic going on under the covers, and the full details of the implementation are there for anyone to examine in the ATL Server source code shipped with Visual Studio .NET.

One important disclaimer about this section: Most of what follows consists of implementation details and documentation about private APIs. The information isn't to be used directly in user applications. The information also applies only to Visual Studio .NET and may (and likely will) change in future versions. It's for informational and debugging purposes only—any other use is at your own risk.

How an ATL Server Web Service Works

You'll first examine what needs to happen to allow the ATL Server Web service to work the way it does. Let's take the "Hello World" Web service presented in Listing 19-12 and examine what needs to happen at each stage in the lifetime of a SOAP request on the server. The client is by and large the same, except that the order of the operations is reversed: First it generates the output (request) and then it parses the response it gets from the Web service, as shown in Listing 19-13. Unlike the earlier "Hello World" samples, however, you'll include a SOAP header in this one to show how that processing is done. You'll omit namespaces in the example SOAP packets for ease of understanding. Figure 19-1 shows the basic architecture of ATL Server Web service request processing.

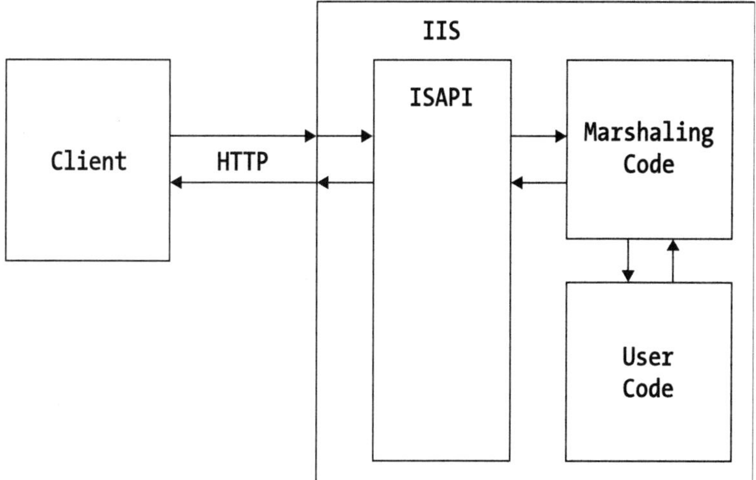

Figure 19-1. The architecture of an ATL Server Web service request

Listing 19-12. SOAP Request Packet

```
< Envelope>
    < Header>
        <InputHeader>StringValue</InputHeader>
    </Header>
    <Body>
        <HelloWorld>
            <InputParam>John</InputParam>
        </HelloWorld>
    </Body>
</Envelope>
```

Listing 19-13. SOAP Response Packet

```
<Envelope>
    <Header>
        <OutputHeader>IntegerValue</OutputHeader>
    </Header>
    <Body>
        <HelloWorld>
            <return>Hello, John!</return>
        </HelloWorld>
    </Body>
</Envelope>
```

When a Web service receives a SOAP request, it must

1. Determine the intended recipient of the SOAP request (the `HelloWorld` Web service method in this case).

2. Parse the XML of the SOAP request and marshal all the headers (`InputHeader`) and parameters (`InputParam`) into real C++ data types.

3. Invoke the intended recipient of the SOAP request (the `HelloWorld` Web service method) with the expected parameters (`InputParam`) and with the expected member variables that correspond to the input headers.

4. After the invocation of the Web service method, it must take the output parameter and return value and generate the SOAP response. This involves taking the C++ data types and converting them to XML.

5. Finally, any memory or resources that were allocated during the processing of the request must be freed.

Similarly, the Web service client must produce the request and consume the response—basically an inverse operation of the server.

ATL Server Implementation

Now let's look at how ATL Server implements all the things that need to happen when processing a Web service request.

ATL Server Web services are implemented using a state machine–based parser. ATL Server uses a stack to maintain information about each state it has entered while parsing the SOAP request. The ATL Server Web service attributes generate metadata information about each Web service class and each method in that class. This information (which you'll examine in detail later in this chapter) includes the name of the method, the SOAP headers used in the method (if any), the parameters of the method, type information for each SOAP header and method parameter, and the invocation type for the method (`rpc/encoded`, `document/literal`, and so on). This metadata is used by the ATL Server framework while parsing the request to determine what the next state that needs to be entered is and how to parse the next piece of information that comes in. For a Web service client, the metadata is generated by sproxy.exe while generating the proxy class.

ATL Server defines several state constants it uses while parsing the request:

- `SOAP_START`: This is the initial state of the request, before any parsing has been done.
- `SOAP_ENVELOPE`: This state indicates that the SOAP `Envelope` element has been encountered.
- `SOAP_HEADERS`: This state indicates that a SOAP `Headers` element has been encountered.
- `SOAP_BODY`: This state indicates that the SOAP `Body` element has been encountered.
- `SOAP_PARAMS`: This state indicates that the parser is ready to begin parsing the parameters. This state is entered after encountering the `MethodName` element in the SOAP request.
- `SOAP_HEADERS_DONE`: This state indicates that the closing tag of the SOAP `Headers` element has been encountered. The framework effectively re-enters the `SOAP_ENVELOPE` state at this point, though it will return an error if any further `Headers` elements are encountered.

Now let's look at the structure of the metadata ATL Server uses in parsing the request. There are two main objects that the framework uses for metadata information: `_soapmapentry` and `_soapmap`. In turn, these objects use the following enumerations: `SOAPFLAGS` and `SOAPMAPTYPE`.

`SOAPFLAGS` is used to specify type information about a particular entry in the `_soapmapentry` struct. For example, if an entry represents an `in` parameter, `SOAPFLAG_IN` would be set in its `dwFlags` value. Each value in the `SOAPFLAGS` enumeration serves a similar purpose, either for the metadata or for the parsing state.

- SOAPFLAG_NONE: This value is used to indicate that a particular field has no other flags.
- SOAPFLAG_IN: This value is used to indicate that the field represents an in parameter or in header.
- SOAPFLAG_OUT: This value is used to indicate that the field represents an out parameter or out header.
- SOAPFLAG_RETVAL: This value is used to indicate that the field represents the return value of the Web service method.
- SOAPFLAG_DYNARR: This value is used to indicate that the field is a dynamic array.
- SOAPFLAG_FIXEDARR: This value is used to indicate that the field is a fixed-size array.
- SOAPFLAG_MUSTUNDERSTAND: This value is used to indicate that the field represents a mustUnderstand header.
- SOAPFLAG_UNKSIZE: This value is used to indicate that no size was specified for an array element in a SOAP request. This will commonly be the case for arrays in document/literal style.
- SOAPFLAG_READYSTATE: This value is used to indicate that the parser is in a *ready state;* that is, it's used to indicate that the parser is prepared to begin reading the "value" of a parameter or header.
- SOAPFLAG_FIELD: This value is used to indicate that the entry represents a field in a struct or enumeration.
- SOAPFLAG_NOMARSHAL: This value is used to indicate that the entry shouldn't be put on to the wire as part of the SOAP response or read from the write as part of the SOAP request. size_is elements are examples of entries that would have this flag set.
- SOAPFLAG_NULLABLE: This value is used to indicate the entry represents a field that is *nullable;* that is, it can be omitted from the SOAP request and be set to NULL in the SOAP response. Strings are examples of nullable elements.
- SOAPFLAG_DOCUMENT: This value is used to indicate that the entry is part of a document-style request. Currently, this implies document/literal.

- `SOAPLAG_RPC`: This value is used to indicate that the entry is part of an `rpc`-style request. Currently, this implies `rpc/encoded`.
- `SOAPFLAG_LITERAL`: This value is used to indicate that the entry is part of a `literal`-style request. Currently, this implies `document/literal`.
- `SOAPFLAG_ENCODED`: This value is used to indicate that the entry is part of an `encoded`-style request. Currently, this implies `rpc/encoded`.
- `SOAPFLAG_PID`: This value is used to indicate that the entry is part of a `document/literal` parameters-in-document (PID)–style request. This means that the parameters will appear under a `MethodName` element in the request.
- `SOAPFLAG_PAD`: This value is used to indicate that the entry is part of a `document/literal` parameters-as-document (PAD)–style request. This means that the parameters will appear directly under the SOAP `Body` element without an enclosing `MethodName` element.
- `SOAPFLAG_CHAIN`: This value is used to indicate the first entry in a PAD-style request.
- `SOAPFLAG_SIZEIS`: This value is used to indicate a `size_is` entry for an array.

The `SOAPMAPTYPE` enumeration is used to indicate what type of object the `_soapmap` instance is representing.

- `SOAPMAP_ERR`: An internal error. This should never be encountered.
- `SOAPMAP_ENUM`: This value is used to indicate the instance represents an enumeration.
- `SOAPMAP_FUNC`: This value is used to indicate the instance represents a Web service method.
- `SOAPMAP_STRUCT`: This value is used to indicate the instance represents a struct.
- `SOAPMAP_HEADER`: This value is used to indicate the instance represents a collection of SOAP headers.
- `SOAPMAP_PARAM`: This value is used to indicate the instance represents a parameter.

Now let's look at the _soapmap and _soapmapentry objects. Listing 19-14 presents the definition of the _soapmap struct.

Listing 19-14. Definition of the _soapmap Struct

```
struct _soapmap
{
    ULONG nHash;
    const char * szName;
    const wchar_t * wszName;
    int cchName;
    int cchWName;
    SOAPMAPTYPE mapType;
    const _soapmapentry * pEntries;
    size_t nElementSize;
    size_t nElements;
    int nRetvalIndex;

    DWORD dwCallFlags;

    ULONG nNamespaceHash;
    const char *szNamespace;
    const wchar_t *wszNamespace;
    int cchNamespace;
};
```

Here's an overview of the fields in Listing 19-14:

- nHash: This field is used to store a hash value that's used for more efficient string comparisons for the object's name.
- szName: This field stores the ASCII version of the name of the object the map represents (function name, struct name, enumeration name, and so forth).
- wszName: This field stores the wide-character version of the name of the object the map represents.
- cchName: This field stores the length of szName string.
- cchWName: This field stores the length of the wszName string (it can be different from szName on the client side).
- mapType: This field indicates the type of the map (from SOAPMAPTYPE).

- pEntries: This field stores a pointer to an array of _soapmapentry objects that represent the fields, values, or parameters for _soapmap.

- nElementSize: This field indicates the size of the memory block that needs to be allocated to represent the object (the size of a struct, for example) and its fields or parameters.

- nElements: This field indicates the count of the entries in the pEntries array.

- nRetvalIndex: This field is used to represent the index into pEntries of the return value for the SOAPMAP_FUNC map. A–1 indicates there's no return value.

- dwCallFlags: This field is used to indicate what type of invocation method is being used, document/literal or rpc/encoded.

- nNamespaceHash: This field is used to store a hash value that's used for efficient string comparisons for the object's namespace.

- szNamespace: This field is used to store the ASCII version of the object's namespace.

- wszNamespace: This field is used to store the wide-character version of the object's namespace.

- cchNamespace: This field is used to store the length of the namespace strings.

Listing 19-15 shows the definition of the _soapmapentry struct.

Listing 19-15. Definition of the _soapmapentry Struct

```
struct _soapmapentry
{
    ULONG nHash;
    const char * szField;
    const WCHAR * wszField;
    int cchField;
    int nVal;
    DWORD dwFlags;

    size_t nOffset;
    const int * pDims;

    const _soapmap * pChain;
```

```
    int nSizeIs;

    ULONG nNamespaceHash;
    const char *szNamespace;
    const wchar_t *wszNamespace;
    int cchNamespace;
};
```

Here's an overview of the fields in Listing 19-15:

- `nHash`: This field is used to store a hash value that's used for efficient string comparisons for the entry's name.
- `szField`: This field is used to store the ASCII version of the entry's name.
- `wszField`: This field is used to store the wide-character version of the entry's name.
- `cchField`: This field is used to store the length of the `szField` and `wszField` strings.
- `nVal`: This field is used to store the entry's type from the `SOAPTYPES` enumeration.
- `dwFlags`: This field is used to store flags for entry (`in`, `out`, `retval`, and so on).
- `nOffset`: This field is used to store the offset of the entry into the block of memory used to represent its parent type (struct, function, or header). You'll examine this field in more detail later in the chapter.
- `pDims`: This field is used to specify the array dimensions for an entry that is a fixed-size array. You'll look at the structure of this information later in the chapter.
- `pChain`: This field links to another `_soapmap` instance for entries that are structs or enumerations.
- `nSizeIs`: This field specifies the index of the `size_is` element for an array in the list of entries.
- `nNamespaceHash`: This field is used to store a hash value that's used for efficient string comparisons for the entry's namespace.

- szNamespace: This field is used to store the ASCII version of the entry's namespace.

- wszNamespace: This field is used to store the wide-character version of the entry's namespace.

- cchNamespace: This field is used to store the length of the namespace strings.

ATL Server stores the information from these fields in a state stack that's built while parsing the request. The stack contains elements of type CSoapRootHandler::ParseState, as shown in Listing 19-16.

Listing 19-16. Definition of the ParseState Struct

```
struct ParseState
{
    void *pvElement;
    DWORD dwFlags;
    size_t nAllocSize;
    size_t nExpectedElements;
    size_t nElement;
    const _soapmap *pMap;
    const _soapmapentry *pEntry;

    // mark when we get an item
    CBitVector vec;

    size_t nDepth;

// omitted...
};
```

Here's an overview of the fields in Listing 19-16:

- pvElement: This field contains the pointer to the beginning of the allocated memory block for the element currently being parsed.

- dwFlags: This field contains the flags for the element, plus additional flags set during parsing (such as SOAPFLAG_READYSTATE).

- nAllocSize: This field indicates the size of the memory block allocated for the element. For the root element, it will be the size of the memory block for the struct fields or method parameters. For a dynamic-size array, it will the amount of memory currently allocated for the array elements.

- nExpectedElements: This field indicates the number of child entries that are expected for the entry represented by the state. For a struct, this will be the number of fields; for a method, this will be the number of in parameters; and for an array, this will be the number of array elements.

- nElement: This field indicates how many child entries have been encountered for the object. This is checked against nExpectedElements when the entry's closing tag is encountered.

- pMap: The _soapmap for the element.

- pEntry: The _soapmapentry representing the element.

- vec: A bit vector that's modified when child elements are encountered. When an entry's closing tag is encountered and nElement < nExpectedElements for the state, the bit vector is examined to ensure that any omitted elements were nullable elements.

- nDepth: The current depth of the parsing.

Let's look at how these pieces fit together by examining how ATL Server handles the "Hello World" example you saw earlier. Listing 19-17 shows the Web service definition and the Web service definition after compilation with the attribute provider.

Listing 19-17. The HelloWorld Web Service

```
// HelloWorld.h : Defines the ATL Server request handler class
//
#pragma once

namespace HelloWorldService
{
// all struct, enum, and typedefs for your web service
// should go inside the namespace

// IHelloWorldService - web service interface declaration
//
[
    uuid("A035C807-3516-422C-A527-AB93D57F2798"),
    object
]
__interface IHelloWorldService
{
```

```
    // HelloWorld is a sample ATL Server web service method. It shows how to
    // declare a web service method and its in parameters and out parameters
    [id(1)] HRESULT HelloWorld([in] BSTR InputParam,
        [out, retval] BSTR *bstrOutput);
    // TODO: Add additional web service methods here
};


// HelloWorldService - web service implementation
//
[
    request_handler(name="Default", sdl="GenHelloWorldWSDL"),
    soap_handler(
        name="HelloWorldService",
        namespace="urn:HelloWorldService",
        protocol="soap"
    )
]
class CHelloWorldService :
    public IHelloWorldService
{
public:
    BSTR InputHeader;
    int OutputHeader;

    // This is a sample web service method that shows how to use the
    // soap_method attribute to expose a method as a web method
    [ soap_method ]
    [ soap_header(value="InputHeader", in=true, out=false) ]
    [ soap_header(value="OutputHeader", in=false, out=true) ]
    HRESULT HelloWorld(/*[in]*/ BSTR InputParam,
        /*[out, retval]*/ BSTR *bstrOutput)
    {
        CComBSTR bstrOut(L"Hello ");
        bstrOut += InputParam;
        bstrOut += L"!";
        *bstrOutput = bstrOut.Detach();
        if (InputHeader && InputHeader[0])
            OutputHeader = _wtoi(InputHeader);
        else
            OutputHeader = 0;

        return S_OK;
    }
```

```
    // TODO: Add additional web service methods here
}; // class CHelloWorldService

} // namespace HelloWorldService
```

```
// omitted...

// HelloWorld.h : Defines the ATL Server request handler class
//
#pragma once

namespace HelloWorldService
{
// all struct, enum, and typedefs
// for your web service should go inside the namespace

// IHelloWorldService - web service interface declaration
//
[
    uuid("A035C807-3516-422C-A527-AB93D57F2798"),
    object
]
__interface IHelloWorldService
{
    // HelloWorld is a sample ATL Server web service method. It shows how to
    // declare a web service method and its in parameters and out parameters
    [id(1)] HRESULT HelloWorld([in] BSTR InputParam,
        [out, retval] BSTR *bstrOutput);
    // TODO: Add additional web service methods here
};


// HelloWorldService - web service implementation
//
[
    request_handler(name="Default", sdl="GenHelloWorldWSDL"),
    soap_handler(
        name="HelloWorldService",
        namespace="urn:HelloWorldService",
        protocol="soap"
    )
]
```

```
class CHelloWorldService :
    public IHelloWorldService,
    /*+++ Added Baseclass */ public CSoapHandler<CHelloWorldService>
{
public:
    BSTR InputHeader;
    int OutputHeader;

    // This is a sample web service method that shows how to use the
    // soap_method attribute to expose a method as a web method
    [ soap_method ]
    [ soap_header(value="InputHeader", in=true, out=false) ]
    [ soap_header(value="OutputHeader", in=false, out=true) ]
    HRESULT HelloWorld(/*[in]*/ BSTR InputParam,
        /*[out, retval]*/ BSTR *bstrOutput)
    {
        CComBSTR bstrOut(L"Hello ");
        bstrOut += InputParam;
        bstrOut += L"!";
        *bstrOutput = bstrOut.Detach();
        if (InputHeader && InputHeader[0])
            OutputHeader = _wtoi(InputHeader);
        else
            OutputHeader = 0;

        return S_OK;
    }
    // TODO: Add additional web service methods here

    //+++ Start Injected Code For Attribute 'soap_handler'
    const _soapmap ** GetFunctionMap() throw();
    const _soapmap ** GetHeaderMap() throw();
    void * GetHeaderValue() throw();
    const wchar_t * GetNamespaceUri() throw();
    const char * GetNamespaceUriA() throw();
    const char * GetServiceName() throw();
    HRESULT CallFunction(
        void *pvParam,
        const wchar_t *wszLocalName,
        int cchLocalName,
        size_t nItem);

    //--- End Injected Code For Attribute 'soap_handler'
```

```
};

//+++ Start Injected Code For Attribute 'request_handler'


HANDLER_ENTRY_SDL("Default",
                  CHelloWorldService, ::HelloWorldService::CHelloWorldService,
                  GenHelloWorldWSDL)


//--- End Injected Code For Attribute 'request_handler'


//+++ Start Injected Code For Attribute 'soap_handler'
struct __HelloWorldService_CHelloWorldService_HelloWorld_struct
    {
    BSTR InputParam;
    BSTR bstrOutput;
};

extern __declspec(selectany) const _soapmapentry
__HelloWorldService_CHelloWorldService_HelloWorld_entries[] =
    {

        {
            0xF6041A8C,
            "bstrOutput",
            L"bstrOutput",
            sizeof("bstrOutput")-1,
            SOAPTYPE_STRING,
            SOAPFLAG_RETVAL | SOAPFLAG_OUT | SOAPFLAG_NULLABLE,
            offsetof(
                __HelloWorldService_CHelloWorldService_HelloWorld_struct,
                bstrOutput),
            NULL,
            NULL,
            -1,
        },

        {
            0xD41C0B61,
            "InputParam",
            L"InputParam",
            sizeof("InputParam")-1,
```

```
            SOAPTYPE_STRING,
            SOAPFLAG_NONE | SOAPFLAG_IN | SOAPFLAG_NULLABLE,
            offsetof(
                ___HelloWorldService_CHelloWorldService_HelloWorld_struct,
                InputParam),
            NULL,
            NULL,
            -1,
        },
        { 0x00000000 }
    };

extern __declspec(selectany) const _soapmap
___HelloWorldService_CHelloWorldService_HelloWorld_map =
    {
        0x46BA99FC,
        "HelloWorld",
        L"HelloWorld",
        sizeof("HelloWorld")-1,
        sizeof("HelloWorld")-1,
        SOAPMAP_FUNC,
        ___HelloWorldService_CHelloWorldService_HelloWorld_entries,
        sizeof(___HelloWorldService_CHelloWorldService_HelloWorld_struct),
        1,
        0,
        SOAPFLAG_NONE | SOAPFLAG_RPC | SOAPFLAG_ENCODED,
        0xE6CAFA1C,
        "urn:HelloWorldService",
        L"urn:HelloWorldService",
        sizeof("urn:HelloWorldService")-1
    };

extern __declspec(selectany) const _soapmapentry
___HelloWorldService_CHelloWorldService_HelloWorld_atlsoapheader_entries[] =
    {
        {
            0x45334E39,
            "InputHeader",
            L"InputHeader",
            sizeof("InputHeader")-1,
            SOAPTYPE_STRING,
            SOAPFLAG_NONE | SOAPFLAG_IN | SOAPFLAG_NULLABLE,
            offsetof(CHelloWorldService, InputHeader),
            NULL,
```

```
            NULL,
            -1,
            0xE6CAFA1C,
            "urn:HelloWorldService",
            L"urn:HelloWorldService",
            sizeof("urn:HelloWorldService")-1
        },
        {
            0x647BAD1A,
            "OutputHeader",
            L"OutputHeader",
            sizeof("OutputHeader")-1,
            SOAPTYPE_INT,
            SOAPFLAG_NONE | SOAPFLAG_OUT,
            offsetof(CHelloWorldService, OutputHeader),
            NULL,
            NULL,
            -1,
            0xE6CAFA1C,
            "urn:HelloWorldService",
            L"urn:HelloWorldService",
            sizeof("urn:HelloWorldService")-1
        },
        { 0x00000000 }
    };

extern __declspec(selectany) const _soapmap
___HelloWorldService_CHelloWorldService_HelloWorld_atlsoapheader_map =
    {
        0x46BA99FC,
        "HelloWorld",
        L"HelloWorld",
        sizeof("HelloWorld")-1,
        sizeof("HelloWorld")-1,
        SOAPMAP_HEADER,
        ___HelloWorldService_CHelloWorldService_HelloWorld_atlsoapheader_entries,
        0,
        0,
        -1,
        SOAPFLAG_NONE | SOAPFLAG_RPC | SOAPFLAG_ENCODED,
        0xE6CAFA1C,
        "urn:HelloWorldService",
        L"urn:HelloWorldService",
        sizeof("urn:HelloWorldService")-1
```

```
    };
extern __declspec(selectany) const _soapmap *
___HelloWorldService_CHelloWorldService_funcs[] =
    {
        &___HelloWorldService_CHelloWorldService_HelloWorld_map,
        NULL
    };

extern __declspec(selectany) const _soapmap *
___HelloWorldService_CHelloWorldService_headers[] =
    {
        &___HelloWorldService_CHelloWorldService_HelloWorld_atlsoapheader_map,
        NULL
    };

ATL_NOINLINE inline const _soapmap ** CHelloWorldService::GetFunctionMap()
{
    return ___HelloWorldService_CHelloWorldService_funcs;
};

ATL_NOINLINE inline const _soapmap ** CHelloWorldService::GetHeaderMap()
{
    return ___HelloWorldService_CHelloWorldService_headers;
}

ATL_NOINLINE inline void * CHelloWorldService::GetHeaderValue()
{
    return this;
}

ATL_NOINLINE inline HRESULT CHelloWorldService::CallFunction(
        void *pvParam,
        const wchar_t *wszLocalName,
        int cchLocalName,
        size_t nItem)
{
    wszLocalName;
    cchLocalName;

    HRESULT hr = S_OK;

    switch(nItem)
{
    case 0:
```

```
        {
            ___HelloWorldService_CHelloWorldService_HelloWorld_struct *p =
                (___HelloWorldService_CHelloWorldService_HelloWorld_struct *)
                pvParam;
            hr = HelloWorld(p->InputParam, &p->bstrOutput);
            break;
        }
    default:
        hr = E_FAIL;
    }

    return hr;
}

ATL_NOINLINE inline const wchar_t * CHelloWorldService::GetNamespaceUri()
{
    return L"urn:HelloWorldService";
}

ATL_NOINLINE inline const char * CHelloWorldService::GetNamespaceUriA()
{
    return "urn:HelloWorldService";
}

ATL_NOINLINE inline const char * CHelloWorldService::GetServiceName()
{
    return "HelloWorldService";
}

  //--- End Injected Code For Attribute 'soap_handler'
  // class CHelloWorldService

} // namespace HelloWorldService
```

As you can see, the attribute provider injects the metadata (_soapmap, _soapentry) as described earlier in this chapter. ___HelloWorldService_CHelloWorldService_HelloWorld_entries contains information about the input and output parameters of the HelloWorld method of the Web service, and ___HelloWorldService_CHelloWorldService_HelloWorld_map contains information about the HelloWorld method itself, including a link to the _soapmapentry array for the parameters. ___HelloWorldService_CHelloWorldService_HelloWorld_atlsoapheader_entries contains information about the individual SOAP headers for the HelloWorld method, and __HelloWorldService_CHelloWorldService_HelloWorld_atlsoapheader_map contains higher-level SOAP header information for the HelloWorld method.

In addition to the metadata, the attribute provider also injects several functions:

- GetFunctionMap: This method returns a pointer to the _soapmap array for the methods of the Web service that are exposed over SOAP.
- GetHeaderMap: This method returns a pointer to the _soapmap array for the header information for all the methods of the Web service that are exposed over SOAP.
- GetHeaderValue: This method returns a void* pointer that points to the instance of the Web service (i.e., the this pointer). This is used in assigning and extracting header values for marshaling because headers are stored as member variables.
- GetNamespaceUri: This method returns a wide-character string for the namespace URI of the Web service.
- GetNamespaceUriA: This is an ASCII version of GetNamespaceUri.
- GetServiceName: This method returns the name of the Web service specified in the name parameter of the soap_handler attribute.
- CallFunction: This method invokes the Web service method for the current SOAP request.

Upon receiving an HTTP request, the ATL Server framework will attempt to retrieve a SAXXMLReader object from ATL Server's per-thread data. This object will be used to parse the SOAP request. ATL Server will then attempt to extract the SOAPAction header from the HTTP request. For ATL Server Web services, the SOAPAction headers are always of the following form:

```
SOAPAction: "#MethodName"
```

ATL Server uses the SOAPAction header to determine which function is being invoked. If the header is absent, ATL Server will attempt to continue processing. The framework will determine which function is being invoked from the SOAP request body later on. It will only fail if it encounters any SOAP headers as part of the request, because at that point, the SOAP body hasn't been encountered and it isn't possible to determine which method is being invoked.

Let's assume you received an appropriate SOAPAction:

```
SOAPAction: "#HelloWorld"
```

The framework will then push an initial parse state on the stack. Because the parsing will not have encountered any SOAP headers yet, it will set the pvElement value of the ParseState to the instance of the Web service class (as the offsets and elements in this case are member variables of the class). Figure 19-2 shows the start state of the state stack.

```
pvElement = web service class instance
dwFlags = 0
pMap = pointer to "header" map of service
nElements = pMap->nElements
pEntry = NULL
```

Figure 19-2. The initial state of the state stack

Once all this has been set up, the framework is ready to begin parsing the request. For the purposes of this example, assume the request is well-formed and skip over the error-handling portions of the code.

The first element encountered is the Envelope element, and the framework sets the current state to SOAP_ENVELOPE. Next, the parser encounters the Headers element. The state is set to SOAP_HEADERS. The InputHeader element is next and the framework invokes the CSoapRootHandler::ProcessParams function. The ProcessParams function attempts to look up InputHeader in the _soapmapentry array. If it's found, a value is set in the current state's bit vector indicating that this particular element was received (based on its ordinal position in the _soapmapentry array). Once it's found, the ProcessParams method checks the type and sees that it's a string and invokes the ProcessString function. ProcessString sets the active SAX parser to be the CSAXStringBuilder class. Because the string might contain embedded XML, it's necessary to parse it as XML elements and build the final string before copying it into the appropriate memory location for the SOAP header. The ProcessString function also pushes a new state on the stack that includes the SOAPFLAG_READYSTATE flag to indicate it's ready to set the string value. The new state's pvElement value is set to the value of the InputHeader member variable. This is done by using the nOffset value in the metadata and adding that offset to the pvElement value in the current state. Figure 19-3 shows the state stack after encountering the InputHeader element.

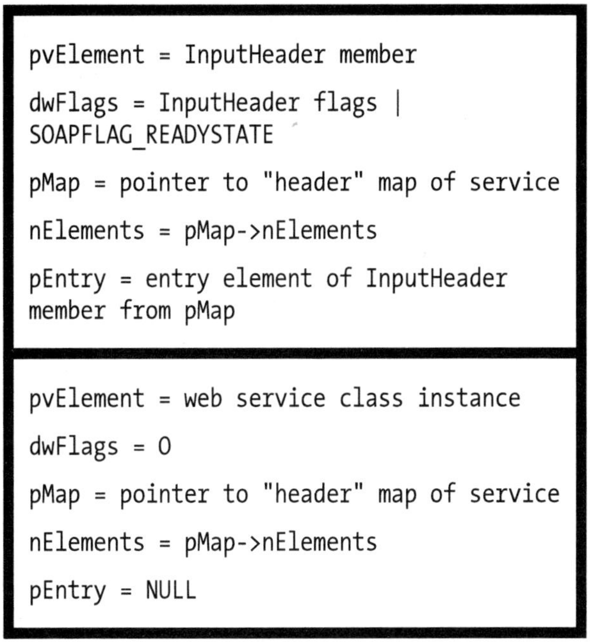

```
pvElement = InputHeader member
dwFlags = InputHeader flags |
SOAPFLAG_READYSTATE
pMap = pointer to "header" map of service
nElements = pMap->nElements
pEntry = entry element of InputHeader
member from pMap
```

```
pvElement = web service class instance
dwFlags = 0
pMap = pointer to "header" map of service
nElements = pMap->nElements
pEntry = NULL
```

Figure 19-3. The state stack after the InputHeader element

Once the CSAXStringBuilder class encounters the final element of the string, it invokes the characters function of CSoapRootHandler. The characters function sees the type of the element is the SOAPTYPE_STRING enumeration value and that the state includes the SOAPFLAG_READYSTATE flag. It then invokes the AtlSoapGetElementValue function, which switches on the type of the element, and then invokes the AtlGetSAXValue template function, which does the actual data conversion from the XML data to the C++ type. In this case, for SOAPTYPE_STRING, it's simply a matter of putting the string into a BSTR. The state's pvElement value is passed in as the memory location of the BSTR.

The endElement method is invoked for the closing InputHeader tag, which in turn invokes the CheckEndElement method of CSoapRootHandler. The CheckEndElement function ensures that the data received in the XML packet is valid. This function does most of its work when validating the end tags of structs, ends of header blocks, and ends of method blocks. You'll examine this function in more detail later. After CheckEndElement is called, the current state is popped from the stack.

The endElement method is then invoked for the closing Header tag. Because the current state is SOAP_HEADERS, the CheckEndHeaders method is invoked. This method sets the state to SOAP_HEADERS_DONE.

The next element encountered is the Body element, and the framework sets the state to SOAP_BODY. When the HelloWorld element is encountered next, the framework invokes the DispatchSoapCall method, which looks up the HelloWorld method in the Web service class's metadata and allocates a struct based on the nElementSize field that will hold the method's parameters. It then pushes this state on the stack and sets the current state to SOAP_PARAMS. Figure 19-4 shows the state of the state stack after encountering the HelloWorld element.

```
pvElement = allocated struct for params
dwFlags = 0
pMap = pointer to methods "function" map
nElements = pMap->nElements
pEntry = NULL
```

Figure 19-4. The state stack after encountering the HelloWorld element

The next element encountered is the InputParam element. The framework invokes the ProcessParams function, which then continues in the same way as when it was invoked for the InputHeader element. The processing for the closing tags in the Body section is the same as for that in the Header section, with the exception that when the closing HelloWorld tag is encountered, the CheckEndElement function does additional processing. It ensures that the number of parameters received is the same as the number of in parameters specified by the metadata. If the number of elements is fewer than expected, the CheckEndElement function will walk the _soapmapentry array and compare the in parameters against what has been set in the bit vector. For any missing element, it ensures that that element is considered a nullable element. If there are any missing non-nullable elements, an error is returned.

Once the XML processing is completed and all the XML data has been converted to C++ types, the Web service method is invoked using the CallFunction method. This method will invoke the actual Web service method using the pvElement value at the top of the state stack to create the parameters. Listing 19-18 shows how the framework invokes the user's method after the request has been parsed.

Listing 19-18. Invocation of User Code

```
ATL_NOINLINE inline HRESULT CHelloWorldService::CallFunction(
        void *pvParam,
        const wchar_t *wszLocalName,
        int cchLocalName,
        size_t nItem)
    {
    wszLocalName;
```

```
    cchLocalName;

    HRESULT hr = S_OK;

    switch(nItem)
    {
    case 0:
        {
            __HelloWorldService_CHelloWorldService_HelloWorld_struct *p =
                (__HelloWorldService_CHelloWorldService_HelloWorld_struct *)
                pvParam;
            hr = HelloWorld(p->InputParam, &p->bstrOutput);
            break;
        }
    default:
        hr = E_FAIL;
    }

    return hr;
}
```

Once the method returns, the SOAP response has to be generated. This is done using the `GenerateResponse` method. The `GenerateResponse` method first walks the `out` headers for the Web service method by invoking the `GenerateResponseHelper` method using the value retrieved from the injected `GetHeaderValue` method and the header metadata for the method. Different response packets are generated depending on whether the Web service is implemented specifying `rpc/encoded` or `document/literal`. The framework uses different types of response generator classes for the different encodings. All the classes inherit from the private `CResponseGenerator` base class, which defines this basic interface:

- `StartEnvelope`: Begin the SOAP `Envelope` element.
- `StartHeaders`: Begin the SOAP `Headers` element.
- `EndHeaders`: End the SOAP `Headers` element.
- `StartBody`: Begin the SOAP `Body` element.
- `EndBody`: End the SOAP `Body` element.
- `EndEnvelope`: End the SOAP `Envelope` element.
- `StartMap`: Begin a subelement for a `_soapmapentry` that has a `_soapmap` (such as a struct or a function).

- EndMap: End a subelement for a _soapmap.
- StartEntry: Start an element for a _soapmapentry (such as a struct field or a method parameter).
- EndEntry: End an element for a _soapmapentry.

Different methods in this interface are overridden for rpc/encoded or document/literal generation.

The GenerateResponseHelper method walks each of the entries in the root _soapmap and uses the pvElement field from the root of the state stack in combination with the _soapmapentry's nOffset field to generate the XML packet from the C++ data. In the case of headers, the pvElement is the value retrieved from the injected GetHeaderValue method, and for method generation, the pvElement is the value allocated in the DispatchStencilCall method for storing the parameters extracted from the XML data. For each _soapmapentry that isn't a UDT (such as an enumeration or a struct), the AtlSoapGenElementValue function is called to generate the output. This function is similar to the AtlSoapGetElementValue function in that it switches based on the SOAPTYPE of the element and then dispatches to the AtlGenXMLValue template function, which generates the XML data from the C++ data type passed in.

Finally, after the response has been generated, it's necessary to clean up any memory that has been allocated during the processing of the request. This is the same basic operation as generating the response. The framework walks each of entries based on the metadata, but instead of outputting the XML representation of the C++ type using AtlSoapGenElementValue, the AtlSoapCleanupElement function is called. The AtlSoapCleanupElement function switches on the type and invokes the AtlCleanupValue template function for any data type that has to be deallocated or freed in any way.

Error Checking

The ATL Server framework must perform error checking during the processing of the response to ensure that the SOAP is well-formed and is what's expected and supported for the Web service. In cases where the SOAP packet is malformed or makes use of a part of the SOAP standard that isn't supported by ATL Server, the framework must return an appropriate SOAP fault to the client.

One of the errors the framework checks for is that all SOAP headers that are sent with the mustUnderstand attribute set are expected by the server. If, during the processing of the request, the framework encounters a SOAP header that it doesn't recognize, it will then check to see if the header has the mustUnderstand attribute set. If it doesn't, the framework will simply skip the header using the CSkipHandler class; if it does, the framework will return a SOAP fault indicating that a mustUnderstand header was encountered that wasn't expected by the Web service. This checking happens in the ProcessParams function, which invokes the CheckMustUnderstandHeader function, which looks for the mustUnderstand attribute.

The framework needs to check that the same element isn't specified more than once within the SOAP packet. It performs this check using the bit vector described earlier in this chapter. Once an element is encountered, the position in the bit vector corresponding to it (based on its ordinal position in the pEntries array of the _soapmap struct) is then set to true. The bit vector is always checked before processing an element; if the element has already been processed, an error is returned. The bit vector is also checked during the endElement SAX content handler method to ensure that all array elements that were expected were received and that any omitted elements (for a struct or a function) are nullable.

The framework must also ensure that the SOAP packet doesn't contain data for elements that are specified as null or href in the SOAP message. The framework accomplishes this using a member variable (m_bNullCheck) that is set to true in href and null situations. This variable is then checked in the startElement SAX content handler method implementation. If it's true, then the framework returns an error, because it's expecting endElement to be the next SAX method to be invoked (endElement will clear m_bNullCheck).

Similarly, the framework needs to check that elements that should be followed by character data (such as integer values) don't have children. This is done using a member variable (m_bCharacters) that is set to true in these situations. This variable is then checked in the endElement and startElement SAX content handler method implementations. If it's true, then the framework returns an error, because it's expecting characters to be the next SAX method to be invoked.

Another malformed packet check occurs for UDTs. If a struct is encountered and it isn't an href, then the top-level struct element must be followed by child elements. This verification is accomplished using a member variable (m_bChildCheck) that's set to true when a non-href UDT is encountered. The member variable is checked in endElement. If it's true, the framework returns an error, because it's expecting startElement to be the next SAX method to be invoked.

Structs and Enums

The framework supports enumerations in much the same way it deals with other simple types, such as integers. The primary difference is that it must assign the value based on the *name* of value, rather than doing some other string conversion operation. Listing 19-19 presents an example Web service that uses an enumeration.

Listing 19-19. Web Service Using an Enumeration

```
// EnumTest.h : Defines the ATL Server request handler class
//
#pragma once

namespace EnumTestService
{
// all struct, enum, and typedefs for
// your web service should go inside the namespace

[ export ]
enum TestEnum { EnumVal1, EnumVal2, EnumVal3 };

// IEnumTestService - web service interface declaration
//
[
    uuid("3484E1E4-D46C-44DD-871D-52799101ADCE"),
    object
]
__interface IEnumTestService
{
    // HelloWorld is a sample ATL Server web service method. It shows how to
    // declare a web service method and its in parameters and out parameters
    [id(1)] HRESULT EnumTest(
        [in] TestEnum InputEnum,
        [out, retval] TestEnum *OutputEnum);
    // TODO: Add additional web service methods here
};


// EnumTestService - web service implementation
//
[
    request_handler(name="Default", sdl="GenEnumTestWSDL"),
    soap_handler(
        name="EnumTestService",
        namespace="urn:EnumTestService",
        protocol="soap"
    )
]
class CEnumTestService :
    public IEnumTestService
{
```

```
public:
    // This is a sample web service method that shows how to use the
    // soap_method attribute to expose a method as a web method
    [ soap_method ]
    HRESULT EnumTest(
        /*[in]*/ TestEnum InputEnum,
        /*[out, retval]*/ TestEnum *OutputEnum)
    {
        *OutputEnum = InputEnum;
        return S_OK;
    }
    // TODO: Add additional web service methods here
}; // class CEnumTestService

} // namespace EnumTestService
```

Listing 19-20 shows the attribute-injected metadata for the enumeration.

Listing 19-20. Injected Code for a Web Service Using an Enumeration

```
__if_not_exists(__EnumTestService_TestEnum_entries)
{
extern __declspec(selectany) const
_soapmapentry __EnumTestService_TestEnum_entries[] =
    {
        { 0xDA154F6B, "EnumVal3", L"EnumVal3",
          sizeof("EnumVal3")-1, 2, SOAPFLAG_FIELD,
          0, NULL, NULL, -1 },

        { 0xDA154F6A, "EnumVal2", L"EnumVal2",
          sizeof("EnumVal2")-1, 1, SOAPFLAG_FIELD,
          0, NULL, NULL, -1 },

        { 0xDA154F69, "EnumVal1", L"EnumVal1",
          sizeof("EnumVal1")-1, 0, SOAPFLAG_FIELD,
          0, NULL, NULL, -1 },

        { 0x00000000 }
    };

extern __declspec(selectany) const _soapmap __EnumTestService_TestEnum_map =
    {
        0xF8EFE655,
        "TestEnum",
```

```
        L"TestEnum",
        sizeof("TestEnum")-1,
        sizeof("TestEnum")-1,
        SOAPMAP_ENUM,
        ___EnumTestService_TestEnum_entries,
        sizeof(::EnumTestService::TestEnum),
        1,
        -1,
        SOAPFLAG_NONE,
        0xF29B2B15,
        "urn:EnumTestService",
        L"urn:EnumTestService",
        sizeof("urn:EnumTestService")-1
    };
}
```

The ___EnumTestService_TestEnum_entries _soapmapentry array maps the enumeration value names to their actual integer value. When an enumeration is encountered, instead of calling AtlSoapGetElementValue, the characters SAX content handler function walks this array to match the enumeration value name to its integer value. It returns a failure if it doesn't find a matching value name. When generating the SOAP response, it matches the integer value to the name to get a string representation of the enumeration value.

The framework supports structs in the same way it supports Web service methods. Because Web service methods are modeled as structs, you can think of structs as a kind of nested function within the SOAP packet. Listing 19-21 presents an example Web service that uses a struct.

Listing 19-21. Web Service Using a Struct

```
// StructTest.h : Defines the ATL Server request handler class
//
#pragma once

namespace StructTestService
{
// all struct, enum, and typedefs for your web
// service should go inside the namespace

[ export ]
struct TestStruct
{
    int IntegerValue;
```

```
    BSTR StringValue;
};

// IStructTestService - web service interface declaration
//
[
    uuid("FFCF67A4-D9C9-4F54-BE04-E30A6B62E9C2"),
    object
]
__interface IStructTestService
{
    // HelloWorld is a sample ATL Server web service method.
    // It shows how to declare a web service method and its
    // in parameters and out parameters
    [id(1)] HRESULT StructTest(
        [in] TestStruct InputStruct,
        [out, retval] TestStruct *OutputStruct);
    // TODO: Add additional web service methods here
};


// StructTestService - web service implementation
//
[
    request_handler(name="Default", sdl="GenStructTestWSDL"),
    soap_handler(
        name="StructTestService",
        namespace="urn:StructTestService",
        protocol="soap"
    )
]
class CStructTestService :
    public IStructTestService
{
public:
    // This is a sample web service method that shows how to use the
    // soap_method attribute to expose a method as a web method
    [ soap_method ]
    HRESULT StructTest(
        /*[in]*/ TestStruct InputStruct,
        /*[out, retval]*/ TestStruct *OutputStruct)
    {
        OutputStruct->IntegerValue = InputStruct.IntegerValue;
        if (InputStruct.StringValue)
```

```
        {
            OutputStruct->StringValue = SysAllocString(InputStruct.StringValue);
            if (!OutputStruct->StringValue)
                return E_OUTOFMEMORY;
        }
        else
        {
            OutputStruct->StringValue = NULL;
        }

        return S_OK;
    }
    // TODO: Add additional web service methods here
}; // class CStructTestService

} // namespace StructTestService
```

Listing 19-22 shows the attribute-injected metadata for the `TestStruct` struct.

Listing 19-22. Injected Code for a Web Service Using a Struct

```
extern __declspec(selectany) const _soapmapentry
    ___StructTestService_TestStruct_entries[] =
{
    {
        0x8A8BD84B,
        "IntegerValue",
        L"IntegerValue",
        sizeof("IntegerValue")-1,
        SOAPTYPE_INT,
        SOAPFLAG_FIELD,
        offsetof(::StructTestService::TestStruct, IntegerValue),
        NULL,
        NULL,
        0    },
    {
        0xE257E474,
        "StringValue",
        L"StringValue",
        sizeof("StringValue")-1,
        SOAPTYPE_STRING,
        SOAPFLAG_FIELD | SOAPFLAG_NULLABLE,
        offsetof(::StructTestService::TestStruct, StringValue),
        NULL,
```

```
        NULL,
        0   },
    { 0x00000000 }
};

extern __declspec(selectany) const _soapmap
    ___StructTestService_TestStruct_map =
{
    0x15962585,
    "TestStruct",
    L"TestStruct",
    sizeof("TestStruct")-1,
    sizeof("TestStruct")-1,
    SOAPMAP_STRUCT,
    ___StructTestService_TestStruct_entries,
    sizeof(::StructTestService::TestStruct),
    2,
    -1,
    SOAPFLAG_NONE,
    0x57848C05,
    "urn:StructTestService",
    L"urn:StructTestService",
    sizeof("urn:StructTestService")-1
};
```

As you can see, the metadata is largely the same as the kind of metadata injected for Web service methods, with `___StructTestService_TestStruct_entries` containing information about the fields of the struct and `___StructTestService_TestStruct_map` containing information about the struct itself.

An example SOAP request/response for this Web service might look like Listings 19-23 and 19-24.

Listing 19-23. SOAP Request

```
<Envelope>
    <Body>
        <StructTest>
            <InputStruct>
<IntegerValue>0</IntegerValue>
<StringValue>String</String>
            </InputStruct>
        </StructTest>
    </Body>
</Envelope>
```

Listing 19-24. SOAP Response

```
<Envelope>
    <Body>
        <StructTest>
            <OutputStruct>
<IntegerValue>0</IntegerValue>
<StringValue>String</String>
            </OutputStruct>
        </StructTest>
    </Body>
</Envelope>
```

On processing the request, when the framework encounters the `InputStruct` element, it will push a new state on the stack with the `pMap` field set to `___StructTestService_TestStruct_map` and the `pvElement` field set to the value of `InputStruct` in the parameter struct for the Web service method. It then continues processing as normal using the new top state of the stack to process `IntegerValue` and `StringValue`. When it encounters the `InputStruct` close element, it verifies the fields of `InputStruct` and then pops the struct state off of the stack to continue processing the SOAP request.

When generating the response, the framework again treats the struct like a nested Web service method. When it encounters a struct while walking the metadata for the Web service method, it recursively invokes `GenerateResponseHelper` with the `_soapmap` for the struct.

Structs of structs are handled in a similar nesting fashion.

Arrays

ATL Server supports two kinds of arrays: fixed-size arrays (which includes multidimensional) and variable-length arrays. In terms of the SOAP request processing and response generation, there's relatively little difference between these two types of arrays, except that with fixed-size arrays, a specific number of elements is expected and if the number of elements received exceeds or falls below this number, an error will be returned by the framework. With variable-length arrays, the array elements are allocated as necessary.

When an array element is encountered, the framework will push an array state onto the stack in much the same way it handles structs. The `pvElement` field of the new state will point to the base of the array, and each element that's encountered from this point on will be incremented off `pvElement` based on the ordinal of the element (the `nElement` field of the `ParseState` is incremented for each array entry encountered) and the size of the data being stored in the array. The rest of the processing continues as normal for the actual data in the array, which may contain structs that contain arrays and so forth.

WSDL Generation

The ATL Server framework will automatically generate the WSDL for the Web service. The WSDL is generated dynamically at runtime based on an SRF template and attribute-injected metadata and functions for the Web service. For example, in the HelloWorld example from earlier in this chapter, the attribute-injected code includes the following line:

```
HANDLER_ENTRY_SDL("Default", CHelloWorldService,
::HelloWorldService::CHelloWorldService, GenHelloWorldWSDL)
```

This macro is similar to the HANDLER_ENTRY macro in the HANDLER_MAP for ATL Server request handlers and, in fact, the HANDLER_ENTRY_SDL macro will eventually delegate to the HANDLER_ENTRY macro. However, it also contains additional information such as the name of the handler from which to retrieve the WSDL (GenHelloWorldWSDL, or whatever is specified in the sdl parameter of the soap_handler attribute) and the Web service class from which to retrieve the metadata (CHelloWorldService).

The CSDLGenerator class and its base class _CSDLGenerator then use this information at runtime to retrieve the name of the Web service, its namespace URI, and its metadata. It then processes a WSDL SRF template, which uses the metadata to generate the WSDL.

Conclusion

In this chapter, you examined the internal workings of the ATL Server Web service support. You should now have a better understanding of how this Web service support works and why it has the limitations it has. You also should have a better idea of where to go to work around any limitations (or bugs) should the need arise.

In Chapter 13 you saw some performance tuning tips and tricks that you can use in your ATL Server application. These were in the form of some general guidelines and some specific issues that we had seen other development teams run into. In the next chapter you'll take a closer look at performance tuning your ATL Server application, including how to use and not use many of the ATL Server classes themselves.

CHAPTER 20

Performance Tuning ATL Server Web Applications

ATL SERVER PROVIDES AN efficient, high-performance framework for writing Web applications and Web services. However, ATL Server can't provide facilities for every scenario encountered by users, and it can't guard against every programming idiom that may hinder performance.

In this chapter we discuss techniques that will help you write high-performance code within the ATL Server framework. We examine how you can leverage portions of the ATL Server library in writing new user code and how to best use the services provided by ATL Server (such as caching, dynamic services, and per-thread services) to write Web applications that perform well. Additionally, we look at performance pitfalls, such as specific programming techniques to avoid when writing high-performance Web applications. Finally, we examine methods of accurately measuring the performance of Web applications and diagnosing problem areas: which metrics are relevant, testing tools and hardware, and testing setup.

What Performance Is

When dealing with definitions of performance, it's important to keep in mind some important caveats. First, it's practically impossible to duplicate the same environment in a lab performance-testing setting that users of an application will encounter; therefore, whatever performance numbers come from a lab setting won't necessarily reflect the performance users can expect. However, these kinds of performance numbers still serve as the best guide in improving your application's performance.

Second, even if it were possible to faithfully duplicate an end-user environment in a laboratory setting, the specific performance metrics you choose to measure may not necessarily be the same metrics that would be most relevant in improving performance from an end-user perspective.

And the third and most important caveat is this: The information about performance in this chapter is provided as *general* performance guidelines, suggestions, and testing scenarios—no general framework can accurately reflect all the performance-related considerations for specific applications. Performance testing and performance tuning must be considered in relation to the specific application.

Having put forth all these caveats, we feel it's important to note that there are still many useful generalizations that can be made about performance testing and performance tuning that will apply to most applications. The information in this chapter is still useful and accurate for the majority of applications built with ATL Server. It's just important to be able to recognize when it isn't.

A Typical Web Request from a Performance Perspective

In this section you'll look at a typical ATL Server Web request from a performance perspective. You'll learn where your time will usually be spent in a typical ATL Server Web request.

When a Web request first reaches the server, it must first go through the infrastructure of IIS before it reaches ATL Server (see Figure 20-1). Additionally, it must go through IIS when it's writing output, completing the request, and making queries for request information to IIS (HTTP headers and so forth). The exact overhead of the time spent in IIS depends on the type of request, the size of the request, the number of queries made to IIS about request information, and the size of the response. However, for a typical Web request, the overhead is between 5 percent and 10 percent of the execution time of the Web request. In general, most of the time is spent cracking the request parameters and headers, determining the ISAPI extension to which it will dispatch the request, and creating the ISAPI control structures to pass to the ISAPI extension.

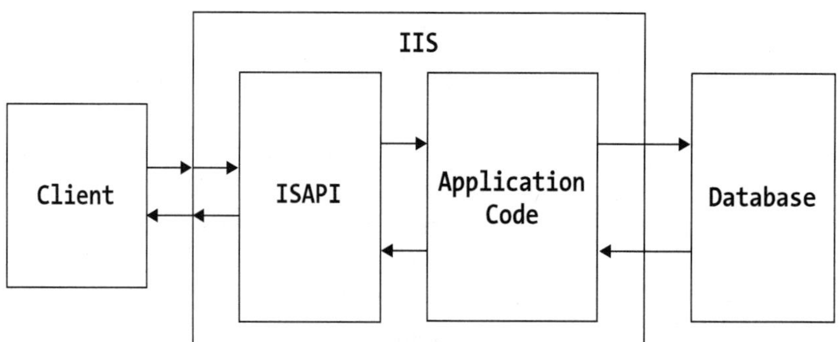

Figure 20-1. A typical Web application request involving databases

After IIS has done its initial processing of the request, it dispatches it to the ATL Server ISAPI DLL. Once it reaches the ATL Server ISAPI DLL, the request goes through several stages of processing. When the ATL Server ISAPI extension receives the request, it first creates an ATL Server–specific information structure for the request and puts it in its own thread pool, thus freeing IIS to continue handling other requests on the IIS thread pool. ATL Server then has slightly different behavior depending on whether it's processing the request as an SRF request or as a DLL request (see Chapter 5 for more details).

From a performance perspective, there's no significant difference at the ISAPI level in the request processing between SRF and DLL requests. In fact, for a typical request—one for which the application DLL has been loaded and cached and the parsed stencil (if it's an SRF request) has been cached—there's very little direct overhead in the ISAPI extension before or after invoking the request handler. Almost all the overhead comes from the creation of the request handler class itself. For a synchronous request (which is the typical case), the request handler class is created off a per-thread heap for maximum performance (we discuss per-thread heaps in more detail later in this chapter).

Once the request handler class has been created, the processing moves from the ISAPI extension to the application DLL and request handler class. For the purposes of this section, assume that the request handler will be doing SRF processing and that the parsed stencil has been cached. The ATL Server framework retrieves the parsed stencil from the cache and then begins invoking the tag methods for the rendering. The ATL Server framework overhead here is very small—it's just the cost of walking the stencil tags and invoking the tag methods.

Because database processing is so common in Web applications, assume that the request handler is also doing some database processing during the request. For this section, also assume that database access is through the ATL OLE DB Consumer Templates. The main overhead involved in database access relates to opening database connections and building and executing the query. ATL Server provides facilities for caching database connections to minimize the cost of opening connections. For an application that makes good use of ATL Server's connection caching mechanism, the majority of the cost will be in the SQL statements that are executed in the Web request. Though we discuss some database performance issues later in this chapter, optimization of SQL statements is outside the scope of this book. However, the same considerations that apply to SQL optimization in general apply to the use of SQL within ATL Server.

Once the request handler has finished its processing and returned control to the ISAPI extension, ATL Server does its final processing, which usually involves informing IIS of the request completion (and may also involve writing some headers and content to the request) and freeing any memory allocated for the request (usually the request handler class and the ATL Server–specific information structure).

For a typical Web request, the ATL Server framework takes an additional 5 percent to 10 percent of the execution time over the portion of the execution time taken by IIS.

Now that we've broken down a typical Web request into its parts from a performance perspective, you can look at how to optimize each portion (specifically, how *not* to slow things down). Later on in this chapter, you'll look at other scenarios that occur frequently in Web development but aren't as common as this "typical" request.

ATL Server Facilities

In this section you'll examine the services and tools provided by ATL Server to facilitate creating high-performance Web applications.

One of the ways to improve performance is to cache long-lived data in the `CIsapiExtension` class instead of creating or retrieving it on every request. For more information on the ATL Server caching facilities, see Chapter 12.

The ATL Server framework also provides simple ways to take advantage of per-thread data and per-thread services. The benefit here is that synchronization costs are avoided because each thread maintains a separate instance of the data or the service. For example, ATL Server uses a per-thread heap to allocate the request handler class when dealing with synchronous requests, thus avoiding the costs of synchronizing on the Win32 heap. ATL Server also provides a data source cache as a per-thread service. The cache eliminates the cost of opening and closing a database connection in every request, and by making it per-thread, the cost of any interthread marshaling is also eliminated.

In addition, ATL Server provides facilities to leverage knowledge about the lifetime of a request. For example, instead of using the normal heap or even the per-thread heap that ATL Server provides, it's possible to write a custom allocator that's optimized for a per-request usage. That is, it's fairly straightforward to write an "arena" allocator that simply moves a pointer for allocations and does nothing on any free operation. The pointer is reset at the beginning of a request. Using an arena allocator, it's possible to eliminate even more overhead than when you're using a per-thread, unsynchronized Win32 heap.

Pitfalls and Programming Idioms to Avoid

This section covers various programming pitfalls and idioms you'll want to avoid when you write high-performance Web applications. To a large extent, it's a matter of understanding that what may work fine in client applications can have a very detrimental impact in server applications.

There are some general programming idioms to avoid when you program Web applications. The major performance killers for server-side applications generally fall into a few major categories: excessive memory allocation, locks, and I/O.

Excessive Memory Allocation

Performing memory allocations for every Web request will have a significantly detrimental effect on performance so, whenever possible, you should avoid memory allocation on a per-request basis. Consider using the stack-based buffers instead of allocating from a heap. ATL 7.0 provides some classes to assist in this.

The `CFixedStringT` class allows you to use the functionality of `CString` while avoiding memory allocations in most common scenarios. For example, if you're reasonably certain the data you want to put into a character buffer is less than `MAX_PATH`, you can declare a string of type `CFixedStringT<CStringA, MAX_PATH>`, which won't do any allocations unless the string exceeds `MAX_PATH` characters.

The `CTempBuffer` class provides functionality for generic memory buffers similar to what `CFixedStringT` provides for `CString`s. The `CTempBuffer` class takes template arguments that specify the type of data for the memory buffer, the size of the initial memory buffer, and the type of allocator to use. If the memory required exceeds that specified by the template argument, `CTempBuffer` will allocate from the heap. For example, if you're reasonably certain that the data you want to put into a `BYTE` buffer is less than 128 bytes, you can declare an object of type `CTempBuffer<BYTE, 128, CCRTAllocator>`. In fact, in this situation, the object can be declared just as `CTempBuffer<BYTE>` because the default template parameters for the size and allocator type are 128 and `CCRTAllocator`, respectively. The type of allocator to use depends on your code, but in general it's fine to leave the default allocator in place. If there's a particular reason you need to use the `GlobalAlloc` or `LocalAlloc` functions, you can use the `CGlobalAllocator` or `CLocalAllocator` classes, respectively.

For stack-based allocations, the `_alloca` function is also an option. However, the `_alloca` function should be used only with small allocations, never in a loop, and never in a recursive function. If there isn't enough stack space for `_alloca` to perform the allocation, a stack overflow exception will result. In general, it's preferable to use the `CFixedStringT` or `CTempBuffer` class for stack-based buffers.

Locks

Locks represent another performance killer for server-side applications. Any kind of per-request synchronization will negatively affect performance and should be avoided whenever possible. However, there are times when the cost of synchronization is worth the benefit derived from the object being synchronized. For example, synchronizing on cache is worth it if the cost of creating/retrieving the cached data on every request is prohibitively expensive. ATL Server uses several caches internally that, although they take a performance hit on synchronization, improve the overall performance of the framework. Examples include the stencil cache, the DLL cache, and the file cache.

When locks are necessary, such as in the ATL Server cache scenarios, it's important to minimize their overhead. You should keep a few important considerations in mind. First, don't spend too much time in the lock. The longer a thread holds onto a lock, the longer other threads are waiting for that lock. The ATL Server caches, for example, do as much work as possible outside the lock and take the lock only when absolutely necessary. Another way to minimize the cost of synchronization is to use reader/writer locks. Unfortunately, neither the Win32 API nor ATL/MFC provide a built-in reader/writer lock. There are many open-source implementations of reader/writer locks for Win32 available, however.

Even though there are many ways to minimize the cost of locks, it's best to avoid their use altogether. Using per-thread services, for example, eliminates the need for synchronization on those services. For examples of per-thread services, see Chapter 12.

I/O

Another important consideration to keep in mind when you write server-side applications is that the same APIs that work fine on the client won't necessarily behave well on the server. It's important to be aware of what APIs you're calling and their cost. There are some APIs that you should avoid altogether.

When you write code in C++, especially server-side code, it's also important to keep in mind the hidden costs involved in C++. Though these hidden costs rarely have a significant effect on performance, it's still important to keep in mind what the code is doing under the covers. In particular, it's important to pay attention to what functions are being called when you're using overloaded operators. A simple += operation may actually be extremely expensive.

It's also important to be aware of what constructors and cast operators are implicitly invoked. For example, `CString` will do implicit casts, conversions, and even create temporary `CString`s when assigning `CString`s of different types or when assigning a character buffer of a different type to a `CString`. For example,

```
CStringW wstr = "ASCII string";
```

will construct a temporary `CString` for the ASCII string before it makes the assignment—a very expensive operation.

Though in general it's important to keep such considerations in mind when you write the code, using the `_ATL_CSTRING_EXPLICIT_CONSTRUCTORS` preprocessor directive before including any ATL files will ensure no temporaries are constructed for situations like those in the preceding code snippet. In general, however, you should always be aware of what the code you write is doing under the covers to avoid any unforeseen performance problems.

Finally, any use of C++ exceptions should be limited to truly exceptional situations, such as out-of-memory errors and uncommon errors. Any errors that are "expected" or are likely to occur in any given request should be handled through the normal error-handling procedures because C++ exceptions are too expensive in dealing with common errors.

In general, the most important thing is to be aware of what the code you write is doing and never assume that some function will have good performance simply because it comes from ATL, the C runtime (CRT), or the Win32 API.

Measuring Performance

In this section we discuss how to measure the performance of your application. We describe the tools and techniques you can use, some metrics that relate to performance, and how to interpret testing results.

Tools such as Application Center Test (ACT, which ships as part of Visual Studio .NET Enterprise Edition) allow you to get some performance data on your applications by recording and running scripts that make requests to your Web site and record and collate performance information on the requests. Most of these kinds of tools allow you to specify a number of client machines from which requests will be made during the test; ACT also allows you to specify the number of threads on each client and the number of connections on each thread. ACT allows you to record scripts just by clicking through your Web application in Internet Explorer. If your application doesn't lend itself to being tested in this way, you may have to create the scripts by hand. This manual approach involves adding `GET`/`POST` entries to specific URLs with specific data. Most Web stress tools have similar facilities for custom scripts.

ACT, like most tools, allows you to specify a duration for the test and a warm-up time. It's important to enter a reasonable warm-up time so that your application will be in its *steady state* when the main test is run. That is, any data that will generally be retrieved from the cache will already be cached, all DLLs that will generally be loaded during a request will already be loaded, all SRF files that will generally be parsed will be in the cache, and so forth. Using a reasonable warm-up period ensures that the performance data won't be impacted by start-up time costs. For the duration of the test, usually a short period of time is enough to get accurate performance data. A 10–30 second warm-up time and 1–5 minute duration should be adequate for the majority of applications. If your application needs to do more at start-up or takes a particularly long time to handle requests, you would need to adjust your settings accordingly. But for a typical ATL Server application (that is, SRF files and simple database requests), these settings should suffice.

Another setup issue has to do with keep-alive connections. Unfortunately, ACT doesn't allow you to easily set this option, but most commercial tools will allow you to specify connections should be kept alive between requests, thus eliminating the cost of reopening the connection on every request.

Once you've run your test, the tool will report a summary regarding the total number of requests made and the number of success codes returned, failure codes returned, and so forth. The first thing to check is that the return codes reported are as expected—that is, if you aren't expecting any failures, make sure there are no failures reported. ACT, like most tools, has a variety of metrics that are reported. What metrics are relevant depend on your application, but generally the most useful performance metrics are Requests Per Second, Average Response Time, Time To First Byte, and Time To Last Byte. Some other relevant metrics for diagnosing performance bottlenecks are Total Requests, Total Bytes Received, and Total Bytes Sent.

Requests Per Second is the most generally useful metric to measure the performance of your application because it tells you how much load it can handle. Average Response Time, Time To First Byte, and Time To Last Byte are useful metrics for testing the responsiveness of your Web site. Depending on what's most relevant to your Web application, you would weigh these performance metrics differently. If it's more important that your application be able to handle a very large user load, then Requests Per Second will be very useful, but if it's more important for your application to be snappy and responsive for the user, Time To First Byte and Time To Last Byte may be more relevant to you.

When you're diagnosing performance issues, Total Requests, Total Bytes Received, and Total Bytes Sent are useful metrics to help determine where your performance bottleneck is. Using the aforementioned metrics in combination with the duration of the test, you can determine the network usage in terms of megabits per second for your application and compare that against the capabilities of your network connection to determine if your application is network bound:

(((Total Bytes Received + Total Bytes Sent)*8) / 1024) / (Duration in Seconds) = Megabits Per Second

You can also use the Win32 performance counters to determine network usage during the test. Though you'll almost never reach the maximum capabilities of your network and there are other considerations (such as network packet size, other network operations, and so on), this metric can help you narrow down your performance bottleneck when you use it in combination with other metrics, such as CPU usage on the Web application server and the database server. For a typical ATL Server application, if the CPU usage on the Web application and database servers isn't 100 percent, then your bottleneck may lie elsewhere, such as in the network. This isn't always the case, however, as you may be spending a lot of idle time in locks on the Web server if you've written custom caches.

The Windows performance counters can be very helpful in narrowing down performance problems. You can use the counters to track issues such as excessive file I/O, memory leaks, page faults, and so forth, all of which can severely impact performance. The ATL Server framework also provides performance counters to track data within the framework itself. The ATL Server performance counters include information about requests per second, average response time, the number of active threads, and the number of requests waiting for an active thread, among other things.

Another consideration to keep in mind is the request size. Using too many query parameters, form variables, or cookies can result in the request size being larger than necessary. This is also true of the response size. Try to make the response as small as possible. Avoid sending too many cookies back to the user and try to minimize the page size as well. One good way to reduce the size of your pages is to eliminate unnecessary white space from your pages, as HTML will ignore most white space anyway.

A final consideration is client-side performance. From the end user's perspective, poor client-side performance can be just as much a problem as poor server-side performance. Coverage of efficient HTML design is outside the scope of this book, but some common problems include excessive script code, overly complicated tables, too many frames, too many images, or images that are too large.

One final tool that's helpful in performance tuning any application is a profiler. Many commercial profilers are available that can provide good data on your Web application hot spots. If you need to specify the process to which you have to attach, you'll need to attach to the process in which the ATL Server ISAPI DLL is running. If your application is running in-process, this will be inetinfo.exe on Windows 2000 and earlier, and w3wp.exe on Windows Server 2003. If your application is running out-of-process, this will one of the dllhost.exe processes on Windows 2000 (you can determine which dllhost.exe process has your DLL loaded by using `tasklist -m <isapidllname>`).

Conclusion

Measuring the performance of your Web application means defining the performance criteria that are relevant to your application and testing them accurately. In this chapter we discussed the various relevant metrics in performance testing, how to accurately measure them, and how to improve the performance of your application based on this data. Even though every application is unique, you can apply the general guidelines put forth in this chapter to nearly any ATL Server–based application.

One of the more interesting technologies that Microsoft has released in recent times is the Passport technology. The Microsoft Passport service enables application developers to authenticate using a central service instead of creating their own. In the next chapter you'll see how you can use ATL Server to access the functionality provided by Passport.

CHAPTER 21

ATL Server and Passport .NET

PASSPORT IS A UNIQUE SERVICE offered by Microsoft that allows users to create an identity that they can use to authenticate themselves with any Passport-enabled applications. This allows users the convenience of creating and using one identity across a number of unrelated applications. As a developer, instead of spending valuable development time developing an authentication system and user database, you can use Passport and focus your efforts on your application development.

Passport is an exciting service that benefits both developers and customers. This chapter explains how to integrate Passport seamlessly into your ATL Server Web applications.

Using Passport

If you've ever visited a Passport-enabled site such as Hotmail (`http://www.hotmail.com`) or MSN (`http://www.msn.com`), you'll notice the same Sign In button. Clicking that button will take you to a page or dialog box that prompts you for your user name and password. If you successfully authenticated with Passport, the site will typically display content tailored to your profile. For example, once you sign in with MSN, the news and weather displayed are tailored to suit the geographic information stored in your Passport profile.

This functionality is simple, but quite powerful and convenient. Using Passport gives your users a consistent and familiar user interface that they can use to authenticate themselves. Because Passport identities aren't restricted to individual applications, your users have to maintain only one set of credentials that they can use for any Passport-enabled application.

How to implement this scenario is what we focus on in this chapter. On your own time, you should explore the other services that Passport offers, such as the sign-in service that restricts content for underage users. The scenario that we describe requires the interaction of the following pieces of technology:

- Your Web application.

- Passport Manager running on your application.

- The Passport server hosted by Microsoft (sometimes this is also referred to as a Passport "environment").

- The application your user is using to access your Web application. This is usually a Web browser, but some applications, such as instant messaging clients, may use Passport as well.

To develop with Passport, you'll need to download and install the Passport SDK. This SDK is available from `http://www.passport.com/business`. You'll also need to configure your Visual C++ .NET project to reference the passport.h and passport.lib files that this SDK installs. Installing the Passport SDK will install Passport Manager.

Passport Manager is the entity that allows you to interact with the Passport servers hosted by Microsoft. For example, your Web application will prompt a user for his or her username and password. Passport Manager will send a remote request with this information to the Passport server that it has been configured to use with this information.

Microsoft hosts "test" Passport servers as well as "production" Passport servers. During your development, you have to configure your Passport Manager to use a test Passport server. Once your development and testing is done, you can reconfigure your Passport Manager to target the production Passport server. This all sounds much more complicated than it is; the technical aspect of reconfiguring your Passport Manager to use a production Passport server is really just a matter of changing a URL. The Passport SDK ships with a convenient tool that you can use to visually configure your Passport Manager. On the nontechnical side, there's an application process that you have to work through in order to be allowed to use the production Passport servers. At the time of this writing, there's a subscription fee that you have to pay in order to use the production Passport servers. The Passport SDK documentation and Web site (`http://www.passport.com`) do an excellent job of explaining the technical and nontechnical steps that you should follow as your application moves from the test environment to the production environment. The SDK documentation and Web site will offer the most up-to-date information in these areas.

If the information that your user entered is valid, the Passport server will return a security token to your Passport Manager. This security token indicates that your user has been successfully authenticated, and the token will expire after a specified amount of time. Passport Manager sends this token to your client as a cookie. The client application, usually a Web browser, is expected to persist this cookie. When the client makes another request to your application, this cookie will be sent as part of the request. The Passport Manager on your server will read the value of this cookie and determine if it's still a valid security token for this user. If the token is valid, then your Web application can use Passport Manager to retrieve information about this user and display content specific to your user, as we discussed earlier. Otherwise, your application can prompt your user to reenter his or her credentials. All of the communication between the client, Passport Manager, and Passport server is done using secure HTTP.

Passport is an evolving technology, so you should always consult the latest documentation and/or Web site to get the most up-to-date information. That said, what we've described so far in this section is a high-level description of how Passport works and it probably won't change for some time.

From the development point of view, all of the network communication that goes on between these pieces is transparent. Passport Manager is exposed as a set of COM interfaces that you can use, so you're isolated from the fact that it's making network requests to remote Passport servers. Passport Manager also makes the way it processes information from your client's cookies transparent.

Now that you have an understanding of how Passport works, you'll take a look in the next section at how you can implement the scenario described earlier.

Initializing Passport Manager

You'll interact with Passport Manager using the `IPassportManager2` interface. You can use this interface in your code by including the passport.h header file and linking with the passport.lib library. As its name suggests, this interface is the core interface for working with Passport Manager.

The code that you'll build in this chapter will be a request handler class that knows how to work with Passport. Once you've built this request handler class, you'll use it to implement the scenario.

First declare your new request handler, as shown in Listing 21-1.

Listing 21-1. Declaration of a Passport-Enabled Request Handler

```
#include <atlstencil.>
#include <passport.h>

template < class THandler,
           class ThreadModel=CComSingleThreadModel,
           class TagReplacerType=CHtmlTagReplacer< THandler > >

class CPassportHandlerT : public CRequestHandlerT< THandler,
                                                   ThreadModel,
                                                   TagReplacerType >

{
protected:
        typedef CRequestHandlerT< THandler,
                                  ThreadModel,
```

```
                                        TagReplacerType> baseType;

        IPassportManager2 *m_passportManager;
};
```

As you can see, you'll keep a pointer to the `IPassportManager2` interface as a member in your new class because you'll need to use Passport Manager in a number of places in the new class.

Next, you'll initialize Passport Manager for each request that you process. This allows Passport Manager to read information it needs from the client HTTP request. You'll override the `InitializeHandler` method in your request handler to accomplish this initialization, as shown in Listing 21-2.

Because ATL Server applications are essentially ISAPI applications, you'll use the `OnStartPageECB` method to initialize Passport Manager. This method expects a pointer to the *extension control block* (ECB) associated with this request. The ECB is a structure that IIS initializes that contains all the information about the request the client is making. The ECB also contains pointers to functions that can be used to read/write data to/from the client. The ECB structure is really the link between IIS and an ISAPI application.

In most cases, you don't have to access the ECB directly when you're developing ATL Server applications. ATL Server provides a class, `CServerContext`, that exposes methods for accessing all of the information and methods in an ECB structure; the `CRequestHandlerT` class stores an instance of this class in a member, `m_spServerContext`, that you can use in your ATL Server applications. However, in cases where you do need access to the actual ECB structure, you can override the `InitializeHandler` method and get access to the ECB from the `pRequestInfo` parameter.

Don't worry if you see members being used in Listing 21-2 that weren't declared in Listing 21-1—we omit some of these declarations for now, but you'll see them in the full code listing at the end of this chapter.

Listing 21-2. Initializing Passport Manager

```
HTTP_CODE InitializeHandler( AtlServerRequest *pRequestInfo,
                             IServiceProvider *pProvider )
{
    HTTP_CODE httpCode = baseType::InitializeHandler(pRequestInfo,pProvider);

    if (httpCode == HTTP_SUCCESS)
    {
        if (!m_passportManager)
        {
```

```
            if (FAILED(CoCreateInstance(CLSID_Manager,
                                        NULL,
                                        CLSCTX_INPROC_SERVER,
                                        IID_IPassportManager2,
                                        (void**)&m_passportManager)))
            {
                return HTTP_S_FALSE;
            }
        }

        DWORD bufferSize(ATL_MAX_COOKIE_LEN);
        CHAR  cookieHeader[ATL_MAX_COOKIE_LEN + 1];
        cookieHeader[0] = 0;

       if (FAILED(m_passportManager->OnStartPageECB((BYTE*)pRequestInfo->pECB,
                                                     &bufferSize,
                                                     cookieHeader)))
        {
            return HTTP_S_FALSE;
        }

        CString url;
        bool    https(false);

        if (!GetURL(url, https))
        {
            return HTTP_S_FALSE;
        }

        m_returnURL  = url;
        m_usingHTTPS = https;

        CCookie passportCookie;
        if( passportCookie.Parse( cookieHeader ) )
        {
            m_HttpResponse.AppendCookie( passportCookie );
        }

        m_HttpResponse.SetCacheControl("no-cache");
        m_HttpResponse.SetContentType("text/html");
    }

    return httpCode;
}
```

Let's have a look at this code line-by-line:

- *Line 4:* You want to preserve the behavior of your base class, so you call back to the base implementation first. If that's successful, then you'll continue on and do your Passport-specific initialization.
- *Lines 8 through 14:* Passport Manager is exposed to you as a COM interface, so you can use `CoCreateInstance` to a get a pointer to `IPassportManager2`.
- *Lines 20 through 29:* Passport Manager needs to know where to read information about the client's request. There are methods on the `IPassportManager2` interface to read client requests from ASP and ISAPI. Passport may require some cookies to be set on the client; these cookies are returned in the `cookieHeader` variable.
- *Lines 31 through 37:* To authenticate with Passport, your users will click a Sign In button. This button is a link to a URL on a Passport server. After it tries to authenticate the user, the Passport server needs to know where the user should go. To do this, you need to give Passport a return URL. In the case of the code you'll build in this chapter, and in most cases in general, this return URL will be the URL that the client used to request your ATL Server application in the first place.
- *Lines 42 through 46:* Set any cookies that Passport Manager requested.
- *Lines 48 and 49:* The last steps in your initialization are to turn off caching and set your content type to indicate that you're returning textual HTML. Turning off caching is helpful especially during the development phase so that the browser won't display cached information about whether you're authenticated with Passport or not.

The code in Listing 21-2 called a `GetURL` function. Let's look at how that method is implemented. Because you're building a request handler that could be used for a number of different applications, you want to get the URL the client requested in a generic way. You'll put this code in the `GetURL` method more for neatness than for anything else. The code for this method is as shown in Listing 21-3.

Listing 21-3. GetURL Implementation

```
bool GetURL(CString& url, bool& bHttps)
{
    CHAR szURL[ATL_URL_MAX_URL_LENGTH];
```

```
    DWORD dwUrlSize = sizeof(szURL) * sizeof(CHAR);

    CHAR szServer[ATL_URL_MAX_HOST_NAME_LENGTH];
    DWORD dwServerSize = sizeof(szServer) * sizeof(CHAR);

    CHAR szHttps[10];
    DWORD dwHttpsLen = sizeof(szHttps) * sizeof(CHAR);

    if (m_spServerContext->GetServerVariable("URL",
                                             szURL,
                                             &dwUrlSize) != FALSE)
    {
        if (m_spServerContext->GetServerVariable("SERVER_NAME",
                                                 szServer,
                                                 &dwServerSize) != FALSE)
        {
            bHttps = false;
            if ((m_spServerContext->GetServerVariable(
                    "HTTPS",
                    szHttps,
                    &dwHttpsLen) != FALSE) &&
                  (!_stricmp(szHttps, "ON")))
            {
                bHttps = true;
            }
            _ATLTRY
            {
                url.Format("http%s://%s%s", bHttps ? "s" : "",
                           szServer,
                           szURL);

                return true;
            }
            _ATLCATCHALL()
            {
                return false;
            }
        }
    }

    return false;
}
```

All of the code in `GetURL` is basically for accessing server variables. *Server variables* are a set of data that IIS stores that provides information about the HTTP connection the client made as well as information about the IIS server itself. You can access the server variables using the `m_spServerContext` member that's part of your `CRequestHandlerT` base class. As we mentioned before, `m_spServerContext` is an instance of the `CServerContext` class, which is essentially an abstraction of the ECB structure.

Let's take a look at this code line-by-line. You should also consult the IIS SDK documentation for a full listing of all the server variables and their definitions.

- *Line 12:* The server variable `URL` will give you the base portion of the URL that the client requested. This doesn't contain the protocol or parameters that were part of that request.

- *Lines 16 through 18:* The `SERVER_NAME` server variable gives you the name of the IIS server you're running. Getting the name in this manner lets you not have to rely on reading the registry or anything on the local machine to determine the name of your IIS installation. The `HTTPS` server variable contains a value of `ON` or `OFF` to indicate whether the request came through a secure channel or an insecure channel, respectively. You'll want to preserve this information for Passport Manager, because if your client came through a secure channel, you don't want Passport Manager to send the client back to your application using an insecure channel.

- *Line 31:* Finally, you build your return URL with a protocol of `http` or `https`, depending on whether or not the user who called your application used a secure channel. A more advanced method that we leave as an exercise for the interested reader is to use the `SERVER_PROTOCOL` server variable to determine this information.

We hope you've seen that working with Passport Manager in ATL Server isn't that difficult. In fact, the code in this section is probably the most complicated code in this chapter. Now that you've initialized Passport Manager, you'll take a look at how you can use it to implement the scenario described earlier in this chapter.

Using Passport to Authenticate

As we discussed earlier in this chapter, one of the benefits of Passport is the ability to give your users a consistent and familiar user interface to use. You'll notice that all Passport-enabled sites use the following Sign In button (note that at the time of this writing, this is the current image):

If the user clicks this button, the Passport Login user interface displays. If the user has authenticated successfully, this button becomes a Sign Out button:

The `CPassportRequestHandlerT` class that you're building in this chapter will expose this functionality as a stencil tag. Remember from earlier in this book that stencil tags are used in SRF files to insert dynamic content into the stream of data that will be sent to the client.

You'll create a stencil tag `{{Passport_LogoTag}}` to insert the Sign In or Sign Out button that Passport provides. By implementing a stencil tag in `CPassportHandlerT`, any ATL Server application that you build using this request handler class will be able to insert a Passport Sign In or Sign Out button by simply including the following stencil tag:

```
{{Passport_LogoTag}}
```

Let's take a look at the code necessary to implement this stencil tag. The first step is to add a replacement map to your `CPassportHandlerT` request handler class:

```
BEGIN_REPLACEMENT_METHOD_MAP(THandler)
     REPLACEMENT_METHOD_ENTRY("Passport_LogoTag", OnLogoTag)
END_REPLACEMENT_METHOD_MAP()
```

As you've probably seen in previous chapters, this replacement map simply associates the `{{Passport_LogoTag}}` stencil tag with the `OnLogoTag` method. The code for the `OnLogoTag` method is shown in Listing 21-4.

Listing 21-4. The OnLogoTag Method

```
1 HTTP_CODE OnLogoTag()
2 {
3     BSTR logoTag(NULL);
4
5     if (FAILED(m_passportManager->LogoTag(m_returnURL,
6                                          m_timeWindow,
7                                          m_forceLogin,
8                                          m_coBrandArgs,
9                                          m_langId,
10                                         m_usingHTTPS,
11                                         m_namespace,
12                                         m_kpp,
13                                         m_useSecureAuth,
14                                         &logoTag)))
15    {
16        m_HttpResponse << "ERROR - could not get LogoTag";
17        return HTTP_S_FALSE;
18    }
19
20    m_HttpResponse << logoTag;
21    ::SysFreeString(logoTag);
22
23    return HTTP_SUCCESS;
24 }
```

The `IPassportManager2::LogoTag` method takes several parameters that you should look at individually. All of the input parameters are optional; if they aren't specified, they will be taken from the Passport Manager registry settings. These registry settings are set using the Passport Manager Administrative tool included with the SDK.

Let's have a look at the code for `OnLogoTag` line-by-line:

- *Line 5:* You'll use the return URL that you built up during your initialization. This will give Passport Manager a URL to redirect the client to after the client has tried to authenticate him- or herself.

- *Line 6:* The time window is used to specify how long the security token is valid after the user successfully authenticates him- or herself.

- *Line 7:* This parameter should be `VARIANT_TRUE` if a return URL was specified and `VARIANT_FALSE` otherwise. If this parameter is `VARIANT_TRUE`, the time window is compared against the last time the user signed in; otherwise, it's compared against the last time the ticket was refreshed.

- *Line 8:* This parameter specifies the query parameters that are added to the logo tag URL for cobranding purposes. Basically, cobranding allows you to integrate the look and feel of your application with the look and feel that Passport uses. Please see the latest Passport SDK documentation for details about cobranding.

- *Line 9:* This parameter determines the language that Passport should use in its Login user interface. The value should be the integer value of the standard locale identifier (LCID) of the language you wish to use.

- *Line 10:* This parameter determines whether or not the return URL is using a secure channel. You obtain this value during your initialization, so you just have to pass it in.

- *Line 11:* This parameter allows you to specify an optional namespace, which helps you avoid name collisions in your HTML.

- *Line 12:* You should use this parameter only if you're implementing Kids Passport. That service is offered by Passport to restrict authentication based on consent levels. See the latest Passport SDK documentation for details on this aspect of Passport.

- *Line 13:* This parameter determines the security level for the Passport Login user interface. The following are valid values:

  0: This is the default. The Login user interface is served using HTTP (though the cookie containing the security token is written using HTTPS).

  1: The Login user interface is served using HTTPS. This requires that the return URL specified is using HTTPS as well.

  2: The Login user interface is a service using HTTPS. This requires that a security key be passed as well as a password.

- *Line 14:* This output parameter contains the URL that specifies the Sign In or Sign Out button. As mentioned earlier, clicking this button will display the Passport Login user interface.

As you can see, there are numerous parameters to the `LogoTag` method; the `CPassportHandlerT` class that you're building will leave these parameters unspecified. That means that their values will be taken from the Passport Manager registry settings. You can configure these settings using the Passport Manager Administrative tool included with the Passport SDK.

With the {{Passport_LogoTag}} stencil tag, an ATL Server application can easily add a Passport Sign In button. You should consult the latest Passport SDK documentation for guidelines as to where this button should appear in your application.

The next step in this scenario, covered in the next section, is to determine whether or not a user is authenticated. You need to know this to decide if you should show content specific to that user.

IsAuthenticated

ATL Server stencils implement basic logic constructs. You can take advantage of this to create a stencil tag that you can branch on, depending on whether or not the user is authenticated. You'll need to do this in order to display user-specific content.

Let's add a stencil tag to CPassportHandlerT called {{Passport_IsAuthenticated}}. This stencil tag will return a boolean value, so it can be used in a stencil as follows:

```
{{if Passport_IsAuthenticated}}
    Thanks for signing in!
{{else}}
    Please sign in!
{{endif}}
```

This stencil tag lets you conveniently divide the generic content from the user-specific content in your pages.

Adding this stencil tag is very similar to what you had to do for {{Passport_LogoTag}}. You need to expand your replacement map as follows:

```
BEGIN_REPLACEMENT_METHOD_MAP(THandler)
     REPLACEMENT_METHOD_ENTRY("Passport_LogoTag", OnLogoTag)
     REPLACEMENT_METHOD_ENTRY("Passport_IsAuthenticated", OnIsAuthenticated)
END_REPLACEMENT_METHOD_MAP()
```

This will associate the {{Passport_IsAuthenticated}} tag with the OnIsAuthenticated method. Listing 21-5 shows how to implement this method.

Listing 21-5. Authenticating a Passport Login Request

```
HTTP_CODE OnIsAuthenticated()
{
    VARIANT_BOOL isAuthenticated(VARIANT_FALSE);
    if (FAILED(m_passportManager->IsAuthenticated(m_timeWindow,
                                                  m_forceLogin,
                                                  m_useSecureAuth,
                                                  &isAuthenticated)))
    {
        return HTTP_S_FALSE;
    }

    return isAuthenticated == VARIANT_TRUE ? HTTP_SUCCESS : HTTP_S_FALSE;
}
```

This code is simple enough that we don't look at it line-by-line. The first three parameters are optional and serve the same purpose as in the `IPassportManager2::LogoTag` method. The last parameter is an output parameter that indicates whether or not the user has been authenticated. You'll return a mapping of this boolean value to the boolean values (`HTTP_S_FALSE`, `HTTP_SUCCESS`) that ATL Server uses in its stencil files.

Now you've seen how to provide a login user interface for your users to authenticate themselves as well as a way to determine if they've successfully done so. The only step remaining in this scenario is to display user-specific content.

Displaying User-Specific Content

When a user creates an account with Passport, he or she is creating a *profile* with Passport. This profile contains information such as nicknames, e-mail addresses, and/or geographical information.

NOTE *Passport strictly guards profile information. Please see the Passport documentation or the Passport Web site for privacy concerns regarding this information.*

You can use the Passport profile information constructively in many ways. You can add a high degree of user-friendliness to your application by using a user's nickname or automatically filling out an address form based on the user's profile information. You can access profile information in Passport .NET by name. Please see the latest Passport SDK documentation for a full list of valid profile names.

To conclude the `CPassportHandlerT` class, you'll add a stencil tag called `{{Passport_GetProfile}}`. This stencil tag will accept a name as a parameter, and assuming that name is a valid profile name, it will return the value for it. This tag can be used in a stencil as follows:

```
Hello {{Passport_GetProfile( "nickname")}}! Thanks for using ATL Server!
```

Adding this stencil tag means adding to your replacement tag as follows:

```
BEGIN_REPLACEMENT_METHOD_MAP(THandler)
    REPLACEMENT_METHOD_ENTRY("Passport_LogoTag", OnLogoTag)
    REPLACEMENT_METHOD_ENTRY("Passport_IsAuthenticated", OnIsAuthenticated)
    REPLACEMENT_METHOD_ENTRY_EX_STR("Passport_GetProfile", OnGetProfile)
END_REPLACEMENT_METHOD_MAP()
```

You'll notice this time that you use the `REPLACEMENT_METHOD_ENTRY_EX_STR` macro. This macro allows you to create a tag that takes a string parameter. Now you have the tag `{{Passport_GetProfile}}` associated with the method `OnGetProfile`, which takes a single string parameter. Listing 21-6 shows how to implement this method.

Listing 21-6. Getting Passport Profile Information

```
HTTP_CODE OnGetProfile(char *profileName)
{
    CComVariant value;

    if (FAILED(m_passportManager->get_Profile(CComBSTR(profileName), &value)))
    {
        return HTTP_S_FALSE;
    }

    switch (value.vt)
    {
        case VT_I1:
            m_HttpResponse << value.cVal;
             break;
        case VT_I4:
            m_HttpResponse << value.intVal;
            break;
        case VT_BSTR:
            m_HttpResponse << value.bstrVal;
```

```
20            break;
21        default:
22            m_HttpResponse << "Unknown type!";
23            break;
24    }
25
26    return HTTP_SUCCESS;
27 }
```

IPassportManager2 exposes get_Profile, which makes your job quite simple. You just have to call this method with the profile name given to use in the profileName parameter and try to display its value. The switch statements in lines 10 through 24 don't cover all the possible data types; for the sake of brevity, the code just converts the most likely ones.

Now you've added all the functionality you need to implement this scenario. In the next section you'll take a look at the complete code listing for your new class.

Putting It All Together

Listing 21-7 contains a few things that we omitted during the course of this chapter for the sake of brevity.

Listing 21-7. The Complete Example

```
#include <atlstencil.>
#include <passport.h>

template < class THandler,
           class ThreadModel=CComSingleThreadModel,
           class TagReplacerType=CHtmlTagReplacer< THandler > >

class CPassportHandlerT : public CRequestHandlerT< THandler,
                                                   ThreadModel,
                                                   TagReplacerType >
{
protected:
    typedef CRequestHandlerT< THandler,
                              ThreadModel,
                              TagReplacerType> baseType;

    IPassportManager2 *m_passportManager;
    CComVariant        m_returnURL;
    CComVariant        m_timeWindow;
```

```
    CComVariant         m_forceLogin;
    CComVariant         m_coBrandArgs;
    CComVariant         m_langId;

    CComVariant         m_usingHTTPS;
    CComVariant         m_namespace;
    CComVariant         m_kpp;
    CComVariant         m_useSecureAuth;

public:
        CPassportHandlerT() :
                m_passportManager(NULL),
                m_forceLogin(true),
                m_langId(GetThreadLocale())
        {}

        virtual ~CPassportHandlerT(void)
        {}

        HTTP_CODE Uninitialize(HTTP_CODE hcError)
        {
            if (m_passportManager)
            {
                m_passportManager->Release();
                m_passportManager = NULL;
            }

            return hcError;
        }

        HTTP_CODE InitializeHandler( AtlServerRequest *pRequestInfo,
                                     IServiceProvider *pProvider )
        {
            HTTP_CODE httpCode = baseType::InitializeHandler(pRequestInfo,
                                                              pProvider);

            if (httpCode == HTTP_SUCCESS)
            {
                if (!m_passportManager)
                {
                    if (FAILED(CoCreateInstance(CLSID_Manager,
                                                NULL,
                                                CLSCTX_INPROC_SERVER,
                                                IID_IPassportManager2,
```

```
                                              (void**)&m_passportManager)))
                {
                    return HTTP_S_FALSE;
                }
            }

            DWORD bufferSize(ATL_MAX_COOKIE_LEN);
            CHAR  cookieHeader[ATL_MAX_COOKIE_LEN + 1];
            cookieHeader[0] = 0;

            if (FAILED(m_passportManager->
                         OnStartPageECB((BYTE*)pRequestInfo->pECB,
                                        &bufferSize,
                                        cookieHeader)))
            {
                return HTTP_S_FALSE;
            }

            CString url;
            bool    https(false);

            if (!GetURL(url, https))
            {
                return HTTP_S_FALSE;
            }

            m_returnURL  = url;
            m_usingHTTPS = https;

            m_HttpResponse.SetCacheControl("no-cache");
            m_HttpResponse.SetContentType("text/html");
        }

        return httpCode;
}

bool GetURL(CString& url, bool& bHttps)
{
    CHAR szURL[ATL_URL_MAX_URL_LENGTH];
    DWORD dwUrlSize = sizeof(szURL) * sizeof(CHAR);

    CHAR szServer[ATL_URL_MAX_HOST_NAME_LENGTH];
    DWORD dwServerSize = sizeof(szServer) * sizeof(CHAR);
```

```
    CHAR szHttps[10];
    DWORD dwHttpsLen = sizeof(szHttps) * sizeof(CHAR);

    if (m_spServerContext->GetServerVariable("URL",
                                             szURL,
                                             &dwUrlSize) != FALSE)
    {
        if (m_spServerContext->GetServerVariable("SERVER_NAME",
                                                 szServer,
                                                 &dwServerSize) != FALSE)
        {
            bHttps = false;
            if ((m_spServerContext->GetServerVariable("HTTPS",
                                                      szHttps,
                                                      &dwHttpsLen) != FALSE)
                                                      &&
                                                   (!_stricmp(szHttps, "ON")))
            {
                bHttps = true;
            }
            _ATLTRY
            {
                url.Format("http%s://%s%s", bHttps ? "s" : "",
                                            szServer,
                                            szURL);
                return true;
            }
            _ATLCATCHALL()
            {
                return false;
            }
        }
    }

    return false;
}

HTTP_CODE OnLogoTag()
{
    BSTR logoTag(NULL);
```

```
    if (FAILED(m_passportManager->LogoTag(m_returnURL,
                                          m_timeWindow,
                                          m_forceLogin,
                                          m_coBrandArgs,
                                          m_langId,
                                          m_usingHTTPS,
                                          m_namespace,
                                          m_kpp,
                                          m_useSecureAuth,
                                          &logoTag)))
    {
        m_HttpResponse << "ERROR - could not get LogoTag";
        return HTTP_S_FALSE;
    }

    m_HttpResponse << logoTag;
    ::SysFreeString(logoTag);

    return HTTP_SUCCESS;
}

HTTP_CODE OnIsAuthenticated()
{
    VARIANT_BOOL isAuthenticated(VARIANT_FALSE);
    if (FAILED(m_passportManager->IsAuthenticated(m_timeWindow,
                                                  m_forceLogin,
                                                  m_useSecureAuth,
                                                  &isAuthenticated)))
    {
        return HTTP_S_FALSE;
    }

    return isAuthenticated == VARIANT_TRUE ? HTTP_SUCCESS : HTTP_S_FALSE;
}

HTTP_CODE OnGetProfile(char *profileName)
{
    CComVariant value;

    if (FAILED(m_passportManager->get_Profile(CComBSTR(profileName),
                                              &value)))
    {
         return HTTP_S_FALSE;
    }
```

```
        switch (value.vt)
        {
            case VT_I1:
                m_HttpResponse << value.cVal;
                break;
            case VT_I4:
                m_HttpResponse << value.intVal;
                break;
            case VT_BSTR:
                m_HttpResponse << value.bstrVal;
                break;
            default:
                m_HttpResponse << "Unknown type!";
                break;
        }

        return HTTP_SUCCESS;
    }

    BEGIN_REPLACEMENT_METHOD_MAP(THandler)
      REPLACEMENT_METHOD_ENTRY("Passport_LogoTag", OnLogoTag)
      REPLACEMENT_METHOD_ENTRY("Passport_IsAuthenticated", OnIsAuthenticated)
      REPLACEMENT_METHOD_ENTRY_EX_STR("Passport_GetProfile", OnGetProfile)
    END_REPLACEMENT_METHOD_MAP()
};
```

Now that you've built your new request handler, you'll come full circle in the next section and see how you can use it to implement the scenario you've been looking at throughout this chapter.

Using CPassportHandlerT

Let's take a look at how you can use your new request handler class to build a simple implementation of this chapter's scenario.

`CPassportHandlerT` can basically be used like the default `CRequestHandlerT` class that Visual Studio uses when generating a new ATL Server project. Here's the definition for your ATL Server application class:

```
#pragma once

#include "passporthandlert.h"

class CatlspassportHandler :
    public CPassportHandlerT<CatlspassportHandler>
{
public:
    HTTP_CODE ValidateAndExchange()
    {
        return HTTP_SUCCESS;
    }

};

BEGIN_HANDLER_MAP()
    HANDLER_ENTRY("Default", CatlspassportHandler)
END_HANDLER_MAP()
```

As you can see, the only change you've made is to use the `CPassportHandlerT` class. Because you're just building a simple example, most of the work will be in the SRF file, as shown in Listing 21-8.

Listing 21-8. Using a Passport-Enabled Request Handler in SRF

```
{{handler atlspassport.dll/Default}}
<html>
   <head>
   </head>
   {{Passport_LogoTag}}
   <br>
   {{if Passport_IsAuthenticated}} Great, you've signed in!
   <br>
   Here's what we know about you:
    <table border="1">
        <tr>
            <td>memberName</td>
             <td>{{Passport_GetProfile(memberName)}}</td>
        </tr>
```

```
        <tr>
            <td>memberIdLow</td>
            <td>{{Passport_GetProfile(memberIdLow)}}</td>
        </tr>
        <tr>
            <td>memberIdHigh</td>
            <td>{{Passport_GetProfile(memberIdHigh)}}</td>
        </tr>
        <tr>
            <td>profileVersion</td>
            <td>{{Passport_GetProfile(profileVersion)}}</td>
        </tr>
        <tr>
            <td>country</td>
            <td>{{Passport_GetProfile(country)}}</td>
        </tr>
        <tr>
            <td>memberName</td>
            <td>{{Passport_GetProfile(memberName)}}</td>
        </tr>
        <tr>
            <td>postalCode</td>
            <td>{{Passport_GetProfile(postalCode)}}</td>
        </tr>
        <tr>
            <td>region</td>
            <td>{{Passport_GetProfile(region)}}</td>
        </tr>
        <tr>
            <td>city</td>
            <td>{{Passport_GetProfile(city)}}</td>
        </tr>
        <tr>
            <td>lang_preference</td>
            <td>{{Passport_GetProfile(lang_preference)}}</td>
        </tr>
        <tr>
            <td>bday_precision</td>
            <td>{{Passport_GetProfile(bday_precision)}}</td>
        </tr>
        <tr>
            <td>{{Passport_GetProfile(birthdate)}}</td>
        </tr>
        <tr>
```

```
59              <td>gender</td>
60              <td>{{Passport_GetProfile(gender)}}</td>
61          </tr>
62          <tr>
63              <td>preferredEmail</td>
64              <td>{{Passport_GetProfile(preferredEmail)}}</td>
65          </tr>
66          <tr>
67             <td>nickname</td>
68              <td>{{Passport_GetProfile(nickname)}}</td>
69          </tr>
70          <tr>
71              <td>wallet</td>
72              <td>{{Passport_GetProfile(wallet)}}</td>
73          </tr>
74          <tr>
75              <td>directory</td>
76              <td>{{Passport_GetProfile(directory)}}</td>
77          </tr>
78          <tr>
79              <td>flags</td>
80              <td>{{Passport_GetProfile(flags)}}</td>
81          </tr>
82      </table>
83      {{else}}
84              Why don't you sign in?
85 {{endif}}
86 </html>
```

Let's take a look at this SRF code line-by-line:

- *Line 1:* This is the usual SRF tag to associate this SRF file with the ATL Server request handler in the DLL.

- *Line 5:* This tag will be replaced by the Sign In or Sign Out button image that Passport provides, depending on whether or not the user has been authenticated with Passport.

- *Line 7:* This is where you can take advantage of the branching properties in SRF. Recall that you implemented `{{Passport_IsAuthenticated}}` to return a boolean value (actually an SRF interpretation of a boolean value). If the user has been authenticated with Passport, you'll display profile information about that user. Otherwise, you'll display a message prompting the user to sign in (line 84).

- *Lines 13 through 80:* This block of SRF code will be executed if the user has been authenticated with Passport. In this block, you're making calls to your `{{Passport_GetProfile}}` tag. This tag will return information about the authenticated user. If you're using the test or beta Passport environment (you most likely are), then you'll get to see only dummy profile values. Once your site has been registered as an official Passport site, you can configure Passport Manager to use the production environment, which has actual profile values.

Conclusion

Using Passport and ATL Server together allows you to build high-performance, user-friendly applications. By using Microsoft Passport, you can add a high degree of user awareness to your application with very little effort.

You've spent a lot of time looking at how to build various types of ATL Server applications and services. In the next chapter, you'll explore how the Web services that you build with ATL Server interoperate with other implementations of Web services.

CHAPTER 22

Interoperability with ATL Server Web Services

THE IDEA BEHIND WEB services is to offer a lingua franca for communication between heterogeneous pieces of software over the Internet. This idea can work only as long as all the implementations respect the rules of the game. This means that for each given SOAP message, a SOAP payload generated by one implementation must be semantically similar to one generated by any other implementation.

This chapter presents a view on the interoperability efforts, with particular focus on the problems encountered during the interoperation testing of the ATL Server implementation. In addition to identifying some of the common interoperability problems, we discuss the ways in which some of these problems were solved and present workarounds for many common problems.

The discussion on SOAP interoperability is based on version 1.1 of the SOAP specification (`http://www.w3.org/TR/2000/NOTE-SOAP-20000508`) and version 1.1 of WSDL (`http://www.w3.org/TR/2001/NOTE-wsdl-20010315`). SOAP interoperability requires that the user has some level of familiarity with Web services (the SOAP specification) and WSDL. Some knowledge of the ATL Server SOAP implementation would be helpful, although this isn't required (see Chapters 10 and 19 for more information on these topics).

In this chapter we provide solutions for some common interoperability issues. By the end of this chapter you should have a good understanding of the implications of interoperability, a clear perspective on the problems that may occur, and knowledge of a few techniques that you can use to solve these and other problems that may arise.

What Interoperability Is

The definition of *interoperability* is straightforward: Two different SOAP implementations can communicate with each other. In practice this means that one SOAP application, developed using one of the SOAP development tools (implementation A) can send a message to a different application developed using another development tool (implementation B), have this message interpreted correctly, and be able to correctly interpret the response that it receives.

More specifically, this means that the following requirements must be met:

- The general structure of the message must be common, both for the sender and for the receiver of the SOAP message. This is usually not a problem: The development tools will most likely respect the `Envelope/Header(s)/Body` structure described in the specification.

- Each communicator is able to understand potential SOAP faults (error/ status information carriers) emitted by the other communicator.

- The data-type encoding matches that specified in the SOAP specification (section 5 of the SOAP specification).

Not all implementations have full support for all the XML Schema data types (in fact, very few do). ATL Server, for example, supports only the most commonly used basic types. So, another interoperability requirement is this:

- The data types used in the SOAP messages belong to the subsets supported by both communicators.

Most SOAP implementations use the WSDL protocol to describe their service. WSDL describes the endpoint of a service (i.e., the URL where SOAP messages are supposed to be sent), the messages that can be sent to that service (i.e., the SOAP methods exposed), the headers (if any) for each of the messages, and the parameters for those messages exposed.

In the WSDL document, the name that each parameter will take and the type of that parameter is specified. If some parameters are compound types (arrays or data structures are examples), the serialization rules for those types are also part of the WSDL. The WSDL document acts like a contract offered by a SOAP service: The service will "understand" a request from the client as long as it respects the rules contained in the WSDL document. This doesn't mean that *any* message respecting the WSDL will be accepted, nor does it mean that there won't be any faults. The destination application may still reject a message based on the semantics of the parameters. For instance, a hypothetical SOAP service performing arithmetical operations will most likely generate a fault if the second parameter of a division operation is 0 (i.e., "divide by zero"), although the type (integer or numeric) matches the WSDL contract correctly.

Thus, if the service exposes a WSDL contract and the development tool knows how to use one, a new requirement should appear in the preceding list:

- The development tool for the sender of the SOAP message must understand the WSDL exposed by the receiver.

Because all ATL Server SOAP applications either expose or consume a WSDL document, this item is relevant and required.

When and Why You Should Care About Interoperability

First of all, you *must* care about interoperability when providing a SOAP development tool. Second, as the developer of a SOAP-based solution, you should also think about interoperability issues, depending on the nature of the solution and, more important, on the production environment for the solution.

Fortunately for developers, most of the SOAP implementations take interoperability very seriously. Unfortunately for developers, this isn't always enough to guarantee headache-free implementations. The SOAP specification and the WSDL specification are very flexible and respecting them doesn't guarantee complete interoperability.

Interoperability often becomes a major issue when a solution is intended to run in an "open" environment. An example would be a SOAP server that will serve multiple clients built using different development tools (and potentially running on many different platforms). A SOAP service exposed over the Internet (e.g., a weather service or news service) will need to have interoperability issues taken into account as key factors during the design stage.

On the other hand, solutions intended to work in a "closed" environment can afford to focus less on interoperability issues. This is the case when the client is developed at the same time as the server, probably using the same development tool. In these cases, any interoperability issues can be discovered and fixed early in the development phase. Even in these cases, however, the planned lifetime (or, more likely, the *unplanned* lifetime) of the solution may still make interoperability an important factor. After all, do you really want your client and server to know about and rely on the implementation details of the other?

ATL Server Interoperability Limitations

In the previous section we covered generic interoperability issues that can and should be treated by any SOAP implementation. In this section we describe known limitations in the ATL Server implementation and ways to work around some of these limitations, when necessary.

Standard Basic Data Types Not Supported by ATL Server

Problems with the support of data types are usually best addressed from the client side, as a server will normally specify (via the WSDL) only types that are fully supported, and the client will have to comply with this specification. The solution presented here, however, will work equally well on the server and the client with the addition of just a few extra steps (discussed at the end of the section).

The ATL Server basic type support mainly focuses on those types that correspond directly with types in the C++ language. Some of the basic types included in the XML Schema Datatypes specification aren't directly supported, as they don't have a natural correspondent in C++ (e.g., `xsd:dateTime`), whereas others are supported by including them into a superset that can be represented in C++ (e.g., `xsd:nonPositiveInteger` is represented as `__int64`). The MSDN documentation contains an article with a list of all the basic types supported by ATL Server: `http://msdn.microsoft.com/library/default.asp?url=/library/en-us/vccore/html/vcconatlserverwebservicetypemapping.asp`.

One of the nice things about developing with ATL Server is that developers can use unsupported types. Therefore, if a developer finds the base implementation restrictive, he or she can write code to improve type support.

Also, for those types that are mapped to supersets (such as `nonPositiveInteger`, which will be represented as `__int64`), the developer can, if necessary, add appropriate restrictions and checks before executing the SOAP request. For example, a function like this:

```
<message name="echoNonPositiveIntegerIn">
  <part name="paramIn" type="s: nonPositiveInteger "/>
</message>
<message name="echoNonPositiveIntegerOut">
  <part name="return" type="s:nonPositiveInteger"/>
</message>
```

will generate (via sproxy.exe) the following code:

```
HRESULT echoNonPositiveInteger(__int64 paramIn, __int64* return);
```

And it can be easily wrapped in a different function that performs a check:

```
HRESULT echoSafeNonPositiveInteger(__int64 in, __int64 *out)
{
  if( in > 0)
    return E_PARAM;
  return echoNonPositiveInteger(in, out);
}
```

Those types that aren't directly supported by ATL Server are treated as strings. Thus, you can use the same technique to wrap the function with some code that converts between the internal chosen representation format for the type and the string to be passed as a parameter. So for a type such as `xsd:dateTime`, the sproxy-generated code would look like this:

```
HRESULT echoDateTime(BSTR bstrIn, BSTR* bstrOut),
```

which you could wrap in something like this:

```
HRESULT echoSafeDateTime(COleDateTime& dtIn, COleDateTime& dtOut)
{
  CString strDateTime = dtIn.Format(...);
  CComBSTR bstrIn;
  BSTR bstrOut;
  bstrIn.Append( strDateTime );
  HRESULT hRet = echoDateTime( bstrIn, &bstrOut);
  if( SUCCEEDED(hRet))
  {
    CW2A szNewTime(bstrOut);
    dtOut.Parse( szNewTime...);
  }
  return hRet;
}
```

CAUTION *In most cases, there's a good reason why ATL Server doesn't try to map an* `xsd` *type onto a "similar" type in C++ (e.g.,* `DateTime`*). When you do these mappings yourself, be careful of sometimes subtle semantic differences between the types that make them less compatible than you might otherwise realize.*

To create an ATL Server–based SOAP server that exposes a method using `xsd:dateTime` (or any other unsupported type), you could apply the same wrapping technique (i.e., writing a wrapper method that performs any required type checking). Take a method echoing an `xsd:dateTime` parameter, which internally will look like this:

```
HRESULT echoDateTime(BSTR bstrIn, BSTR* pbstrOut);
```

Now, the WSDL for this method will look like this:

```
<message name="echoDateTimeIn">
<part name="paramIn" type="s: string"/>
</message>
<message name="echoDateTimeOut">
<part name="return" type="s:string"/>
</message>
```

You can now save the WSDL as a file and manually make a few modifications. For example, you could change all the references to `s:string` to `s:dateTime` before publishing the WSDL. As a result, any client using the published WSDL would send a `dateTime` parameter. The server application would receive the `dateTime` parameter as a string and then be able to convert it into an internal time representation, process it, and convert it back into a string to marshal it back to the client.

NOTE *At first glance, it may seem that all this marshaling to and from strings is going to be inefficient, but remember that SOAP is based on XML, which is a text protocol. Thus, this marshaling to and from strings has to happen regardless of whether the conversion happens in the ATL Server code or your own.*

For a more detailed discussion on ATL Server SOAP marshaling, how to hook into the marshaler, and how you can use this to extend the type support, please see the section "Custom Data Type Marshaling" in Chapter 23.

WSDL Problems

This section covers workarounds for a few problems you may encounter when using WSDL documents that weren't generated by an ATL Server Web service. The problems we cover here are as follows:

- Missing the `soap:location` section of the WSDL
- `Import/include` directives in the WSDL document

The specification for WSDL documents mentions a special entry to describe the endpoint of the Web service. This endpoint is the URL to which the SOAP messages should be sent. This entry has the qualified name `soap:address`, `soap` being the prefix associated with the `http://schemas.xmlsoap.org/wsdl/soap/` namespace. Here's an example:

```
<port name="SomeServiceSoap" binding="s0: SomeServiceSoap">
<soap:address
   location="http://localhost/SomeServer/SomeServer.dll?Handler=Default"/>
</port>
```

This section of the WSDL document is required by the client generator tool (sproxy.exe) in order to generate the proxy class.

An example of a missing `soap:location` entry may be a WSDL designed to be used at multiple endpoints. For example, multiple Web servers may provide the same service, the central authority that coordinates the implementations will publish the common WSDL, and each server has to specify its own endpoint. In this situation, sproxy.exe will fail in generating the proxy class.

To work around this problem, the client developer will have to save the WSDL as a file, manually and add the following section (maybe including dummy data), then run sproxy.exe over the modified file:

```
<definitions...>
  <service name="TestServerService">
    <port name="TestServerServiceSoap" binding="s0:TestServerServiceSoap">
      <soap:address location="http://localhost/ "/>
    </port>
  </service>
</definitions>
```

For now, it doesn't have to identify a valid URL; it's just a syntax element of the WSDL that's required for the WSDL to be accepted as valid. Of course, `http://localhost/` will usually be an invalid Web service endpoint. Once the proxy class is generated, you can programmatically specify the URL, even at runtime, by calling into the `SetUrl` method of the generated class.

Quoting from the WSDL specification: "WSDL allows associating a *namespace* with a document *location* using an *import* statement."

```
<definitions...>
  <import namespace="uri" location="uri"/>
</definitions>
```

Such a mechanism allows, for example, separating the schema part of the WSDL (the types definitions) from the binding part (the messages and the endpoint description). For instance, if multiple services reuse the same type definitions, these can be isolated in a separate schema document and imported for each of the Web services.

The version of ATL Server that comes with Visual Studio .NET doesn't support the import mechanism. The client generator (sproxy.exe) in both releases is able to handle multiple schemas within the same WSDL document correctly.

To work around this issue on the client side, you have to download the WSDL(s) and the imported documents, save them as files, and insert the imported documents instead of the import directives. The WSDL documents are also selected from the WSDL specification. For example, assume that the WSDL looks like this:

```
<< service1.wsdl>>
<definitions...
       xmlns:xsd1= "http://example.com/stockquote/schemas">
  <import namespace="http://example.com/stockquote/schemas"
     location="http://example.com/stock/schemas/quote.xsd"/>
  <message name="GetLastTradePriceRequest">
    <part name="body" element="xsd1:GetLastTradePrice"/>
  </message>
 ...
</definitions>
```

Also assume that the `http://example.com/stock/schemas/quote.xsd` document looks like this:

```
<?xml version="1.0"?>
<schema targetNamespace=http://example.com/stock/schemas
    xmlns=http://www.w3.org/2001/XMLSchema>
  <element name="GetLastTradePrice">
    <complexType>
      <sequence>
        <element name="tickerSymbol" type="string"/>
      </sequence>
    </complexType>
  </element>
  ...
</schema>
```

After you insert the imported document in the WSDL file, the result will look like this:

```
<< service1_with_import.wsdl>>
<definitions... xmlns:xsd1="http://example.com/stock/schemas">
  <schema targetNamespace=http://example.com/stock/schemas
         xmlns=http://www.w3.org/2001/XMLSchema>
  <element name="GetLastTradePrice">
    <complexType>
      <sequence>
        <element name="tickerSymbol" type="string"/>
      </sequence>
    </complexType>
  </element>
```

```
  ...
</schema>

  <message name="GetLastTradePriceRequest">
    <part name="body" element="xsd1:GetLastTradePrice"/>
  </message>
...
</definitions>
```

This document is now valid input for the sproxy.exe tool.

A Specific Interoperability Problem

Even between implementations that use the same XSD, there's a need for interoperability, as perfect interoperation isn't always 100 percent guaranteed. We describe such a problem, resulting from different interpretations of the XSD, in this section. In this case, the problem appears between an ATL Server–based server and an ASP.NET client application, in the scenario where the ATL Server Web service exposes a fixed size array of `unsignedBytes`.

The 2001 version of XSD contains the following definition for a byte (see `http://www.w3.org/TR/2001/REC-xmlschema-2-20010502/#unsignedByte`):

> "*3.3.24* `unsignedByte` *definition:* `unsignedByte` *is derived from* `unsignedShort` *by setting the value of*·`maxInclusive` *to be 255. The base type of* `unsignedByte` *is* `unsignedShort`."

The WSDL generated by ATL Server for a fixed size array of elements, when each element is of type `unsignedByte`, looks like the following (the server-side code is also presented):

```
HRESULT echoByteArray([in] unsigned __int8 arrIn[10], [out, retval] unsigned
__int8 arrOut[10]) <types>
<s:schema targetNamespace="urn:BArrayService"
                attributeFormDefault="qualified"
                elementFormDefault="qualified">
  <s:complexType name="echoByteArray_return_Array">
    <s:complexContent>
      <s:restriction base="soapenc:Array">
        <s:attribute ref="soapenc:arrayType" wsdl:arrayType="s:unsignedByte[10]"/>
      </s:restriction>
    </s:complexContent>
  </s:complexType>
  <s:complexType name="echoByteArray_arrIn_Array">
```

```
        <s:complexContent>
          <s:restriction base="soapenc:Array">
            <s:attribute ref="soapenc:arrayType"
                          wsdl:arrayType="s: unsignedByte [10]"/>
          </s:restriction>
        </s:complexContent>
      </s:complexType>
    </s:schema>
    </types>
    <message name="echoByteArrayIn">
    <part name="arrIn" type="s0:echoByteArray_arrIn_Array"/>
    </message>
    <message name="echoByteArrayOut">
    <part name="return" type="s0:echoByteArray_return_Array"/>
    </message>
```

Therefore, the `echoByteArray_arrIn_Array` type is defined as an `soapenc:Array` with `arrayType="s:unsignedByte[10]"`.

The ATL Server Web service expects a payload that looks like the following:

```
<snp:echoByteArray    xmlns:snp="urn:BArrayService">
  <arrIn soapenc:arrayType="xsd:byte[10]">
    <unsignedByte>1</ unsignedByte >
    <unsignedByte>2</ unsignedByte >
    ...
    <unsignedByte>10</ unsignedByte >
  </arrIn>
</snp:echoByteArray>
```

The ASP.NET client interprets the WSDL fragment as being a BLOB, an object that usually is defined using one of the `xsd:base64Binary` or `xsd:hexBinary` XSD types, and sends a message containing 10 bytes encoded as a BLOB (in this case, base64 encoding). The ASP.NET payload will look like this:

```
<tns:echoByteArray>
  <arIn xsi:type="xsd:base64Binary">
    AQIDBAUGBwgJAA==
  </arIn>
</tns:echoByteArray>
```

which will cause the ATL Server Web service to fault in processing the request.

To solve this problem, from the perspective of the ATL Server Web service, the `unsignedByte` type should be replaced by a different type, say `unsignedShort`, making the function look like this:

```
HRESULT echoByteArray([in] unsigned __int116 arrIn[10],
                              [out, retval] unsigned __int16 arrOut[10])
```

Conclusion

Developers have only recently started to use SOAP and Web services in real-world applications. Although serious efforts were taken to completely solve the interoperability problems, different implementations are still rarely 100 percent interoperable. The common scenarios (the data types that have a correspondence in most of the programming languages, simple or complex aggregated types) are usually interoperable between various implementations. Some minor details (e.g., uncommon types) might still generate problems, but ATL Server was designed to be flexible enough to allow developers to easily work around these problems.

The next chapter will continue our in-depth presentation of the ATL Server Web services. You'll learn how the SOAP support can be extended to perform such tasks as using a different transport protocol or parsing generic XML content.

CHAPTER 23

Extensibility of ATL Server Web Services

IN CHAPTER 22 WE DESCRIBED some of the common issues that developers face when trying to get two different implementations of SOAP to communicate with each other. In this chapter we take a look at extending the ATL Server Web service model. Extensibility not only enables developers to solve some of the interoperability issues that may arise, but also allows for extension of Web services to support custom schemes and requirements.

The flexibility of the ATL Server design is a major asset in solving interoperability issues, and it's the focus of this chapter. In this chapter you'll learn how you can extend the ATL Server SOAP implementation to support nonstandard XML serializations, nonstandard transport channels, and custom data types.

After reading this chapter, you'll have a solution for using SOAP on various transport channels (i.e., replacements for HTTP). You'll also have a solution for hooking into the server-side processing of the parameters of a SOAP method, which allows you to treat a whole XML node passed as a parameter to a SOAP method without needing to instantiate a new parser. The last section shows how to extend the support for user types in the ATL Server implementation.

As you're looking at extending ATL Server Web services, it's useful if you have some level of familiarity with the ATL Server Web service implementation. Therefore, we start the chapter by briefly describing the processing model on the server side and then showing how to hook into this processing model.

ATL Server SOAP Request Processing Model

To get the most out of this chapter, you need a good understanding of ATL Server and the Simple API for XML (SAX) parsing model. Changing the transport channel and performing custom parsing of the SOAP methods parameters are based on a "black-box" approach. These changes don't require you to make modifications to the ATL Server files. The custom types handling, however, does require you to make some modifications to the ATL Server files (specifically, atlsoap.h). Such modifications aren't supported by Microsoft, but they may be very useful, and for advanced developers they often make a lot of sense.

In this section we perform a brief analysis of the ATL Server processing model for a SOAP request. Each Web service is represented on the server side by a class that's implemented using the `soap_handler` and `request_handler` attributes. These attributes make the class behave as a request handler (the working module in the ATL Server architecture) and also as a SOAP handler (i.e., a dedicated parser for SOAP payloads).

Once a SOAP request is received by the ISAPI module of an ATL Server application, the request handler is filtered by the ISAPI DLL out of the request URL. Then, this is mapped to an internal class (the class implemented using the `request_handler` attribute) and the generic `HandleRequest` method is invoked for that class.

The `soap_handler` attribute generates code that makes the class inherit from the `CSoapHandler` class. `CSoapHandler`'s implementation for `HandleRequest` will identify the SOAP method that was invoked (based on the `SOAPAction` header of the HTTP request) and then launch the SOAP payload parser.

The parser is based on SAX, which is an event-driven parser (and is a part of MSXML). Whenever a parsing event occurs, event handlers contained in the parser class (in this case, `CSoapHandler`) are invoked. The most important handlers in parsing an XML payload are as follows:

- `HRESULT __stdcall startElement(...)`: This is called when a new XML element (tag) is encountered.

- `HRESULT __stdcall endElement(...)`: This is called whenever an XML element (tag) is closed.

- `HRESULT __stdcall characters(...)`: This is called when the text content of a tag is encountered by the parser.

Here's the high-level structure of a standard SOAP payload:

```
->SOAP Envelope:
  ->SOAP Body
    ->Method to be invoked
->Parameters
```

`CSoapHandler` behaves as a state machine, moving from the state where it expects the `Envelope` to the state where it expects the `Body` and so on. It takes care of identifying and validating the `Envelope` and `Body` sections of the request. Then once it moves into the `Body` of the request, it calls the following virtual function of the `CSoapHandler`:

```
virtual HRESULT DispatchSoapCall(...)
```

`DispatchSoapCall` takes care of identifying the method that the request should be mapped to. In parsing/rendering the parameters, the pair of functions `AtlGetSAXValue` and `AtlGenXMLValue` are used for retrieving from and rendering to the actual values to XML, respectively. Keeping this model in mind, we can now move forward and look at hooking into the processing.

As we mentioned earlier, the `HandleRequest` function is the entry point for the SOAP request processing. In the next section we show how you can use this function for processing SOAP requests arriving via a different (non-HTTP) transport protocol.

Later in the chapter, we show you how to use the virtual `DispatchSoapCall` to hook into the parsing and handle more flexible payloads (such as those that pass XML nodes as method parameters). Finally, you'll analyze the details of the serialization mechanism and examine one possible solution for marshaling custom data types.

Using a Different Transport Protocol (Non-HTTP)

Under the ATL Server samples in Visual Studio .NET is a documented sample called SoapTransport. The SoapTransport sample shows how to create an alternate entry point function in an ATL Server SOAP server and how to use it for SOAP processing, regardless of the transport protocol. The new entry point behaves in much the same way as `HandleRequest` behaves; its main purpose is to accept parameters that aren't designed for HTTP-specific usage.

Also, the SoapTransport sample provides implementations for SOAP over TCP/IP, over HTTP without a Web server, and even using a floppy disk. In doing so, the sample allows you to preserve the implementation of a SOAP server's methods. You must modify the class definition, making it inherit from a special class, which implements the entry point.

In this section we provide an alternate way of getting the ATL Server SOAP processing out of the HTTP/ISAPI context. The idea behind this solution is to create an environment that, as far as the SOAP server is concerned, behaves exactly as the HTTP context. Once this goal is reached, you can use even existing compiled ATL Server SOAP servers (application DLLs) to process SOAP requests received on any transport channel.

A simple implementation for the current section is available (with the other code samples from the book, which you'll find in the Downloads section of the Apress Web site [`http://www.apress.com`]) as the OverriddenTransport sample. After a few words on how it works, we present the main components of the sample and how you can use it. Some knowledge of the specification for ISAPI is recommended before you read this section.

Overriding the HTTP Transport

In the ATL Server processing model, the HTTP request is received by an ISAPI extension. The ISAPI extension is a dynamic link library (DLL) that exports three functions, and one of these functions (`HttpExtensionProc`) is called whenever a request must be processed. Internally, `HttpExtensionProc` will pass the processing job to a `CIsapiExtension`-based object. This object will read the request using the `EXTENSION_CONTROL_BLOCK` (ECB) provided as a parameter to `HttpExtensionProc` by the Web server. It will load the application DLL that's supposed to handle the request, which will then generate the response by writing through the same ECB.

NOTE *There's a minor exception for this behavior: In a situation where the ISAPI module and the application module reside in the same DLL, the "load the application DLL" step is skipped. But this situation isn't of concern in this section.*

The ECB is exposed in the `CIsapiExtension`-based object through an interface, `IHttpServerContext`. The whole idea behind this section is to provide a custom implementation for `IHttpServerContext` that creates an object that behaves almost exactly as a `CIsapiExtension` derivative, and then uses these two components to load application DLLs (in particular, SOAP servers) and process SOAP requests.

The OverriddenTransport sample is such an engine for loading application DLLs. Using the same pattern as the SoapTransport\FloppyTransport sample on the Visual Studio CD, it loads a SOAP request from a file, and then processes the request and saves the response to another file. So, a file request produced by the SoapTransport\FloppyTransport\FloppyClient from the Visual Studio CD will be accepted as a valid request by this sample. This entire engine is available in the OverriddenTransport\TransportLoader project. Two sample request files (SOAPRequest.txt and WSDLRequest.txt) are provided in the same directory. A simple "Hello, World!" SOAP server is also available to enable you to see the application running without requiring additional code. You should find the code easy to review and understand once we've described the major components of the TransportLoader project.

The application implements two important classes:

```
CLoaderServerContext : public IHttpServerContext
```

and

```
CLoaderExtension: public IServiceProvider, public IIsapiExtension
```

`CLoaderServerContext` behaves as a *server context,* meaning it provides everything an ECB would provide through the same interface that wraps the ECB. So, once an application DLL is loaded, in the most common usage it won't be able distinguish between this ECB wrapper and the one generated by the Web server.

The code for `CLoaderServerContext` closely follows the code from the `CWrappedServerContext` class, defined in atlisapi.h, which is the ATL Server implementation of the `IHttpServerContext` interface. Still, there are a few major differences, which we describe in the next section.

ReadClient/WriteClient

These ATL Server functions call their counterparts (with the same names) that are a part of the ECB (provided by the Web server). Because there's no Web server in the sample, two streams are used, one for the request (`ReadClient`) and another for the response (`WriteClient`). The streams are defined in `CLoaderServerContext` as follows:

```
CReadWriteStreamOnCString   m_requestStream;
CReadWriteStreamOnCString   m_responseStream;
```

`CReadWriteStreamOnCString` is a helper class defined in the sample that provides an `IStream` implementation on top of a `CString` class.

NOTE *Because a* `CString` *can be generated from any given XML buffer, and because a* `CString` *can contain any given XML buffer, a* `CString`*-based mechanism won't require HTTP at all. It can be used with any transport that can carry the XML, including TCP/IP, MSMQ, and even a floppy disk.*

The main application is responsible for filling the `m_requestStream` before executing the request and forwarding the content of `m_responseStream` back to the client upon execution.

GetServerVariable

This function is frequently used by the ATL Server application DLL to access information provided by the Web server, such as the following:

- PATH_INFO: The part of the URL request after the server name and before the query parameters
- URL: The URL of the request
- HTTP_SOAPACTION: The value of the SOAPAction HTTP header
- CONTENT-LENGTH: The value of the Content-Length HTTP header

All of these variables are provided by the Web server. Because you aren't using a Web server in this example, you'll use a map (hash table) to store those variables that will be frequently requested during the SOAP request processing. The map is defined in CLoaderServerContext as follows:

```
typedef CAtlMap<
                CStringA, CStringA,
                CStringElementTraitsI<CStringA>,
                CStringElementTraitsI<CStringA> > HeaderMapType;
HeaderMapType  m_requestHeaderMap;
```

The map is filled either with some default values or values dependant on the request in the CLoaderServerContext::SetUrl public function.

Mapping an HTTP Request Object to a Physical Object

Mapping an HTTP request to a physical object is another function provided by the Web server. The Web server keeps track of the physical location of the virtual Web directories and provides the physical local path of the objects pointed at by URLs. In this case, the application itself needs to parse the request and map it to a physical object.

The CLoaderServerContext class takes care of identifying the object name; therefore, it can filter out the DLL name (HelloWorld.dll) from a URL like this:

```
http://localhost/someVirtualDirectory/HelloWorld.dll?Handler=GetHelloWorldWSDL
```

The main application that uses the CLoaderServerContext class is responsible for mapping the HelloWorld.dll name to a physical path:

```
C:\WokDir\HelloWorld\Debug\HelloWorld.dll
```

Once the mapping is done, the main application has to call into CLoaderServerContext::SetSoapAppDllPath.

So far, the main application is responsible for the following:

- Filling the m_requestStream member of the CLoaderServerContext class (it does this by using an XML stream obtained through any transport—in this case through a call to LoadInputFile in the TransportLoader.cpp file, which loads the XML from a file).

- Calling CLoaderServerContext::SetUrl and passing as parameters the URL of the request and the SOAP Action field. (The URL and the SOAP Action field are "supposed" to come from the client, usually on the same channel as the XML body. In this example, the URL is the first line of the input file and the SOAP Action field is the second. Everything else is supposed to be the body of the request.) At this point, CLoaderServerContext will parse the URL and identify the object name (the DLL name).

- Associating the DLL name (contained, after SetUrl, in CLoaderServerContext::m_strDLLFileName) to a physical path. The main application does this by using a table for mappings (g_arMappings) and then calling CLoaderServerContext::SetSoapAppDllPath.

Let's take a look now at CLoaderExtension. This class is a very simplified version of CIsapiExtension. The main function in this class is

```
BOOL ExecuteRequestDirect(IHttpServerContext  *pServerContext)
```

which closely follows the implementation of CIsapiExtension::DispatchStencilCall in atlisapi.h. Again, this is a very simplified version of the ISAPI extension. To keep the code simple, it doesn't contain a stencil cache and it doesn't fully implement the IServiceProvider interface. The AddService, RemoveService, and GetService methods return E_NOTIMPL, whereas QueryService returns only the DLL cache service. This implementation also differs from the ATL Server version in that it doesn't use the thread pool.

NOTE *You can easily add all of these features, but we've left them out to keep the code simple.*

Just like the `CIsapiExtension` class, `CLoaderExtension` exposes two methods, `Initialize` and `Uninitialize`, to be called before and after usage, respectively.

The main entry point, `ExecuteRequestDirect`, takes as a parameter an `IHttpServerContext` interface, the kind exposed by the `CLoaderServerContext` class. Using the same DLL cache mechanism as in the ATL Server `CIsapiExtension` class implementation, `CLoaderExtension` will load an application DLL and execute what looks like an HTTP request.

In the main application, you need to add the following code (we've omitted error checking for clarity):

```
// The stand-alone ISAPI Extension
CLoaderServerContext srvCtxt;
...
CLoaderExtension  ext;
ext.Initialize();
ext.ExecuteRequestDirect( &srvCtxt);
ext.Uninitialize();
```

After this, if everything runs successfully (all the functions will return `FALSE` in case of an error), `CLoaderServerContext::m_streamResponse` contains the response buffer, the XML payload of the SOAP response. Once again, it's up to the main application to forward this response back to the client, using the transport protocol of choice (in this case, another file).

Once the sample is built and run, it will ask for an input file. The input file should contain the SOAP request in the following format (the content of the SOAPRequest.txt file):

```
http://localhost/HW.dll?Handler=Default
"#HelloWorld"
<soap:Envelope
  xmlns:soap="http://schemas.xmlsoap.org/soap/envelope/"
  xmlns:xsi="http://www.w3.org/2001/XMLSchema-instance"
  xmlns:xsd="http://www.w3.org/2001/XMLSchema"
  xmlns:soapenc="http://schemas.xmlsoap.org/soap/encoding/">
  <soap:Body
    soap:encodingStyle="http://schemas.xmlsoap.org/soap/encoding/">
    <snp:HelloWorld  xmlns:snp="urn:HWService">
```

```
      <bstrInput>SomeInput</bstrInput>
    </snp:HelloWorld>
  </soap:Body>
</soap:Envelope>
```

Notice how the first line of the file contains a URL indicating the application DLL (HW.dll). On the second line, you see SOAPAction:"#HelloWorld" followed by a valid SOAP request. Once the request is executed, the sample application prompts for an output file name, where the SOAP response will be generated.

NOTE *The preceding solution describes how to send a SOAP request. But you can use this file format to send a regular, non-SOAP HTTP request. As an example, take a look at WSDLRequest.txt, which contains an HTTP request that returns a WSDL for the Web service* `http://localhost/HW.dll?Handler=GenHWWSDL`. *In this case, the complete WSDL of the SOAP server will be generated in the response file.*

Please look at the SoapTransport sample that ships with Visual Studio for information on how to create a client for this stand-alone SOAP server.

Custom Parsing on the Server Side

You'll begin this section by examining the problem that you're trying to solve. Take the situation where in a client/server architecture, the client is sending various XML fragments to the server. If the communication protocol of choice is SOAP, the request's payload might look like this:

```
<SOAP:Envelope ....>
  <SOAP:Body....>
    <TreatXMLNode> <!--name of the SOAP method -->
      <xmlNodeStartTag....>
..       custom XML here...
      </xmlNodeStartTag>
    </TreatXMLNode>
  </SOAP:Body>
</SOAP:Envelope>
```

There's no way to strictly define the type of the XML fragment. It could be described by the any element of the XML Schema Datatypes document (see `http://www.w3.org/TR/2001/REC-xmlschema-1-20010502/#Wildcards` for details), but any has no direct correspondent in C++, so ATL Server doesn't support it by default.

A simple workaround for this problem is to have a SOAP method that accepts a string as a parameter. A client could send a regular SOAP request with the XML fragment to be transmitted encoded as a string. The call would then look like this:

```
<TreatXMLNode>
&lt;customXMLRootNode&gt;…content here …&lt;/customXMLRootNode&gt;
</TreatXMLNode>
```

Notice the escape sequences, because the XML is being passed as a string. During this process, the characters that have a special meaning in an XML document will be "neutralized." For example, the brackets used in delimiting the tags (< and >) will be replaced by special entities (< and >, respectively). The string then has to be unescaped on the server side, a new instance of an XML parser has to be launched, and the goal will be achieved.

Although this solution is technically correct, it does have a few disadvantages:

- It encodes an existing XML node to a string, which requires extra memory and processing time on the client side.

- The string has to be decoded on the server side, which requires extra memory and processing time there, too.

- A new instance of the parser (or a different parser) has to be used for parsing the escaped string on the server side.

The third disadvantage requires some discussion: The SOAP payload processing on the server side is, ultimately, an XML parsing. ATL Server uses the SAX parser provided by MSXML, and you can use this parser to get deep into the XML fragment that's passed by the client. But when an unexpected XML tag is encountered, the ATL Server SOAP framework, which ensures the validity of the SOAP payload, will generate an error.

As we mentioned before, ATL Server uses the `DispatchSoapCall` method to map the SOAP request to an actual function call, *before* the framework continues with the processing of the parameters. This mapping must happen—it ensures that the correct server-side function will be invoked. But, immediately after this mapping, you can "hijack" the parsing of the method parameters. This way, the free-form XML fragment could be processed during the same pass over the payload and, by the time the actual method gets invoked, the results of the parsing are already available.

All the code that is presented here is available as a sample called `CustomServerSideParsing`, which you can find with the other code for this book in the Downloads section of the Apress Web site (`http://www.apress.com`).

You'll begin by generating a new ATL Server SOAP server from the Visual Studio's New Project Wizard. In this example you'll call the project "CustomParsingServer". The signature of the SOAP method looks, by default, like this:

```
[id(1)] HRESULT HelloWorld([in]BSTR bstrInput, [out, retval]BSTR *bstrOutput)
```

As you'll take control of the parameter parsing, the default parsing won't take place. This is why, in the new SOAP server, the functions can't take `[in]` parameters. Only `[out]` (optionally `[retval]`) will be permitted.

NOTE *The ATL Server framework takes care of the memory allocated to hold the parameters. For* `[in]` *parameters, memory is allocated during the parsing and released after the method invocation. As the parsing is overridden, the memory won't be allocated anymore, so the attempt to release it at the end will generate an error. This is why only* `[out]` *parameters can appear in the signature of a SOAP method with overridden parsing.*

First you'll change the function's signature. Assume that you want the following information as a result of processing the XML fragment:

- A free text description of the XML content:

```
"Starting new element - <element_name>
  Starting attribute list -
  Attribute --<name > -- <value>
..."
```

- The number of nodes in the XML fragment
- The number of attributes in the XML fragment

The new signature will be

```
HRESULT TreatXMLNode(
    [out, retval] BSTR *bstrOutput,
    [out]unsigned int* pnNodesCount,
    [out]unsigned int* pnAttrCount);
```

Next, you have to define an object that will take care of the parsing of the XML fragment parameter. The SAX parsing model requires that an ISAXContentHandler interface be provided. This interface contains handlers for all the events that may occur during the XML parsing. ATL Server contains the ISAXContentHandlerImpl class, which is intended to be a base for any SAX content handler. This class simplifies the parsing by providing a "do-nothing" implementation for all the events. A real content handler inheriting from ISAXContentHandlerImpl will have to implement only those handlers that are of interest.

The object responsible for parsing the parameter XML fragment is defined in the CustomSAXParser.h file that comes with this example. Its definition is as follows:

```
class CSAXCustomParser : public ISAXContentHandlerImpl
{
public:
  CString     m_strDescription;
  unsigned int  m_nNodesCount;
  unsigned int  m_nAttrCount;
…
}
```

The public members are used to store the information obtained after the parsing of the XML fragment. m_strDescription will hold the free text description of the XML fragment, m_nNodesCount will store the number of nodes encountered in the fragment, and m_nAttrCount will store the number of attributes in the same fragment. CSAXCustomParser will override the processing of the following XML parsing events:

```
HRESULT __stdcall startElement(...)
HRESULT __stdcall endElement(...)
HRESULT __stdcall characters(...)
```

You still need to override startElement and endElement to keep track of the element names in the free text description, and then characters to access the element's content for the same free text description. startElement conveniently provides a pointer to an ISAXAttributes implementation. ISAXAttributes is a SAX interface that allows you to get information about the attributes of an XML element, so with these handlers you have access to all the information required to return the free text description, the attributes, and the element count.

The code inside the implementation of these handlers is straightforward. It just increments the counters or appends a description line to the free text description. The CSAXCustomParser also contains the following public methods:

```
void SetReader(ISAXXMLReader *pReader)
void SetParent(ISAXContentHandler *pParent)
```

SetParent specifies the previous ISAXContentHandler (i.e., the one that lost the control over the parsing when your class took it over). You'll need to let this parent control the payload parsing when you're done with the custom XML fragment.

Now we'll detail how the content handling switches work in SAX. During the SAX parsing there exists a single object that controls everything. Per parsing session, there's a single ISAXXMLReader object that will perform the parsing and invoke an ISAXContentHandler for all the parsing events. The content handler to be invoked is specified by calling ISAXXMLReader->putContentHandler with an ISAXContentHandler* parameter. This is the way you'll pass the XML event-handling job to your CSAXCustomParser object, and this is also the way that you'll reactivate the ATL Server framework handling when the parameter XML fragment is done.

SetReader specifies the single ISAXXMLReader object during this parsing session, so when the fragment is done, the CSAXCustomParser has to call

```
m_pReader->putContentHandler(m_pParent);
```

where m_pReader is reached through SetReader and m_pParent through SetParent.

There's still one problem yet to be solved: You need to decide when the parameter XML fragment is done. SAX will take care of identifying malformed XML before calling the event handlers, so you can assume that, during the usage of the CSAXCustomParser, you're dealing with valid XML. That means that each element start has a corresponding element end. As CSAXCustomParser becomes active immediately after the XML element containing the SOAP method name has been processed, you can imagine an element counter that goes up whenever a new XML element starts and goes down whenever an XML element ends. This way, when the counter reaches zero, you're done with the XML node parameter.

Dealing with this internal node counter is the job of the following protected functions of CSAXCustomParser:

```
DWORD DisableReset(DWORD dwReset = 1)
DWORD EnableReset()
```

These functions increment/decrement an internal counter called `m_dReset`. `DisableReset` should be called whenever a new element starts (i.e., called from `startElement`). For the first time (when `m_dwReset` is 0), `DisableReset` will be called twice (once for the container "start-of-SOAP-method" element and once for the encountered element). This ensures that, even when the XML fragment contains multiple nodes at the top level, the `CSAXCustomParser` object will release handling only when the matching "end-of-method" tag is encountered.

Consequently, `EnableReset` has to be called whenever the `endElement` event occurs. The code in `endElement` is as follows:

```
if (EnableReset() == 0)
{
  // end of the XML Node, the element counter is back to zero
  hr = m_pParent->endElement(wszNamespaceUri, cchNamespaceUri, wszLocalName,
    chLocalName, wszQName, cchQName);
  m_pReader->putContentHandler(m_pParent);
}
else
{
  // Let CSAXCustomParser process the end of element event
}
```

`endElement` must ensure that the end of the XML element associated with the SOAP method will be processed by the ATL Server framework.

Now, let's get back to the SOAP server, the `CCustomParsingServerService` class. First, you'll add a new member to this class:

```
public:
CSAXCustomParser  m_privateParser;
```

NOTE *You aren't required to make the custom parser a member of the SOAP server class. You could design your application so that the custom parser would live for only as long as the parsing took. If you did this, you would need to provide a mechanism for preserving the results of the parsing until the actual function that the SOAP method maps to gets called. In this case, for the sake of simplicity, you'll keep the parser as a member of the class, as it contains the free text description of the parameter XML and the number of attributes and elements as public variables.*

Then override the virtual `DispatchSoapCall` as follows:

```
HRESULT DispatchSoapCall(const wchar_t *wszNamespaceUri,
                    int cchNamespaceUri,
                    const wchar_t *wszLocalName, int cchLocalName)
{
  // Call the base class's DispatchSoapCall
  // This allows the appropriate method to be invoked
  // after the request parsing is done
  HRESULT hRet    = __super::DispatchSoapCall(wszNamespaceUri, cchNamespaceUri,
                                wszLocalName, cchLocalName);
  if( SUCCEEDED(hRet)  )
  {
  // If the method was recognized, launch the custom parser for the content
  m_privateParser.Clear();
  ATLASSERT( GetReader() != NULL );
  m_privateParser.SetReader(GetReader());
  m_privateParser.SetParent(this);
  GetReader()->putContentHandler( &m_privateParser );
}
  return hRet;
}
```

Here you're invoking the base class's implementation for `DispatchSoapCall`, to be sure the method mapping is performed correctly. Then, if everything is fine, you initialize the custom parser and, for the `ISAXXMLReader` object of the current parsing session (which you can obtain with `GetReader()`), you change the content handler to your own object.

TIP *You can use the* `__super` *keyword to explicitly state that you're calling the base class implementation for a function that you're overriding. The compiler will consider all the accessible base class methods and then call the best match. As you can see in this example, it's a very useful keyword to know!*

Now everything is in place, so you continue with the implementation of the SOAP function:

```
[ soap_method ]
HRESULT TreatXMLNode(/*[out, retval]*/ BSTR *bstrOutput,
/*[out]*/unsigned int* pnNodesCount,  /*[out]*/unsigned int* pnAttrCount)
{
  CComBSTR  bstrTemp;
  bstrTemp.Append( (LPCTSTR)m_privateParser.m_strDescription);
  *bstrOutput = bstrTemp.Detach();
  *pnNodesCount = m_privateParser.m_nNodesCount;
  *pnAttrCount = m_privateParser.m_nAttrCount;
  return S_OK;
}
```

The results of the XML parameter parsing have been saved in the public members of the `m_privateParser` object and you can use them in generating the `[out]` values.

You're almost finished, so it's important to take care and clean up after your custom parser. A good opportunity for doing this work is the virtual `Cleanup` function of the `CSoapHandler` class, which is invoked when the SOAP processing, the actual method invocation, and the response generation are complete:

```
public:
virtual void Cleanup()
{
  __super::Cleanup();
  m_privateParser.Clear();
}
```

Everything works! The example included contains a small test client (CustomServerSideParsing\TestClient). It isn't actually a SOAP client; rather, it's an application that writes directly to a socket. It sends a SOAP request similar to one that would be sent by a real client, with a custom XML fragment inside. Listing 23-1 shows what the request looks like.

Listing 23-1. SOAP Payload of a Request Containing an XML Document (Highlighted in Bold)

```
<soap:Envelope
  xmlns:soap="http://schemas.xmlsoap.org/soap/envelope/"
  xmlns:xsi="http://www.w3.org/2001/XMLSchema-instance"
  xmlns:xsd="http://www.w3.org/2001/XMLSchema"
```

```
  xmlns:soapenc="http://schemas.xmlsoap.org/soap/encoding/"
>
  <soap:Body  soap:encodingStyle="http://schemas.xmlsoap.org/soap/encoding/">
    <snp:TreatXMLNode xmlns:snp="urn:CustomParsingServerService">
   <m:customXMLNode xmlns:m="http://MyServer/NamespaceM">
    <m:binaryinfo bintype="exe">
     <m:filename>C:\WINNT\system32\notepad.exe</m:filename>
     <m:filesize>0xc600</m:filesize>
     <m:versioninfo checkSum="0x0" creationdate="2000-10-23T09:33:11.090"
    description="Notepad" manufacturer="Microsoft Corporation" version="4.0"/>
    </m:binaryinfo>
   </m:customXMLNode>
    </snp:TreatXMLNode>
  </soap:Body>
</soap:Envelope>
```

Listing 23-2 shows what the response looks like.

Listing 23-2. SOAP Payload of a Response Containing Results of Parsing the XML Document of Listing 23-1

```
<soap:Envelope
  xmlns:soap="http://schemas.xmlsoap.org/soap/envelope/"
  xmlns:xsi="http://www.w3.org/2001/XMLSchema-instance"
  xmlns:xsd="http://www.w3.org/2001/XMLSchema"
  xmlns:soapenc="http://schemas.xmlsoap.org/soap/encoding/"
>
  <soap:Body
    soap:encodingStyle="http://schemas.xmlsoap.org/soap/encoding/"
  >
    <snp:TreatXMLNode
      xmlns:snp="urn:CustomParsingServerService"
    >
      <bstrOutput>
        … the description here …
      </bstrOutput>
      <pnNodesCount>5</pnNodesCount>
      <pnAttrCount>7</pnAttrCount>
    </snp:TreatXMLNode>
  </soap:Body>
</soap:Envelope>
```

Notice the values for pnNodesCount and pnAttrCount. The free text description is removed from the payload (because of the XML encoding of the new line and tab characters). Listing 23-3 shows this description as displayed onscreen.

Listing 23-3. Free Text Description of the XML Document Sent As a Request Parameter

```
Starting new element : (Namespace - http://MyServer/NamespaceM ) customXMLNode
Starting attribute list
Attribute : (Namespace - , Name - ) http://MyServer/NamespaceM
End attribute list
Content :
Starting new element : (Namespace - http://MyServer/NamespaceM ) binaryinfo
Starting attribute list
Attribute : (Namespace - , Name - bintype) exe
End attribute list
Content :
Starting new element : (Namespace - http://MyServer/NamespaceM ) filename
Starting attribute list
End attribute list
Content : C:\WINNT\system32\notepad.exe
Ending element : (Namespace - http://MyServer/NamespaceM ) filename
Content :
Starting new element : (Namespace - http://MyServer/NamespaceM ) filesize
Starting attribute list
End attribute list
Content : 0xc600
Ending element : (Namespace - http://MyServer/NamespaceM ) filesize
Content :
Starting new element : (Namespace - http://MyServer/NamespaceM ) versioninfo
Starting attribute list
Attribute : (Namespace - , Name - checkSum) 0x0
Attribute : (Namespace - , Name - creationdate) 2000-10-23T09:33:11.090
Attribute : (Namespace - , Name - description) Notepad
Attribute : (Namespace - , Name - manufacturer) Microsoft Corporation
Attribute : (Namespace - , Name - version) 4.0
End attribute list
Ending element : (Namespace - http://MyServer/NamespaceM ) versioninfo
Content :
Ending element : (Namespace - http://MyServer/NamespaceM ) binaryinfo
Ending element : (Namespace - http://MyServer/NamespaceM ) customXMLNode
Content :
```

Notice that it closely matches the XML fragment sent as a parameter.

Custom Data Types Marshaling

This section discusses the marshaling of custom types through the ATL Server SOAP implementation for Web service *clients*. The mechanism used here requires you to modify the ATL Server source code, which Microsoft does not support. You should take this fact into consideration before you use this custom marshaling solution in an application.

We begin by looking at the problem: If a specific data type is frequently used in a Web service, it might be more convenient to the framework to support it "natively" rather than to wrap it for each call. For example, assume that a Web service uses structures that contain a field of type GUID. Let's assume further that the GUID type is defined in an XSD document as follows:

```
<s:simpleType name="guid">
  <s:restriction base="s:string">
    <s:pattern value="[0-9a-fA-F]{8}-[0-9a-fA-F]{4}-[0-9a-fA-F]{4}-
                                        [0-9a-fA-F]{4}-[0-9a-fA-F]{12}" />
  </s:restriction>
</s:simpleType>
```

CAUTION *We use the term "guid" (in lowercase letters) when we talk about the XSD type and the term "GUID" (in uppercase letters) when we talk about the Windows Platform SDK* GUID *structure.*

Thus, a GUID will be rendered and accepted by the server in the form of a string matching a specific regular expression. Sproxy.exe will render this type (guid) as a string (it's a restriction over a string, so it will be treated as a string). A structure containing a string and a guid will be represented in the proxy class as follows:

```
struct someStruct
{
  BSTR strVal;
  BSTR guidVal;
};
```

To ensure the correctness of the data that the proxy class will receive and send, the client-side developer will have to create a wrapper for each function and check the value of the guidVal structure field. On the other hand, it's very likely that the client-side processing will need the guidVal in the GUID (Platform SDK) form to use it as a unique identifier. So, the wrappers should also convert the `guid` string to a real `GUID`. To preserve the consistency, the developer would also have to create some parallel structure that contains a `GUID` with the value contained in the `guidVal` field, and a string. Such a structure might look like this:

```
struct someStructEx
{
  BSTR strVal;
  GUID guidVal;
};
```

This means that there's lots of code to write, and therefore lots of potential problems. A way of "convincing" the proxy class to work directly with the `someStructEx` type will save this effort.

NOTE *An example with all the code described in this section is available as the customMarshaling sample. Only the client part and the WSDL are of interest at this point. The server part simply echoes back whatever the client is sending (i.e., it's only used to prove that this solution actually works).*

Now that you've defined the problem, let's see what kind of solution you can come up with. Let's start with the WSDL. Assume that it contains the `guid` type described previously and a structure containing a common string and a `guid`. Objects of this type (structures) are used as parameters in the methods described in the WSDL. So, besides the `guid` definition, the WSDL also contains the following (see GUIDService.wsdl):

```
<s:complexType name="someStruct">
  <s:sequence>
    <s:element name="strVal" type="s:string"/>
    <s:element name="guidVal" type="s1:guid"/>
  </s:sequence>
</s:complexType>
```

As you intend to modify the marshaling engine that resides in the atlsoap.h file that ships as a part of ATL Server, it's a good idea to make a copy of this file so that the original is available for other applications. An easy way to do this is to create a copy of atlsoap.h in the same directory as the sproxy.exe-generated file. To ensure that you're using the correct version, make sure to change the `#include` as follows:

```
#include <atlsoap.h>
```

to

```
#include "atlsoap.h"
```

In the marshaling engine, all the basic type elements are rendered through one of the `AtlGenXMLValue<>` template functions and are parsed by one of the `AtlGetSAXValue<>` template functions. As `guid` is a simple type (a string restriction), you'll want to provide a flavor of `AtlGenXMLValue` and `AtlGetSAXValue` that renders a `GUID` to a `guid` and reads a `guid` into a `GUID`, respectively.

The supported simple types are denoted internally in ATL Server by the `SOAPTYPES` enumeration in atlsoap.h. For future extensions, `SOAPTYPES` contains an element called `SOAPTYPE_USERBASE`, which is intended to be the last in the enumeration. Therefore, you can be sure that any number greater than `SOAPTYPE_USERBASE` won't generate a conflict with an existing `SOAPTYPE`.

For handling the `GUID` type, you'll define a new `SOAPTYPE` in the proxy-generated header file:

```
#define SOAPTYPE_GUID SOAPTYPE_USERBASE + 1
```

Now you'll need to modify the marshaling in atlsoap.h to support the newly added type.

The global `AtlSoapGetElementValue` function in atlsoap.h behaves as a dispatcher during the parsing of a SOAP payload. Based on the `SOAPTYPE` for a specific element, `AtlSoapGetElementValue` calls the appropriate `AtlGetSAXValue` implementation to parse the XML content representing that element and stores the parsing result in a variable.

The global `AtlSoapGenElementValue` function has a similar dispatcher behavior during the rendering of a payload. Based on the `SOAPTYPE` for a specific variable, it will render the XML content to represent it.

There are two other global helper functions to help deal with various `SOAPTYPES`: `AtlSoapGetElementSize` and `AtlSoapCleanupElement`. `AtlSoapGetElementSize` returns the size to be allocated for a variable holding a specific type (it's used when dynamic allocations occur—for example, in the case of a variable size array), and `AtlSoapCleanupElement` makes sure that all the memory allocated by a variable of a specific type is released (e.g., the `base64Binary` elements are represented as `ATLSOAP_BLOB` structs, which contain buffers, so they have to be cleaned up after usage).

You must modify these four functions to support the new `SOAPTYPE_GUID`. You should keep in mind that `SOAPTYPE_GUID` is a definition local to the proxy-generated header file, so you'll have to use the value of this definition, which is `SOAPTYPE_USERBASE+1`.

NOTE *In the sample atlsoap.h file, all the modifications are preceded by the comment* `// Added for custom marshaling` *to help you identify all the modifications.*

All these functions to be modified are acting as dispatchers, switching on a `SOAPTYPES` value to determine which function should be called. The modifications consist of adding a new branch to the switches (i.e., to the `SOAPTYPE_USERBASE+1` value). For consistency, the new branch will be added right before the *default* branch.

First, based on the order in which the functions are implemented in atlsoap.h, we discuss the `AtlSoapGetElementSize` modifications. This function is supposed to return the size to be allocated for an element of a given `SOAPTYPE`. The newly added branch looks like this:

```
case SOAPTYPE_USERBASE + 1:
  nRet = sizeof(GUID);
  break;
```

So, when the `SOAPTYPES` parameter is `SOAPTYPE_USERBASE+1`, the function will return the size of a `GUID` element (the internal representation of choice for a `guid` XSD type).

The next function to be modified is `AtlSoapGetElementValue`, the parsing dispatcher. The code to be added is as follows:

```
case SOAPTYPE_USERBASE + 1:
  hr = AtlGetSAXValue((GUID*)pVal, wsz, cch);
  break;
```

It's important to mention at this moment that the definition for `AtlGetSAXValue` looks like this:

```
template <typename T>
inline HRESULT AtlGetSAXValue(T * pVal, const wchar_t * wsz, int  cch)
```

This function is responsible for converting `cch` characters in the `wsz` buffer to a value of type `T`. The function is implemented for the basic types supported by ATL Server. The call to the function can deduce the template instance to be invoked based on the type of the `pVal` parameter. As you're casting `pVal` to a `GUID*` in the added code, the `GUID` template implementation will be invoked. Of course, such an implementation isn't available yet, as ATL Server doesn't support GUID, so you'll have to provide it later.

The next function to be modified is AtlSoapGenElementValue, the rendering dispatcher. The code to be added is as follows:

```
case SOAPTYPE_USERBASE + 1:
  hr = AtlGenXMLValue(pStream, (GUID*)pVal);;
  break;
```

At this moment we should mention that the definition for AtlGenXMLValue looks like this:

```
template <typename T>
inline HRESULT AtlGenXMLValue(IWriteStream *pStream, T *pVal)
```

This function is responsible for rendering a value of type T to the stream provided in pStream. The function is implemented for the basic types supported by ATL Server. The call to the function can deduce the template instance to be invoked based on the type of the pVal parameter. As you're casting pVal to a GUID* in the added code, the GUID template implementation will be invoked. Of course, such an implementation doesn't yet exist, so you'll have to provide it later, just as for AtlGetSAXValue.

The last function to be modified is AtlSoapCleanupElement. This function cleans any auxiliary memory needed to represent a value (such as the buffers for an ATLSOAP_BLOB struct). For the GUID type, no auxiliary allocated memory has to be freed, so the code to be added will use the main "do-nothing" path, as shown here:

```
case SOAPTYPE_USERBASE + 1:
  break;
```

This concludes the necessary modifications in atlsoap.h. Now go back to the proxy-generated file. First off, you have to implement AtlGenXMLValue and AtlSoapGetSAXValue for GUID. The code in the sample is straightforward. AtlGenXMLValue attempts to create a string based on the content of a GUID, and then writes that string to the output stream:

```
CString strFormattedGUID;
strFormattedGUID.Format(
"%08lX-%04X-%04x-%02X%02X-%02X%02X%02X%02X%02X%02X",
pVal->Data1, pVal->Data2, pVal->Data3,
    pVal->Data4[0], pVal->Data4[1], pVal->Data4[2], pVal->Data4[3],
    pVal->Data4[4], pVal->Data4[5], pVal->Data4[6], pVal->Data4[7]);
return pStream->WriteStream(strFormattedGUID, -1, NULL);
```

The format is the usual (readable) form used by both the Windows registry and the WSDL you started from.

AtlGetSAXValue uses the CRT function wcstoul to convert the hex numbers appearing in the XML content to their actual values. It contains multiple fragments as you can see here:

```
CStringW  strWork;
wchar_t  *wszEnd;
strWork.SetString(pReadBuff, 8);
pVal->Data1 = (unsigned long)wcstoul( strWork, &wszEnd, 16);
if( *wszEnd != '\0' || errno == ERANGE)
{
  return E_FAIL;
}
pReadBuff += 9; // (Data1 on 8 hex digits) + dash
```

Go back and look at the actual proxy class. It already contains the definition for the structure containing a guid, generated by sproxy as you can see here:

```
struct someStruct
{
  BSTR strVal;
  BSTR guidVal;
};
```

As GUID is now a supported type, you should change the definition to

```
struct someStruct
{
  BSTR strVal;
  /*BSTR*/GUID guidVal;
};
```

This kind of object is rendered and parsed based on a _soapmap structure generated by sproxy. The _soapmap structure contains higher level information about the object to be rendered, such as the container tag name (someStruct), the type of the object (in this case, SOAPMAP_STRUCT) and some serialization flags. It also contains a reference to an array of _soapmapentry structures containing similar information about the fields of the object to be marshaled. You'll need to identify and modify the serialization information for the guidVal field.

The generic _soapmap structure that describes the serialization rules for a given object named SomeObject will be named __someObject_map by sproxy.exe. So, for the _soapmap associated with a someStruct object, you have to look for the definition of __someStruct_map in the proxy-generated file.

Once you find this definition, it's easy to identify the name of the array of entries describing the fields. Based on the declaration of the `_soapmap` structure (also, in atlsoap.h), the array of entries is the seventh field of a `_soapmap`. In the proxy-generated file you're working on, this field is `__someStruct_entries`.

You now need to locate `__someStruct_entries` in the header file. `__someStruct_entries` is an array of `_soapmapentry` structures. One structure describes the serialization rules for each field. You just have to identify the structure describing the serialization rules for `guidVal`. This is easy, as the first field of a `_soapmapentry` structure is the corresponding field to be serialized. The second entry is the one for `guidVal`.

```
{
0x113E60CC,
"guidVal",
L"guidVal",
sizeof("guidVal")-1,
SOAPTYPE_STRING,
SOAPFLAG_FIELD | SOAPFLAG_NULLABLE,
offsetof(someStruct, guidVal),
NULL,
NULL,
-1
}
```

The information here should remain unchanged, except for the fact that you don't want it to be serialized as a string anymore (`SOAPTYPE_STRING`), but as a `GUID` (`SOAPTYPE_USERBASE+1` or `SOAPTYPE_GUID`). So, the modified entry for `guidVal` will look like this:

```
{
0x113E60CC,
"guidVal",
L"guidVal",
sizeof("guidVal")-1,
/*SOAPTYPE_STRING*/SOAPTYPE_GUID,
SOAPFLAG_FIELD | SOAPFLAG_NULLABLE,
offsetof(someStruct, guidVal),
NULL,
NULL,
-1
}
```

Now, almost everything is in place for using the `GUID`.

Atlsoap.h provides two template functions, allowing the client-side developer to clean up an object. These two functions are already implemented for the types supported by ATL Server—you might want to implement them for the `GUID` type as well. In this particular case (`GUID`), they aren't required. `GUID` doesn't hold any allocated memory, so the cleanup won't do anything really useful, but ignoring these functions for more complex types can easily result in memory leaks. These two functions are

```
template <typename T>
inline HRESULT AtlCleanupValue(T * /*pVal*/)
```

and

```
template <typename T>
inline HRESULT AtlCleanupValueEx(T *pVal, IAtlMemMgr *pMemMgr)
```

These functions do the same thing (i.e., they clean the allocated memory), but `AtlCleanupValue` assumes that the memory was allocated with the CRT memory manager (e.g., `malloc`), therefore it should be used for memory allocated by the client application (i.e., `[in]` parameters). The memory allocated through the ATL Server processing framework (e.g., variable size arrays transmitted through SOAP) comes from a memory manager object that, by default, is the CRT as well, but it can be overridden in order to use a private, customized heap. For memory allocated like this, the cleanup function must also know which memory manager was used in allocations. This is why `AtlCleanupValueEx` takes an `IAtlMemMgr` pointer. For example, when a proxy class returns a dynamically allocated array, that array should be cleaned with the memory manager of the proxy object, as follows:

```
AtlCleanupValueEx(...object.., proxyObject.GetMemMgr())
```

But as we already pointed out, in the case of `GUID` there's nothing for these cleanup functions to do:

```
inline HRESULT AtlCleanupValue<GUID>(GUID *pVal)
{
pVal;
return S_OK;
}
inline HRESULT AtlCleanupValueEx<GUID>(GUID *pVal, IAtlMemMgr *pMemMgr)
{
pVal;
pMemMgr;
return S_OK;
}
```

Now that the proxy class fully supports GUIDs, it's ready to use. The client application code will look something like this:

```
CGuidService  service;
someStruct    stIn, stOut;
CoCreateGuid(&stIn.guidVal);
stIn.strVal = SysAllocString(L"TestVal");
HRESULT hRet = service.RetGuidSoap(stIn, &stOut);
... processing here, using stOut.guidVal as a GUID
```

Conclusion

Class libraries are supposed to be generic, easy to use, and flexible enough to solve many problems. Real-life applications, on the other hand, tend to be very specific and often don't fit exactly into a class library scope. You have seen in this chapter how you can extend the ATL Server class library to solve specific problems that may occur in a real-life application. Such extensions go beyond the originally intended usage of the library, and they weren't tested as thoroughly as the documented features. Nevertheless, we think they're very handy tools for skilled developers.

This chapter concludes the Web services discussion. In the next chapter you'll learn about another very powerful component of ATL Server: the support for authoring and sending e-mails.

5. Now that the proxy class fully supports all files, it's ready to use. The client application code will look something like this:

```
[illegible]
```

Conclusion

Class libraries are supposed to be [illegible] many programs. [illegible] and often [illegible] however [illegible] may [illegible] go beyond the [illegible] intended [illegible] used as the [illegible] [illegible] tools [illegible]

[illegible]

CHAPTER 24

SMTP and MIME Support in ATL Server

ATL SERVER PROVIDES SUPPORT for sending Multipurpose Internet Mail Extensions (MIME)-encoded e-mail using the SMTP protocol. This feature can be very useful in a Web application where you need to send a confirmation back to the user.

In this chapter you'll learn how to use this feature to manage connections to SMTP servers and send e-mail. You'll be able to send both regular e-mail and e-mail with attachments. There are numerous ways you can use this feature in your applications—user confirmation and logging are just a couple common ones that come to mind.

To use the sample code in this chapter, you'll need to have access to an SMTP server. If you're using IIS, you can simply configure the virtual SMTP service that's installed with IIS to work in your domain.

NOTE *Unlike most other ATL Server functionality, SMTP support doesn't require that IIS be enabled.*

Connecting to an SMTP Server

You'll start by looking at the simple snippet of code in Listing 24-1 to see how you can establish a connection to an SMTP server.

Listing 24-1. Initializing a Connection to an SMTP Server

```
#include <atlsmtpconnection.h>
#include <atlmime.h>

CoInitialize(NULL);

CSMTPConnection smtpConnection;
if (!smtpConnection.Connect("localhost"))
{
  printf("Could not connect to SMTP server!\n");
}
```

Listing 24-1 is obviously very short, but we'll take a quick line-by-line look at it:

- *Lines 1 and 2:* All of the public support for SMTP and MIME in ATL Server is implemented in the atlsmtpconnection.h and atlmime.h header files. These classes make use of some of the constants and utility functions defined in atlsmtputil.h.

- *Line 4:* ATL Server uses the MLang services to help with the conversion between the local character set and Unicode. These services are exposed via COM interfaces, so COM must be initialized before ATL Server can query for these services. In general, MLang provides services for writing internationalized software for the Internet. We recommend looking up documentation in MSDN for the `IMultiLanguage` interface as a good start for learning about MLang.

- *Line 7:* The name of the SMTP server you're connecting to will depend on your network setup. You can optionally specify a timeout for the connection; by default, the timeout is 10 seconds.

You'll spend this chapter looking at the major classes in ATL Server that support SMTP and MIME. You'll also take a look at how to implement some of the more common scenarios that SMTP and MIME are used for. In the next section you'll examine the `CSMTPConnection` class.

Managing Connections with CSMTPConnection

Most of the SMTP functionality in ATL Server is implemented using the `CSMTPConnection` class. `CSMTPConnection` manages connections and allows messages to be sent. In this section you'll look at how `CSMTPConnection` manages connections for you.

`CSMTPConnection` provides methods for connecting to an SMTP server, disconnecting from it, and determining whether or not you have a valid connection.

CAUTION *An important point to remember is that* `CSMTPConnection` *isn't thread-safe, so you must be careful not to allow multithreaded access to it in your application.*

Let's look at each method associated with managing connections in CSMTPConnection:

```
BOOL Connect(LPCTSTR lpszHostName,
                        DWORD  dwTimeout = 10000) throw()
```

Connect must be called and it must execute successfully before you can send messages using CSMTPConnection. This method establishes a connection to the SMTP server specified by lpszHostName. A boolean value is returned to indicate success or failure. You can also specify an optional timeout value. Because CSMTPConnection is not thread-safe, if you must send messages from multiple threads in your application, you should maintain one CSMTPConnection per thread. You can, however, safely call Connect multiple times (after a successful connection, subsequent calls are ignored). Another connection won't be made until you call Disconnect. This method simply ends your connection to the SMTP connection and returns a boolean to indicate success or failure:

```
inline BOOL Disconnect() throw()
```

This method returns a boolean to indicate whether or not you have a valid connection to an SMTP server:

```
inline BOOL Connected() throw()
```

Now that you've seen how to establish a connection to a SMTP server, you'll look at how to actually send messages over that connection in the next section.

Sending MIME Messages

CSMTPConnection provides a number of different methods for sending messages. Each method varies in the level of control you have over the message being sent.

The following method is the simplest way to send an e-mail message. The parameters of this method correspond to familiar e-mail message properties; none of these parameters can be NULL. You can specify multiple recipients in lpszRecipients using a string delimited by a comma, semicolon, or space. If you need to set your own delimiter characters, then you should override the method AtlSmtpIsRecipientDelimiter in atlsmptutil.h that determines the valid delimiter characters.

```
inline BOOL SendSimple(LPCTSTR lpszRecipients,
                       LPCTSTR lpszSender,
                       LPCTSTR lpszSubject,
                       LPCTSTR lpszBody,
                       int  nTextLen = -1) throw()
```

The following method allows you to use a CMimeMessage object to represent the message you want to send. You can optionally override the recipients and sender specified in that object with the lpszRecipients and lpszSender parameters, respectively. The CMimeMessage class provides you with a convenient way of working with MIME messages. The next section of this chapter covers CMimeMessage, so we don't look at this class in depth right now.

```
inline BOOL SendMessage(CMimeMessage& msg,
                        LPCTSTR  lpszRecipients = NULL,
                        LPCTSTR  lpszSender = NULL) throw()
```

The following method gives you the most control over how you send messages with CSMTPConnection. None of the string parameters can be NULL. lpszRawData is expected to contain all of the text of your message. The format of this text must conform to RFC 822 (http://www.rfc.net/rfc822.html). You should use this method if you want to specify exactly what your message will look like as it's transferred over the network.

```
inline BOOL SendRaw(LPCTSTR lpszRawData,
                    DWORD   dwLen,
                    LPCTSTR lpszRecipients,
                    LPCTSTR lpszSender) throw()
```

Now that you have an understanding of how to send messages using CSMTPConnection, you'll take a closer look at how you can build more sophisticated messages using the CMimeMessage class.

CMimeMessage

CMimeMessage gives you access to the various parts of a MIME message. You can use this class to construct a MIME message with multiple attachments and text segments. Let's begin by looking at how to construct instances of this class.

Constructing MIME Messages

The CMimeMessage constructor allows you to optionally specify an object that implements the IMultiLanguage interface:

```
CMimeMessage(IMultiLanguage *pMultiLanguage = NULL) throw()
```

IMultiLanguage is part of the MLang services. As mentioned earlier, MLang is an API that makes writing internationalized Internet applications easier. Because of the nature of MLang, creating objects that implement IMultiLanguage can be computationally expensive. You can use CoCreateInstance to create an instance of IMultiLanguage and reuse it across multiple CMimeMessage objects.

By using MLang, CMimeMessage allows you to easily add text from various character sets to your MIME message. This is one major advantage of using a MIME message over sending regular ANSI text.

The following method allows you to create a copy of a CMimeMessage instance. A new instance of CMimeMessage is created and populated from the current instance. Because a memory allocation is required, there's a possibility of an exception being thrown from this method. You'll notice this pattern in ATL Server in general; all methods that require memory allocation will be marked as being ones that could throw exceptions.

```
virtual ATL_NOINLINE CMimeBodyPart* Copy() throw( ... )
```

The following method lets you easily specify a display name for your message. A display name isn't required.

```
inline BOOL SetDisplayName(LPCTSTR szDisplayName) throw()
```

Once you've constructed an instance of CMimeMessage, you have many options available for sending text and adding attachments. We describe these methods later in the chapter.

Addressing Your Messages

CMimeMessage derives from the CMimeHeader base class. This base class implements methods to construct the elements of a MIME message as defined in RFC 822 (http://www.rfc.net/rfc822.html). You can use this base class if you want to create your own MIME message classes. CMimeMessage inherits and exposes the following methods. Most of these methods relate to familiar elements of e-mail messages, so we don't spend too much time explaining them.

```
inline BOOL SetPriority(ATL_MIME_PRIORITY nPriority) throw()
inline ATL_MIME_PRIORITY GetPriority() throw()
```

These methods set and get the priority of your message. The priority levels are as follows:

- ATL_MIME_HIGH_PRIORITY
- ATL_MIME_NORMAL_PRIORITY
- ATL_MIME_LOW_PRIORITY
- ATL_MIME_PRIORITY_ERROR

The value chosen sets the X-Priority header in your MIME message.

The following methods set and get the friendly sender name of your message. The friendly names are not required, but they are used by most e-mail clients.

```
inline BOOL SetSenderName(LPCTSTR szName, UINT uiCodePage = 0) throw()
inline LPCSTR GetSenderName() throw()
```

The following method appends a user-defined header to your message. You should use the X- prefix convention in your header. Like other MIME headers, the user-defined header that you specify must not contain any line break (CR/LF) characters. You also have the option of specifying any code page that your system supports.

```
inline BOOL AppendUserDefinedHeader(LPCTSTR szHeaderName, LPCTSTR szHeader,
                                                  UINT uiCodePage = 0) throw()
```

The following methods allow you to work with the direct recipients of your message. GetRecipients returns a comma-delimited list of recipients.

```
inline BOOL AddRecipient(LPCTSTR szAddress,
                                 LPCTSTR szName = NULL,
                                 UINT uiCodePage = 0) throw()
inline LPCSTR GetRecipients() throw()
inline BOOL   ClearRecipients() throw()
```

The following methods allow you to work with the Cc recipients of your message. GetCc returns a comma-delimited list of recipients.

```
inline BOOL AddCc(LPCTSTR szAddress, LPCTSTR szName = NULL, UINT
inline LPCSTR GetCc() throw()
inline BOOL ClearCc() throw()
```

The following methods allow you to work with the Bcc recipients of your message. `GetBcc` returns a comma-delimited list of recipients.

```
inline BOOL AddBcc(LPCTSTR szAddress) throw()
inline LPCSTR GetBcc() throw()
inline BOOL ClearBcc() throw()
```

These methods allow you to work with required recipients of your message:

```
inline DWORD GetRequiredRecipientsStringLength() throw()
ATL_NOINLINE BOOL GetRecipientsString(LPSTR szRecip, LPDWORD pdwLen) throw()
```

These methods allow you to work with the sender of your message:

```
inline LPCSTR GetSender() throw()
inline BOOL SetSender(LPCTSTR szSender) throw()
```

These methods allow you to work with the subject of your message:

```
inline BOOL SetSubject(LPCTSTR szSubject, UINT uiCodePage = 0) throw()
inline LPCSTR GetSubject() throw()
```

Sending Text

The `AddText` method adds a text segment to your MIME message and optionally specifies a code page for that text. The text specified by `szText` can't be `NULL`. You can specify any code page in `uiCodePage` that your system supports. By default, you use the default ANSI code page on your system, which ATL Server determines by calling the `GetACP()` Win32 API function.

```
inline BOOL AddText(LPCTSTR szText,
                    int     nTextLen   = -1,
                    int     nPos       = 1,
                    UINT    uiCodePage = 0) throw()
```

Besides sending text, MIME allows you to add attachments to your message, which we cover in the following section. This ability gives you many more options for sending information back to your user.

Adding Attachments

The following method allows you to add different types of attachments to your MIME message:

```
inline BOOL AttachFile(LPCTSTR szFileName,
                       LPCTSTR szDisplayName   = NULL,
                       LPCTSTR szContentType   = NULL,
                       Int  nEncodingScheme = ATLSMTP_BASE64_ENCODE,
                       UINT  uiCodepage = 0)
```

AttachFile allows you to specify a file to attach to your MIME message. You can optionally specify a display name, content type, encoding scheme, and code page.

szDisplayName specifies the display name that is used by e-mail clients such as Outlook to display information about a given attachment. If no display name is specified, you'll use the name rawdata as a default.

szContentType describes the content of the attachment. If one isn't specified, try to determine the content type by looking up the file extension under the HKEY_CLASSES_ROOT registry key and reading its content type value. If the extension isn't registered or there isn't a content type value, default the content type to application/octet-stream.

nEncodingScheme specifies how the file will be encoded. You can specify one of the following:

- ATLSMTP_BASE64_ENCODE: Encodes using base64, as described in RFC 2045 (http://www.ietf.org/rfc/rfc2045.txt)
- ATLSMTP_UUENCODE: Encodes using the scheme specified in the POSIX P1003.2b/D11 specification
- ATLSMTP_QP_ENCODE: Encodes using the "Q" encoding scheme specified in RFC 2047 (http://www.ietf.org/rfc/rfc2047.txt)

All of these encoding schemes, as well as other schemes, are implemented in functions defined in atlenc.h and can be used independently anywhere in your application.

Listing 24-2 is a very simple example showing how you can use Base64Encode to encode a piece of data. If the encoding was successful, the resulting encoded data is output to the console.

Listing 24-2. Using Base64Encode to Encode a Piece of Data

```
#include <atlenc.h>

int _tmain()
{
    char *data   = _T( "Hello World!" );
    int   dataLen = strlen( data );

    //
    // First determine how much memory to allocate to
    // hold the encoded data.
    //
    int encodedDataLen  = Base64EncodeGetRequiredLength( dataLen );
    char* encodedData = new char[ encodedDataLen + 1 ];

    if( TRUE == Base64Encode( ( const BYTE*)data,
                              dataLen,
                              encodedData,
                              &encodedDataLen ) )
    {
        encodedData[ encodedDataLen ] = 0;
        printf( "Successfully encoded!\n%s", encodedData );
    }
    else
    {
        printf( "Error encoding!" );
    }

    return 0;
}
```

The following method allows you to attach one `CMimeMessage` to another. A copy of `pMsg` is made and attached so that the caller remains responsible for the memory management of `pMsg`. A minor bug in this method is that it should be declared as `throw()` rather than `throw( ... )`. In other words, the declaration of this method says that it might throw an exception, when in fact it never will.

```
inline BOOL AttachMessage(CMimeMessage* pMsg) throw( ... )
```

As with CSMTPConnection, CMimeMessage gives you a way of sending a raw attachment, as shown in the following code snippet. This gives you complete control of how you obtain the data that's to be attached. A great use of this method is to read the contents of a file that you'll attach to all messages that your application sends at start-up. This saves the overhead of reading the file each time you want to attach it (you can just use a memory buffer or something else more efficient than a file).

```
inline BOOL AttachRaw(void*   pRawData,
                      DWORD   dwDataLength,
                      int     nEncodingScheme = ATLSMTP_BASE64_ENCODE,
                      BOOL    bCopyData = TRUE,
                      LPCTSTR szDisplayName = NULL,
                      LPCTSTR szContentType = _T("application/octet-stream"),
                      UINT    uiCodepage = 0)
```

Now that you've had a chance to look at the classes that make up ATL Server's support for sending SMTP messages, you'll take a look at a complete example. In the next section, you'll learn how you can extend ATL Server's SMTP functionality to send HTML messages instead of regular text.

Extending ATL Server's SMTP Support: Sending HTML Messages

In this example, we demonstrate how you can extend the SMTP support in ATL Server to send HTML messages rather than just plain text messages.

ATL Server uses implementations of the CMimeBodyPart class to encapsulate the various "parts" of a MIME message. A MIME message is typically made up of several of these parts. Plain text and file attachments are good examples of MIME message parts. These two attachment types are implemented with the CMimeText and CFileAttachment classes, respectively.

A limitation of CMimeText is that it allows you to only send plain text. This, however, does provide us with a good opportunity to demonstrate how to extend ATL Server's SMTP functionality. To do so, you'll create a new class called CMimeTextEx that can support sending different types of text messages. Later on, you'll see how to use this class in a MIME message. First, you'll take a closer look at the common base class that all MIME parts, including the base class CMimeText, implement.

CMimeBodyPart is defined as shown in Listing 24-3.

Listing 24-3. Definition of CMimeBodyPart

```
class CMimeBodyPart
{
public:
  virtual ~CMimeBodyPart() = 0 {}
  // WriteData - pure virtual method to dump the data for a body part.
  virtual BOOL WriteData( HANDLE  hFile,
  LPOVERLAPPED  pOverlapped,
  LPCSTR  szBoundary,
  DWORD   dwFlags = 0) = 0;
  // GetContentType - pure virtual method to get the content of a body part
  virtual LPCSTR GetContentType() = 0;

 // GetCharset - virtual method to get the character set of a body part
 // (defaults to ATLSMTP_DEFAULT_CSET).
  virtual LPCSTR GetCharset()
  {
    return ATLSMTP_DEFAULT_CSET;
  }
  virtual CMimeBodyPart* Copy() = 0;
protected:
  // MakeMimeHeader - pure virtual method to create a MIME header for a
  // body part.
  virtual BOOL MakeMimeHeader(CStringA&  header,
   LPCSTR  szBoundary) = 0;
};
```

You'll use `CMimeText` as your base class and just inherit most of the implementation from this class. Your class will only differ in the value returned by `GetContentType` and the way you build the header in `MakeMimeHeader`.

Implementing your `CMimeTextEx` class is actually quite simple. Listing 24-4 presents the class definition.

Listing 24-4. Definition of CMimeTextEx

```
class CMimeTextEx : public CMimeText
{
protected:
   CStringA m_strContentType;

public:
     CMimeTextEx(LPCSTR contentType)
  {
```

```
  m_strContentType = contentType;
}

virtual inline LPCSTR GetContentType() throw()
{
  return m_strContentType;
}

virtual ATL_NOINLINE CMimeBodyPart* Copy() throw( ... )
{
  CAutoPtr<CMimeTextEx> pNewText;
  ATLTRY(pNewText.Attach(new CMimeTextEx(this->m_strContentType)));
  if (pNewText)
    *pNewText = *this;

  return pNewText.Detach();
}

  const CMimeTextEx& operator=(const CMimeTextEx& that) throw( ... )
  {
     if (this != &that)
     {
       *(CMimeText*)this = *(CMimeText*)&that;
        m_strContentType  = that.m_strContentType;
      }

      return *this;
  }

  // Make the MIME header
  virtual inline BOOL MakeMimeHeader(CStringA& header,
                                     LPCSTR    szBoundary) throw()
  {
    char szBegin[ATL_MIME_BOUNDARYLEN+8];
    if (*szBoundary)
    {
      // this is not the only body part
      memcpy(szBegin, "\r\n\r\n--", 6);
      memcpy(szBegin+6, szBoundary, ATL_MIME_BOUNDARYLEN);
      *(szBegin+(ATL_MIME_BOUNDARYLEN+6)) = '\0';
     }
     else
     {
       // this is the only body part, so output the full MIME header
```

```
        memcpy(szBegin, "MIME-Version: 1.0", sizeof("MIME-Version: 1.0"));
      }

        _ATLTRY
        {
           header.Format("%s\r\nContent-Type:\
         %s;\r\n\tcharset=\"%s\"\r\nContent-Transfer-Encoding: 8bit\r\n\r\n", \
           szBegin, m_strContentType, m_szCharset);
           return TRUE;
        }
        _ATLCATCHALL()
        {
             return FALSE;
        }
    }
};
```

The implementation of this class is quite simple. The constructor takes the content type of the text part and uses it to set the content type of the header file when the message is being sent. You can use the `Initialize` method inherited from `CMimeText` to set the text of the message that you want to send.

As you saw earlier in this chapter, instances of `CMimeBodyPart` are added to a `CMimeMessage` object, which you can send using the `CSMTPConnection` class. `CMimeMessage` is implemented to accept only a finite set of MIME parts. This limitation gives us another opportunity to extend ATL Server's functionality. Listing 24-5 shows a class that derives from `CMimeMessage` that allows you to insert your HTML text part into the MIME message.

Listing 24-5. Extending CMimeMessageEx to Allow HTML

```
class CMimeMessageEx : public CMimeMessage
{
 public:
 // Add some custom part to the message at position nPos in the body parts list
 // pPart - the part
 // bCopy - copy the part or add the pointer itself
 // nPos  - the position in the message at which to insert the text (optional)
 inline BQOL AddCustomBodyPart(CMimeBodyPart *pPart,
                               BOOL          bCopy = TRUE,
                               int           nPos  = 1) throw()
 {
   BOOL bRet = TRUE;

```

```
    if( !pPart )
      return FALSE;

    if (nPos < 1)
    {
      nPos = 1;
    }

    _ATLTRY
    {
      CAutoPtr<CMimeBodyPart> spNewComponent;
      if( bCopy )
        spNewComponent.Attach( pPart->Copy() );
      else
        spNewComponent.Attach( pPart );

      if( !spNewComponent )
      {
        return FALSE;
      }

      POSITION currPos = m_BodyParts.FindIndex(nPos-1);

      if (!currPos)
      {
      if (!m_BodyParts.AddTail(spNewComponent))
          bRet = FALSE;
      }
      else
      {
       if (!m_BodyParts.InsertBefore(currPos, spNewComponent))
         bRet = FALSE;
      }
      }
      _ATLCATCHALL()
      {
        bRet = FALSE;
      }

      return bRet;
  }
};
```

Your extension to `CMimeMessage` adds a new method that allows you to add a custom `CMimeBody` part to the message. You'll use this method to insert instances of your `CMimeTextEx` class into your message.

Listing 24-6 puts your two extension classes together into a full example.

Listing 24-6. The Complete Example

```
1 CMimeMessageEx htmlMsg;
2
3 htmlMsg.SetSender("bogdanc@microsoft.com");
4 htmlMsg.SetSenderName("Bogdan Crivat");
5 htmlMsg.AddRecipient("bogdanc@microsoft.com",  "Bogdan Crivat");
6 htmlMsg.SetPriority(ATL_MIME_NORMAL_PRIORITY);
7 htmlMsg.SetSubject("Hello World!");
8
9 char *pText = "<html>
10               <body>\
11                 <h1>Hello!</h1>\
12                 <br><br>\
13                 <p>Test</p>\
14                 <img href='http://msimg.com/m/r/logo/msft/logo.gif'>
15                    Hello World!\
16                 </img>\
17               </body>\
18               </html>";
19
20 CMimeTextEx htmlText("text/html");
21 htmlText.Initialize(pText, strlen(pText), NULL, 0);
22
23 htmlMsg.AddCustomBodyPart(&htmlText);
24 smtpConnection.SendMessage(htmlMsg);
```

Let's have a look at Listing 24-6 line-by-line:

- *Lines 1 through 7:* You initialize `CMimeTextEx` in the same way as you would `CMimeText`.

- *Lines 9 through 18:* This is contrived, but you'll statically declare some HTML to send in your message.

- *Lines 20 and 21:* You've defined the `CMimeTextEx` constructor to take a content type as a parameter. Because you're sending HTML, you'll use `text/html` as your content type. The `Initialize` method allows you to specify the text that you want to send.

- *Lines 23 and 24:* Calling `AddCustomBodyPart` adds your HTML to the message. You can call this method repeatedly to add multiple text parts to the message. As usual, `SendMessage` will send your MIME message.

As you can see, extending ATL Server to support sending HTML messages over SMTP isn't a difficult task. In the next section you'll look at a few ways of minimizing the performance impact of sending SMTP messages in your application.

Tips for Improving Performance

No matter which technique or technology you choose to send SMTP messages in your application, it's going to be a time-intensive operation. More than likely, the time needed to connect to the SMTP server is going to be the dominant time in this operation. Let's look at a technique that you can apply to improve the performance of sending e-mail in your application.

Creating a Delivery Queue

To minimize the impact of sending SMTP messages on your application's overall performance, you should consider queuing SMTP messages for delivery. Ideally, this delivery would be done in a separate thread or process. ATL Server provides functionality to make building a queuing system into your application very simple:

```
Using CSMTPConnection::WriteFile/CSMTPConnection::SendMessage
```

`CSMTPConnection::WriteFile` allows you to write out the complete SMTP transcript to a file. `CSMTPConnection::SendMessage` can read from a file that contains an SMTP transcript and send it to the appropriate SMTP server. This pair allows you to easily build an SMTP queuing system into your application.

Let's look at how you can queue up SMTP messages for later delivery. Consider the code in Listing 24-7 for sending an SMTP message.

Listing 24-7. Sending an SMTP Message

```
1 CMimeMessage msg;
2
3 msg.SetSender("bogdanc@microsoft.com");
4 msg.SetSenderName("Bogdan Crivat");
5 msg.AddRecipient("bogdanc@microsoft.com",  "Bogdan Crivat");
6 msg.SetPriority(ATL_MIME_NORMAL_PRIORITY);
7 msg.SetSubject("Hello World!");
8
9 CAtlTemporaryFile smtpFile;
10 smtpFile.Create();
11
12 smtpConnection.WriteToFile( smtpFile.TempFileName(), msg);
```

The notable lines of Listing 24-7 are 9 through 12. In these lines, the `CAtlTemporaryFile` class gives you a convenient way to create a temporary, uniquely named file. The `CSMTPConnection::WriteToFile` method allows you to write out your message object to a file, rather than sending it directly. The contents of the file created by this code look like this:

```
DATA
Date: Tue, 14 Aug 2001 22:58:48 -0700
From: Bogdan Crivat <bogdanc@microsoft.com>
Subject: Hello World!
To: "Bogdan Crivat" <bogdanc@microsoft.com>
X-Priority: 3
MIME-Version: 1.0
Content-Type: text/html;
  charset="iso-8859-1"
Content-Transfer-Encoding: 8bit

<html>
    <body>
       <h1>Hello!</h1>
       <br><br>
       <p>Test</p>
       <img href='http://msimg.com/m/r/logo/msft/logo.gif'>Hello World!</img>
    </body>
</html>
```

This is the exact text that `CSMTPConnection` will send to a SMTP server when it's actually sending the message. For security reasons, you should make sure that these files are written to a directory structure whose file permissions deny access to the account that IIS is running under.

Now you have one half of SMTP message queuing system. Each time you call `WriteToFile`, you'll create a file with an SMTP transcript like the previous one. Let's now look at the code for a simple client that will process these transcripts.

Processing the Delivery Queue

In the interest of brevity, you'll create a simple console application to process these SMTP transcripts. You could use the Windows Task Scheduler to run this process on a regular basis to process messages, or you could create a Windows service with this functionality. Consider the code in Listing 24-8.

Listing 24-8. A Simple Application for Processing a Delivery Queue

```
int main(int argc, _TCHAR **argv)
{
   ASSERT(argc);
   ASSERT(argv);

   if (argc != 1)
   {
     printf("usage: smtpclient <smtp server name> <smtp file directory>\n");
     return 1;
   }

   _TCHAR *smtpServerName = NULL;
   smtpServerName = argv[1];

   _TCHAR *smtpFileDirectory = NULL;
   smtpFileDirectory= argv[2];

   HRESULT hr = E_FAIL;
   hr = CoInitialize(NULL);

   ASSERT(SUCCEEDED(hr));
   if (FAILED(hr))
   {
     return 1;
   }
```

```
26
27    CSMTPConnection smtpConnection;
28    if (!smtpConnection.Connect(smtpServerName))
29    {
30      return 1;
31    }
32
33    BOOL  hasMoreFiles = TRUE;
34    HANDLE tempHandle   = NULL;
35    WIN32_FIND_DATA findFileData;
36    ZeroMemory(&findFileData, sizeof(findFileData));
37
38    CHandle fileHandle(FindFirstFile(smtpFileDirectory, &findFileData));
39
40    while (fileHandle != INVALID_HANDLE_VALUE &&
41           hasMoreFiles)
42    {
43        smtpConnection.SendMessage(findFileData.cFileName);
44
45        hasMoreFiles = FindNextFile(fileHandle, &findFileData);
46    }
47 }
```

Let's look at the important parts of this code line-by-line:

- *Lines 12 through 16:* Take the name of your SMTP server and directory where the SMTP transcripts are located as command-line parameters.

- *Lines 33 through 38:* Use the Win32 API to find all of your SMTP transcript files.

- *Line 43:* For each SMTP transcript file, call `CSMTPConnection::SendMessage` to send the SMTP message. You can optionally specify alternate recipients and senders as parameters to this method. By default, `CSMTPConnection` will assume that the recipients and senders are in the SMTP transcript file.

That's all the code necessary to implement a queued SMTP delivery system in your application. When you execute the actual SMTP send operation in a separate client executable, your main application is free to process requests without having to wait for a response from a SMTP server.

Conclusion

ATL Server's support for SMTP and MIME is quite extensive. In a few lines of code, you can send SMTP messages from your application. Going further, you can take advantage of ATL Server's MIME support to send rich messages composed of text, HTML, files, and attachments. ATL Server integrates MLang services, so you can easily develop applications for the international market. ATL Server also exposes several functions that encode and decode data in a variety of formats. You've seen how you can use these functions in any type of application. When performance is critical, you can use ATL Server's offline SMTP features to implement a SMTP message queuing system.

In the next chapter you'll round out your education of ATL Server by moving away from server-side applications and looking how you can apply ATL Server in client-side applications.

CHAPTER 25

Developing HTTP Client Applications in ATL Server

ATL SERVER COMES WITH a set of classes intended to facilitate development of HTTP client applications. A common example of when these classes are used is in a SOAP client. The default SOAP client class generated by sproxy.exe uses this set of classes for HTTP communications.

This chapter provides an overview of the features of the HTTP client. It also provides some code snippets (and analysis) for a few common scenarios in developing HTTP client applications. You can find a complete reference for the classes and methods we discuss in this chapter in Visual Studio .NET's MSDN documentation (`ms-help://MS.VSCC/MS.MSDNVS/vccore/html/vcconatlhttpclientoverview.htm`).

NOTE *All the code snippets presented in this chapter send HTTP requests to a virtual directory called "HTTPClient" on the local machine, and build and deploy the ClientParams sample application. For compiling and running the sample code, please create a folder called "HTTPClient" in the root directory of IIS on your machine. Usually, the IIS root folder is in %HOMEDRIVE%:\Inetpub\wwwroot, where %HOMEDRIVE% is the drive where you've installed Windows. Then, copy the content of the HTTPClient sample folder into this directory.*
If you don't have IIS installed on your machine, you'll need to modify the sample code to point to the server of your choice. Also, if accessing the IIS machine requires you to use an HTTP proxy server, we provide details on how to do this for an ATL Server application in the "A Simple HTTP Client" section.

In the next section we discuss the classes involved in developing HTTP clients.

Classes for Developing HTTP Clients

The framework for supporting HTTP clients in ATL Server applications consists of a client class (`CAtlHttpClientT`) and a set of "feature" classes that encapsulate different aspects of the behavior of the client class. The `CAtlHttpClientT` class is defined as follows:

```
template <class TSocketClass> class CAtlHttpClientT;
```

The `template` parameter is the class to be used for socket communications. ATL Server provides a single class to be used as a socket class (`ZEvtSyncSocket`). Therefore, it also provides a `typedef` for the HTTP client using this socket class:

```
typedef CAtlHttpClientT<ZEvtSyncSocket> CAtlHttpClient;
```

NOTE *The* `ZEvtSyncSocket` *class is an internal class and it's not supported by the MSDN documentation. It's strongly recommended that you not use this class directly. The supported (and recommended) way of using* `CAtlHttpClientT` *is to either use the default template instantiation (i.e.,* `CAtlHttpClient`*, the* `typedef`*-ed version) or instantiate the template with your own socket class. Avoid explicitly instantiating the template with the* `ZEvtSyncSocket` *class or using this class directly in your applications. It may be dropped or replaced in later versions of ATL Server.*

For most of this chapter, you'll deal with the `typedef`-ed version of HTTP client, `CAtlHttpClient`. The main functionality of the HTTP client class is the `Navigate` method, which sends an HTTP request and collects the response from the server.

An HTTP request is defined by multiple elements: the destination, the content of the request, and the method of sending the content (HTTP verb) being the most important. You'll see in the following section how you can populate these request components using ATL Server classes.

A Simple HTTP Client

In this section we describe the steps you need to take when you develop a basic HTTP client application. To start, a simple call to the `Navigate` method of the `CAtlHttpClient` class will send an HTTP request to the specified URL:

```
CAtlHttpClient client;
if( client.Navigate( "http://localhost/HTTPClient/test.html" ) )
    printf( "Return Code -- %d\n", client.GetStatus() );
```

Most likely, this code will display something like this:

```
Return Code -- 200
```

with 200 being the HTTP code for success.

In this section, we incrementally analyze how you can build the URL parameter from components, how you can customize the HTTP request to use a different HTTP verb (`POST`, for instance, instead of the default `GET` verb), and how you can retrieve the whole HTTP response (not only the status code). You can perform all these operations with the different overloads of the `Navigate` method.

There are three overloads for the `Navigate` method:

```
bool Navigate(
   LPCTSTR szURL,
   ATL_NAVIGATE_DATA * pNavData = NULL
) throw(...);
bool Navigate(
   LPCTSTR szServer,
   LPCTSTR szPath,
   ATL_NAVIGATE_DATA * pNavData = NULL
) throw(...);
bool Navigate(
   const CUrl* pUrl,
   ATL_NAVIGATE_DATA * pNavData = NULL
) throw(...);
```

In all of the overloads, the `pNavData` parameter has the same meaning, which we discuss later.

The first overload (the one used in the code snippet) works fine when the URL to receive the request is simple enough to be hard-coded inside the application or entered as a parameter (user input).

This isn't the case for most applications. Assuming that the path to the object is constant (something that isn't very common), at least the server name should be entered as a parameter (so that the HTTP call can be easily routed to a different server). The second overload is helpful for this scenario—it allows separation between the server name and the server path to the request object.

You can assemble components of more complex URLs in strings to use in either of these overloads. However, the task of merging strings (such as username, password, local object paths, and query parameters) and numbers (such as the port number) into a URL that's compliant with the HTTP specification can prove time-consuming and bug-prone. Fortunately, ATL Server provides a class, `CUrl`, that does most of this work for you. `CUrl` provides methods to separately access and modify components of a URL and also to get a complete URL string built from those components.

For instance, you can build a rather complex URL like the following:

```
https://someone:secret@www.microsoft.com:8080/visualc/stuff.htm#contents
```

using a CUrl object in a few calls as follows:

```
CUrl    url;
url.SetScheme(ATL_URL_SCHEME_HTTPS);
url.SetUserName("someone");
url.SetPassword("secret");
url.SetHostName("www.microsoft.com");
url.SetPortNumber(8080);
url.SetUrlPath("/visualc/stuff.htm");
url.SetExtra("#contents");
```

This code should be easier to maintain. Also, by separating all the URL components, this code allows for tighter validation of each field (e.g., with regular expressions).

NOTE CUrl *isn't the main subject of this section. However, we should note that it supports generating a full URL string out of the components, with a few different escaping schemes that make it compatible with older WinINet code (*InternetCreateUrl*). It also supports the reverse operation, (i.e., parsing an existing URL string and separating the various components of the string), via the* CrackUrl *method, the equivalent of the WinINet* InternetCrackUrl *API.*

The third overload of the CAtlHttpClient::Navigate method takes as a parameter a pointer to a CUrl object.

Let's look now at the last parameter in all three overloads: the ATL_NAVIGATE_DATA structure pointer. This structure contains information about the HTTP request to be sent. The various fields of an HTTP request appear as fields of the structure. The structure members can be classified as follows:

- Request content (such as data to be posted or additional HTTP headers)
- Helpers for sending content (such as the packet size for the request or callbacks for streaming data to the server)

- Helpers for receiving content (such as the packet size for reading the response or callbacks for data streamed by the server, or the maximum time to wait for a response)

- Behavioral flags that describe the actions to be performed by the HTTP client for specific server response codes (such as automatically handling redirections)

By manipulating the members of this structure, you have full control over the behavior of the HTTP client.

The behavior modification flags prove extremely useful in making the HTTP client as easy to use as a browser (with automatic redirection or authentication and no concern for the response content until it's downloaded) or as flexible as a detailed set of Internet APIs. Furthermore, a class provided in ATL Server, `CAtlNavigateData`, encapsulates the `ATL_NAVIGATE_DATA` structure and provides public methods for accessing and modifying these fields. The next sections provide more detail on how you can use the `CAtlNavigateData` structure.

The invocation of one of the `Navigate` methods will return a boolean `true` if the request is sent and any response comes from the server.

When `true` is returned from the `Navigate` method, it means that the request was completed successfully and the server returned a success code. However, `false` may have multiple meanings. Therefore, you can make a complete conclusion on the status of the request only after you inspect both the result of `Navigate` and the result of `GetStatus`. For the Visual Studio .NET release of ATL Server, Table 25-1 describes the possible states. However, this may change in later releases and service packs.

Table 25-1. The Meaning of Different Status Values After a Failing Navigate Call

NAVIGATE	GETSTATUS	MEANING
`false`	`ATL_INVALID_STATUS` (< 0)	No valid response (can't connect to the server, timeout occurred, there was an error parsing the response, and so forth).
`false`	301–303	Autoredirect is disabled *or* it failed.
`false`	401, 407	Negotiate authentication failed.
`true`	200–206, 304, or 305	SUCCESS (and the respective HTTP meaning).
`false`	Any code not mentioned previously	ERROR (the specific HTTP meaning of that code. For instance, 500 is Internal Server Error).

If the status is greater than 0, the error message that comes from the server can be retrieved in the same way as the regular HTTP response content.

Once you've invoked `Navigate`, if some response is available, you can obtain it by using `GetResponseLength` and `GetResponse`, two methods offered by the HTTP client class.

The code snippet at the beginning of this section, when modified to display the response, looks like this:

```
CAtlHttpClient client;
client.Navigate( "http://localhost/HTTPClient/test.html" );
if (client.GetStatus() != ATL_INVALID_STATUS)
{
    // Display any response, not only for success
    DWORD    dwResponseLength = client.GetResponseLength();
    const BYTE*    pResponse = client.GetResponse();
    char*    pText = new char[dwResponseLength+1];
    // ensure the trailing zero for printf
    memcpy( pText, pResponse, dwResponseLength);
    pText[dwResponseLength] = 0;
    printf("\n\n%s\n\n", pText);
}
```

The output looks like this:

```
HTTP/1.1 200 OK
Server: Microsoft-IIS/5.1
Date: Wed, 13 Nov 2002 10:03:31 GMT
Content-Type: text/html
Accept-Ranges: bytes
Last-Modified: Sun, 20 Oct 2002 18:39:03 GMT
ETag: "708e89f66778c21:8ca"
Content-Length: 54

<html>
<body>
        This is a Test Page
</body>
</html>
```

As you can see, the response contains all the HTTP incoming traffic (including status code, headers, and so forth). If some "HTTP 100 Continue" responses are issued before the actual content, these are going to be displayed too. This might prove useful in debugging an application or in handling some HTTP error code. But, for a successful request, usually only the actual body of the response matters (in the preceding output, the text between `<html>` and `</html>`). To get the filtered body of the response, simply replace `GetResponseLength()` and `GetResponse()` with `GetBodyLength()` and `GetBody()`, respectively, in the preceding code snippet.

We've discussed so far the main code path for sending an HTTP request and retrieving the response with the ATL Server HTTP client classes. The code snippets presented so far should provide enough information for you to create simple applications and expect success in most cases. Please consult the MSDN documentation for up-to-date details on all the methods of `CUrl`, `CAtlNavigateData`, and the other classes discussed here.

The next section covers sending and receiving complex data, such as multiple form/query parameters or chunked content.

Transmitting and Receiving Data

In this section we explain some strategies that we hope will make your life as a developer easier when you handle large or complex data that you have to send via the HTTP client.

Handling Query and Form Parameters

The most common way of sending data through HTTP consists of collections of name/value pairs, passed either as query parameters (part of the URL) or as form parameters (part of the request body).

To show how to use query or form parameters with the HTTP client, we present a small ATL Server request handler without SRF file support that contains the code in Listing 25-1 in the `ValidateAndExchange` function.

Listing 25-1. ValidateAndExchange Implementation That Iterates the Request Parameters

```
m_HttpResponse << "<html><body>";
POSITION pos;
LPCSTR    szName, szValue;

m_HttpResponse << "<H1>Form Variables</H1><br>";
pos = m_HttpRequest.GetFirstFormVar( &szName, &szValue);
while( pos != NULL )
{
    m_HttpResponse << szName << "=" << szValue << "<br>";
    pos = m_HttpRequest.GetNextFormVar(pos, &szName, &szValue);
}
```

```
m_HttpResponse << "<H1>Query Params </H1><br>";
pos = m_HttpRequest.GetFirstQueryParam( &szName, &szValue);
while( pos != NULL )
{
    m_HttpResponse << szName << "=" << szValue << "<br>";
    pos = m_HttpRequest.GetNextQueryParam(pos, &szName, &szValue);
}
m_HttpResponse << "</body></html>";
```

As you can see, the code in Listing 25-1 iterates through both the query and the form parameters and displays them in a user-friendly form.

How Are Parameters Sent in HTTP?

Let's assume that you want to send as parameters values for Name and Age. You can send these values as part of the URL in a request, as follows:

```
GET /ClientParams/ClientParams.dll?Name=UserName&Value=25 HTTP/1.1
```

Or you can send them as part of the request body, generating an HTTP request like this:

```
POST /ClientParams/ClientParams.dll HTTP/1.1
Content-Length: 15
Content-Type: application/x-www-form-urlencoded

Name=foo&Age=25
```

The format of the name/value collection containing the parameters is the same, both in the URL and in the request body. The differences are in the other headers of the HTTP request. There are also some other differences related to the HTTP server implementation. For instance, usually a URL must be shorter than a certain limit accepted by a Web server. The length of the request body doesn't have to comply with the same restriction.

The client application (in this case, the ATL Server HTTP client application) has to build the string that contains the name/value pairs in the following form:

```
<ParameterName>=<ParameterValue>
```

followed optionally by other pairs separated by an ampersand (&).

If special characters occur inside the name or the value (the HTTP specification provides a list of all the special characters—here, we only deal with the `=` and `&` characters, which would affect sever-side parsing of the pairs), then these special characters have to be encoded to their ASCII code. Therefore, the `=` character inside a name or a value should be represented as `%3D` and the `&` character should be encoded as `%26`. The client application should take care of the encoding rules when creating the parameter's text representation.

Let's see now what the code for sending the `Name` and `Age` parameters looks like in the ATL Server HTTP client.

NOTE *In all the code snippets presented in this section, we assume three variables declared as follows:*

```
CAtlNavigateData    navData;
CAtlHttpClient      client;
CUrl                url;
```

For sending the parameters as part of the URL, one simple implementation can provide directly the full URL containing the parameters:

```
url.CrackUrl(
 "http://localhost/ClientParams/ClientParams.dll?Name=UserName&Age=25");
client.Navigate( &url, &navData );
```

Alternately, you can specify the parameters part of the URL separated from the main part, which is convenient when the parameters are generated dynamically:

```
url.CrackUrl("http://localhost/ClientParams/ClientParams.dll")
    LPCSTR szParamData = "?Name=UserName&Age=25";
url.SetExtraInfo(szParamData);
client.Navigate(&url, &navData);
```

ding the same content inside the request body (as form
ok like this:

```
calhost/ClientParams/ClientParams.dll")
 "Name=UserName&Age=25";
e = _T("application/x-www-form-urlencoded");
```

```
navData.SetMethod(ATL_HTTP_METHOD_POST);
navData.SetPostData((BYTE*)szPOSTData, _tcslen(szPOSTData), szContentType);
client.Navigate(&url, &navData);
```

With the preceding code snippets, the problem of sending parameters is reduced to generating the string containing them encoded according to the HTTP standard (name and value separated by `=` and couples separated by `&`).

The `CHttpRequestParams` class in atlisapi.h provides the implementation for a collection of name/value pairs, plus methods for both rendering the HTTP-encoded string for these pairs and parsing such a string. This class is used by the request handlers to parse the request parameters, and it can be used on the client side in generating the string containing the request parameters.

So, the new code for adding `Name` and `Age` might look Listing 25-2.

Listing 25-2. Using CHttpRequestParams for Generating a Collection of HTTP POST Parameters

```
CHttpRequestParams    requestParams;
requestParams.SetAt("Name", "UserName");
requestParams.SetAt("Age", "25");

char    *szPOSTData = NULL;
DWORD    dwSize = 0;
// Get the number of actual characters
requestParams.Render(szPOSTData, &dwSize);
szPOSTData = new char[dwSize+1]; // leave room for trailing \0
dwSize += 1; // mark the room for trailing \0
requestParams.Render(szPOSTData, &dwSize); // render the string
navData.SetMethod(ATL_HTTP_METHOD_POST);
navData.SetPostData((BYTE*)szPOSTData,
                _tcslen(szPOSTData), szContentType);
client.Navigate(&url, &navData);
```

The `CHttpRequestParams` class has a limitation: It isn't able to render the ? separator required for sending parameters … nd the parameters as part of the URL … place the last part of the co…

Listing 25-3. Using CHttpRequestParams for Generating a Collection of HTTP GET Parameters

```
// Get the number of actual characters
requestParams.Render(szPOSTData, &dwSize);
szPOSTData = new char[dwSize+2];   // leave room for ? prefix trailing \0 and ?
szPOSTData[0] = '?';        // add the URL parameters separator
dwSize += 1;            // mark the room for trailing \0
requestParams.Render(szPOSTData + 1, &dwSize);    // render the string
url.SetExtraInfo(szPOSTData);
```

NOTE *By default,* `CHttpRequestParams` *is implemented as a hash table (*`CAtlMap`*, mapping strings to strings). In this implementation, assigning for the second time a value to the same parameter will override the initial value. However, you can use it for multiple parameters with the same name. To do so, you have to define* `ATL_HTTP_PARAM_MULTIMAP` *before you include atlisapi.h. When you define* `ATL_HTTP_PARAM_MULTIMAP`, `CHttpRequestParams` *is no longer a* `CAtlMap` *derivative; rather, it's a* `CRBMultiMap` *derivative.*

Sending and Receiving Large Payloads

In this section we discuss methods exposed by `CAtlNavigateData` for sending or receiving large payloads. ATL Server provides multiple ways of customizing the transfer of such content. First, we briefly look at how you can customize the read/write buffer size and the implications this might have on the behavior of the client application.

The `CAtlNavigateData` class, an instance of which you can use for controlling a `Navigate` invocation, allows setting the size of the buffers used for socket operations. You can do this by invoking the following methods:

```
DWORD SetReadBlockSize(DWORD dwBlockSize ) throw( );
DWORD SetSendBlockSize(DWORD dwBlockSize ) throw( );
```

The default size of the socket buffers is `ATL_HTTP_DEFAULT_BLOCK_SIZE` (4096), which proved an appropriate number for the most common scenarios.

Now, it's possible that the data becomes available faster than the socket code can process it. In this case, the bottleneck for the application performance is the socket operation. If this is the case, increasing the size of the buffer used in the socket operation will improve the performance of the application. You can obtain the current values for the buffer size by invoking the similar Get methods.

You can use the block size functions only when the CAtlNavigateData object has the ATL_HTTP_FLAG_SEND_BLOCKS flag set (which is on by default).

Reading or sending a large amount of content takes an accordingly long time. Therefore, it's important to have some way of recording the progress of the operation, especially in applications that provide a user interface. Using a common practice for this kind of scenario, CAtlNavigateData allows the usage of callback functions for recording the progress of reading and writing requests. These two callbacks (one for reading and one for writing) have to be implemented by the client application and they should have the following prototype:

```
typedef bool (WINAPI *PFNATLSTATUSCALLBACK)( DWORD dwBytesSent,
                                   DWORD_PTR dwParam);
```

Once you've implemented the callbacks, you can "attach" them to the CAtlNavigateData object with the following code:

```
PFNATLSTATUSCALLBACK SetReadStatusCallback(
   PFNATLSTATUSCALLBACK pfn,
   DWORD_PTR dwData ) throw( );

PFNATLSTATUSCALLBACK SetSendStatusCallback(
   PFNATLSTATUSCALLBACK pfn,
   DWORD_PTR dwData ) throw( );
```

Both functions will return the previously used callback function (NULL, by default). The dwData parameter will be passed to the callback functions as the dwParam parameter. This parameter is intended to serve as a "cookie" when using the same callback function with multiple instances of the CAtlHttpClient class (by identifying the instance that generated a specific progress notification). It's of type DWORD_PTR, a type that allows you to safely store either a numeric value or a pointer, both on 32-bit and 64-bit systems.

Alternately, you may decide to use chunked-transfer encoding of the request content, which allows you to deal with blocks of variable size. For this, you should set the ATL_HTTP_FLAG_SEND_CALLBACK flag on the CAtlNavigateData object. This flag and the one for using blocks are mutually exclusive. Also, you should use the CAtlHttpClient class's NavigateChunked method.

With chunked content, the application can successively send blocks of different sizes. This proves useful when you don't know the total size of the request before you start the request. The code for socket operations communicates with the rest of the application by using a callback mechanism for passing the blocks to and from the socket. To do this, you'll have to implement callback methods defined as follows:

```
typedef bool (WINAPI *PFNATLCHUNKEDCB)(BYTE** ppData, DWORD *pdwSize,
 DWORD_PTR dwParam);
```

Once you've implemented a chunked callback, you can "attach" it to a `CAtlNavigateData` object by calling

```
PFNATLCHUNKEDCB SetChunkCallback(
   PFNATLCHUNKEDCB pfn,
   DWORD_PTR dwParam ) throw( );
```

The MSDN documentation that comes with Visual Studio .NET mistakenly doesn't include the `dwParam` parameter in the definition of the `PFNATLCHUNKEDCB` prototype. It's actually a required parameter of the callback function, and it has the same role there as in the callbacks for progress notifications: It allows you to use the same callback function for multiple instances of the `CAtlHttpClient` class.

In the next section we cover security-related issues and describe the authentication objects that you can use within ATL Server HTTP client applications. We also offer suggestions for further transport security enhancements.

Securing the HTTP Communication

This section provides information on how to use the `CAtlHttpClient` class to issue authenticated HTTP requests and how to perform secure HTTPS communication.

Authentication

`CAtlHttpClient` supports two authentication schemes: Basic Authentication (based on username and password) and NTLM (Windows credentials) authentication. Additional authentication schemes can be supported, or different implementations for the supported schemes can be used, but you'll have to provide classes for handling the authentication objects. These authentication objects have to be derivatives of `CAtlBaseAuthObject`.

The HTTP client class contains a map of authentication objects indexed by the authentication scheme that they support. Such a map might contain at a given moment objects to support different forms of authentication. For example, it may contain a CNTLMAuthObject for the NTLM authentication scheme and a CBasicAuthObject for the Basic Authentication scheme. When the server attempts to authenticate the client, the CAtlHttpClient code will walk the list of authentication objects and try to find one that matches the server requirements.

The code for adding authentication to an HTTP client generally looks like this:

```
CAtlHttpClient     client;
CNTLMAuthObject authObj;
if( !client.AddAuthObject(ATL_HTTP_AUTHTYPE_NTLM, &authObj) )
{
    // error handling here
}
```

This code supports the NTLM authentication scheme by using the credentials of the current running thread (which are most likely the credentials of the currently logged user).

To provide the credentials of an alternate user, or to retrieve authentication information for a user, you can use an implementation of the IAuthInfo interface either in the construction of the authentication object or passed as a third parameter to AddAuthObject. IAuthInfo exposes methods that return the username, the password, and the authentication domain, and this information is further used by the authentication object. Such an implementation might invoke a username/password dialog box or load this information from a different source. You must use an IAuthInfo implementation for Basic Authentication.

Secure Communication (HTTPS)

HTTPS isn't directly supported by the ATL Server HTTP client. The designers considered that the most common scenario for using ATL Server in a client application is a SOAP client, and alternate solutions for HTTPS are available in SOAP (CSoapWininetClient and CSoapMSXMLInetClient both are wrapping HTTP stacks that support HTTPS).

However, if a given application requires HTTPS support and using CAtlHttpClient, you can accomplish this by implementing a socket wrapper class that hides the HTTPS layer from the CAtlHttpClient class.

As we stated at the beginning of this chapter, CAtlHttpClient is defined as

```
typedef CAtlHttpClientT<ZEvtSyncSocket> CAtlHttpClient;
```

ZEvtSyncSocket is the default socket wrapper class, which doesn't support HTTPS. However, by creating a custom class that supports it (say, CSecureSyncSocket), you can define an HTTPS-enabled HTTP client as follows:

```
typedef CAtlHttpClientT<CSecureSyncSocket> CAtlHttpsClient;
```

You can find an example of this in the MSDN documentation, in the SecureSOAP sample (ms-help://MS.VSCC/MS.MSDNVS/vcsample/html/vcsamSecureSOAPSample.htm). In this sample, the solution described previously is used for implementing SOAP HTTPS communication with a CAtlHttpClientT class.

Conclusion

ATL Server is mainly intended for server-side use. However, you can exploit the flexible architecture and the performance benefits on the client side as well.

As you learned in this chapter, the existing code supports the most common scenarios of a HTTP client application, and the modular design allows you to easily extend the CAtlHttpClientT class and overcome the limitations of the implementation.

One of the big differences between traditional desktop applications and Web applications is the increased importance of security. Whether you're concerned about customer information, private company data, or even technical intellectual property, security plays an important role in modern Web applications. In the next chapter we take a brief look at some of the key ways you can make your application more secure. We discuss some of the technologies that ATL Server provides support for, and we describe some of the successful techniques we've used to find security issues.

CHAPTER 26

Securing Your Web Application

SECURITY IS ONE OF THE most important "features" of any Web application. ATL Server is designed for high-end Web applications and services, and these mission-critical applications almost always require mission-critical security.

This chapter will introduce you to some of the key requirements in securing a Web application, and it includes an examination of some of the security support provided by ATL Server. Unless you're already an expert in security, however, we recommended that you buy a book devoted to the topic. Creating secure applications on any platform requires a significant amount of thought and effort, and Windows is no exception. The Windows security-related APIs have many semantics that the average developer may not be aware of.

Security Best Practices

We start this chapter by discussing some of the best practices you should follow when creating secure applications. Some of these are techniques that we used in creating the ATL Server library itself, and others are techniques that we recommend developers take advantage of when creating end-user applications. Many of the suggestions in the following list may seem like common sense, but they're items that time and time again application developers forget.

- *Analyze threats:* Security is difficult and, as with any difficult process, you're best off spending your time where it's most effective. With security, you'll want to spend most of your time focusing on the most vulnerable areas of your application. The only way to do this is to complete some level of threat analysis on your application. Threat analysis should involve documentation of the findings and should point out all possible threats. Ranking these threats by priority is a secondary task after identifying possible methods of attack.

- *Check errors:* One of the most common mistakes that application developers make is not checking for errors (either in return values or via exceptions) from their calls. If an API can return an error, then there are situations where it can fail. Unless you understand the implementation of the API completely (including all semantics), it's best to check for errors and respond appropriately. Having your application terminate is better than giving control over to a hacker!

- *Use tools:* Two categories of tools are very useful for securing your application. The first category of tools is *stress tools.* Reliable applications tend to be secure applications because they handle unusual situations (e.g., stress) safely. Testing your application in stressful conditions (e.g., low memory) is a good way to see if you're checking for uncommon API failures (there are some great tools that simulate OS API failures for you). It's very possible that your server will hit these conditions, or that a hacker can figure out a way to make your server enter into these conditions. Compiling /GS and using tools such as BoundsChecker and PC-lint can help improve the quality of your code, which in turn can help make it more reliable and more secure. The second category of tools is *hacker tools.* A number of Web sites are devoted to hacking and hacking tools. Even if you can't or don't want to play around with some of these tools, you should consider using tools such as Perl to create attack scripts and testing if various threats are exploitable. You should create some template Perl scripts so that it's easy for team members to test the scenario that they're interested in without having to put together the entire request packet.

- *Use secure functions:* Sure, you use the security APIs, but do you make calls to CRT functions such as strcpy or sprintf? Many of these APIs have no validation whatsoever, and you're often better off using the safe versions of these function (e.g., strncpy, shlwapi.h, or strsafe.h in the platform SDK). `CFixedString` has better performance characteristics than `CString` in many situations, but both provide more security than many custom string classes or `char *`. Using these functions eliminates many of the most common buffer overrun bugs in code.

- *Perform code reviews:* The best way to test for security is to perform code reviews. These reviews should include individual reviews as well as group reviews. Although reviewing an entire code base is always ideal, it's often unrealistic. For this reason, you should pay attention to high-risk areas (once again, the threat analysis comes in handy). Following all user input from when it's received to when the request is complete is critical to any application. You should also look at what happens when invalid requests are sent to your application (invalid headers, form or query variables, and so on) and what happens when very large requests are sent to your server. You should create tests for all these situations. You should also be sure to do some ad-hoc testing, where once again Perl is your friend.

- *Test all cases:* This is probably the most obvious suggestion, but it's the easiest one to forget. Often, traditional application development teams are caught in the mindset of testing for positive scenarios. With server-side applications, and with Web applications in particular, it becomes very important (in some cases, more important) to test for negative cases. Are your authentication mechanisms working? Does your application handle invalid data correctly? On errors, is your application returning too much information to the user?

These are just some of the key work items that your team should keep in mind to ensure that the end result of your efforts is a secure application. Often just the education team members receive in creating a formal security plan justifies the cost of doing the work. The end result is a development team that is better able to find, review, and fix security issues *before* they hurt the application.

Authentication

Authentication can be useful on the Internet (for protecting access to a site or, more commonly, for protecting access to areas of a site), but it's even more popular on an intranet, where access is often managed with fine-grained control.

ATL Server supports NTLM authentication and Basic Authentication. *NTLM authentication* is a secure authentication mechanism that uses Windows security to authenticate the user. It's useful when you know that users of the site will be using Windows to access the site. You can usually determine this for intranet applications, but it's not always as feasible for Internet applications (although if you're providing a section of your site to "vendors" or "partners," it can be very useful). The `CNTLMAuthObject` class in atlhttp.h is where NTLM authentication is implemented. `CNTLMAuthObject` is derived from `CAtlBaseAuthObject`, which provides the general requirements for any authentication function (initialization and authentication).

Basic Authentication is a simpler authentication mechanism that takes a username/password combination to control access to the site. This authentication mechanism provides no encryption by default, which is why it's important to ensure that you're using an encryption mechanism such as HTTPS when you use this protocol. Basic Authentication can be very useful for controlling access to parts of a Web site or customizing a site for a particular user. `CBasicAuthObject` in atlhttp.h is where Basic Authentication is implemented. The application must implement an `IAuthInfo` interface (and pass it to the `CBasicAuthObject`) in order for the call to succeed. This class also derives from `CAtlBaseAuthObject`.

You'll note that if either of these functions fail, the application will return a 401 error with an indicator that authorization is required. This is generally a sound policy, as it limits the information that anyone can glean from the failure. In particular, the user has no information as to what authentication mechanism is being used and why it failed (information that may help a potential hacker).

NTLM Authentication

Using NTLM on the server side is usually done in one of two ways. One option is to use the IIS administration tool to set the permissions on a given vroot. IIS will then be responsible for receiving and interpreting authentication information. This does mean that a user either has access to the entire application or doesn't have access to the entire application. The other option is to do the authentication in your actual application. The code for this is fairly simple and looks something like Listing 26-1.

Listing 26-1. Confirming That NTLM Authentication Is Being Used

```
CString str;
CString ntlm = "NTLM";
BOOL b = m_HttpRequest.GetAuthenticationType(str);
if (b == FALSE)
{
  return HTTP_UNAUTHORIZED;
}
if (str == ntlm)
{
  // Set the content type
  m_HttpResponse.SetContentType("text/html");
  return HTTP_SUCCESS;
}
return HTTP_UNAUTHORIZED;
```

This code should be simple to follow.

CAUTION *You'll need to disable anonymous access on the vroot in order to have the code in Listing 26-1 work correctly.*

The other side of NTLM authentication is authenticating from the client. Internet Explorer automatically pops up an NTLM authentication credentials window, but what about a custom client application?

This is where `CNTLMAuthObject` comes into play. You can either use the default setting (log in as the current user) or implement `IAuthInfo` in order to authenticate in a different manner (log in as a different user or prompt for credentials):

```
int main(void)
{
  CoInitialize(NULL);
  NTLMAuthService::CNTLMAuthService svc;
#ifdef SECURE
  CNTLMAuthObject auth;
  svc.m_socket.AddAuthObj("NTLM", &auth);
#endif
  CComBSTR bstrIn, bstrOut;
  bstrIn = "World!";
  svc.HelloWorld(bstrIn, &bstrOut);
  printf("%S", bstrOut);
  return 0;
}
```

With this client you're using an `ifdef` block to contain the code that sends the authentication information. This way, you can easily check that the call only succeeds when you have your authentication information included.

If you look at the code for this chapter (you can download the code for this book from the Downloads section of the Apress Web site [`http://www.apress.com`]), you can see that we've used a similar `#define` around the Web service server, so that you can easily check that it's authenticating against NTLM. Notice that if you disable the code on the server, the client will never authenticate correctly (and thus the call will always fail).

Basic Authentication

Basic Authentication follows exactly the same pattern as NTLM authentication. You can use either IIS or Internet Explorer to handle authentication on the server side and the client side, respectively, or you can use the classes provided to implement the authentication manually.

CAUTION *One warning about Basic Authentication is that it transmits the user information (username and password) as plain text. This means that you must use an encryption scheme if you want to use this method of authentication.*

In general, the same principles apply when you want IIS to handle authentication as when you want to do it yourself.

CAUTION *When we talk about "do-it-yourself" security, we're really referring to using the supplied APIs that handle the security for you. For the vast majority of developers, implementing a custom security system isn't recommended.*

In the next sections you'll look at code snippets that show how the server and client code looks.

Server-Side Authentication Code

You don't have to verify if the user is using Basic Authentication in your code—you can always have IIS do the verification for you. If you support multiple types of authentication (e.g., Basic Authentication or NTLM authentication), you might want to treat the two types of users differently, and in these cases using code to verify the authentication type may be useful, as shown in Listing 26-2.

Listing 26-2. Verifying the Use of Basic Authentication

```
 [
  request_handler(name="Default", sdl="GenbasicauthWSDL"),
  soap_handler(
    name="basicauthService",
    namespace="urn:basicauthService",
    protocol="soap"
  )
]
class CbasicauthService :  public IbasicauthService
{
private:
  BOOL Auth;
  CHttpRequest m_HttpRequest;
public:
  // override HandleRequest
  HTTP_CODE HandleRequest(AtlServerRequest *pRequestInfo,
       IServiceProvider * pProvider)
  {
    // We need to create an m_HttpRequest in order to Authenticate
    HTTP_CODE hRet = m_HttpRequest.Initialize(pRequestInfo->pServerContext, 0, 0);
    CString str;
    CString type = "Basic";
```

```
    BOOL b = m_HttpRequest.GetAuthenticationType(str);
    Auth = FALSE;
    if ((b == TRUE) && (str == type))
    {
      Auth = TRUE;
    }
    return __super::HandleRequest(pRequestInfo, pProvider);
  }
```

Client-Side Authentication Code

The client code is a little more complex than a normal Web service client, as you need to pass the authentication information yourself. In Listing 26-3, we've put a note for where you should prompt the user for his or her username and password and copy them into your structure. Remember that this information will exist in plain text and will transmit in plain text, which is why an encryption system is critical.

Listing 26-3. The Client Side of Basic Authentication

```
class BasicAuth : public IAuthInfo
{
  HRESULT GetUsername(LPTSTR lpBuffer, DWORD *pdwBuffSize)
  {
    if (*pdwBuffSize < 10)
    {
      *pdwBuffSize = 10;
      return E_OUTOFMEMORY;
    }
    GET USERNAME AND COPY USERNAME INTO lpBuffer
    *pdwBuffSize = strlen(lpBuffer);
    return S_OK;
  }

HRESULT GetPassword(LPTSTR szPwd, DWORD *pdwBuffSize)
  {
    if (*pdwBuffSize < 10)
    {
      *pdwBuffSize = 10;
      return E_OUTOFMEMORY;
    }
    GET PASSWORD AND COPY INTO szPwd
    *pdwBuffSize = strlen(szPwd);
```

```
    return S_OK;
  }

  HRESULT GetDomain(LPTSTR lpBuffer, DWORD *pdwBuffSize)
  {
    if (*pdwBuffSize < 10)
    {
      *pdwBuffSize = 10;
      return E_OUTOFMEMORY;
    }
    _tcscpy(lpBuffer,"PRANISHK-V1\0");
    *pdwBuffSize = strlen(lpBuffer);
    return S_OK;
  }
};

int main(void)
{
  CoInitialize(NULL);
  basicauthService::CbasicauthService svc;
  BasicAuth ba;
  CBasicAuthObject auth(&ba);
  svc.m_socket.AddAuthObj("BASIC", &auth);
  CComBSTR bstrIn, bstrOut;
  bstrIn = "World!";
  svc.HelloWorld(bstrIn, &bstrOut);
  printf("%S", bstrOut);
  return 0;
}
```

Encryption

Authentication provides one half of the story, and in this section you'll examine the second half: encryption. Encryption even plays a role in the authentication story when you're using authentication systems such as Basic Authentication that don't encrypt the username and password data when they transmit.

There's one encryption system that is predominant on the Internet, be it encrypting authentication information, encrypting credit card information, or keeping other information on a Web site protected. That system is HTTPS.

Both IIS and Internet Explorer support HTTPS. Again, it's more interesting when you want to have programmatic HTTPS support—for example, in a client application. In this section you'll create a simple ATL Server Web service and expose it over HTTPS. You'll use the HTTPS support in WinHTTP to access this service from the client.

To set up an HTTPS server you'll need to have a trusted certificate on your machine. Usually you'll use a company such as VeriSign to get certificates, but for development and testing purposes, you can create your own certificate server (this requires that you have a server version of Windows installed). Use the Add/Remove Windows Components dialog box (available under the Add/Remove Programs option in the Control Panel) to install the certificate server components on your machine.

Your machine is now a certificate authority, and you can make a request against your certificate authority to request a certificate. The easiest way to request a certificate is to use your Web browser. If you look under your IIS settings, you'll notice that the machine that you made a certificate server (say, "MyCertServer") has a new vroot called something like "CertServ". If you go to `http://MyCertServer/CertServ` you'll see a number of options, including Request a Certificate. You can also use the certreq.exe utility to request a certificate from a server.

If you open your certification authority (from Administrative Tools, or go back to the original Web site), you'll see a pending request. You can then choose to issue the certificate. Once the certificate is granted, you can install the certificate.

If you now go to IIS, select the properties for the Default Web Site, and go to Directory Security, you'll see that you can either request a certificate or assign an existing certificate. Your machine now requires that SSL be used for communication.

For more information on this topic, we recommend looking at the SecureSoap sample included with the Visual Studio .NET Product samples. This sample also demonstrates how to access a secure server from a custom client application (in this case, a Web service).

NOTE *If you use WinHTTP for your HTTP services (WinHTTP provides an excellent implementation, particularly for security support), then you'll probably need to download the proxycfg.exe tool from MSDN (`http://msdn.microsoft.com`). This tool is required to access HTTP and HTTPS servers through a proxy server (if you're using WinHTTP). There is currently no programmatic way to go through a proxy server with WinHTTP. To find the utility, just search for "proxycfg" on the MSDN site.*

Conclusion

You should now have a good understanding of the security classes provided by ATL Server. ATL Server also has a number of new security classes designed for working with Windows security objects such as ACLs that we don't cover in this book. You should also understand the basics of setting up a secure server (with HTTPS encryption) and using an ATL Server client to access this server.

This chapter was designed to give you a brief introduction to security and some of the common security issues that arise when you design ATL Server applications. This chapter isn't intended to be a replacement for a book devoted to the subject, and we recommend that you read a book dedicated to security to learn more about it.

We hope that you now have an excellent understanding of the ATL Server library and how to use it to make the most in your applications. You've seen how ATL Server can be used to make Web application and Web service development easier. You've learned how you can take advantage of ATL Server classes in non-Web contexts. Finally, you've learned how to make the most of this powerful framework through the advanced topics presented in this book.

In the next and final chapter we present a number of frequently asked questions and their answers. Although this is by no means a complete list of questions people ask about ATL Server, it contains responses to some of the top questions that developers ask the team.

CHAPTER 27
ATL Server FAQ

THIS CHAPTER PRESENTS some of the frequently asked questions (FAQ) we've received about ATL Server. Many of these questions have been posted on various newsgroups. We've grouped them here by component. Some of the answers we present direct you to a specific chapter in the book or to articles posted on the Web. We've tried to keep the answers here as short and concise as possible. Whenever possible, we try to point you to a place where the information we're referring to is presented in more detail.

A few of the solutions we present here involve rewriting/overriding some classes from the library. In such cases, we present the solutions in a more verbose manner; the answers will usually contain instructions detailed down to classes and functions.

Generic ATL Server Application FAQ

The following sections present some generic questions we've received regarding ATL Server applications.

What Does "Assertion in Atlisapi.h, Line 663" Mean?

The ISAPI extension part of ATL Server is responsible for dispatching the requests to the actual request handlers. The call into the actual request handler (which involves execution of the user code) is "guarded" in a Try...Catch block to prevent IIS from crashing in case of an exception. The code that performs this "guarding" looks like this:

```
_ATLTRY
{
    (static_cast<IIsapiExtension*>(pvParam))->DispatchStencilCall(pRequestInfo);
}
_ATLCATCHALL()
{
    ATLTRACE(_T(
      "Warning. An uncaught exception was thrown from DispatchStencilCall\n"));
    ATLASSERT(FALSE);
}
```

The assertion displayed on the screen is issued by the ATLASSERT line in the preceding code, therefore signaling an exception thrown while processing an HTTP request.

For detailed information on how to troubleshoot such a problem, please refer to Chapter 15.

How Can I Access the Physical Directory of an ATL Server Application?

You have two ways of doing this from a request handler:

- Call m_HttpRequest.GetScriptPathTranslated(). This is the ISAPI-specific way, using data provided by IIS in the EXTENSION_CONTROL_BLOCK.

- Call GetModuleFileName and pass CRequestHandlerT::m_hInstHandler as the HINSTANCE parameter.

Now, a SOAP server isn't a CRequestHandlerT derivative. To get the physical path of a SOAP server, you have to override HandleRequest, which is defined in atlsoap.h as follows:

```
HTTP_CODE HandleRequest(
      AtlServerRequest *pRequestInfo,
      IServiceProvider * /*pProvider*/)
```

Then invoke pRequestInfo->pServerContext->GetScriptPathTranslated.

How Can I Access the Client's SSL Certificate in a Secure Web Application?

According to the ISAPI specification, the ISAPI DLL gets information about client requests by invoking ServerRequestFunction on the extension control block (ECB) pointer received with the request. The HSE_REQ_GET_CERT_INFO_EX server function specifies the certificate context for the first certificate in the client's certificate chain.

Now, assuming the ECB pointer is available (pECB in the following code snippet), the code for getting access to the client's certificate would look like this:

```
char CertificateBuf[8192];
CERT_CONTEXT_EX ccex;
ccex.cbAllocated = sizeof(CertificateBuf);
ccex.CertContext.pbCertEncoded = (BYTE*)CertificateBuf;
DWORD dwSize = sizeof(ccex);

if (pECB->ServerSupportFunction(pECB->ConnID, HSE_REQ_GET_CERT_INFO_EX,
   (LPVOID)&ccex, NULL,NULL) == FALSE)
{
    // Handle Error Here
}
else
{
   // ccex now contains valid client certificate information.
}
```

You'll see now how you can retrieve the pointer to the request's ECB. ATL Server preserves the request information in the `AtlServerRequest` structure in its `pECB` member. This structure is passed to all the request handlers as a parameter to the `HandleRequest` method. Therefore, in your implementation of `HandleRequest`, you could cache the pointer to the `AtlServerRequest` parameter and then get access to the ECB pointer whenever necessary.

There are two kinds of ATL Server Web applications that, by default, don't override the `HandleRequest` method: a SOAP server and an application with support for stencil processing. The "SOAP FAQ" section of this chapter deals with the SOAP server, so we'll focus now on the applications with support for stencil processing.

These applications use classes decorated with the `request_handler` attribute, which makes them inherit from `CHtmlTagReplacer`. In its internal implementation of `HandleRequest`, `CHtmlTagReplacer` caches the `AtlServerRequest` parameter (actually, it creates a copy of that parameter). Therefore, you can execute the preceding code for accessing a client's certificate at any time inside the request handler by replacing `pECB` with `m_RequestInfo.pECB`.

Mail Support FAQ

The following section contains the answer to the most frequently asked question we've received about mail support in ATL Server.

How Do I Send HTML Mail Messages with ATL Server?

The SMTP infrastructure in ATL Server doesn't support directly creating messages with HTML content. However, you can easily extend the framework with a new class that adds support for custom content types. Please see Chapter 24 for a detailed sample that shows how to do this.

SOAP FAQ

The following sections contain FAQ relating to ATL Server and SOAP.

How Do I Make a SOAP Client Point to a Different URL?

Briefly, you do this by calling `SetUrl` on the SOAP proxy class and passing the new URL as a parameter.

The class generated by sproxy.exe has a URL hard-coded in the constructor. This is the URL contained by the input WSDL document under the `soap:location` field. However, the proxy class doesn't actually perform the transport and, therefore, it isn't using the URL to perform the HTTP connection. The SOAP proxy class is defined as follows:

```
template <class THttpClient>
class CMyServiceT : public THttpClient
```

The preceding definition allows invoking any public method of the HTTP client class on the SOAP proxy class.

It's the `HttpClient` template parameter class that handles the connection and uses the URL to connect to the SOAP server. So, changing the URL is actually something that has to be supported by the HTTP client class.

This transport class has to conform to the SOAP client archetype (described in MSDN under the ATL Server library reference). The definition of the archetype specifies only that this class should take a URL as a constructor parameter, to support the hard-coded URL described previously. A method allowing the changing of the URL isn't a requirement under the archetype definition in MSDN, but all three implementations of the SOAP client archetype that come with ATL Server implement the `SetUrl` method.

How Do I Use an HTTP Proxy in a SOAP Client?

Briefly, you do this by calling `SetProxy` on the SOAP proxy class and passing the proxy server and the port as parameters.

Very much like `SetUrl` (the function described in the previous section), `SetProxy` is not a SOAP client archetype requirement; rather, it's a method implemented by the `CSoapSocketClientT` and `CSoapWininetClient` classes that come with ATL Server.

It also has an implementation (albeit a nonfunctional one) in the `CSoapMSXMLInetClient` class. To set the HTTP proxy for the `ServerXMLHTTP` component, please see the MSDN article titled "Using the WinHTTP Proxy Configuration Utility" (`http://msdn.microsoft.com/library/en-us/xmlsdk30/htm/serverxmlhttpproxy.asp`).

How Do I Use SOAP over a Custom Transport Protocol?

The SOAP transport sample in MSDN covers this topic. The sample provides a low-level way of directly using the SOAP infrastructure classes in ATL Server in a stand-alone application.

An alternate mechanism for controlling the SOAP transmission is presented in Chapter 23. It's a higher-level approach that basically consists of writing a stand-alone application that encapsulates the functionality of an ISAPI DLL, meaning it loads a prebuilt SOAP application DLL and launches the SOAP request-handling code in the same way a Web server would.

How Do I Use WinINet, ServerXMLHTTP, or a Custom HTTP Stack in a SOAP Client?

The typical SOAP proxy class, generated by sproxy.exe, is defined as follows:

```
template <class THttpClient>
class CMyServiceT : public THttpClient
```

It is the `THttpClient` template parameter class that handles the connection and uses the URL to connect to the SOAP server. So, changing the URL is actually something that has to be supported by the HTTP client class.

Also, the sproxy.exe-generated header contains a specialization of the preceding template:

```
typedef CMyServiceT<CSoapSocketClientT<> > CMyService;
```

Most applications use `CMyService` as a proxy class—that is, the specialization based on the `CSoapSocketClientT` HTTP client, the lightweight SOAP HTTP client that comes with ATL Server. However, you can use different HTTP stacks by passing different template parameters when instantiating the SOAP proxy. Two such alternate HTTP stacks, based on the WinINet and ServerXMLHTTP libraries, are available in ATL Server. They are `CSoapWininetClient` (using WinINet) and `CSoapMSXMLInetClient` (using ServerXMLHTTP, which comes with MSXML 3.0 or higher). To use these classes, you'll have to change the typical client code, which looks like this:

```
CMyService soapProxy;
```

and make it look like this:

```
CMyServiceT<CSoapWininetClient> soapProxy;
```

You don't have to use one of the ATL Server–provided classes for your HTTP communication. You can implement your own class or use a third-party transport class, as long as it conforms to the SOAP client archetype described in MSDN at `ms-help://MS.VSCC/MS.MSDNVS/vclib/html/vclrfatlserversoapclientarchetype.htm`.

How Do I Use HTTPS/SSL in a SOAP Client?

The default SOAP transport client, `CSoapSocketClientT<>`, doesn't support SSL. However, HTTPS URLs and secure communication are supported by the alternate transport classes that use the WinINet and the ServerXMLHTTP libraries, respectively. So, the typical client code that looks like this:

```
CMySoapProxy    srv;
```

should be changed to look like this:

```
CMySoapProxy<CSoapWininetClient> srv;
```

or this:

```
CMySoapProxy<CSoapMSXMLInetClient> srv;
```

Also, the SecureSOAP sample that ships as part of ATL Server shows a way to use a custom, SSL-enabled socket class for performing HTTPS communication with the lightweight `CSoapSocketClientT` class.

The recommended way of doing SSL is by using `CSoapMSXMLInetClient`, as the ServerXMLHTTP library is designed to be used both in server applications and in client applications.

How Do I Select a Specific Certificate for an SSL Connection?

Like setting the proxy and changing the SOAP server's URL, specifying the certificate to be used in a secure HTTP connection is very specific to the transport class used for SOAP communication. We demonstrate how to do so here for the `CSoapMSXMLInetClient` class, which is the recommended class to use when performing secure SOAP with ATL Server. The client code should look like this:

```
CMyProxyClassT<CSoapMSXMLInetClient> srv;
// Invoking with the default settings.
// MSXML looks in the certificate store and
// uses the first available certificate
hRet = srv.InvokeMethod( params);

if( FAILED(hRet) )
{
    CComVariant certFriendlyName;

    // This way you can force the MSXMLInetClient
    // to use a specific certificate
    certFriendlyName.bstrVal =
         ::SysAllocString(L"Some Specific Certificate's Friendly Name");
    hRet = srv.m_spHttpRequest->setOption(
           SXH_OPTION_SELECT_CLIENT_SSL_CERT,
           certFriendlyName);
}
// Calling again, with the new client certificate
hRet = srv.InvokeMethod(params);
```

Please note that, due to a design bug, you can't call `SetOption` before the first invocation, because the `m_spHttpRequest` pointer member of `CSoapMSXMLInetClient` is instantiated only on the first request.

By default, the `CSoapMSXMLInetClient` class will use the first certificate in the local store (and that one will be used to negotiate the first invocation).

How Do I Access the Client's Certificate in a SOAP Server?

We've already presented the generic solution for this problem in the "Generic ATL Server Application FAQ" section of this chapter. The only SOAP server–specific part is getting the pointer to the ECB.

You learned earlier that the ECB for the current HTTP request is preserved in the `AtlServerRequest` structure that's passed as a parameter to the `HandleRequest` method. A SOAP server class inherits from the `CSoapHandler` class, and `CSoapHandler`'s `HandleRequest` doesn't cache the `AtlServerRequest` parameter, so you'll have to do this.

Start by adding a new member to your SOAP server class, defined as follows:

```
AtlServerRequest m_RequestInfo;
```

Then override the `HandleRequest` method. Don't forget to call the default implementation after caching the parameter.

```
HTTP_CODE HandleRequest(AtlServerRequest *pRequestInfo,
            IServiceProvider * pProvider)
{
        // copy the AtlServerRequest into the safe version
        memcpy(&m_RequestInfo, pRequestInfo, sizeof(m_RequestInfo) );
        return __super::HandleRequest(pRequestInfo, pProvider);
}
```

Now `m_RequestInfo` contains a copy of `AtlServerRequest` for the current request, therefore you can obtain the ECB as `m_RequestInfo.pECB`.

How Do I Use Custom Encryption/Compression with SOAP?

On the client side, you can achieve this by writing a custom SOAP transport class. As we mentioned in previous sections of this chapter, a custom SOAP transport class should conform to the SOAP client archetype, as described in the MSDN documentation. What you want to do here is not necessarily replace the HTTP transport mechanism, but extend it by adding encoding capabilities (such as encryption or compression). This is why the simplest way of getting a custom SOAP transport class is to inherit from an existing one—say, inherit from `CSoapSocketClientT` (if you decide to inherit from another transport class, the same functions should be overridden).

The code generated by sproxy serializes the SOAP request into the stream returned by the transport class's `GetWriteStream` method. So, to get a SOAP payload to be in any way encoded (encrypted and/or compressed) before sending it to the server, you'll have to override the `GetWriteStream` method and return your own `IWriteStream` derivative. This class will perform the encoding (either on-the-fly or by storing the entire payload in memory and encoding it all at once).

Now, the other method to be overridden is `SendRequest`. This can preserve most of the code from the base class's `SendRequest`. Due to optimization issues, the code that comes with ATL Server assumes that the stream returned by `GetWriteStream` is a `CWriteStreamOnCString` class and uses `CWriteStreamOnCString::m_str` for sending the actual request's body. You'll have to replace this with some call to a method returning the encoded (encrypted and/or compressed) body from your stream class. Optionally, your new `SendRequest` implementation might send some other HTTP headers to warn the server of the encoding used in the request's body.

On the server side, the easiest way of matching the client encoding is to write an ISAPI filter, which can identify the encoded requests and decode them before passing them to the actual SOAP server. The MSDN documentation contains detailed information about building an ISAPI filter, and the ISAPIFilter sample that comes with ATL Server shows how to build a filter using the ATL Server classes.

An alternate solution (which involves some extra work) is to modify the SOAP server's `HandleRequest` method. You would have to use almost exactly the original code from atlsoap.h (`CSoapHandler::HandleRequest`, starting at line 6379). You should replace the code that instantiates a stream wrapper on top of the HTTP request with code to instantiate your custom stream class, which, besides reading from the request's body, will perform decoding. So, the following line (6412 in atlsoap.h):

```
CStreamOnServerContext s(pRequestInfo->pServerContext);
```

will be modified in your overridden `HandleRequest` with something like this:

```
CDecodingStreamOnServerContext s(pRequestInfo->pServerContext);
```

How Do I Develop an Asynchronous SOAP Client?

This subject is described in detail by some of the authors of this book in an article entitled "Using ATL Server to Build an Asynchronous SOAP Client in Unmanaged C++" (`http://msdn.microsoft.com/msdnmag/issues/02/04/SOAP/default.aspx`). This article explains how to asynchronously invoke SOAP methods and then, upon completion, collect the results.

How Do I Send XML Fragments/Unescaped Strings As Part of a SOAP Message?

This question arises often from the need to send preformatted XML documents as function parameters.

In Chapter 23 in the "Custom Data Types Marshaling" section, you learned a way of extending the ATL Server SOAP infrastructure to support the `GUID` type exactly like any other built-in type. The answer to this FAQ (how to send unescaped strings as part of SOAP messages) is very similar to the method described in Chapter 23.

You'll have to define a custom type, say `SOAPTYPE_RAWSTRING`, by following the steps you used to define `SOAPTYPE_GUID` in the aforementioned section. There is a difference, though. As `GUID` was a completely new type, you could rely on the compiler to load the appropriate instantiation of the template function `AtlGenXMLValue` when serializing. The unescaped string is still a string (a BSTR, actually), so the compiler will use the existing serialization code for BSTR, which escapes XML content. The solution to this problem is to not rely on the compiler for this. You'll start by defining the following:

```
inline HRESULT AtlGenRawStringXMLValue (
                IWriteStream *pStream, wchar_t **pVal)
```

This function should inherit most of the code from the existing string implementation:

```
inline HRESULT AtlGenXMLValue<wchar_t *>(
              IWriteStream *pStream, wchar_t **pVal)
```

but it shouldn't contain the `EscapeXML` part, which actually performs the escaping.

Now, you should modify the serialization code for `AtlSoapGenElementValue` by adding the following branch:

```
case SOAPTYPE_RAWSTRING:
  hr = AtlGenRawXMLValue(pStream, (BSTR*)&pVal);
  break;
```

This doesn't cover the parsing of unescaped XML, so the deserialization for the new `SOAPTYPE_RAWSTRING` type will be the same as for regular strings. This is the default behavior for an unknown type that isn't an error and isn't

SOAPTYPE_USERBASE. However, the correct way to do this is to add a branch to the case instruction in AtlSoapGetElementValue, as follows:

```
case SOAPTYPE_RAWSTRING:
  hr = AtlGetSAXValue((BSTR *)pVal, wsz, cch);
  break;
```

Now, once a SOAP proxy is generated, you can modify the maps from the generated code (see the instructions in the "Custom Data Type Marshaling" section in Chapter 23) and change SOAPTYPE_STRING to SOAPTYPE_RAWSTRING for the parameters that you don't want escaped in your SOAP payload.

How Do I Perform Custom Server-Side Parsing?

A solution for this problem is described in detail in Chapter 23 in the section "Custom Parsing on the Server Side." That solution actually describes the answers for a couple of FAQ:

- How do I parse XML sent as SOAP method parameters (xsd:any)?
- How do I reuse the main SAX parser?

Conclusion

In this chapter we covered many of the common questions that people have asked us (the ATL Server team) about developing ATL Server–based applications. The answers are concise and often link to other material, but they provide the basic methodology behind tackling each of these problems.

With this chapter you have completed the book. We hope that you've enjoyed the experience and that you've learned a lot about ATL Server. We also hope that the ATL Server library has been able to meet and then exceed the requirements of your application.

Most of today's applications don't require low-level control, high performance, and high flexibility. However, those that do tend to be critical ones that power a core application or service. We hope that with the techniques we outlined in this book and your newfound knowledge of the power, performance, flexibility, and control of the ATL Server library, you'll be able to create these mission-critical applications quickly, easily, and with fewer bugs than ever before.

SOAPPF [illegible]. However, the correct way to do this is to add a branch to the [illegible] case[illegible] as follows:

[illegible]

[illegible] you're done [illegible] you can [illegible] erated, [illegible] Chapter 2[illegible] [illegible] that you['ve] declared [illegible] in your SOAP payload.

How Do I [illegible] Side [illegible]ing?

[illegible]

[illegible]

[illegible] the [illegible]

[illegible]

Index

Symbols and Numbers

A

B

C

G

H

N

O

P

Q

T

U

V

W

X

Z